EVOLUTIONARY PSYCHIATRY

Evolutionary Psychiatry challenges a medical model which has supplied few effective answers to long-standing conundrums. A comprehensive introduction to the new science of Darwinian Psychiatry, this second edition includes important fresh material on a number of disorders, along with an entirely new chapter on research.

Anthony Stevens and John Price argue that psychiatric symptoms are manifestations of ancient adaptive strategies which are no longer necessarily appropriate but which can best be understood and treated in an evolutionary and developmental context. Readily accessible to both the specialist and non-specialist reader, *Evolutionary Psychiatry* describes in detail the disorders and conditions commonly encountered in psychiatric practice and shows how evolutionary theory can account for their biological origins and functional nature.

Anthony Stevens is a psychiatrist, Jungian analyst, and author of numerous books, including *On Jung, Ariadne's Clue: A Guide to the Symbols of Humankind*, and *An Intelligent Person's Guide to Psychotherapy*. **John Price** has worked for the Medical Research Council Psychiatric Genetics Unit, and as a Consultant Psychiatrist in the NHS. He is a former Senior Lecturer in Psychological Medicine at the University of Newcastle upon Tyne and was recently Chairman of the Section on Psychotherapy of the World Psychiatric Association.

To the younger generation, who will carry it through

EVOLUTIONARY PSYCHIATRY

A new beginning

Second Edition

Anthony Stevens and John Price

BRUNNER-ROUTLEDGE
ALERE FLAMMAM
Taylor & Francis Group

First edition published 1996
Second edition published 2000
by Routledge
11 New Fetter Lane, London EC4P 4EE

Simultaneously published in the USA and Canada
by Taylor & Francis Inc.
325 Chestnut Street, Philadelphia, PA 19106

Reprinted 2001
by Brunner-Routledge
27 Church Road, Hove, East Sussex, BN3 2FA
325 Chestnut Street, Suite 800, Philadelphia, PA 19106

Brunner-Routledge is an imprint of the Taylor & Francis Group

© 2000 Anthony Stevens and John Price

Typeset in Times by RefineCatch Limited, Bungay, Suffolk

Printed and bound in Great Britain by Biddles Ltd, www.biddles.co.uk

British Library Cataloguing in Publication Data
A catalogue record for this book is available from the Britsh Library

Library of Congress Cataloging in Publication Data
Stevens, Anthony.
  Evolutionary psychiatry: a new beginning/Anthony Stevens and John Price.
    —2nd ed.
    p. cm
  Includes bibliographical references and index.
  ISBN 0–415–21978–7 (hc)—ISBN 0–415–21979–5 (pbk.)
  1. Mental illness—Etiology. 2. Genetic psychology. 3. Mental illness—
    Genetic aspects.
  I. Price, John, 1930– II. Title.

RC454.4 .S73 2000
616.89′001—dc21

99–086488

ISBN 0–415–21978–7 (hbk)
ISBN 0–415–21979–5 (pbk)

CONTENTS

CONTENTS

Part IV Spacing disorders

Part V Reproductive disorders

Part VI Dreams, treatment, research, and the future

ILLUSTRATIONS

FIGURES

TABLES

PREFACE TO THE
FIRST EDITION

The inspiration for this book has arisen out of our shared conviction that psychiatry is entering the most exciting phase in its history. A 'paradigm shift' is under way, which is carrying the speciality beyond the medical model, with its emphasis on the diagnosis and treatment of dubious disease entities, towards an entirely new conceptual framework which defines the basic components of human nature in terms of their evolutionary origins and their essential developmental needs.

So far, no introductory text on psychiatry has acknowledged the emergence of this revolutionary development, nor has it sought to reveal the penetrating new insights that evolutionary psychiatry can provide into the causes of human psychopathology.

The present volume is our joint attempt to fill this vacuum. It is not a general textbook of psychiatry. A number of disorders are not discussed (for example, the organic psychoses, the amentias of childhood and the dementias of middle and old age) and the treatments available at the present time, though mentioned, are not described in detail (for example, the antidepressant, anxiolytic and neuroleptic drugs, the use of ECT, and the various forms of psychotherapy, behaviour therapy, liaison psychiatry, and so on). These subjects are well covered in other publications.

Evolutionary psychiatry is a new discipline standing at the threshold of its existence. So far its contribution has been more in the realm of understanding than in the generation of new empirical or therapeutic initiatives. Accordingly, we have confined ourselves primarily to the explanatory implications of evolutionary theory for the personality disorders, neurotic conditions and 'functional' psychoses commonly encountered in psychiatric practice. Many of the ideas we discuss have been proposed by others, and these are duly acknowledged in the text. Where we must bear our full share of responsibility is for the hypotheses developed in Chapters 5, 13, and 16 – namely the **rank theory** of manic-depression, the **group-splitting hypothesis** of schizophrenia, and the **sex-rank fusion hypothesis** of sadomasochism. The classification of psychiatric conditions as **disorders of attachment and rank** (Part II) and **spacing disorders** (Part IV) is also our own.

The book has the following plan: after outlining the main concepts and theoretical assumptions of evolutionary psychiatry in Part I, we describe each of the disorders covered in Parts II to V, reviewing what is known of their aetiology before examining them in the light of evolutionary theory. Finally, in Part VI, we examine ways in which the evolutionary perspective can contribute to our understanding of sleep and dreams and to new developments in psychiatric treatment and research.

We acknowledge that much of our theorizing at this early stage may be somewhat crude, as were the maps drawn by early cartographers of the world. Occasionally we have also allowed ourselves to indulge in speculative thinking, not always in the presence of hard data with which to support our reasoning. We have felt justified in taking this liberty in view of the comparative infancy of our subject and in the light of William Blake's dictum that what is now proved was once only imagined. Now that the evolutionary paradigm has entered the mainstream of behavioural science, we may expect our hypotheses to undergo refinement (or refutation) and to be replaced by others. What we wish to share with the reader is our excitement at the regenerative impact evolutionary thinking is having on the epistemological foundations of our discipline. It is, we believe, a new beginning.

PREFACE TO THE
SECOND EDITION

We have taken the opportunity provided by publication of the second edition of this book to make changes to the original text. In addition to new material on obsessional, anxiety, phobic, eating and mood disorders, we have added chapters on Paedophilia and Research, as well as extending and reorganizing the chapter on Treatment. Paedophilia continues to be an area of great media interest, which has resulted in misconceptions about the disorder as well as the demonization and persecution of those unfortunate enough to be afflicted with it. Sociological research on the whole has exacerbated this state of affairs, for it has been less interested in understanding the paedophile than in detecting him, controlling him, and protecting children from him. While not wishing to minimize the social problem that paedophilia represents, we have nevertheless attempted to examine the condition from an evolutionary perspective and in the same non-judgemental spirit as we have adopted in the chapters on Homosexuality and Sadomasochism.

We have also revised our classification of personality disorders, grouping **schizotypal personality disorder** with the spacing disorders and not as a borderline state. This readjustment we feel to be nosologically justified and logically compatible with our views on the adaptive functions of spacing disorders.

Although the first edition was generally well received, it was not without its critics. Some of these criticisms we felt to be just, and we have accordingly taken account of them. In particular, we have made a partial retreat from the group selectionist position we adopted in proposing our group-splitting hypothesis of schizophrenia. Though we still consider that the emergence of schizotypal leaders could increase the rate at which groups split and thus enhance the possibility that group selection may occur, this is not indispensable to our hypothesis. The reproductive success of charismatic leaders, who, once they have established their cult, exercise *droit de seigneur* over its members, would be sufficient to explain the survival of schizotypal genes in all human populations.

Perhaps the most challenging area for evolutionary psychiatry at its present stage of development is that of research. Accordingly, we have written a chapter devoted to some of the problems to which psychiatric research may be profitably directed in the light of the new evolutionary paradigm.

As was fully anticipated by us on publication of the first edition, we have been castigated by some colleagues for indulging in speculative thinking in the absence of empirical data and, as one reviewer put it, 'seeking the glory of the winning tape without running the race'! While having some sympathy with their irritation, we remain unrepentant, and continue to think ahead of the data in certain areas. Rather than being lampooned as 'Just-So' stories, we would wish our suggestions to be considered as 'bold hypotheses' (to use Karl Popper's term), which it may be possible to state in scientifically verifiable (or refutable) forms. We realize that this approach will not satisfy those who take a conservative view of scientific progress, believing that no theoretical possibility should be advanced unless supported by already existing data. However, science develops only episodically in this cumulative manner, each episode being punctuated by the emergence of a new paradigm. When paradigms change, as Kuhn (1962) has argued, a significant shift occurs in the criteria which determine the legitimacy both of the problems confronted by the science concerned and of the solutions proposed for them: 'When a new candidate for a paradigm is first proposed', wrote Kuhn, 'it has seldom solved more than a few of the problems that confront it, and most of those solutions are still far from perfect.'

One major obstacle that a new paradigm invariably encounters is what Kuhn calls the 'professionalization' of the old paradigm that it seeks to replace. 'Professionalization leads', he says, 'to an immense restriction of the scientist's vision and to a considerable resistance to paradigm change.' The science becomes increasingly rigid. As a result, the obsolete paradigm is seldom displaced merely through falsification, proof, or argument, because its defenders invariably devise *ad hoc* modifications to their theory so as to accommodate whatever new data, concepts, or insights may be put to them. Accordingly, we feel justified in reassessing already-existing data in the light of evolutionary theory, and in suggesting ways in which research programmes may be designed to test the 'bold hypotheses' which we and others have developed.

One of the most irritating accusations to have been levelled at us was that, with publication of our book, we had 'jumped on the evolutionary bandwagon'. This was particularly galling in view of the fact that one of us could claim to have been in on the conception and original construction of the bandwagon (Price, 1967), while the other helped to get it trundling along the road on which it continues to gather speed (Stevens, 1982). In the last four years this acceleration has become dizzyingly impressive, with growing academic and media interest in the applications of evolutionary theory to economic, social, and political behaviour, as well as to psychology and psychiatric disorders. Landmark publications have been *How the Mind*

Works (1997) by Stephen Pinker, *Darwinian Psychiatry* (1998) by Michael McGuire and Alfonso Troisi, *Handbook of Evolutionary Psychology* (1998) edited by Charles Crawford and Denis Krebs, and *Evolutionary Psychology: The New Science of the Mind* (1999) by David Buss. The importance of the evolutionary paradigm for new approaches in psychotherapy have been explored in several publications, including *An Intelligent Person's Guide to Psychotherapy* (1998) by Anthony Stevens, a special issue of the *British Journal of Medical Psychology* (1998), *Genes on the Couch: Explorations in Evolutionary Psychotherapy* (1999), edited by Paul Gilbert and Kent Bailey, *Evolution of the Psyche* (1999), edited by David Rosen and Michael Luebbert, and *Subordination and Defeat: An Evolutionary Approach to Mood Disorders and their Therapy* (2000), edited by Leon Sloman and Paul Gilbert. Both of the 1999 publications include chapters by ourselves. Evolutionary insights are also being taken up by child psychiatrists, as evidenced by the paper by Jensen *et al.* (1997), 'Evolution and revolution in child psychiatry: ADHD as a disorder of adaptation'.

There can be little doubt that we are witnessing a revolution in our under-standing of human nature. This is a long overdue fulfilment of the great revolution inaugurated by Charles Darwin nearly a century and a half ago. That it has taken the behavioural sciences so long to catch up with him is, as we have argued, due to the powerful resistance put up by those wedded to the moribund paradigm known as the Standard Social Science Model, which, with hindsight, can now be perceived to have been the 'phlogiston theory' of twentieth-century social science. Not only has the SSSM been responsible for denying to psychology its phylogenetic foundations but also for the restricted vision imposed on psychiatrists by their training. Whereas no surgeon or physician would be let loose on patients without devoting years to the study of comparative anatomy and physiology, psychiatrists have been expected to do their work without any grounding in the evo-lutionary basis of the human mind and its disorders. The time is dawning when they will no longer have to labour under such an extreme disadvan-tage, for we are now on the point of realizing Darwin's own prophecy: 'In the distant future I see open fields for far more important researches', he wrote in the final pages of *The Origin of Species*. 'Psychology will be based on a new foundation . . . Light will be thrown on the origin of man and his history.'

ACKNOWLEDGEMENTS

This book embodies the fruits of our thinking over a span of three decades, and, inevitably, we have sometimes drawn on material previously published by us separately (this being our first collaborative venture) in journals and books. These sources are listed under our names in the Bibliography. We should like to express our thanks to Routledge for permission to use material from *Archetype: A Natural History of the Self* and *On Jung*, and to Hamish Hamilton and Penguin for material from *Private Myths: Dreams and Dreaming* by Anthony Stevens.

In addition, our thanks are due to the American Psychiatric Association, Washington DC, for permission to quote from the *Diagnostic and Statistical Manual of Mental Disorders*, Fourth Edition, and to the Random House Group Ltd for permission to quote from *Attachment and Loss: Volume 1, Attachment,* by John Bowlby.

We should also like to thank those of our colleagues who have read and commented on earlier drafts of chapters appearing in this book. Of these our particular thanks are due to Professors Paul Gilbert, Spencer Millham, David Rosen, and David Sloan Wilson, as well as to Dr Michael Chance and Dr Mark Erickson. While we have taken note of their suggestions, the views expressed in the chapters which follow are, unless otherwise stated, our own, and our commentators should not be held responsible for them.

Finally, our warmest thanks are reserved for Norma Luscombe, who word-processed numerous drafts of this text with unfailing care and good taste, for Bill MacKeith, who copy-edited the first edition, and for Edwina Welham, our editor at Routledge, who has given her enthusiastic support to the project from the moment it was first proposed to her. Publication of the second edition was supported with no less enthusiasm by Kate Hawes, and was seen through the production process by her highly efficient team consisting of Mandy Collison, Joanne Forshaw, Mike Shardlow and Katherine Carson, and we are deeply indebted to them.

Part I

EVOLUTIONARY PSYCHIATRY: AN INTRODUCTION

1

HISTORICAL BACKGROUND

THE MEDICAL MODEL IN PSYCHIATRY

All psychiatrists are doctors. Their long and arduous training conditions them to base their work on the medical model – namely, the idea that it is the doctor's function to examine, to diagnose, and to treat. A psychiatric examination, like any medical examination, is designed to elicit signs and symptoms and to establish the history and course of a diagnosable disease. Once a diagnosis is made, a course of treatment is prescribed, and the patient followed up to assess progress, or otherwise, as the case may be.

The grubby, unemployed youth, who thinks people are staring at him and laughing at him and who hears accusing voices coming out of other passengers' Walkmans on the tube, is diagnosed as schizophrenic and put on phenothiazine drugs. The lonely, divorced woman, who wakes early in the morning, wishing she were dead, and is too frightened to go out and do the shopping in case she breaks down in public, is diagnosed as suffering from depression associated with agoraphobia and put on antidepressant and anxiolytic medication.

In this way, psychiatrists emulate the clinical precision of their medical and surgical colleagues, persuading themselves that they are dealing with clinical entities, which, like diabetes and myxoedema, possess a known origin, a definable course, and a definite cure. Unfortunately, this is largely an illusion. For although psychiatrists may define and classify mental illnesses such as schizophrenia, depression, and obsessive-compulsive disorder, they have little or no idea of what these conditions could be or why human beings should suffer from them.

This does not mean, however, that examining patients and classifying their mental symptoms are futile activities. Observation, differentiation, and classification are natural modes of intellectual progression: they are the means by which our cognitive faculties seek to impose order on chaos. Phenomena have to be recognized and distinguished before they can be explained. Carl Linnaeus had described nearly a million different plant and animal species before Darwin came along and cut through this vast complexity

3

with his tremendous insight that all species are related, and that the more complex evolved out of simpler forms by the twin processes of genetic mutation and natural selection occurring in an environment with finite resources. If the labour of description, annotation, and classification had not continued throughout the eighteenth and early nineteenth centuries the necessary data would not have existed for Darwin's genius to work on.

In medical science this procedure started with Hippocrates and his disciples. They carefully studied their patients, recording the signs and symptoms of their disease. When certain of these indices were found to recur in conjunction with one another, the physician was in the position to recognize (and diagnose) a typical clinical syndrome. We also owe to Hippocrates the idea that diseases have a course through time: they have a natural history. The physician must not only make a careful physical examination in the here and now, but he must elucidate details of the illness's first manifestation and its history since the onset. Then the patient must be followed carefully, noting what changes occur, either spontaneously or as a result of therapeutic intervention. In this way, knowledge could be acquired which might make it possible to distinguish one disease entity from another and to make a realistic assessment of the likely prognosis. In this manner the basis of sound medical practice was laid. Where Hippocrates fell short of the modern physician was in the aetiological system he used to account for the afflictions he was able to diagnose. He attributed madness, for example, to increased humidity of the brain.

In the seventeenth century, the English physician Thomas Sydenham applied the Hippocratic approach to demonstrate that, when one illness can be distinguished from another on the basis of careful clinical examination, it becomes possible to move beyond ancient humoural theories to establish actual pathological changes which underlie each disease. In this way he was able to describe such conditions as malaria, scarlet fever, and gout. Only when the underlying pathology has been described does it become feasible to devise scientifically validated treatments likely to produce a cure – though for the conditions Sydenham described, the cure was a long time in coming. However, his was a decisively important argument. The description of the clinical characteristics of myxoedema and Grave's disease preceded the discovery that they were due respectively to under- and over-activity of the thyroid gland. Once this was established, it became possible to cure myxoedema by administering thyroid extract and Grave's disease by removing part of the thyroid tissue. Interestingly, Sydenham saw his approach as analogous to that employed by the botanists of his time. The physician, he said, should be able to describe physical diseases 'with the same exactness as we see it done by botanic writers in their treatises on plants.'

The psychiatrists of the eighteenth and nineteenth centuries were inspired by a similar sense of mission. By making systematic observations of the mentally ill, they were able to describe their symptoms and behaviour with a precision that other psychiatrists were able to understand and replicate. This prepared the way for Emil Kraepelin to perform his great work of synthesis and to publish his conclusion in the 1890s that there existed two major functional psychotic disorders, which he called **dementia praecox** and **manic-depression**.

Medical science has historically progressed through five stages:

1 Recognition of specific symptoms
↓
2 Definition of syndromes
↓
3 Identification of tissue pathology
↓
4 Demonstration of the causes of tissue pathology
↓
5 Establishment of an appropriate cure.

All five stages have been completed with regard to a number of medical conditions, but with psychiatric disorders the story has been less encouraging. There has been considerable progress in accomplishing the first two stages, but the last three have been marked with only variable and often disappointing success. The descriptive classification of mental illnesses introduced by Kraepelin certainly brought order into a previously chaotic back ward of psychiatric practice, but it offered no definite indications as to the aetiology or treatment of the illnesses it defined. Since then the search for structural lesions in the brain and for biochemical disturbances of cerebral functioning has yielded some progress towards establishing a genetic and neurophysiological basis for the major psychoses. The role of psychological and social factors influencing the onset of psychiatric illness is now better appreciated than hitherto, and powerful psychoactive drugs have been developed which go some way to remove symptoms and relieve suffering. However, it is widely acknowledged that as a branch of medicine psychiatry has failed to achieve the scientific status confidently predicted for it by such pioneers as Kraepelin, Bleuler, and Maudsley at the beginning of the twentieth century.

In this failure, psychiatry has been no more culpable than its sister disciplines psychology and sociology. Outstanding figures in the history of these areas of enquiry – men like J.B. Watson, B.F. Skinner, Karl Marx, Emile Durkheim, Sigmund Freud, and C.G. Jung – achieved eminence primarily because they proposed theoretical models capable of guiding the clinical, experimental, and field work of those who subscribed to them. But none of these has achieved the degree of general acceptance enjoyed by paradigms in physics (the Newtonian and Einsteinian paradigms), biology (the Darwinian paradigm of evolution through natural selection), or astronomy (the Copernican paradigm).

In the course of this book we shall argue that the main reason for the paradigmatic failure of psychiatry and the behavioural sciences generally is attributable to their persistent reluctance to come to terms with the scientific revolution wrought in biology by Charles Darwin. Their formulations are still tinged with special creationism, their findings lack the unifying cohesion of a conceptual framework linking the basic features of human life with the natural history of our own and other animal species. There are powerful religious and political reasons why this has been so in the past, but these have now lost their salience, and developments in ethology, behavioural ecology, and sociobiology have at last made it possible, we believe, to bring psychology and psychiatry into the mainstream of contemporary biological science.

THE PHYLOGENETIC DIMENSION

The first systematic attempt to place human psychopathology on a biological footing was that of Sigmund Freud. That it failed was because of his dogmatic insistence on the central motivating importance of sex, his obsolete conceptions of the functioning of the central nervous system acquired working in Brücke's laboratory in the 1880s, and because, throughout his life, his evolutionary formulations remained unashamedly Lamarckian. A significant, but less appreciated, contribution, was made by Freud's dissident colleague, Alfred Adler, who annexed Nietzsche's 'will to power' in order to introduce the notions of self-esteem, feelings of inferiority, and the need to compensate for them, into the aetiology of neurosis. In this he anticipated the importance attributed to social ranking behaviour by modern behavioural biology. That Adler's formulations have been neglected by evolutionary psychologists is because he was by nature an educationalist and politician rather than a biologist.

A major breakthrough in the early decades of this century was the hypothesis proposed by C.G. Jung of **archetypes** functioning as dynamic units of **the phylogenetic psyche**, which Jung misleadingly termed the 'collective unconscious'. Archetypes are conceived as neuropsychic units which evolved through natural selection and which are responsible for determining the behavioural characteristics as well as the affective and cognitive experiences typical of human beings.

Unlike Freud, who maintained that the crucial events of human developmental psychology were confined to childhood and adolescence, Jung took the view that development proceeds throughout the life-cycle as a whole. The archetypal endowment with which each of us is born prepares us for the natural life-cycle of our species in the natural world in which we evolved. A programmed sequence of stages, each mediated by a new set of archetypal imperatives, seeks fulfilment in the development of characteristic patterns of

6

personality and behaviour. Each set of imperatives makes its own demands on the environment. Should the environment fail to meet them, then the consequent 'frustration of archetypal intent' (Stevens, 1982) may result in psychopathology. For example, the infant–mother archetypal system will achieve fulfilment only if activated by the presence and behaviour of a maternal figure; and the heterosexual archetypal system can achieve fulfilment only through the presence of a suitable mate. Should any of these figures be absent, then the archetypal system concerned will remain dormant and development may be arrested or follow an aberrant course.

In the Jungian view, the purpose of life is the fullest possible realization of the archetypal programme that is compatible with ethical responsibility. Psychopathology results, on the other hand, when the environment fails, either partially or totally, to meet one (or more) basic archetypal need(s) in the developing individual. This view is in close agreement with that developed by the British psychiatrist, John Bowlby, in the 1950s. Before then, Jung's ideas had for the most part been neglected or derided because they subverted the prevailing academic consensus which was deeply hostile to the notion that innate structures could have any part to play in human psychology or human social behaviour.

Until Bowlby's arrival on the scene, it had been generally accepted that infant attachment behaviour, like practically all other forms of human behaviour, was learned through a form of 'operant conditioning' associated with natural rewards and punishments, the caretaker's presence and nurturing behaviour being experienced as rewarding, and her absence or lack of maternal attention being experienced as punishing. As with most theories espoused by academic psychologists at that time, the primary reward held to be responsible for eliciting infant attachment was food, and, as a consequence, it came to be known as the 'cupboard love' theory. Practically all psychologists, psychiatrists, and psychoanalysts accepted the cupboard love theory as accounting for the facts, and it went unquestioned for decades.

Then, in 1958, Bowlby published his now famous paper entitled 'The nature of the child's tie to his mother', in which he attacked the cupboard love theory and suggested instead that infants become attached to their mothers, and mothers to their infants, not so much through learning as by instinct. Mothers and infants had no need to learn to love one another: they were innately programmed to do so from birth. The formation of mother–infant attachment bonds, Bowlby maintained, is a direct expression of the genetic heritage of our species.

The initial reaction to Bowlby's paper was one of widespread condemnation, particularly from social scientists. What upset them was Bowlby's use of the term 'instinct' and the readiness with which he borrowed concepts from the relatively new science of **ethology** (the study of behaviour patterns in organisms living in their natural environments) and applied them to human psychology. But he remained adamant that such comparisons between different species were biologically justifiable; and in attacking the cupboard love theory he was able to cite many examples from the ethological literature of the existence of strong infant–mother bonds which had been formed through mechanisms bearing no relation to feeding gratification and which developed in the absence of any conventional rewards such as those postulated by the learning theorists. This was corroborated by Stevens (1982) who, in a study of Greek children raised in an orphanage, found that a substantial proportion of them became primarily attached to nurses who had cuddled and played with them but seldom fed them.

One of the most influential ethological texts, *The Study of Instinct* by Niko Tinbergen, was published in 1951. In it Tinbergen proposed that every animal species possesses a repertoire of behaviours. This behavioural repertoire is dependent upon structures evolution has built into the central nervous system of the species. Tinbergen called these structures **innate releasing mechanisms**, or **IRMs**. Each IRM is primed to become active when an appropriate stimulus – called a sign stimulus – is encountered in the environment. When such a stimulus appears, the innate mechanism is released, and the animal responds with a characteristic pattern of behaviour which is adapted through evolution to the situation.

Although no one made the connection at the time, Tinbergen's position was very close to Jung's view of the nature of archetypes and their mode of activation. A mallard duck becomes amorous at the sight of a mallard drake (the green head being the sign stimulus that releases in her central nervous system the innate mechanism responsible for the characteristic **patterns of behaviour** associated with courtship in the duck), and a ewe becomes attached to her lamb as she licks the birth membranes from its snout. In the same way, Bowlby argued, a human mother presented with her newborn infant perceives its helplessness and its need for her care, and during the hours and days that follow is overwhelmed by feelings of love, attachment, and responsibility. Bowlby, like Jung, held that such patterns of response had been prepared for by nature. As Jung himself insisted, the archetype 'is not meant to denote an inherited idea, but rather an inherited mode of functioning, corresponding to the inborn way in which the chick emerges from the egg, the bird builds its nest, a certain kind of wasp stings the motor ganglion of the caterpillar, and eels find their way to the Bermudas. In other words, it is a "pattern of behaviour". This aspect of the archetype, the purely biological one, is the proper concern of scientific psychology' (Jung, 1953–78, CW 18, para. 1228). When due allowance is made for the greater adaptive flexibility of our species, therefore, the ethological position is very close to Jung's view of the nature of archetypes and their mode of activation. Having been neglected for the greater part of this century, the archetypal hypothesis is being rediscovered and rehabilitated by those psychologists and psychiatrists who have adopted the ethological orientation to their subject matter and allowed an evolutionary perspective to illuminate their thinking.

Tinbergen's original ideas were greatly extended during the 1970s and 1980s by the sociobiologists Charles Lumsden and Edward Wilson, who argued that all behaviour, both human and non-human, depended on what they called **epigenetic rules** that control the psychosocial development of the individual. This idea was itself an extension of an earlier proposal by the biologist C.H. Waddington that the development of all living organisms is determined by **epigenetic pathways.**

All these concepts – IRMs, patterns of behaviour, epigenetic rules, and epigenetic pathways – although derived from animal observations, are all compatible with the archetypal hypothesis. For in the course of human evolution, at no time have we ceased to be mammals or primates. Indeed, as we shall see in the next chapter, the human brain incorporates still functioning and much earlier mammalian and reptilian brains.

Most articulate of the evolutionary psychologists and psychiatrists are Paul Gilbert and John Archer in Great Britain, Russell Gardner, Brant Wenegrat, David Buss, Randolph Nesse, and Michael McGuire in the United States, and Alfonso Troisi in Italy. Each of them has detected and announced the presence of neuropsychic propensities virtually indistinguishable from archetypes. Gilbert refers to them as 'psychobiological response patterns', Gardner as 'master programmes' or 'propensity states', while Wenegrat borrows the sociobiological term 'genetically transmitted response strategies'. Buss refers to 'evolved psychological mechanisms', Nesse to 'prepared tendencies', and McGuire and Troisi to 'evolved psychological capacities'. These response patterns, master programmes, propensity states, response strategies, evolved psychological mechanisms, prepared tendencies, and evolved psychological capacities are held responsible for crucial, species-specific patterns of behaviour that evolved because they maximized the fitness of the organism to survive, and for its genes to survive, in the environment in which it evolved. These strategies are inherently shared by all members of the species, whether they be healthy or ill. Psychopathology intervenes when these strategies malfunction as a result of environmental insults or deficiencies at critical stages of development.

The importance of this work is not only its extension of archetypal theory to psychiatric aetiology but the historic fact that it represents the first systematic attempt to acknowledge the phylogenetic dimension in psychiatry and to put psychopathology on a sound evolutionary basis. This, we believe, will do much to restore the shaky morale of the mental health profession as a whole. That there has been a decline in the status of psychiatry is due to the rebellion against established authority in the 1960s, which found expression in, among other things, the 'anti-psychiatry' movement, which called into question basic concepts at the heart of psychiatric practice. Thomas Szasz, for example, argued that mental illness did not exist, while R.D. Laing maintained that schizophrenics were displaying a set of healthy responses to a sick society. Though these propositions were rejected by most

9

authorities, they nevertheless achieved wide currency and went some way towards undermining the self-confidence of many psychiatrists, forcing them to question whether they were indeed worthy to occupy the position of commander-in-chief of their own clinical units. This was perhaps a necessary corrective to the arrogance of some consultants in mental hospital practice, but in too many cases it led to clinical funk and an abdication of proper responsibility for the unhappy people in their care.

The psychiatrist's vulnerability was further increased by the failure of biochemists and neuroscientists to demonstrate a clear physical aetiology for the neuroses and functional psychoses. While most psychiatrists continued to insist that these conditions were true medical diseases, and that, one day, a physical cause would be found for them, they could not but acknowledge that their belief was based on faith rather than scientific evidence. This embarrassing situation has persisted, despite recent advances, and, as a consequence, psychiatrists have felt they had little option but to languish in a no man's land situated somewhere between medicine and sociology.

Against this background, it is our contention that the introduction of the new evolutionary paradigm will be of inestimable value to the future of psychiatry, since a number of crucial advantages will accrue from it:

1 It will make possible a much clearer definition of the essential parameters of mental health by integrating the findings of psychiatry with those of ethology, sociobiology, and cross-cultural anthropology.

2 It will facilitate study of the developmental progress of the human organism in relation to the socio-economic environment in which development proceeds, contrasting contemporary environmental circumstances with those which prevailed during the period that marked our evolution as a species (the so-called 'environment of evolutionary adaptedness' or 'the ancestral environment'). This in turn will serve to generate hypotheses concerning the environmental provisions necessary for healthy development and for the prevention and treatment of mental disorders.

3 It will enable us to incorporate what is known about human developmental psychology with what is known about development in other animal species, thus rendering it possible to propose hypotheses to explain the genesis of typical modes of psychopathology.

4 Since the new paradigm gives equal weight to psychological and physical events, it will permit new research findings from both psychology and neuroscience to be integrated with one another and with the whole body of psychiatric knowledge.

5 Establishment of the new paradigm will have a rejuvenating impact, we believe, on all psychiatric research and practice, transforming the subject into a dynamic and exciting new discipline capable of attracting some of the best minds from the younger generation of doctors – something which the speciality, in its present jaded form, has conspicuously failed to do.

2

HUMAN NATURE
ITS EVOLUTION AND DEVELOPMENT

BASIC PROPOSITIONS

We are highly evolved social animals. We have a large brain (relative to our body weight) which bears indelible traces of our long evolutionary history from the reptiles through the mammals to the primates. Encoded within this brain are core schemata which predispose us to think, feel, and behave in specific ways. These archetypal predispositions evolved in the same way as the anatomy and physiology of our bodies. As with all other animal species, our innate propensities (which together make up the human **genome**) are dependent on environmental variables for their expression. Since these basic archetypal units are responsible for typically human modes of behaviour and experience, they are inevitably a primary focus of study for psychologists and psychiatrists.

From the biological standpoint, the ultimate 'purpose' of our existence is the perpetuation of our genes. The transmission of our genes to the next generation is the **ultimate cause** of our behaviour. The archetypal propensities with which we are endowed are adapted to enable us to survive long enough in the environment in which we evolved ('the environment of evolutionary adaptedness') to give our genes a fair chance of transmission to our offspring.

THE EVOLUTION OF ARCHETYPAL PROPENSITIES

What comes to be fixed in the genetic structure of the species is the *predisposition* to certain species-specific forms of behaviour and experience. How has evolution brought this about? Darwin's answer was through **natural selection**. As a result of genetic mutations, which occur spontaneously and at random, an individual may acquire a characteristic or a propensity which makes it better adapted than its fellows to respond appropriately to a certain typical situation – such as, for example, attack from a predator. Being thus advantaged, this individual will tend to survive and pass its new genetic configuration to members of subsequent generations, who, possessing the desirable characteristic, will compete more effectively in the struggle for

11

existence. As a result the new attribute eventually becomes established as a standard component in the genetic structure of the species.

In this manner, our archetypal propensities have become adapted to the typical situations encountered in human life. The repeated selection of fortuitous mutations, occurring through hundreds of thousands of generations and over millions of years, has resulted in the present genome of the human species. And the genome expresses itself as surely in the structure of the human psyche and in human patterns of behaviour as it does in the anatomy of the human physique.

But this is not the whole story. In addition to natural selection, which promotes the evolution of characteristics which prove beneficial to an animal in the struggle for existence, Darwin posited two other modes of selection, which have come to be called **intrasexual selection** and **mate selection**. Intrasexual selection promotes the evolution of characteristics which benefit an animal when it competes with others of the same sex for the favours of a sexual partner (such as size, strength, dominance, assertiveness); while mate selection promotes the evolution of characteristics which make an animal attractive to the opposite sex as a potential breeding partner (such as plumage, colouring, physique). Success in the struggle for survival linked with success in competing for the attraction of sexual partners enhances an individual's **reproductive fitness** – that is, it will increase the number of copies of his or her genetic material that the individual passes on to *direct* descendants.

However, the Darwinian strategies of sexual reproductive fitness which focused on the *individual* have proved inadequate to explain certain elements of animal behaviour, such as self-sacrifice and various forms of **altruism**. As a result, it has been found necessary to replace the Darwinian notion of reproductive fitness with the neo-Darwinian concept of **inclusive fitness**. In the contemporary evolutionary view, what matters more than the survival of the individual *per se* is the survival of that individual's *genes*. Inclusive fitness refers to the number of copies of his genetic material that an individual causes to be passed on, not only to his direct descendants, but to *other* than direct descendants as well – for example, to nephews, nieces and cousins, all of whom share a proportion of his genes. This has given rise to a variety of **response rules**, **strategies**, and **tactics** (Wenegrat, 1984) for the performance of social behaviours which promote the probability of gene survival – for example, the care and protection of children, peer bonding and peer play, status-seeking, competing for valued resources, courtship, sexual bonding and marriage, sharing and storing food, seeking shelter, co-operating, reciprocal altruism, discriminating against strangers, the splitting of groups when they achieve a critical size, the expression of outgroup hostility and ingroup loyalty, cleaning, washing, grooming, teaching (pedagogy), ritualized tournaments, subscribing to the beliefs and practices of myth, religion, and ritual, and so on. Since in the environment of evolutionary adaptedness (the EEA) human beings lived in small groups in which some genetic relationship existed between all members, these strategies were usually directed towards kin or shared with kin.

As a concept, fitness implies relativity: your fitness is greater than your friend's if more of your genes appear in the next generation. The genetic arithmetic of individual fitness is straightforward: parents share 50 per cent of their genes with each offspring and 25 per cent with each grandchild. If you have a nephew, he will share, on average, 25 per cent of your genes. One of his offspring will have 12.5 per cent of your genes. Therefore, if he has five offspring, a greater number of your genes will be replicated in the next generation than if you had only one son (12.5 per cent $\times$ 5 = 62.5 per cent as opposed to 50 per cent). In practice, this gives rise to trade-offs which influence behaviour in predictable ways. Thus, parents tend to invest more in their offspring than in less genetically close relatives, and children who live with one natural and with one step-parent are more likely to be abused than children living with two natural parents (Daly and Wilson, 1989).

ULTIMATE CAUSES AND PROXIMATE MECHANISMS

Evolutionary psychiatry makes a distinction between ultimate causes and proximate causes of behaviour. Ultimate causes have shaped the human genome over millions of years of selection pressure, whereas proximate causes operate on and through the phenotype, that is, on and through the life experience of the individual. The 'ultimate' predispositions encoded in the brain of the newborn infant provide the basic plans on which 'proximate' development proceeds. Ultimate predispositions also act as constraints which limit the scope of proximate functions and their development. So far in its history, psychiatry has confined itself to the study of proximate mechanisms, such as the alteration of receptor function through use of pharmacological agents.

A number of proximate mechanisms have been distinguished as being specific to certain psychosocial domains – such as the identification of caretakers, the differentiation of strangers from familiars, the calculation of costs and benefits in reciprocal interactions, and so on. These domain-specific proximate mechanisms have been called **algorithms** (Cosmides and Tooby, 1989) and have been compared to the actualized functions of Jungian archetypes (Walters, 1994). Algorithms sensitize the organism to monitor specific situations, and they function as *biases to learn* certain behavioural responses rather than others. Indeed, many of the behaviours previously thought to be learned – for example, infant attachment behaviours, stranger avoidance, submissive behaviours – can now be more appropriately understood as developmental refinements of pre-programmed algorithms. It is important to remember that genes are not rigid determinants of social behaviour, but *conveyors of potential* to behave in species characteristic ways.

The major concern of evolutionary psychiatry is the nature and function of proximate mechanisms rather than the fulfilment of ultimate causes. Apart from any other consideration, this reflects clinical reality. After all, patients do not complain about failure to promote their inclusive fitness but about their inability to meet the demands of social, emotional, and economic life. Natural selection has equipped us, it is true, with archetypal propensities which, in appropriate contexts, will stand a good chance of prompting behaviours which promote inclusive fitness. But much depends on the context, and in that sense life is a lottery. The Almighty may not play at dice, as Einstein asserted, but, if human behaviour is anything to go by, God is a gifted statistician. The pursuit of biosocial goals has the unconscious consequence of facilitating inclusive fitness while failure to attain these goals can certainly result in mental distress. But it is failure to meet the biosocial imperatives by which we are guided, rather than failure to transmit our genes, that is the source of human psychopathology and suffering.

The nature and number of the primary biosocial goals responsible for initiating human behaviour are still open to dispute. Gilbert (1989) has postulated four distinct types. These are **care-eliciting**, **care-giving**, **competitive power-seeking**, and **co-operating**. We are doubtful that these goals are as distinct as Gilbert believes. Like Bowlby, we consider care-eliciting, care-giving, and co-operating, as derivatives and developmental expressions of the archetypal system responsible for affiliation and bonding. We see competitive power-seeking, on the other hand, as an aspect of the hierarchical, ranking, or dominance–submission archetype. Moreover, Gilbert leaves out of account courtship and mating, the stranger archetype, and the biosocial system responsible for the evasion of enemies, for outgroup hostilities, and paranoia. One might almost agree with Jung when he said that there are as many archetypes as there are common situations in life.

INNATE PROPENSITIES AND THE BRAIN

Like the social structures for which it is responsible, the human brain is a hierarchical system: this is a reflection of its architecture, its evolution, and its enormous functional complexity. Dominating the entire apparatus are the two massive cerebral hemispheres, with their convoluted cortical covering, which contain no less than 75 per cent of the approximately 20 thousand million neurones in the brain. Beneath these relatively recent additions much older parts of the brain exist which still possess their full functional integrity. A crude distinction between these older and newer components was made many years ago by James Olds (1922–1976) who called them the 'hot' and 'cold' brains respectively. By the 'hot' brain Olds was referring to the mid-brain which could in many ways be identified with the Freudian 'id': it appears to function in accordance with the 'pleasure principle', in that it is impulsive, incautious, and unashamedly appetitive. The hot brain wants its own way, and it wants it *now*. The 'cold' brain, or cerebral cortex, on the other hand, is more rational and more susceptible to social conditioning: like Freud's 'reality principle' it mediates the passions of the hot brain to the environment, and causes them to heed the constraints of outer necessity.

A far more sophisticated and empirically productive distinction than that of James Olds was made in the 1960s by the American neuroscientist, Paul MacLean, who conceived of the brain not as a unity but as *three brains in one*, each with a different phylogenetic history, each with 'its own special intelligence, its own special memory, its own sense of time and space, and its own motor functions' (MacLean, 1976). MacLean's famous diagram of the three brains, which together make up what he calls the **triune brain**, is reproduced in Figure 1. Another American neuroscientist, Jim Henry of Los Angeles, has argued that the dominant left cerebral hemisphere represents a fourth and phylogenetically most recent system which is peculiar to our species (Henry and Stephens, 1977).

In line with these suggestions, it is likely that the brain evolved in four stages:

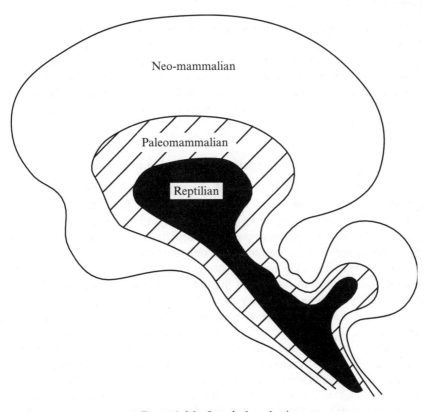

Figure 1 MacLean's three brains
Source: MacLean, 1973

1　The reptilian brain

This, our most primitive cerebral component, evolved in our reptilian ancestors about 300 million years ago. We share it with all other terrestrial vertebrates and it has remained remarkably unchanged by the march of evolution. It contains nuclei which are vital to the maintenance of life, such as those controlling the cardiovascular and respiratory systems. The main structural components of the reptilian brain are the **basal ganglia**, including the olfactostriatum (the olfactory tubercle and nucleus accumbens) and part of the corpus striatum (the caudate nucleus, putamen, globus pallidus, and satellite collections of grey matter).

At the early evolutionary stage represented by the reptilian brain emotions had not yet emerged, nor had cognitive appreciation of future or past events. Behavioural responses at this level are largely governed by instinct and appear to be relatively automatic. The typically reptilian behaviours of territorial acquisition and defence, as well as dominance striving, agonistic threat displays, and mating are manifested at this stage of development. As Bailey (1987) says:

> Our drives, inner subjective feelings, fantasies and thoughts are thoroughly conditioned by emanations from the R-complex [the reptilian brain]. The reptilian carry-overs provide the automatic, compulsive urgency to much of human behaviour, where free will steps aside and persons act as they have to act, often despising themselves in the process for their hatreds, prejudices, compulsions, conformity, deceptiveness and guile.

2　The paleo-mammalian brain

This is made up of those subcortical structures which comprise the **limbic system**. This includes not only the hippocampus, the hypothalamus, and the thalamus, but also the pituitary gland, which has been aptly described as 'the conductor of the endocrine orchestra'. The limbic system is a homeostatic mechanism *par excellence*: it not only maintains a sensitive control of hormone levels but also balances hunger against satiation, sexual desire against gratification, thirst against fluid retention, sleep against wakefulness. It also plays an indispensable role in memory storage.

By this evolutionary stage, the major emotions of fear and anger have emerged as well as those of love and attachment, together with their associated behavioural response patterns, bonding and mating. MacLean (1985) particularly draws attention to three forms of behaviour that most clearly distinguish the evolutionary transition from reptiles to mammals. These are: (1) nursing and maternal care, (2) audiovocal communication for maintaining mother–offspring contact, and (3) play. The most primitive and basic mammalian vocalization, MacLean asserts, is the **separation call**, which originally served to maintain mother–offspring proximity and which later came to maintain contact between members of a group. MacLean believes that play evolved as a means to promote group harmony and affiliation. It is the thalamocingulate division of the limbic system that performs the essential role in these mother–offspring and peer group behaviours, and there is no counterpart of this limbic subdivision in the reptilian brain. The other subdivisions of the limbic system – the amygdalar and septal subdivisions – are involved, respectively, in behaviour promoting self-preservation and the procreation of the species.

Conscious awareness is more in evidence at this stage and behaviour is less rigidly determined by instincts, though these are still very apparent. The limbic system includes the oldest and most primitive part of the evolving cerebral cortex – the so-called *paleocortex*.

In all mammals, including man, this part of the brain is, therefore, a structure of the utmost complexity, controlling basic psychophysical responses and attitudes to the environment. An animal, deprived of its cerebral cortex, can still find its way about, eat, drink, and avoid painful stimuli, but it has difficulty in attributing *meaning* to things: a natural predator will be noticed, for example, but not apparently perceived as a threat.

3 The neo-mammalian brain

This is the *neocortex*. It is responsible for cognition and sophisticated perceptual processes, as opposed to emotional (limbic) and instinctive (basal ganglia) behaviour. Behaviour arising in the neocortex is usually described as 'conscious', 'voluntary', and 'rational', reflecting the fact that there is a sense of personal control over such behaviour. At this level there is a high degree of awareness, unlike the partial awareness and limited sense of control that characterizes emotional behaviour, and the relative lack of control, and often only retrospective awareness, that is typical of instinctive behaviour.

4 The human brain

By this stage lateralization of function between the two hemispheres has occurred, with the development of the left dominant hemisphere responsible for rational, empirical thinking, as well as the use of language and speech.

Attempts to integrate the two disciplines of neurophysiology and ethology have resulted in the focus of intense research interest on the limbic system as the region subserving species-specific patterns of behaviour. MacLean's conclusions were largely derived from animal studies, but the work of Flor-Henry (1976) and Schwartz *et al.* (1975), indicated that they were no less applicable to man. These researchers demonstrated that human emotional responses are dependent on neuronal pathways linking the limbic system with parietal and frontal areas of the right cerebral cortex. It appears, moreover, that this whole complicated right hemispheric/limbic affectional system is under the control of the left frontal cortex, which suggests that the 'cold' dominant hemisphere has a role in repressing or inhibiting the emotionally toned activities of the 'hot' paleo-mammalian brain.

MacLean's triune brain concept is not without its critics. Butler and Hodos (1996), for example, point out that the brains of present-day reptiles have undergone independent evolution in the past 250 million years and can hardly be assumed to be identical with the brain of the common ancestor we share with the reptiles. While this is undeniably true, the basic principles formulated by MacLean remain valid. The increase in size and complexity developed by the human brain since the reptilian stage has equipped us with three *central processing assemblies*, or decision-making units, each of which responds in its characteristic way to changes in the environment. Though the activity of these three assemblies is to some extent co-ordinated, each retains a degree of autonomy. Later, we shall examine how their activity may result in psychopathology (see particularly pp. 242–49).

The triune brain provides a home for what we might call the 'triune mind'. Many thinkers, including Plato, St Augustine, La Rochefoucauld, Freud, and Jung, have observed that the mind seems to possess separate functional components which compete with one another for overall control of behaviour. Variously attributed to such organs as the 'head', the 'heart', and the 'bowels', reason, emotion, and instinct may display differing intentions when it comes to choosing a mate during courtship or displaying valour on the field of battle: 'Le coeur a ses raisons, que la raison ne connait point.' MacLean's anatomical studies give useful support to this long-standing concept of three minds in one (the neurological 'holy trinity').

It begins to look, therefore, as if Jung was right when he guessed that the archetypal systems of the collective unconscious, if they could be given a local habitation and a name, must have their neuronal substrate in phylogenetically old parts of the brain. It is not, of course, possible to designate any precise neurological location for any of the archetypes. The neural structures involved in archetypal functioning must have an extremely complex and widely ramifying neurological basis involving millions of neurones in the brain stem and limbic system and both cerebral hemispheres.

HUMAN ONTOGENESIS: THE ETHOLOGICAL VIEW

Ethology views the human being as a psychophysical system with a built-in biological clock: both its structure and its life-cycle are predetermined by the evolutionary history of its genes. As the biological clock ticks away and the life-cycle unfolds, so the system accepts and incorporates into itself the life experience of the individual. But what we experience as the whole process is only the end result. We are aware only of the ontogenetic aspects of our own maturation, being largely unconscious of the phylogenetic blueprint on whose basis it proceeds. This goes some way to explain the naïve readiness of psychologists for most of this century to give credence to behaviourist or learning theorist accounts of human development, which looked no further in their formulations than the conditioning to which each individual has been subjected in his or her life time.

In contrast to the *tabula rasa* model adopted by behaviourism, evolutionary psychiatry conceives of the human organism as a highly complex system constructed in such a way as always to be ready, at successive stages of the life-cycle, to process certain kinds of data, to experience certain psychophysical states, and produce certain kinds of behaviour. Maturation requires that, like a computer, the organism be capable of storing the data once they have been processed and, having stored them, of progressing to the next stage to deal with the next set of circumstances that might arise. In this manner, development proceeds by way of a largely predetermined series of sequences, each of which is linked to a stage in the natural life-cycle of the species, and each manifested in species-specific patterns of behaviour, such as maternal bonding, speech acquisition, peer play, and so on. 'Ultimately', wrote Jung, 'every individual life is at the same time the eternal life of the species' (CW11, para. 146).

At any given moment in any population of human beings there will be individuals who have reached different stages in the developmental sequence; each will possess a certain store of data and will consequently emit behaviours which will stimulate others who have reached a stage appropriate to respond to them (Henry and Stephens, 1977). The product of interaction between such individuals will be certain typical relationships or attachments. As Bowlby, who was the first to introduce this ethological view of ontogenesis into psychiatry, pointed out, 'Behaviour patterns mediating attachment of young to adults are complementary to those mediating care of the young by adults; in the same way, systems mediating adult masculine behaviour in one individual are complementary to those mediating adult feminine behaviour in another' (1969, p. 179). Bowlby emphasized that innate behavioural systems are never intelligible in terms of a single individual but only in terms of a population of individuals interacting with one another.

In formulating his ideas, Bowlby was much influenced by C.H. Waddington's (1957) **theory of epigenesis** which conceives of preprogrammed **epigenetic pathways** along which ontogenetic development proceeds. This corresponds to the Jungian concept of **the Self** – the sum total of archetypal potential – which possesses its own ontological dynamic. The Self proposes and the environment disposes. The archetypes of the phylogenetic psyche are actualized in the complexes (pathological or normal as the environment determines) of the ontogenetic psyche, and tend to maintain the individual on whatever developmental pathway he is already progressing. In this way, the complexes come to possess the enduring self-regulatory property which Waddington termed **homeorhesis**.

Waddington's theoretical approach became widely influential among ethologists. It prompted, for example, the proposal put forward by H.F. and M.K. Harlow (1965) that the social adaptation of rhesus monkeys depended upon the sequential activation of five distinct affectional systems. These are as follows:

1 **The maternal system**, which ensures survival by providing nutrition and protection, encourages security through close physical proximity, and promotes development through infant–mother interactions.
2 **The infant–mother system**, which integrates the preprogrammed behaviours of the infant prompting it to seek and maintain the mother's proximity.
3 **The peer system**, which plays a crucial role in promoting exploration of the environment and the development of social and motor skills.
4 **The heterosexual system**, which operates intermittently in some species and more durably in others, to ensure mating and reproduction. While many birds and some primates mate for life, most mammals are promiscuous. In birds and rodents mating is primarily determined by hormonal rhythms, whereas in primates the formation of heterosexual bonds is influenced by the success or failure of bonds previously formed with mother or peers. As the Harlows put it: 'Primates which have never loved early, never love late.'
5 **The paternal system**, which has the function of providing protection against predators, preventing infants from falling victim to aggression within the group, and assuring the privileged position of mothers and infants. It manifests itself in a paternal interest in infants and in a willingness to play with them.

Though these postulates were based on experiments with rhesus monkeys, it seems highly probable that similar ontological steps occur in the social maturation of human beings. Though the Harlows considered each of these systems to be separate and distinct in their mode of operation, Bowlby's researches demonstrated that affectional systems are apt to influence each other in the course of human development. This observation formed the basis of his **attachment theory** of human social behaviour and human psychopathology.

Maturation proceeds, therefore, through a sequence of **innate expectations**, which the environment either fulfils or fails to meet. Most important among these expectations are the following: adequate warmth and nourishment for survival; a family consisting of mother, father, and peers; sufficient space for exploration and play; security from enemies and predators; a community to supply language, myth, religion, ritual, codes of behaviour, values, initiation into adulthood, social status, an economic role, and, eventually, a mate. Of all these archetypal anticipations, the most crucial is that the environment will provide a family.

THE FAMILY

Anthropology demonstrates that family formation is a universal character-istic of humanity. Different cultures favour different kinds of family, it is true, but all societies support family ties of one sort or another, where at least one man and at least one woman care for children. It seems, therefore, that the family is an archetypal configuration; its very universality and per-sistence indicate that the family is biologically established as a species-specific characteristic and that it is only secondarily modified by cultural or ecological factors as to the indigenous form that it takes.

Family-like groupings exist in other primates, but in no other animal is family life so highly structured and institutionalized as in humanity. The reason for this must be connected with the relative helplessness and apparent prematurity of human infants, which place a far greater burden on the human mother than that endured by any of her mammalian sisters. To bear it alone and without support would, in the environment of evolutionary adaptedness, have been difficult and often fatal, especially for a woman who, in the absence of contraception, gave birth to a new child every two or three years. The well-being of her young demanded that she be provided with a protector and helpmate. Seen in this light, the family seems the obvious solution and it is probable that populations which have assumed ordered patterns of family life have possessed a selective advantage over those which have not.

It is hardly surprising, therefore, that we have acquired characteristics whose function is to sustain mature heterosexual partnerships once they have been formed: these include the genetic acquisition of a tendency to make lasting heterosexual bonds, the 'hypersexuality' of human beings, and the development of marriage laws which served to hold partners together despite frictions and misunderstandings, and to reduce sexual jealousy and competition between males, thus enabling them to go about their essen-tially *collaborative* business of hunting and warfare without having to waste too much time keeping an eye on their womenfolk and each other. Marriage promotes the cohesiveness of a society and its competitive effi-ciency, and it is not hard to see why such an invaluable institution should have evolved.

It is highly probable, therefore, that for as long as our species has existed children have been reared in families. And if, as evolutionary psychiatry maintains, the human infant is phylogenetically prepared to meet the typical circumstances of its **Umwelt**, then it is reasonable to assume that this innate structure will anticipate in some measure the presence and the behaviour of parents of both sexes. It follows that children in whom this anticipation is not met will be at risk.

ATTACHMENT

All schools of analysis agree that there is no finer start in life than to have been born to parents who loved, trusted, and respected one another, who were open and honest in their personal dealings, and consistent in their attitudes to each other and to their children. Developmental psychology is sufficiently advanced for us to know that children who grow up in reasonably stable families are likely to enjoy mental health, in that they are free of incapacitating neurotic symptoms, and that they tend to become secure, self-reliant adults who display social maturity through their ability to be helpful and co-operative with others. It is these characters that psychiatry regards as 'normal'. Freudian analysts speak of them as possessing a 'strong ego'; Kleinians consider them to have 'introjected a good object'; in Erik Erikson's terms, they have established 'basic trust'; Fairbairn would have described them as displaying 'mature dependence'; and for Bowlby and his attachment theorists, they have succeeded in constructing a model of themselves as being able to provide help and as being worthy of receiving help from others should the need arise. In Jungian terms, they are well started on the path to individuation.

However, a large and growing section of the population is less fortunate. **Neurotic illness**, which disturbs the emotional and mental well-being of people without depriving them of their reason, is without doubt one of the greatest scourges of contemporary humanity. Just how common it is cannot be accurately determined; those statistics which do exist are almost certainly underestimates since they are derived from the minority of sufferers who present themselves for treatment. In the majority of such people who are actually seen by psychiatrists, a history is elicited of deficient parental care – deficient in the sense that the quality of care provided was such as to frustrate those archetypal imperatives, inherent within the biogrammar of the maturing brain, which are concerned with the formation of attachment bonds, the establishment of basic trust, and the development of a secure ego conceiving of itself as being both acceptable to others and capable of coping with the eventualities of life.

Of all these developmental imperatives, that concerned with cementing the bond to mother is primary and indispensable. In the normal course of events, a mother is well prepared to become attached to her baby by the months of waiting for its arrival. Her investment is apparent from the moment of birth. In all species of mammal the mother rapidly learns to recognize her own baby and develops a tenacious proprietorial right to it. If any attempt is made to take the infant away she will display violent hostility. Equally, if she is presented with an infant belonging to another female she will decisively reject it.

As time goes on, the mother's attachment to her child is confirmed and strengthened in response to the numerous signals which it emits (because it is programmed to do so) which release in her feelings of love and tenderness as well as the appropriate maternal behaviour that her role demands. From the very beginning, the infant is powerfully motivated to seek physical contact with the mother and not to relinquish contact once it has been obtained. In the ancestral environment human mothers and infants spent as much time in close physical contact as do gorillas and chimpanzees. This has been observed in hunter-gatherer societies which have survived into the present century: babies are not kept in a cradle or a pram as with us but, as with monkeys and apes, are carried about piggy-back fashion. Although human infants are less able to hang on to their mothers than infant primates – they are not so strong and their mothers lack a fur coat – nevertheless all human beings have vestigial grasp reflexes strong enough to support their own weight. This primary need to be cuddled, when fully satisfied, forms the foundation of the child's developing 'basic trust', and it is a need which persists into adulthood. As George Brown (Brown and Harris, 1978) has shown, individuals who can depend upon the physical and verbal expression of attachment from an intimate enjoy a vital social asset protecting them from depression and neurotic distress.

To the formation of the mother–child bond, love provides the indispensable catalyst. 'It is as if,' wrote Bowlby (1951), 'maternal care were as necessary for the proper development of personality as vitamin D for the development of bones.' As Bowlby was able to demonstrate, among children reared in institutions without love, many are retarded in their physical, intellectual, and social development when compared with children reared in normal families, and are more susceptible to physical and mental disease. Many workers have pointed to an association between institutional care, maternal deprivation, and the later development of an affectionless **sociopathic** personality with its feeble superego and disagreeable penchant for impulsive antisocial behaviour.

Similarly, numerous experimental studies of a variety of social mammals have shown that failure or impairment of the bond to mother results in predictable abnormalities in the offspring. For example, as the Harlows observed, rhesus infants, deprived of their mothers but provided with mechanical substitutes, may survive into adult life but their social and sexual capacities are permanently damaged: both males and females are sexually incompetent and make hopeless parents, treating their young with the same indifference as they would inanimate objects. Similar case histories are commonly elicited by psychiatrists from human subjects.

SEPARATION

The power of the mother–child behavioural system is never more apparent than when a young animal or child is separated involuntarily from its mother. The loud protest and dreadful despair which forced separations

23

induce are *primary responses* which are not reducible to other causes: they are directly due to the a priori nature of the attachment bond – that is to say, to the frustration of the child's absolute need for the maternal presence. The extent of the child's suffering and the damage caused is related to the duration of the separation: brief separations are bad enough; long ones can be devastating. Separated children predictably pass through three stages, which Bowlby described as protest, despair, and detachment, and he showed how the experience of separation can affect the personality for life. In particular, the development of basic trust tends to be impaired, the child becoming a prey to **neurotic anxiety** and to doubts about its capacity to elicit care and affection – a state which Bowlby termed **anxious attachment**. The result can be the adoption of a defensive posture of detachment from others, the child becoming self-absorbed and self-reliant to an unusual extent. Such individuals appear odd to their fellows, who may be disconcerted by their remote, somewhat aloof manner, and they commonly experience difficulty in achieving social integration at school and within their local community. A high proportion of them as adults display a **schizoid personality**.

As Bowlby subsequently pointed out, each of the three phases of response to separation is related to a central issue of psychoanalytic and psychiatric theory: *protest* raises problems of **separation anxiety**; *despair* that of **depression**, grief, or mourning; *detachment* that of defence and **schizoid personality disorder**. These are crucial areas of psychopathology and they can all be understood as the natural consequences of thwarted archetypal intent.

MORALITY

Parents are deeply implicated in passing on to their children the values, beliefs, and attitudes of society. All societies codify themselves; and their continuity depends upon the ability of new members to assimilate the code. Were this not so, the alternative would be anarchy and a collective incapacity for competition or defence. Because of its fundamental importance for the survival of any human community, the moral code has everywhere been accorded the dignity of divine sanction. Indeed, as we shall see, it seems highly probable that a propensity to religious forms of symbolism and belief exists as an innate potentiality in human nature.

Under parental tutelage, the child acquires its own version of the moral code and builds it into an intrapsychic **moral complex**. Freud called this complex the **superego**, and thought that it emerged during the Oedipal phase of libidinal development in response to a fear of being castrated as a punishment for forbidden incestuous desires. A more probable explanation is that the superego possesses an innate substrate in the neurophysiological system, since the universally apparent phenomena of **guilt** and **shame** would otherwise be incomprehensible. Like anxiety, depression, hunger, and sexual desire, guilt and shame are emotional characteristics of our species, and, as a consequence, some innate structures must be responsible for their existence and their release. Had the superego no foundation in phylogeny, we should be condemned to live in a state of psychopathic amorality, incapable of mutual toleration or trust, and it is unlikely that our species could ever have come into existence, let alone survived.

SOCIAL STATUS

The commitment of social scientists to the notions of cultural relativity and behavioural plasticity (together with a tendency to idealize the apparently egalitarian spirit of hunter-gatherer communities) has meant that the universal importance attributed to rank and status in human societies has been largely overlooked. Recent acknowledgement of this oversight has encouraged some anthropologists to re-examine the evidence from hunter-gatherer societies that have survived into the twentieth century: this has resulted in the discovery that these societies are in fact less egalitarian than they seemed. For example, successful hunters among the Ache of South America share their kill with all other members of their community instead of keeping the best portions for themselves. This, on the face of it, displays a nice sense of responsibility and social justice. However, closer investigation reveals that although success in the hunt may not bring the hunter greater economic power, it does, nevertheless, bring him respect and charisma. The community shows tolerance for his extra-marital activities and acceptance of his illegitimate offspring, which are not only more numerous but more likely to survive than the children of less valiant hunters. Also lacking in any obvious social hierarchy are the communities of Aka pygmies in Central Africa, in the sense that they have no chieftain or headman. They do, however, have a *kombeti*, a man who is deferred to in political matters who is usually an outstandingly good hunter, and who is by custom allowed to keep more than an equal share of his kill and to have more wives and more offspring than any other men in the group (Wright, 1994).

That the propensity to form social hierarchies is a universal and evolutionarily stable characteristic is indicated not only by cross-cultural studies but by the spontaneous social behaviour of pre-school children. When left to play in groups, with minimal interference from adult observers, some children automatically assume dominant roles. Those who rise to the top tend to be tougher, in that they are less likely to back down in a conflict. Not infrequently they are also more attractive, more talented, and more popular. Such dominant individuals are likely to be imitated and obeyed by other members of the group, who thereby demonstrate their acceptance of a sub-dominant role (Jones, 1985; Lippitt *et al.*, 1958). Similar patterns of hierarchical behaviour are to be observed among gangs of adolescents (Savin-Williams, 1979). The practice of initiation rites by many societies at this stage of the epigenetic programme would seem designed to institutionalize

25

a status hierarchy among males in the interests of social stability, economic efficiency, and defence, and also to enhance the reproductive success of the dominant members of the group. In all animal communities in which social hierarchies exist, the major benefit derived by a male from success in the competition for status is the degree of access it grants him to sexually desirable females.

Evidence for the phylogenetic antiquity of ranking behaviour comes from ethological studies of our closest relatives – the chimpanzees, the bonobos (pygmy chimpanzees), and the gorillas – among whom hierarchies of varying degrees of complexity are indispensable to their social organization (de Waal, 1988). As a consequence, the phylogenetic history of human social competitiveness has come to assume special interest for evolutionary psychiatrists. For, as we shall see, it appears to be deeply implicated in the psychopathology of a number of psychiatric disorders (such as the **affective disorders**, **cluster 'B' and 'C' personality disorders**, **obsessional** and **phobic disorders**) as well as **reproductive disorders** (such as **exhibitionism** and **sadomasochism**).

MENTALITIES, SOCIAL ROLES, AND PSYCHOPATHOLOGY

Our evolved capacities are context specific: they operate on the a priori assumption that an organism will live out its life-cycle in its *Umwelt* – the environment which it evolved to live in. What evolutionary psychology has to solve is the problem of how our innate propensities are activated by certain anticipated features of the environment to produce behaviour appropriate to the context in which it occurs. We know that behaviour evolved first and that the capacity to make sense of it evolved later. We also recognize that behaviour evolved to maximize survival and to facilitate the transmission of genes to the next generation. The advantage of making sense of behaviour (either one's own or that of one's conspecifics) is that it enables us to monitor what is going on in a given environmental situation and to select what experience has taught us to be the most appropriate form of behaviour to meet the circumstances. In other words, our evolved predispositions are committed to the perception of meaning, the selection of adaptive strategic options, and the consequent performance of socially appropriate or advantageous roles.

In order to understand these highly sophisticated processes, evolutionary psychiatry conceives of the human mind-brain as an organization of specialized propensities which are shaped by experience into emotional and cognitive schemata. This approach represents a modern rediscovery of Jung's contention that archetypes in the phylogenetic psyche are built by experience into the ontogenetic psyche where they function as **complexes** (associations of images and ideas bound together by a common affect). These schemata, or complexes, have variously been termed 'modules' (Fodor, 1985), 'special intelligences' (Gardner, 1985), and 'small minds' (Ornstein, 1986). We shall call them **mentalities**. Mentalities create and monitor the social roles we perform in such a way as to promote our inclusive fitness. It is as if each of us were a travelling orchestra with a number of well-rehearsed symphonies and concertos in our repertoire from which we select, for each performance, the programme we consider most appropriate for the audience, the venue, and the fee (that is, the pay-off in terms of cost/benefit).

This orchestral analogy is adequate as far as it goes, but it should not be taken too literally, for our capacity to adopt innate themes and improvise variations upon them is apparently infinite. We do it in life, in literature, in the cinema, and in our dreams. Nevertheless, our archetypal propensities pervade all these productions, not least the roles we play whenever we come into contact with other people.

The relationship between **biosocial goals** and **behavioural systems**, on the one hand, and **social roles**, on the other, is of special importance for evolutionary psychology, for while some workers have focused on goals (Gilbert, 1989), and behavioural systems (Bowlby, 1969), others have concentrated on roles (Gardner, 1988; Champion and Power, 1995) as their primary data. The biosocial goal and its related behavioural system provides the social role for the individual to perform. Gardner has analysed eight specific roles, which he defines as states of communication, that are readily perceived and understood by conspecifics. Each role, Gardner believes, can be implicated in major psychiatric states as well as in the typical social activities apparent among normally adjusted humans and animals.

Gardner labels these communication states with the term **PSALIC**, which stands for *Programmed Spacings and Linkages in Conspecifics*, or *Propensity States Antedating Language in Communication*! Gardner defines a PSALIC as 'A primitive communicational state, mediated by deeply homologous neural structures, that, when stimulated and activated, causes the organism to demonstrate an unusual readiness to assume distinctive roles relating to functional activities involving one or more of its conspecifics' (1988, p. 212).

The PSALICs listed by Gardner are: Nurturant, Nurturance Recipience, Sexual, Alpha, Alpha-reciprocal, Ingroup Omega, Outgroup Omega, and Spacing (Avoidant). These are listed in Table 1 together with their animal and human (both normal and abnormal) expressions.

As will be apparent from a glance at Table 1, Gardner's eight PSALICs relate to the biosocial goals of **attachment** (Nurturant and Nurturance Recipience), **reproduction** (Sexual), and **dominance-striving** (Alpha, Alpha-reciprocal, and Ingroup Omega), as well as to the defence strategy of **flight** or **withdrawal** (Outgroup Omega, Spacing). Gardner stresses the point made by most evolutionary psychiatrists, that a normal human counterpart exists for any psychiatric disorder or symptom we may care to examine. Where Gardner makes an interesting extension of this principle is in his suggestion that a normal animal counterpart exists as well, thus underlining the phylogenetic antiquity of these homologous states (they are, in Gardner's language,

Table 1 Gardner's eight PSALICs

PSALIC	Abnormal human	Normal human	Normal animal
Nurturant	Kidnapping without financial aims	Parenting Caretaking	Nest-tending Parenting
Nurturance recipience	Dependency Anaclitic depression	Normal offspring behaviour with parents (and other caretakers)	Normal care-seeking behaviours
Sexual	Perversions Rape	Being in love Sexual intercourse	Oestrous behaviour Male sexual behaviour
Alpha	Mania Early stages of alcohol intoxication	High-profile normal Charismatic leader	Dominant member of a social grouping
Alpha-reciprocal	Loss of values, as in a mob or with an inappropriate leader Conversion disorder	Followers Audiences Hypnotic trance	Non-Omega subordinates in a grouping
Ingroup Omega	Melancholic depression	Very low ranker who exhibits submissive behaviour to others in the group	Lowest ranker in a social hierarchy
Outgroup Omega	Paranoia Persecutory delusions	Persecuted member of an outgroup	Persecuted member of an outgroup (non-member of an ingroup)
Spacing (Avoidant)	Schizoid behaviour Autism	Hermit Isolated living	Avoidant behaviour towards conspecifics

Source: Gardner 1988

dependent on 'deeply homologous neural structures', which are 'highly conserved'). Indeed, they are so 'hardwired' as to allow inter-specific communication between related species (as in the exceptionally rich relationship it is possible for a human to enjoy with a dog). Homology implies that a trait that two taxa have in common was once a trait of their common ancestor.

Gardner also emphasizes that PSALICs are not independent of one another but can often overlap, which makes them harder to study, but also indicates that their underlying neuronal systems are both independent and inter-related. Thus, aggressive self-assertion, and success in controlling subordinates in the social hierarchy (Alpha), are associated with success in competing for mates (Sexual PSALIC) not only in normal human and animals but in **hypomanic** patients as well. The ingestion of **alcohol** tends to release similar behaviour patterns (Steele, 1986) – assertiveness, aggression, risk-taking, and heightened interest in sex.

Similarly, an individual forced into an inferior rank by his superiors will normally exhibit submissive behaviours to other higher-ranking members of his group (In-group Omega). He will also display **grief** if deprived of an attachment figure (Nurturance Recipience). Yet if either condition becomes so disagreeable or incapacitating as to draw him to the attention of a psychiatrist, he will be diagnosed as suffering from a **depression**.

As far as out-group and avoidant behaviours are concerned, normal people, if driven out of a group, will feel persecuted, or they may choose to withdraw from society to live the life of a hermit, but if they become deluded and odd they will be classified as suffering from **paranoia** or **schizophrenia**.

It is Gardner's contention that people experience **delusions** and **hallucinations** when normal subcortical processes are exaggerated or misinterpreted by cerebral cortical processes. A psychiatric illness results when a PSALIC programme is inappropriately released and acted upon.

All major psychiatric syndromes may thus be conceived as inappropriate expressions of evolved propensities concerned with adaptive behaviour in the domains of group membership (**Part II Disorders of attachment and rank**), group exclusion (**Part IV Spacing disorders**), and mating (**Part V Reproductive disorders**).

3

PRINCIPLES OF
PSYCHOPATHOLOGY

ANIMALS IN ZOOS

At London Zoo there is a concrete mound, surrounded by a moat, known as Monkey Hill. It measures about 30 by 18 metres. In 1925 the zoo authorities put 100 hamadryas baboons on this pitiful excrescence and expected them to settle in good-naturedly and entertain the public. They declined.

It was to have been an all-male population but, with a standard of care which proved typical of the whole operation, 6 females were accidentally included. Vicious battles for dominance took place between the males, which continued for months, and before two years had elapsed, 44 of them were dead. But, by then, a stable dominance hierarchy had been established and an uneasy peace prevailed.

However, the unfortunate creatures seemed unhappy and, in a wholly misguided attempt to cheer them up, the authorities put 30 more females on the island. Within a month, 15 of these had been torn to pieces by the resident males fighting to possess them. By 1930, only 39 males and 9 females survived, and that year 3 males and 4 females were killed.

What does this say about baboon psychology? Are they such vicious brutes that they are incapable of controlling their passions and living in peace with one another? If so, how could this species survive? Ethological observations have established that out of captivity hamadryas baboons live in well-ordered social groups based on a stable dominance hierarchy, and seldom challenge heterosexual bonds once they have been formed (Kummer, 1995). Clearly, the behaviour of the baboons on Monkey Hill was grossly abnormal. What went wrong?

The most likely explanation is that the circumstances in which the zoo required them to live constituted a monstrous frustration of their basic archetypal expectations. The ethogram of the hamadryas baboon – that is to say, the total archetypal endowment of the species – presupposes large areas of land on which to establish a group territory, win position in the social hierarchy, and, when successful in both these achievements, to collect a harem of females. Instead of the 540 square metres afforded by Monkey

Hill, a troop of 100 baboons would normally require a range of 50 square kilometres – 50,000 square metres – an area nearly one hundred times as great.

In normal circumstances, baboons develop intense group loyalties and are hostile to strangers from other troops. That the animals on Monkey Hill fought each other with such psychopathic savagery was because they had been trapped and assembled from different wild troops and crowded together in a tiny area where there were more males than females and where they couldn't possibly keep out of each other's way.

We must conclude, therefore, that the frustration of archetypal intent caused by the zoo environment in which this tragic population was placed resulted in gross and unmistakable psychopathology.

This sad story is an allegory of what can happen to human beings – who also evolved to live in the wide open spaces of the East African savannah – when made to live in that urban habitat which Desmond Morris (1969) called *The Human Zoo*. Directly comparable disasters to that suffered by the baboons in London Zoo have been observed in human communities forced to abandon their traditional way of life and live in circumstances alien to them. One such people was the Ik, a group of hunter-gatherers in Uganda who were excluded from their range of 40,000 square kilometres, placed in shack settlements, and taught subsistence farming. They rapidly became demoralized, depressed, anxious and ill, and behaved with psychopathic indifference to their children and their spouses. Similarly, the fragmentation of the Aboriginal culture in Australia and Amerindian cultures in the United States has left in its wake the psychiatric sequelae of alcoholism, suicide, and despair.

Evidence such as this provides us with a model for psychopathology, which we may state as follows: mental health depends upon the provision of physical and social environments capable of meeting the archetypal needs of the developing individual; psychopathology can result when these needs are frustrated.

This formulation gives rise to two fundamental questions:

1 What are the archetypal needs of the developing individual?
2 What environments, physical and social, are capable of guaranteeing their fulfilment?

These would seem to be the two questions that in the twenty-first century psychology and psychiatry will have to address. The paradigm in terms of which the answers to these questions will have to be framed is that of Darwinism: for the Darwinian paradigm is the bedrock on which all biological sciences are now based, and no psychological explanation can hope to survive if it is incompatible with it. Evolutionary psychiatry holds, as we have seen, that every living organism has an anatomical structure and a behavioural repertoire which are uniquely adapted to the environment in which it evolved. This is the environment in which individuals have a built-in expectation that they will live out their life-cycle. Any alteration in the environment has consequences for the organism. Some changes may be compatible with survival and reproduction, others may not. And changes which do not result in elimination of the species may nevertheless produce distortions in its typical modes of behaviour which may lead to disorders of various kinds, whether they be psychiatric, social, or ecological.

Human versatility, coupled with a sophisticated capacity for innovation, has resulted in dramatic transformations in the environments which human beings now inhabit. These environments display an astonishing diversity in comparison with the stable characteristics of the African savannah where we evolved and lived out the greatest part of our existence as hunter-gatherers. Indeed, the speed at which man-made environments have altered in recent centuries has far outstripped the pace at which natural selection can proceed in the time-honoured Darwinian manner.

These considerations present problems to any researcher wishing to establish precisely what the characteristics of the environment of human adaptedness were actually like. Yet if we truly wish to understand what manner of creature we are then the effort has to be made, for the challenges provided by our primordial environment selected the archetypal propensities still present in human beings to this day.

How can we proceed? How can we hope to establish the inventory of archetypal imperatives with which we have been equipped by evolution? One invaluable source of information has come from anthropological accounts of hunter-gatherer communities which have survived into the present century – people like the !Kung bushmen of Botswana. But how can we know that such people were (when they were studied) as we were when we evolved? The answer is that we cannot. If physical particles change their behaviour when observed by physicists, then the behaviour of hunter-gatherers is hardly likely to remain undisturbed when scrutinized by Western anthropologists. Moreover, we cannot know how much modern ways had already begun to influence them before the anthropologists arrived on the scene. It is only an assumption that surviving hunter-gatherers were living closer to the original human state than populations practising agriculture and animal husbandry. But it is, we believe, a fair assumption.

This does not mean that we would fall into the trap of regarding the ancestral environment as a stereotypical or unitary phenomenon. Clearly, the EEA must have varied from group to group in accordance with custom and precise geographical location. However, studies of hunter-gatherer communities as geographically disparate and culturally varied as the Inuit 'Eskimos' of the Arctic and the Ache of Paraguay as well as the !Kung bushmen of the Kalahari Desert have revealed consistent, typically human patterns of existence. This is compatible with the view that much has remained constant during the evolution of the human psyche: the universal factors of mating and marriage, child-rearing, living in small communities, the initiation of young males into manhood, the marriage of young females by the time they are fertile, and so on.

How can we know that these consistencies are due to genes and not to cultural diffusion? We cannot. Both factors are almost certainly involved. If a pattern or characteristic such as maternal attachment, dominance striving, and sexual bonding, is found to satisfy three sets of criteria, it is likely to be genetically based. These criteria are *universality*, *phylogenetic continuity*, and *evolutionary stability* (Wenegrat, 1984).

1 **Universality**: the pattern in question is found in all known cultural groups.
2 **Phylogenetic continuity**: the record of evolution shows no sharp break between human and other mammalian species with regard to the pattern concerned. Thus attachment behaviour between mothers and infants, between peers, and between mature males and females can be traced backwards from human beings through primates to their earliest mammalian origins. The major breakthrough of ethology has been to demonstrate that such patterns of behaviour can be codified and their evolution studied in the same way as the evolution of anatomical structures, such as bones, lungs, and brains.
3 **Evolutionary stability:** patterns that are evolutionarily stable are sustained through the selective penalization and ultimate elimination of individuals who fail to manifest them.

Since we are a supremely social animal, the most important characteristics of the evolutionary environment for us to define are the social characteristics. In what kinds of groups did we evolve? Astonishing though it is, remarkably few anthropologists have shown any interest in establishing the basic social parameters of the environment of human adaptedness. One brave exception is Robin Fox, who has attempted to define the kind of society that is typical of hunter-gatherer communities. He refers to this society as 'the basic state': 'Where in time is the basic state to be found?' asks Fox (1989).

> The answer is straightforward: in the Late Paleolithic, some fifteen to forty thousand years ago. It is really that simple. We were fully formed modern *Homo sapiens sapiens*; we had reached the top of the food chain – we were doing quite a bit better than the other carnivores. Then with frightening rapidity, it all began to go wrong . . .
>
> (*ibid.*, p. 215)

Fox argues that in the Upper Paleolithic, a balance existed between the organism, the social system, and the environment. Then two things happened to disturb this balance. First, the Ice Age occurred, which increased the density of human populations by squeezing large numbers of peoples

33

into south-west Europe, the Middle East, and parts of Asia; and, second, the principles of agriculture and animal husbandry were discovered.

The improved economy and increased numbers which these developments produced led in turn to the emergence of the characteristics typical of civilized societies, such as, classes, castes, power elites, armies, empires, and the exploitation of subject peoples. Ever since, 'these emergent properties – seized as their subject matter by the social scientists – have been on a collision course with the social needs of the paleolithic hunter.' What we call 'history', concludes Fox, is merely the most recent catalogue of the products of this 'collision' (*ibid.*, p. 220).

THE ANCESTRAL SOCIETY

Extrapolating from the extant ethnographic accounts of hunter-gatherer communities, Fox deduces that the groups in which our species lived for 99.5 per cent of its existence consisted of about forty to fifty individuals, made up of approximately six to ten adult males, about twice that number of child-bearing females, and about twenty juveniles and infants. These were 'organic extended kinship groups' and they constitute what we might call 'the ancestral society' of our kind.

Such groups did not, of course, function in isolation. They came into frequent contact with other similar groups – hence the universal human rituals of greeting, visiting, feasting, making alliances, marriages, and wars.

These compact, intimate, extended kinship groups of forty to fifty members knew one another intimately and shared the same values, rules, customs, and mores, their beliefs being sustained by myth, ritual, and religion. In all of them the family was the central institution, whether polygamous, monogamous, or polyandrous. When they got larger than this there was a natural tendency for groups to split and for one section of the community to move away to find another range. It is in order to live in such societies as this that nature has equipped us, and this fact is a crucial issue for evolutionary psychiatry.

A BASIC PRINCIPLE

A basic principle of psychopathology may be summed up in the following postulate: *Psychopathology results when the environment fails, either partially or totally, to meet one (or more) archetypal need(s) in the developing individual.* (As we shall make clear in the next chapter, two basic archetypal needs, frustration of which can give rise to psychopathology, are the need for attachment and the need for status or rank.)

The first psychiatrist to propound this principle was John Bowlby, who added the corollary that the further the rearing environment deviates from the environment of evolutionary adaptedness the greater is the likelihood of pathological development. If we are to understand the psychiatric disorders from which our contemporaries suffer, then we have to take into account the ways in which Western society frustrates the needs of paleolithic man or woman still persisting as living potential within us in our present environmental circumstances.

CONTEMPORARY FRUSTRATIONS OF ARCHETYPAL INTENT

Although mental illness occurs and is acknowledged in hunter-gatherer communities, it appears to be less of a problem to them than it is to us, and it would seem plausible to propose that our modern urban environment is less conducive to the mental health and well-being of the contemporary human animal than was the environment of evolutionary adaptedness. This, at any rate, is our view, though it would be wrong to give the impression that it is shared by all evolutionary psychiatrists. McGuire and Troisi (1998), for example, are sceptical of this position which they caricature as the 'genome-lag hypothesis'. The sort of arguments that have been advanced against the hypothesis are the following:

1 That the contemporary environmental characteristics likely to induce pathogenesis have never been defined.
2 That despite urbanization, increased migration, and technological change, the number of people with whom one regularly interacts (approximately 40), as well as the number of close non-kin relationships (approximately 5), is likely to be about the same now as it was in the Pleistocene.
3 That there is little reason to suppose that the incidence of disorders is any higher in modern social conditions than it has been in the past.
4 That human beings cannot be maladapted to contemporary environments because they created them.

We would disagree with each of these statements. In the first place, it is not hard to suggest a number of contemporary social and environmental characteristics which could be productive of psychopathology in an animal with such a detailed, complex, and socially demanding epigenetic programme as our own. Many possibilities immediately come to mind: the disruption of community-based kinship bonds as a result of migration, job mobility, experiments in town planning, and so on; the disruption of families through divorce and separation together with the rapidly increasing incidence of single-parent families; the loss of female support groups of the kind provided by traditional communities; the lack of adequate provision for the secure and intimate care of children whose mothers go out to work; the occurrence of negative life events such as losing one's job, being passed over for promotion, mortgage rate increases, house repossessions, exam or interview failures, difficulty in acquiring the necessary skills demanded by employers, and sedentary work in artificial light and controlled atmospheres; the loss of myth, ritual, and religion; the lack of contact with nature, the seasons, and the primordial environment. All these factors are potentially productive of stress, insecurity and 'anomie' as well as skewed or distorted development. It seems likely that the various neuroses, psychopathies, drug dependencies, the occurrence of child and spouse abuse, to say nothing of the ever rising crime statistics, are not unconnected with Western society's inability to satisfy the archetypal needs of our kind. Many of these points have been impressively emphasized by Glantz and Pearce (1989).

Second, the argument that modern individuals still interact on a regular basis with about the same number of people as hunter-gatherers may be true, but it fails to take account of the factors already listed. Moreover, the people with whom one regularly interacts are not kin, they generally live some distance away and, as often as not, can only be seen by appointment. They seldom live next door or upstairs (many of our contemporaries have no knowledge of their neighbours) and in order to get to them one has to endure a hostile environment of noise and traffic pollution, unfriendly strangers, and the often fraught experience of finding a parking place.

Thirdly, the attempt to minimize the incidence of disorders in contemporary society does not coincide with our understanding that estimates of individuals who suffer from anxiety or depression, or who fail to sustain lasting relationships for the rearing of children, are rising all the time.

There is, indeed, evidence that the incidence of depressive disorders may be increasing in the West (Klerman, 1988) and in developing countries (Schwab, 1989). Sartorius *et al.* (1983) estimated in a report for the WHO that there are altogether 100 million depressives in the world and that the number may be increasing because of rapid economic and demographic changes. Data derived from 39,000 people living in five different areas of the world indicated that more young people in every country have suffered a depressive episode than have their elders. The more developed the country, the greater were the chances of young people becoming depressed (Nesse and Williams, 1995).

Finally, the suggestion that human beings cannot be maladjusted to modern environments because they created them has become something of a cliché among those hostile to the development of evolutionary psychiatry. For example, an anti-Darwinian polemic by Malik (1998) stated: 'It seems bizarre to hold that the brain is "wired up" to invent modernity and not to cope with it.' However, it is possible to cite many examples of human populations which have made such effective use of their adaptive capacities for economic, social, and ecological exploitation as to render their environment hostile to their continued well-being (Russell and Russell, 1998). In the fourth century AD, for instance, a party of Marquesans colonized Easter Island in the Pacific. The population grew rapidly and by the end of the first millennium they were building temples and erecting the gigantic heads, which are now a major tourist attraction. By the sixteenth century, the population had reached about 8,000, on a not very fertile island of about 160 square kilometres. From the seventeenth century onwards, however, famine, massacres, cannibalism, and epidemics reduced the population to its present number of about 2,000. The main reasons for this catastrophe were connected with the adaptive successes of previous generations, who had so depleted the palm forests, that it was no longer possible to build the ocean-going boats necessary to exploit the rich off-shore fisheries. Indigenous bird species had either been extinguished or driven to distant islets that could not be reached. Russell and Russell provide many other examples to demonstrate how our adapted abilities can produce maladapted environments with dire consequences for whole societies. They consider this to be a warning of what might happen to humanity as a whole.

Suicide is yet another indicator of the mental health problems that are increasingly afflicting populations in developed and developing countries. Those most at risk are among the single, widowed, separated, and divorced (Shneidman, 1989). Younger males are again more vulnerable. Males generally more often kill themselves than females (in the United States the ratio is 3:1), while females are more prone to make suicide attempts (between 80,000 and 100,000 a year in the United Kingdom).

However, we would not wish to imply that our society is an unmitigated disaster. In fact, when it comes to meeting our basic needs, the contemporary environment does not differ from the ancestral environment as radically as one might imagine. For example, the physical requirements of warmth, shelter, and nourishment are met in the West better than ever before in history. The social needs for parents, peers, and potential mates are also met in the majority of individuals. However, the number of people in whom these basic needs are not met is large and growing, as indeed is the psychiatric problem which they represent.

A key factor concerned in the causation of most psychiatric illness is **stress**. The probability is that the greater the gap between archetypal needs and environmental fulfilment of those needs, the greater the stress and the more incapacitating the illness.

Although many people suffering from stress come to the attention of psychiatrists, many of them, perhaps the majority, do not; nor do they necessarily manifest the signs of psychiatric illness. As Jung noted in the 1930s, the people who came to consult him were not, on the whole, suffering from disorders susceptible to neat clinical diagnosis. Rather they were suffering from the aimlessness and futility of their lives. He came to regard this as a malaise typical of the twentieth century bourgeoisie and intelligentsia. He called it 'the universal neurosis of our age'. Jung had no hesitation in attributing the universal neurosis of our age to the emergence of social institutions which alienated us from our archetypal nature. Secular urban life breeds 'disalliance with the unconscious', he wrote, and 'disalliance with the unconscious is synonymous with loss of instinct and rootlessness' (CW7, para. 195).

This insight has a long and respectable pedigree. In the eighteenth century, Denis Diderot (1713–1784) maintained that the benefits of civilization had been acquired at the cost of man's natural happiness. Civilized man of necessity remained an unhappy creature. The theme that, to be civilized, man had to renounce his basic instincts was taken up by Nietzsche and developed by Freud in *Civilization and Its Discontents* (1930) as well as by Jung in *Modern Man in Search of a Soul* (1933). The Austrian ethologist Konrad Lorenz (1903–1989) compared our plight to that of a wild species that has been domesticated, like hens, cows, and pigs, living a wholly artificial existence which makes few demands on its instinctual equipment, while Desmond Morris, as we have seen, compared our lot to that of animals condemned to languish in a zoo of their own making.

Our sense of bereavement for the lost habitat of our species might explain the bouts of nostalgia which take hold from time to time for primitive life, primitive people, and for primitive art – for the mythic life of Jean-Jacques Rousseau's 'noble savage'. It is one motive that promotes a fascination with anthropology. But we should not allow it to encourage us to idealize the life of the hunter-gatherer, which, if not solitary, was often as Thomas Hobbes (1588–1679) described it – nasty, brutish, and short.

Study of the EEA is not important as providing an example of Paradise Lost but as establishing the kind of social milieu that our evolved propensities have equipped us to inhabit. Comparison of the EEA with contemporary social environments will, in our view, provide valuable insights into the aetiology of those psychiatric disorders which result from the inappropriate activation of previously adaptive strategies in present environmental conditions.

THE LAWS OF PSYCHODYNAMICS

We are now in a position to propose five laws of psychodynamics:

1 Whenever a behavioural trait is found to be characteristic of all human communities, irrespective of culture, race, or historical epoch, then the possibility should be considered that it is the expression of an innate propensity or archetype.
2 Archetypes possess an inherent dynamic whose goal is to actualize themselves in both psyche and behaviour.
3 Mental health results from the fulfilment of archetypal goals.
4 Psychopathology results from the frustration of archetypal goals.
5 Psychiatric symptoms are persistent exaggerations of adaptive psychophysiological responses.

These laws, which appear to us to be explicitly about human psychic functioning, may in fact be applications to the psyche of laws whose operation is apparent throughout nature. Thus, the acorn will become the best oak tree it can, given the kind of soil, the condition of the climate, the proximity and height of the surrounding trees, and so on. Deficiencies in any of these environmental conditions will result in stunting or susceptibility to disease, such as 'dieback', the mystery disease afflicting many oak trees in Britain at the present time.

It is important to recognize that the frustration of archetypal intent can occur at any stage of the life-cycle, and not only in childhood as Freud supposed. Psychopathology is not invariably related to earlier traumatic experience. Unlike Freud, Jung recognized this, stressing that development proceeds throughout the *whole* life-cycle, and that every stage has its own archetypal goals. The truth of this view has been confirmed empirically. We have already drawn attention to the studies of George Brown (Brown and Harris, 1978) and his colleagues, which demonstrated that individuals who could depend on the physical and verbal expression of attachment from an intimate companion enjoyed a vital social asset protecting them from depression and neurotic distress. They found that it was not at all uncommon for anxiety and depression to be caused, not by childhood deprivation, but by a major life event occurring in adulthood which revealed that one's personal relationships are unsupportive and uncaring.

The fifth law – that psychiatric symptoms are persistent exaggerations of adaptive psychophysiological responses – was not only proposed by Freud and by Jung but has been reaffirmed by contemporary etho-psychiatrists. For example, both Brant Wenegrat (1984) and Russell Gardner (1988) see all psychopathological syndromes, whether psychotic, neurotic, or psychopathic, as statistically abnormal manifestations of innate response strategies shared by *all* individuals whether they are mentally healthy or ill. For psychiatry, the central aetiological question is: What causes these adaptive strategies to become exaggerated in people who are diagnosed as being 'mentally ill'?

THE AETIOLOGY OF PSYCHIATRIC DISORDERS

The crucial issue of how to account for the aetiology of psychiatric disorders in individual cases is a primary concern of evolutionary psychiatry. The 'genome-lag' or, 'exiles from Eden', hypothesis may go some way to explain the high incidence of psychiatric disorders in postindustrial and developing societies, but it leaves a number of questions unanswered. For example, given the extent to which our society has deviated from the EEA, how is it that so many of us remain disorder-free? And how may we explain that psychiatric disorders exist and are recognized in hunter-gatherer societies still living in environments which closely approximate to the EEA?

These questions have generated a number of theoretical suggestions. We will limit ourselves to six of these, namely, theories of (1) normal distribution, (2) genotype–environment interaction, (3) activation and inhibition of psychological mechanisms, (4) social homeostasis, (5) inclusive fitness, and (6) ontogenesis.

1 Normal distribution theory

Adaptive strategies such as fight, flight, freeze, withdrawal, dominance, submission, and attachment will be **normally distributed** through every human population. Most individuals will be placed in the middle of the distribution curve and will be reasonably well adapted to prevailing environmental conditions. Exaggerated or inadequate endowment with these strategies might account for psychopathology among individuals placed towards the tails of the distribution of adaptive traits. For example, one investigator examined birds that die during migration and discovered that their wingspan was either too long or too short. Successful migrators had a wingspan of average length. It is theoretically possible that tendencies to anxiety, depression, sensitivity to adverse life events, to criticism, and so on, could be similarly distributed. This approach is linked to the **critical threshold** concept: those too sensitive to criticism go under; those too insensitive take too little care; those with an **anxiety neurosis** will suffer the symptoms of arousal in response to a minimal stimulus, while those with an **anti-social personality disorder** will experience no symptoms of arousal when confronted by a major threat.

2 Genotype–environment interaction theory

Since psychiatry is not dealing with behaviour that is equally apparent in all members of the species, it has to pay particular attention to genetic and environmental variations in order to explain differences between individuals. Etho-psychiatry conceives individual differences in behaviour and in personality development as being the consequences of alternative strategies which are determined by genes, or by the environment, or by randomly occurring events. For example, if we have two genetic behavioural strategies such as introversion and extraversion, and two environments, one fertile and overcrowded, the other arid and underpopulated, the consequences for the mental health of the individual might be as follows:

Table 2 Possible interaction of two genetic strategies and two environments

| | Habitat | |
Phenotype	Fertile and overcrowded	Arid and underpopulated
Extravert	adjustment	neurosis
Introvert	neurosis	adjustment

An individual can find himself in an environment to which the average member of the human species can readily adapt but to which he, because of his own particular constitutional make-up, is ill-adapted. He is mismatched, not because he is in an environment other than the EEA, but because he is in an environment to which he is constitutionally unsuited. (NB: Throughout this book, when using the convention of referring to a person of indeterminate gender as 'he' we wish to make it clear that we also mean 'she'.)

3 Activation and inhibition of psychological mechanisms

An active psychological mechanism may express itself as a symptom. For example, a woman who suffers from panic attacks if she goes out to do her shopping is suffering from activity of an adaptive mechanism which evolved to make our ancestors wary of open spaces lacking in cover. She can pre-empt this activity either by getting a neighbour to do her shopping for her or by taking a tranquillizer. An adaptive mechanism may operate as a low level or autonomous strategy, but it does not necessarily preclude the operation of alternative strategies at a higher level of central nervous functioning.

The selection of one strategy rather than another in a given environmental situation is a highly complex process. As already noted in Chapter 2, comparative neuroanatomists like Paul MacLean have come to realize that, in the phylogenetic development of the human brain, new layers have been added to previously existing ones, rather than replacing the old parts altogether. This means that new functions have been added to and not replaced old ones. As a result, human responses to variations in the environment involve both primitive and modern processes operating in parallel. For instance, if we find ourselves in dazzling sunlight, we can draw on a list of strategies of increasing complexity and decreasing phylogenetic antiquity:

constriction of the iris;
blinking;
turning away of the head;
shading the eyes with the hand;
moving into the shade; and
purchasing a pair of sunglasses.

These are processes operating relatively independently of one another at different levels of complexity and involving different levels of the brain. Moreover, the operation of a process at one level may pre-empt a process operating at another. For example, blinking may be pre-empted by the purchase of sunglasses, or it may be increased by paralysing the iris constrictor with a dose of atropine. In addition, the initiation of a strategy at one level may terminate one operating at another. Thus, blinking may be terminated by moving into the shade.

41

Similar considerations apply to the prevention or development of psychiatric symptoms. For example, one high-level strategy for dealing with defeat in social competition is an act of voluntary submission, while a lower-level strategy for dealing with the same situation is a depression of mood. Just as blinking may be pre-empted or terminated by putting on a pair of sunglasses, so a conscious and deliberate act of submission can pre-empt or terminate a depression. However, a depressive episode may be the direct consequence of a personality characteristic, such as pride, ambition, or a proneness to guilt, which induces the depression by effectively ruling out voluntary submission as an available option.

4 Social homeostasis theory

An example of this theory is Freud's suggestion that the turning of anger on to the self prevents one from destroying the object of one's love. Instead of destroying both the love object and the bond, one becomes depressed, which preserves both. This is a **homeostatic** mechanism because change at the individual level has the effect of preserving homeostasis at the dyadic or group level. It is the central concept of the ranking theory of depression (see Chapter 5), which proposes that a depressive reaction serves to preserve the stability of the group by preventing constant struggles for status in the social hierarchy. Allen's (1995) theory that depression preserves people from being ostracized by their group also falls into the homeostatic category.

5 Inclusive fitness theory

This might also be called 'making the best of a bad job' theory or 'exit from the gene pool' theory. An individual assesses his phenotype and if, having pitted himself against his peers, he comes to the conclusion that it is unsatisfactory, he is less likely to reproduce. He becomes depressed, goes off to be a hermit, refrains from mating, or commits suicide, thus exiting from the gene pool. The selective arguments for this strategy are, first, that since his phenotype is unsatisfactory, the chances are that he would not have proved reproductively successful, and, second, that his inclusive fitness is raised because by refraining from reproduction, or by removing himself from the community, he leaves more space and resources for his kin. This possibility fits well with sexual selection theory, namely, that it is people of unsatisfactory phenotype who are deselected.

6 Ontogenetic theory

Like all other approaches to psychopathology, evolutionary theory accepts that experiences during development can shunt individuals towards different strategies (Buss, 1991; Tooby and Cosmides, 1990a). There is evidence that father absence during childhood shunts individuals towards a more promiscuous mating strategy, whereas the presence of an investing father during childhood shunts individuals towards a more monogamous mating strategy (Belsky *et al.*, 1991). Many studies confirm that boys who grow up without fathers, particularly during their early years, are more prone to sex-role confusion, less likely to form lasting relationships, and more inclined to socially disruptive behaviour (Biller, 1974; Burton, 1972; Leichty, 1960).

All these theoretical possibilities may contribute to the genesis of disorder in an individual case. For example, the amount of depression needed to maintain social homeostasis will be provided in different degrees by different individuals depending on their phenotype. Some will be very prone to become depressed when criticized, while others will be much less susceptible. In a sense, social homeostasis theory can be seen as a special instance of 'tail of the distribution' theory. Few theories in psychiatry are mutually exclusive. The one over-arching theory is **sexual selection theory**, which maintains that in every generation for the last 300 million years, the population has been stratified by social competition into those who are successful and those who are not. It is in examining the behavioural strategies of the unsuccessful that we move into the realm of psychopathology. There will be behavioural variation in the population in each generation and some people will be mentally disadvantaged in comparison with others. What form the disadvantage will take the theory does not specify, but it is likely to reflect capacities on the two dimensions of dominance (rank) and attachment (affiliation).

4

ATTACHMENT, RANK, AND PSYCHIATRY

The immediate cause of a large number of psychopathological conditions is a subjective prediction of probable failure in competing for two highly valued social resources: **attachment** and **rank**. Anticipated failure in these two crucial areas gives rise to two sets of aetiological contributions to psychiatric disorders.

ATTACHMENT

The credit for bringing attachment into the ambit of evolutionary psychiatry rests firmly with John Bowlby. He not only established that attachment is instinctive and 'prepared for' in both mother and child but also that the behavioural system responsible for making and sustaining the attachment bond is goal-corrected, in the sense that it is designed to maintain both physical proximity and social communication between the bonded partners. Because of its crucial significance for survival, mother–child bonding has evolved in a great variety of species.

Bowlby devoted the greater part of his life to the study of bond formation and to the consequences of its disruption, and he provided a wealth of evidence to show how a person's self-concept is profoundly influenced by these early experiences. Stable attachment bonds in childhood are associated, as already noted in Chapter 2, with emotional security and the development of an inner model of the self as worthy and capable of giving and receiving affection in a bonded relationship, whereas unstable bonds tend to result in emotional insecurity, development of a flawed self-concept, and indulgence in the kind of 'clinging' behaviour with significant others that Bowlby called **anxious attachment**. Fear that an attachment bond may be under threat can result in anger and aggression as well as anxiety, while loss of an attachment figure is associated with grief, despair, depression, and, ultimately, detachment. Renewal of an attachment bond, on the other hand, can be experienced as a source of profound joy.

By protecting her child from predators and the unwelcome attention of strangers, the mother, or mother-substitute, provides a **secure base** from which the child can, with impunity, make exploratory forays into the environment. The child's growing sense of security in the world (what Erik Erikson called **basic trust**) is dependent on the formation of a warm, intimate, and lasting bond in infancy. Any situation which is potentially threatening to the infant's survival (such as illness, aloneness, the intrusion of strange animals or strange people) can release distress calling, crying, and searching behaviour designed to re-establish proximity to the mother and to evoke protective, nurturing behaviour from her.

Physical contact, a major component of attachment formation, is one of the most potent means of reassurance and fear-reduction. It has long been recognized that stroking, holding, and cuddling by a care-giver are experienced by most (but not all) children as the desired response to anxiety and distress, from whatever situation it may arise. Gilbert (1989) comments that such physical reassurance may affect opiate activity in the cingulate cortex and that attachment anxiety may, as a consequence, be an important factor in the later development of **drug** or **alcohol addiction**.

Moreover, ready access to physical proximity is of vital importance not only for the child's emotional security but also for his or her **sexual development**. It could be that a primary function of breast feeding is that, in addition to providing nourishment, it ensures regular and intimate physical contact in conditions of deep satisfaction and contentment to both parties. As Montagu (1979) wryly observed: 'Man cannot live by milk alone.' That such close mother–infant contacts can involve sexual arousal, at least in boys, was recognized by Freud, and it is highly probable that the manner in which physical contact is expressed and experienced during early life may decisively influence an adult's ability to enjoy sexuality within the intimacy of a close relationship. Mothers who cuddle for the pure pleasure of physical contact are likely to produce children who themselves delight in such intimacy. Should the mother, however, be censorious or rejecting of the child's erotic pleasure then the grown child may be able only to engage in sexual activity outside of bonded relationships (as with prostitutes) or in sexuality of a deviant kind (e.g. **fetishism**, **sadomasochism**, **exhibitionism**, and so on).

Summarizing his position, Bowlby (1979) wrote:

> The key point of my thesis is that there is a strong causal relationship between an individual's experiences with his parents and his later capacity to make affectional bonds and that certain common variations in that capacity, manifesting themselves in marital problems and trouble with children as well as in neurotic symptoms and personality disorders, can be attributed to certain common variations in the ways in which parents perform their roles.

We shall now examine the ways in which parental behaviour can induce these unfortunate consequences.

PATHOGENIC PARENTING

The characteristic patterns of deficient parenting which neurotic subjects commonly reveal in their histories may be summarized as follows:

1 **Parental absence or separation from the child**: one or both parents may go away and leave the child, or put it in hospital or an institution. The earlier the loss and the longer or more frequent the separations the more serious are the consequences for the mental health of the child and future adult.
2 **Parental unresponsiveness to the child's attachment needs**: one or both parents persistently fail(s) to respond to the child's care-eliciting behaviour, and may, indeed, be actively disparaging and rejecting of such behaviour.
3 **Parental threats of abandonment used as sanctions to coerce or discipline the child**: one or other parent makes a practice of threatening to withdraw love, to abandon the family, to commit suicide, or even to kill the spouse or child.
4 **Parental induction of feelings of inferiority or guilt in the child**: the child is subjected to excessive criticism and made to feel bad or unwanted; in extreme cases assertions are made that the child's behaviour is or will be responsible for the illness or death of one or other parent.
5 **Parental 'clinging' to the child**: the parent (usually the mother) displays 'anxious attachment' to the child, exerting pressure on it to be the primary care-giver in their relationship, thus inverting the normal pattern.
6 **Parental inconsistency in the expression of love:** one or both parents vacillate between relative neglect of the child's attachment needs and periodic expressions of love, which may be excessive by way of compensation.

Any one of these forms of parental frustration of a child's basic archetypal needs can result in anxious, insecure individuals who report themselves to be lacking in confidence, shy, inadequate, or unable to cope. They often have difficulty in forming and maintaining lasting relationships, and under stress they are prone to develop **neurotic symptoms** such as **phobias**, persistent **anxiety**, and **depression**.

In addition, the emotional state of the parents, as well as their predominant mode of personality adjustment, have a direct impact on their children. The mother is particularly influential in this regard, for she mediates the world, in all its momentous ambiguity, to the child. In this crucially significant role as mediator, an extremely anxious mother will tend to induce **defensive arousal** and **fear** in her children, while a depressed mother will have difficulty in responding to their needs in such a way as to foster their development of 'basic trust'. The world for such children will necessarily remain ambiguous, uncertain, and potentially threatening.

Another critical factor is the kind of mothering that the mother herself received as a child, for these patterns can readily be passed on from generation to generation. Adequate mothering tends to produce adequate mothers.

The care a mother provides, or fails to provide, is also affected by such factors as the degree to which she feels secure in her bond to her husband, whether the child is of the desired gender, the number of children she already has, and her economic circumstances. A vital aspect of a mother's nurturing behaviour is her capacity to intuit her child's subjective state (whether the child is hungry, soiled, tired, angry, or frightened, and so on) and her ability to respond appropriately to it. This **mirroring function**, by which she helps the child to understand the nature of what it is experiencing, can go wrong for any of the above reasons, with potentially grave psychopathological consequences. With so much at stake, it says a great deal for the adaptive power of the heterosexual and parental affectional systems that so many children grow up to enjoy the degree of health and happiness that they do.

RANK

The phylogenetic history of competitiveness for rank and resources has become of growing interest to evolutionary psychiatrists since the 1960s. The story, though it took millions of years to unfold, is relatively simple to tell. Three hundred million years ago our ancestors competed for resources (food, territory, mates), on an individual basis, as many vertebrates continue to do to this day. Then, as group living became established and territory began to be shared, individuals ceased competing directly for territory and instead started to compete for rank. Once acquired, high rank brought with it access to the resources that were desired.

Competition for rank took the form of threat displays and physical combat in dyadic contests or tournaments, referred to by ethologists as **ritual agonistic behaviour** or **RAB**. Success in such tournaments provided a measure of an individual's **resource holding power** or **RHP**.

Animals have the capacity to assess their own RHP in relation to the RHP of potential adversaries. This enables them to make a realistic 'guess' at the probable outcome of getting involved in a fight – whether to attack, to flee, or to submit. Since RAB is conspicuously apparent among reptiles, the capacity for evaluating relative RHP must reside in the reptilian brain.

Repeated successes in dyadic contests result in high RHP and access to prime breeding sites and prime mates, both of which contribute to increased reproductive fitness. Defeats, on the other hand, result in a lowering of RHP and changes in the animal's physical and behavioural state. Lizards, for example, lose their colour in these circumstances and may die (MacLean, 1985). The defeated state has been called the **yielding subroutine of RAB** (Price and Sloman, 1987) or the **involuntary subordinate strategy** or **ISS** (Price *et al.*, 1994).

The human equivalent of RHP is self-esteem, and defeat can have similar effects on both the behaviour and self-esteem of human beings as it has on the behaviour and RHP of reptiles, mammals, and primates. This has frequently been observed among men in defeated armies. An essential aspect of high self-esteem is the subjective awareness of being able to control desired social outcomes, while low self-esteem is the awareness of not being able to control such desirable assets, and is associated with submissive or subordinate forms of behaviour, as well as with a liability to anxiety, depression, or social withdrawal.

In all social animals, threat from a conspecific perceived as holding higher RHP results in two alternative kinds of defensive behaviour: **submission** and **escape.** Submission differs from escape precisely because the animal stays put. The dominant individual will tolerate the continued presence of the defeated individual and cease to threaten him provided he puts on a postural display which indicates submission.

Subordinate animals tend to be driven to the periphery of the group to which they belong and, as a consequence, are most at risk from predators and hostile groups of conspecifics. This means that such peripheral subordinates must maintain a continuous state of high **arousal**, so as to facilitate rapid escape and the avoidance of injury.

The tense posture and anxious vigilance observed among subordinate animals is eminently understandable. Not only must they be alert to the possibility of attack from outside the group, but they must continuously engage in self-monitoring and self-protective vigilance against the possibility of attack from dominant members within the group. This state of high but undischarged arousal is directly analogous to the nervous arousal observed in **anxious patients** and to the constant rumination, checking behaviour, and intense preoccupation reported by patients with **obsessive-compulsive disorder**. As Gilbert (1989) has suggested, the various forms of checking characteristic of these patients are derived from the need to anticipate danger. The perfectionism of obsessional neurotics represents a desire to put themselves beyond attack or rebuke. Such people are commonly terrified of making mistakes, presumably because they fear an overwhelming attack on their RHP or self-esteem from persons in authority.

Observations such as these not only help to establish an evolutionary link between behaviour and psychopathology but also provide some insight as to why many psychiatric states (such as anxiety, depression, obsessive thoughts, and compulsive behaviour) are often found to co-exist in the same patient. It is also possible that the agitation and early morning insomnia characteristic of patients with **depression** are linked to the fact that the predators which were a threat to our ancestors were particularly active in the twilight hours. Rather than representing discrete disease entities, these states are better understood as chronic exaggerations of innate behavioural potentials with which all human beings are equipped by virtue of their humanity.

HEDONIC AND AGONIC COMPETITION

Sometime in the last ten million years, a new form of social competition has arisen: instead of trying to intimidate rivals, the competitor seeks to attract them. This form of competition is apparent, for example, among chimpanzees, and its significance was first recognized by Michael Chance (Chance and Jolly, 1970). In addition to threat display, male chimpanzees indulge in a form of display that is not threatening at all and does not demand the submission of a subordinate. Rather it is a form of social solicitation, which, Chance noted, results in affiliative behaviour 'in which there is a continuing interaction between individuals, such as grooming, play, sexual or mothering behaviour with the displayer.'

In the course of extensive observations on social groups of primates, Chance recognized that they had two quite distinct modes of functioning, which he termed **agonic** and **hedonic**. The agonic mode is characteristic of hierarchically organized societies where individuals are concerned with warding off threats to their status and inhibiting overt expressions of aggressive conflict; while the hedonic mode is associated with affiliative behaviour in more egalitarian social organizations where agonic tensions are absent. Not only do patterns of social interaction differ in each mode, but the mentalities of those individuals involved in the interaction also differ in such fundamental areas as emotion, cognition, perception, memory, and goal-seeking.

In the agonic mode, Chance observed that the social balance between dominant and subordinate individuals is maintained by a process which he called **equilibration**: the group is held together by the threat of attack from dominant individuals, and any attempt on the part of a subdominant to escape from the group elicits attack. As the subdominant approaches the implicit boundary of the group, a mere gaze from a dominant will usually be enough to slow him, stop him, and revert both his path and his attention to the centre. This phenomenon, which Chance termed **reverted escape** is typical of the agonic mode. It contrasts with the freedom of individuals to drift apart within the group, and even to leave it for a time, which is possible in the hedonic mode.

Chance has made an important distinction between **agonic** and **agonistic** modes of social interaction. The agonic mode prevails when the potential for agonistic violence is present but *inhibited*: as a result, individual members of the group are kept in a high state of psychological tension, but outbreaks of physical aggression are prevented. In the agonic mode, says Chance,

> individuals are always together in a group yet spread out, separate from one another, keeping their distance from the more dominant ones to whom they are constantly attentive. They are ready, at an instant, to avoid punishment by reacting to those threats that are dealt out from

time to time down the rank order. This they do with various submissive and/or appeasing gestures, and by spatial equilibration . . . which, arising from withdrawal followed by the reversion of escape, serve to prevent escalation of a threat into agonistic conflict, yet with tension and arousal remaining at a high level. The continuous high tension, without the accompanying agonistic behaviour, is the unique characteristic of this mode, for which the term agonic is reserved – *as arousal must be balanced by inhibition to preserve this state.*

(1988, pp. 6–7)

While acknowledging the epistemological pitfalls involved in translating ethological findings to human social organizations and psychology, many researchers have come to see the two modes as possessing great heuristic value in their implications for psychosocial theory and research.

These two contrasting forms of social organization find numerous parallels in the history of ideas: for example, Empedocles' distinction between love and strife, from which Freud derived his Eros and Thanatos instincts, Aristotle's distinction between the political and hedonic life, and the classic sociological distinction made by the German social theorist Ferdinand Tonnies (1855–1936) between *Gemeinschaft* and *Gesellschaft*. The Freudian dichotomy was taken up by Bakan (1966), who argued that two opposing modalities (his term) are at work in human social relations: *agency* (when individuals are concerned with self-protection, self-assertion, and power-seeking, tend to become separated or alienated from others, and to use repression), and *communion* (when individuals feel at one with others, indulge freely in forms of contractual co-operation, and dispense with repression). Milgram (1974) accounted for the obedience of his subjects by invoking an *agentic* state in which the subject focused attention on the experimenter and allowed the relationship with this authority figure to determine his judgement when given the task of punishing others. A close parallel is apparent between Bakan's agency mode, Milgram's agentic state, and Chance's agonic mode.

In short, the evidence points to the existence of **two great archetypal systems**: that concerned with attachment, affiliation, care-giving, care-receiving, and altruism; and that concerned with rank, status, discipline, law and order, territory, and possessions. These may well be the basic archetypal patterns on which social adjustment and maladjustment, psychiatric health, and sickness depend. Both can function healthily when evoked in appropriate circumstances, but either can give rise to pathology when their goals are frustrated or when they are inappropriately activated.

The discovery of two types of competition, one by intimidation and one by attraction, provides a deeper insight into the nature of the distinction between the two modes. The evolutionary replacement of intimidation by attraction allowed the **hedonic mode** to emerge. In the hedonic mode, the competitor seeks to disarm potential rivals and attract potential mates as well as achieving status in the eyes of other members of the group. Group approbation of the competitor's displays has the effect of raising his self-esteem. Should his displays be met with disapprobation, on the other hand, the individual becomes less attractive to potential mates, loses status in the eyes of the group, and suffers a reduction in his self-esteem.

With the evolution of competition by attraction, a new capacity for self-assessment emerged, which Gilbert (1989) has called **social attention holding potential** or **SAHP**. An individual's SAHP is a measure of his ability to hold attention and attract investment from other members of the group. Attractive people (people with high SAHP) are granted prestige (the systemic correlate of SAHP). They assume leadership roles and have access to more resources than their less successful competitors. In environments similar to the EEA, they tend (as with the Ache and !Kung bushmen) to have more wives, sire more children, and their children are more likely to survive. Their fitness, therefore, increases.

The criteria on which positive and negative assessments are made are, to a certain extent, culture dependent, in the sense that they are based on certain ground rules which are formalized in customs, ethical standards, and laws. These ground rules are incorporated into the personal (ontogenetic) psyche in the form of a moral complex similar to the Freudian **superego**, and to transgress the rules is to incur the disagreeable experience of shame or guilt. **Shame** is experienced when one fails to measure up to the standards of the group; **guilt** is suffered when one breaks the rules. Both shame and guilt are associated with a lowering of SAHP, reduced self-esteem, and dysphoria. We suggest that these responses to failure in hedonic competition *are evolutionary developments of the more primitive forms of anxiety and depression that evolved to manage failure in agonic competition.*

Agonistic competition has been present and evolving for 300 million years, and is deeply embedded in the genome; whereas hedonic competition has only been in existence for about one-thirtieth of that time. For affiliative, co-operative societies to function effectively, therefore, they must have powerful social sanctions against agonistic competition. This is why initiation rites, religious commandments, laws against assault and battery, 'Queensberry rules', and 'good manners' are an indispensable feature of all human communities. Where these sanctions break down, the result is the sort of agonistic behaviour typical of street corner gangs, football hooligans, prison populations, and others who have not experienced the social conditions conducive to the development of hedonic competition.

The two-mode concept thus has profound implications for both mental health and psychopathology. Groups in which hedonic competition prevails are the kind of groups in which most human beings live and, given the choice, in which they would almost certainly prefer to live. Only authoritarian personalities, high in Social Dominance Orientation (Pratto *et al.*,

1994), are likely to prefer living in an agonistic society. With agonistic behaviour relegated to the street corner, the school playground, and other places where society lacks either the power or the will to intervene, individuals can flourish in the hedonic mode, secure in the belief that agonistic behaviour will not occur *because it is against the cultural norms of the society*. This leaves human beings free to pursue co-operative activities and to engage in hedonic competition, which, fame being the spur, has resulted in their dedication to science, art, story telling, and all those manifold activities which give pleasure to others and bring status to their originators. It seems that humans have been selected to be co-operative, decent, loyal, and wishing to give pleasure to others. Our genes may be selfish, but hedonic competition has seen to it that our phenotypical behaviour, on the whole, is not. For our phenotypes have the capacity to be hedonic. Given the right upbringing, a child will learn to derive self-esteem from the approbation of others. But, lacking this example, he or she may well revert to the primitive source of self-esteem which results from the intimidation of others.

It can be seen, therefore, that the psychiatric states of anxiety and depression are natural and universal experiences which human beings share with all mammalian species. Both are pathological exaggerations of biological conditions which, in the EEA, contributed to survival. Both are adaptive reactions to loss or deprivation. Both occur in young mammals when they are forcibly separated from their mothers and in individuals living in hierarchically organized groups when deprived of rank or status. How can this contribute to survival? Having lost its mother, and after the initial cries of protest are over, the depressed infant lies still, silent and waiting, conserves body energy, and avoids the attention of predators. By this strategy the animal can survive until reunited with its mother or adopted by a surrogate parent, moved by its depressed state.

Similarly, a depressive reaction to loss of status enables the demoted individual to adapt passively to the lower rank, thus avoiding further attack from the more powerful individual who has displaced him or her. This in turn contributes to peace and social cohesion. **Depression**, therefore, is linked with the ubiquitous mammalian tactic of submission, while its opposite, **mania**, is linked with the tactic of dominance. **Manic-depression** is inextricably tied into the dominance–submission rank-ordering system and to its linked systems, aggression and appeasement.

The two-mode concept thus provides us with an evolutionary paradigm of the affiliative and ranking structures at the root of the manic-depressive disorders: mania derives from a sense of being dominant *and* adorable (lit. *omni-potent*), depression from being subdominant *and* unlovable. In fact, disordered functioning of the fundamental components of the two modes (attachment and rank) can go a long way to elucidate the characteristic features of a large number of psychiatric disorders. In some, factors relating to attachment formation and hedonic behaviour predominate (e.g., **attachment anxiety**, **separation anxiety**, the **depression** of bereavement or loss), while in others, factors relating to status-seeking and agonic behaviour predominate (e.g., **mania**, **type A personality disorder** and the **depression** triggered by lost status), but most conditions are, as we shall see in the next five chapters, a result of frustration of archetypal needs for both attachment *and* status, and they affect an individual's capacity to function adequately in either the hedonic or the agonic mode.

AN ORTHOGONAL SCHEMA FOR THE MAJOR DISORDERS

Essentially, the possible outcomes of competition through threat and aggression (RAB to gain RHP) or competition through attraction (self-display for group approbation to gain SAHP) are four in number:

1 social co-operation and integration;
2 dominance;
3 submission; and
4 withdrawal and social isolation.

These can be represented orthogonally, with physical competition for dominance on the vertical axis, and competition by attraction for approval and social integration on the horizontal axis (Figure 2).

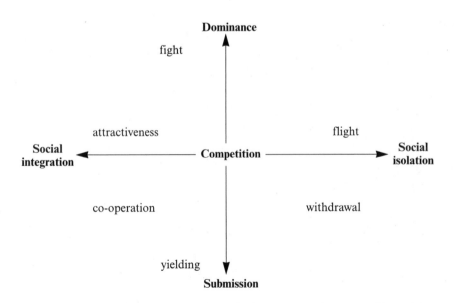

Figure 2 A schema for possible outcomes of competition through dominance and attraction

53

This schema is an elaboration of earlier proposals by Leary (1957), Crook (1980), Birtchnell (1990; 1993), and others. The horizontal dimension may also be labelled approach–withdrawal, closeness–distance, friendliness–hostility, ingroup–outgroup orientation, love–hate, and so on. In other words, the horizontal dimension is concerned with affiliation, the vertical dimension with power. The 'closeness–distance' label is applied to the horizontal dimension by Birtchnell (1990), who calls the vertical dimension 'upperness–lowerness'. Birtchnell postulates a further, diagonal dimension, which he calls 'control–lack of control'. He argues that feeling in control of the various interpersonal possibilities is linked with positive affects; while feeling that one lacks control of them is associated with negative affects, such as hate, anxiety, and depression. Birtchnell's horizontal needs for relatedness and distance resemble Jung's 'extraversion–introversion' dimension in his theory of psychological types. The implication is that extraverts would be more prone to depression than introverts when their needs for relatedness are frustrated, and that introverts would be more prone to schizoid withdrawal when their needs for distance are frustrated.

Since dominance has to do with **intrasexual selection** (competing with conspecifics for breeding resources) and love has to do with **mate selection**, these two co-ordinates are fundamental constructs. The broad application of

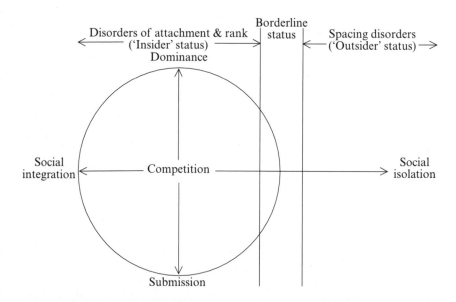

Figure 3 A schema for the classification of the major disorders

these basic dimensions to human psychopathology results in the following postulates:

1 **successful affiliation** tends to be associated with social adjustment and mental health;
2 **failure in affiliation** tends to be associated with schizoid personality disorder, schizotypal or schizophreniform illness and an introverted, inner-directed mode of personality adjustment;
3 **submission** tends to be associated with low self-esteem, feelings of shame and humiliation, dependent personality disorder, anxiety, depression, masochism, and a liability to be victimized or abused; and
4 **dominance** tends to be associated with high self-esteem, type A personality, hypomania, sadism, and a liability to victimize and abuse others.

A crucial factor is whether or not the individual continues to feel himself or herself to be an 'insider' (that is, a member of the ingroup, a committed member of the community, whether loved or unloved, of high status or low), or an 'outsider' (not a member of the ingroup, not a committed member of the community, not involved in attachment relationships or status conflicts). If an 'insider' develops a psychiatric disorder, it will tend to be a **disorder of attachment and rank**, whereas an 'outsider' will tend to develop a **spacing disorder** (Figure 3). Individuals who are uncertain as to their allegiance and who hover uneasily on the cusp between 'insider' and 'outsider' status will, if they develop a psychiatric disorder, tend to present with a **borderline state**. This schema will govern the plan for Parts II to IV of this book.

Part II

DISORDERS OF ATTACHMENT AND RANK

5

MOOD DISORDERS

Mood disorders, also referred to as affective disorders (from the Latin *affectus*, meaning emotion or mood) are the commonest conditions encountered in psychiatry. It has been estimated that the life-time risk of being afflicted with one of them is in the order of 12 per cent for men and 20 per cent for women. Essentially, they are exaggerations of the universal human capacity to experience sadness and elation. Psychiatry classifies these moods as illness when they are judged to be extreme, incapacitating, of long duration, disproportionate to the circumstances, and found to be unresponsive to advice or outside influence. The polar extremes of mood range from the profound misery of severe **depression** to the ecstatic self-confidence and limitless energy of **mania**.

That episodes of depression and mania can alternate was observed by the French psychiatrist J.P. Falret (1794–1870), who introduced the term *la folie circulaire* to describe the condition. At the end of the nineteenth century, Emil Kraepelin (1855–1926) grouped recurrent depression and recurrent mania ('periodic mental illnesses') together with 'circular insanity' in a single category, which he called **manic-depressive psychosis**. Kraepelin taught that three principle areas were affected by the illness: level of mood, psychic activity, and motor activity. In mania all three are elevated, while in depression all three are depressed. Kraepelin also described 'mixed states' in which manic and depressive features coincided in the same patient at the same time.

Despite Kraepelin's masterly nosological contribution, conceptual confusions have always surrounded the affective disorders, and disputes about the best way of classifying them invariably arise when groups of psychiatrists meet to discuss them. The problem has always been the lack of a coherent psychopathological theory to account for them. There is, however, broad agreement as to the clinical features typical of depression and mania.

CLINICAL FEATURES OF DEPRESSION

The main features of a depressive illness of moderate severity are low mood, reduced energy, pessimistic thinking, and disturbances of sleep and appetite.

The appearance of depressed people is characteristic: they look miserable. The brow is furrowed, the corners of the mouth turned down, the shoulders are hunched, the head hangs forwards, the gaze is directed downwards, and the usual gestures of social intercourse are reduced.

There is a general inhibition of activity (so-called **psychomotor retardation**): slow thought processes are reflected in slow, quiet, and monotonous speech, a disinclination to converse, and in long delays before giving answers to questions. There is difficulty in concentration, a reduction in attention span, and a consequent loss of efficiency in coping with ordinary tasks and duties. In severe depression, psychomotor retardation may be so marked as to become depressive stupor and mutism.

The depressed mood is altogether more intense, more pervasive, and more sustained than ordinary sadness, and is bound up with gloomy thoughts of worthlessness, guilt, and helplessness. A distinction is to be made between mood and emotion. Whereas the emotion of sadness is focused on an object, the mood of depression is either unfocused or self-focused (Ekman and Davidson, 1994). 'Biological symptoms' invariably accompany the condition. These include insomnia, anorexia, constipation, amenorrhoea, and loss of sexual libido.

In all depressive disorders, the most characteristic form of sleep disturbance is early morning waking, associated with agitated and pessimistic thinking, which prevents a resumption of sleep. Some depressed people also experience difficulty in getting off to sleep when they go to bed. However, a number report that they sleep excessively ('hypersomnia'), though they wake up unrefreshed.

Just as thoughts tend to be their most gloomy first thing in the morning, so the mood remains at its most depressed through the early hours of the day, gradually lightening in the course of the afternoon or evening; this **diurnal rhythm** is characteristic of depressive disorders.

While most depressed people have a poor appetite and lose weight, a small proportion of them eat excessively and gain weight – so-called 'comfort eating'.

A marked lack of self-esteem is accompanied by feelings of failure, hopelessness, and self-reproof. Depressed people express deep pessimism about their capacity to cope with the future, predicting they will be unable to hold a job, discharge their social and financial obligations, or remain competent and healthy. They may be intensely preoccupied with real or imagined delinquencies in the past, guilt about mistakes, letting people down, or petty acts of dishonesty. Preoccupied with an endless stream of worries, the present confronts them with insuperable difficulties, to which they respond with vacillation, perplexity, and brooding self-absorption. They are trapped on 'a ceaseless roundabout of painful thought' (Mapother and Lewis, 1937). In this state, depressives are obdurate that nothing can be done to help them: if one attempts to reason with them in an effort to persuade them that things are not really as bad as they seem, one encounters hydra-headed objections to every argument and to every course of action one may propose. Altogether, life no longer seems worth living and thoughts of suicide may provide the only source of relief. For this reason, severely depressed patients are beyond psychotherapy and require urgent antidepressant medication and, when the condition is considered life-threatening, ECT.

Although most depressed people sit still and silent, showing inhibition of all movements, some may be agitated, indulging in various forms of fidgeting, hand-wringing, and pacing about, tending to cling onto doctors and nurses, earnestly demanding help and reassurance. There is invariably some degree of anxiety in all depressive conditions, but the restless, semi-purposive activity of agitated depression is more common in elderly patients than younger ones.

Hypochondriacal preoccupations are not uncommon, often focusing on the bowels, which, in depressed people, may well be constipated. In severe or psychotic depression, these preoccupations may reach delusory intensity so that patients become convinced that they have an inoperable cancer, AIDS, or some other fatal disease. Similarly, feelings of guilt and worthlessness can become exaggerated into frank delusions of sin, impoverishment, and ruin. The depressive illness may then be 'explained' as a moral 'judgement' – as being no more and no less than what one deserves. Auditory hallucinations may intervene and these commonly back up the thought content of the delusions. It has been well said that 'depression is a central assault upon the well-being of the self' (Sims, 1995). In its severest form it is possibly one of the most dreadful afflictions humanity can suffer.

CLINICAL FEATURES OF MANIA

In all essentials, mania and the milder form, hypomania, present a clinical picture which is the mirror-image of depression, as can be seen from a glance at Table 3. The mood is elated, self-esteem inflated, and energy levels are high. In mania, the appearance is florid and rather wild, with flamboyantly colourful dress, bold gestures, vigorous movements, erect posture, a domineering, authoritative manner, and a constant flow of confident, exuberant and utterly tactless speech, which it is virtually impossible to interrupt. Numerous expansive, self-important ideas are expressed, which jump vertiginously from one topic to another (**flight of ideas**). The future is viewed with supreme optimism, ambitious plans formulated in capricious abundance, huge commitments entered into without any possibility of meeting them, money is spent like water, and uninhibited fury expressed against anyone who may object or offer criticism. Normal sleep patterns are disturbed in that manic people are usually busy for most of the night, but this is not experienced as a problem as sleep is regarded as both unnecessary and a waste of time. Both appetite and sexual libido are increased, and

Table 3 Contrasting features of depression and mania

	Depression	Mania
Mood	Depressed	Elated
Self-esteem	Low	High
Energy	Low	High
Appearance	Drab	Florid
Social manner	Submissive	Domineering
Posture	Slumped	Erect
Gestures	Minimal	Flamboyant
Movements	Retarded	Accelerated
Ideas	Few and fixed	Numerous and fleeting
Speech	Slow	Rapid
Attention	Preoccupied	Distractable
Appetite	Reduced	Increased
Sexual libido	Reduced	Increased
View of the future	Pessimistic	Optimistic
Morality	Feels guilty	Feels above reproach
Plans	None (except suicide)	Abundant
Money	Miserly	Extravagant
Sleep	Can't sleep enough	Doesn't require sleep
Health	Feels ill	Feels well

irresponsible sexual liaisons contracted with ready abandonment. Health is felt to be excellent, and the subjective state is one of extreme well-being.

Not surprisingly, manic people feel no need for a psychiatrist, and are usually condescending and dismissive if one should presume to offer his professional services. Compulsory admission to hospital may be necessary in these circumstances if their families are to be protected from financial ruin.

Just as there are degrees of depression, so elevated mood can range from the cheerful, confident activity of hypomania to the extreme euphoria, the frenzied exuberance and the delusional grandiosity of mania. In severe mania, the delusions and hallucinations that occur are opposite to those of severe depression. Thus, manic patients may be convinced they have a political mission to save the world, that they possess limitless resources, and that history will regard them as among the greatest figures ever to have graced the planet with their existence. Hallucinations, when they occur, are usually compatible with the extreme elevation of mood and comment on the special powers and brilliant future awaiting such a uniquely gifted individual. Physical exhaustion eventually intervenes, the grandiose delusions begin to subside, and the euphoric mood may be interrupted with bursts of irritability, hostility, and sometimes with moments of depression.

CLASSIFICATION

So important and widespread are these disorders, and their aetiology and psychopathology so little understood, that disputes about how best to classify them continue to rage up to the present time. Three major approaches to classification have been tried which seek to differentiate affective disorders in terms of their aetiology, their symptoms, and their course through the life-cycle.

Classification based on aetiology

For many years, a distinction has been made (1) between **endogenous** and **reactive depression**, and (2) between **primary** and **secondary depressive disorders**.

Endogenous depression was held to arise from some genetic or consti-tutional factor conceived as operating quite independently of external life events, while reactive depression was thought to arise purely in response to such events. In practice, few depressions ever belong entirely to one group or the other: both endogenous and reactive factors are usually involved.

The second classificatory system distinguished between depressions which were secondary to other disorders, such as alcoholism, drug dependency, physical disease, or schizophrenia, and primary depression in which no such antecedents could be found. However, this distinction has proved to be of limited clinical use because no clear diagnostic, prognostic or therapeutic criteria have been detected between depressive disorders separated along these lines.

In addition, **seasonal affective disorder (SAD)** is characterized by episodes of depression which recur each year in late autumn, winter, or early spring and are thought to be connected with the reduced hours of sunlight suffered during the winter months by those living at the more extreme latitudes of the northern and southern hemispheres. This form of depression is more likely to be associated with symptoms which are less common than in other depressions, namely, hypersomnia, increased appetite, and a craving for carbohydrate. This is a more successful classification than the others in this section since it relates a cluster of signs and symptoms to a specific aetio-logical factor and to a specific treatment based on phototherapy.

Classification based on symptoms

In addition to making a primary distinction between elevated mood (**mania**) and depressed mood (**depression**), this approach differentiates between dis-orders in terms of symptomatic severity. Hence the traditional psychiatric distinction between **hypomania** and **mania** and between **neurotic** and **psych-otic** depression. More recently it has become fashionable to distinguish between **minor** and **major** depression and between **mild** and **moderate** depres-sion. Such differentiation may have some descriptive uses, but, as with the aetiological classifications (with the exception of SAD), they have not been backed up by evidence establishing them as separate clinical entities. There are, however, biological indications that this classifactory distinction is valid and we shall return to this issue in Chapter 18.

Classification based on course through the life-cycle

This is the kind of classification that has come to dominate the thinking of those responsible for the American DSM-IV and the European ICD manuals of mental disorders, with their elaborate and detailed distinctions between **unipolar** and **bipolar** disorders, **single episode** and **recurrent** disorders, **cyclothymic** and **dysthymic disorders,** and so on.

A unipolar disorder is one in which a depressive illness is or has been present in the absence of any previous manic or hypomanic episode. A bipolar disorder is one in which a depressive illness is or has been present in a patient with a history of at least one previous manic or hypomanic episode. This distinction is not altogether satisfactory because *all* patients with mania or hypomania are classified as suffering from bipolar disorder even if they have never suffered a depressive episode. The questionable rationale for this convention is the assumption that people who have a manic episode will eventually develop a depressive one. A further drawback to this system is that people diagnosed as being unipolar depressives sometimes become manic and have to be reclassified as suffering from bipolar disorder.

Diagnostic categories based on the stage of life reached by the patient have distinguished **depressions of childhood** and **adolescence** as well as **puerperal**, **involutional**, and **senile depressions**. Behind these distinctions is the hope that these depressive disorders may prove to have a distinct aetiology related to the hormonal changes attendant on development or involution of the sex glands. However, no such aetiological differences have so far been demonstrated, though this is not to deny the possibility that they may be at some time in the future.

While these DSM-IV and ICD classifications differ in some respects, they agree in most others. The main similarities are:

1 the distinction between elevated mood (mania) and lowered mood (depression)
2 the distinction between single and recurrent episodes
3 the distinction between mild and more severe disturbances of mood.

Recurrent mild disturbances of mood are classified by both systems as **cyclothymia** (when episodes of depressed mood alternate with episodes of elevated mood) and **dysphoria** (when recurrent episodes are invariably depressive).

All these classificatory distinctions are of only limited usefulness, in our view, in the absence of a unifying evolutionary perspective. Indeed, the long lists of criteria sets, the numerous diagnostic categories, all numbered and specified with the hair-splitting accuracy so characteristic of the American

DSM-IV Bible, have almost become more complicated than the phenomena they seek to describe. In clinical practice, we feel that the best course is to conduct a thorough psychiatric examination and record a careful description of the disorder and its history, rather than to pour copious quantities of intellectual energy into the grail of a perfectly defined (and numbered) classification.

THE EVOLUTIONARY PERSPECTIVE

A major indication that depressive and manic reactions are adaptive is their universal occurrence in human communities in response to certain characteristic life events. For all its regional variations, depression is a specially recognizable entity across cultures: dysphoric mood, inability to take pleasure in anything, low energy, loss of interest, the inability to concentrate, and feelings of anxiety, tension, and worthlessness are *core* symptoms of depression, which are acknowledged and diagnosed in different terminologies in practically all human societies throughout the world (Sartorius *et al.*, 1983). It has also been recognized in our own culture, at least since Hippocrates' description of melancholia over two thousand years ago.

The typical life events which trigger either a depressive or a manic reaction are the perception of one of two probable outcomes: loss or gain. In the immediate, short-term scale of proximate objectives, what is lost or gained may be a spouse or child, a job or financial security, health or reputation. But what the particular loss or gain amounts to, in the long-term scale of ultimate biological objectives, is a decrease or an increase in the resources needed for reproductive success.

In what sense, then, can either depression or mania perform an adaptive function? In the first place, the human capacity to experience the pain of loss and the joy of gain functions as *a punishment and reward system* to discourage or encourage behaviour that will decrease or increase the chances of reproductive success. In the second place, this autonomous punishment and reward system functions as a catalyst promoting adjustment to altered circumstances: the severe and prolonged mental pain of depression will persist until one finally gives up all aspiration to repossess what has been irrevocably lost; while the joy of elation lasts only as long as one holds on to what has been gained.

From the evolutionary standpoint, therefore, it would seem that low mood and high mood evolved as means of adaptation to alterations in one's resource holding power and chances of reproductive success. 'If there is little chance of a payoff, it is best to sit tight rather than to waste energy,' comment Nesse and Williams (1995). If success is in one's grasp, then it is best to pull out all the stops and go for bust. This is the essence of the depressive and manic adaptations.

Of course, this does not mean that all depressive or manic reactions are adaptive, only that they exist, *in potentia*, as evolved mechanisms which can be triggered by perceptions of loss or gain. In psychiatric practice, these reactions can manifest in certain individuals in ways that are so clearly maladaptive that they may result in gross incapacity, suicide, or social and financial ruin.

In approaching the aetiology and clinical consequences of manic-depression, etho-psychiatrists have focused on the fulfilment and frustration of two basic archetypal needs: (1) the need for **affectional bonds**, and (2) the need for **social rank** or **status**. The adaptive function of elevated or depressed mood is to enable an individual to adjust to his circumstances when he is convinced that either one or both of these needs has been decisively fulfilled or irrevocably frustrated.

Many authorities have, in the history of psychiatry, stressed the aetiological significance of one or other of these needs. Freud's (1917) suggestion that depression served to assist the accommodation to loss of a loved person, was taken up and extended by Bowlby in his outstanding series of three volumes, *Attachment and Loss*. The importance of social status was stressed in the early part of this century by Alfred Adler, who introduced the concepts of the **inferiority complex** and of **compensation** for feelings of inferiority, but it was not until the 1960s that Chance's work on the evolution of rank behaviour in primate relationships stimulated Price (1967), to consider the role of involuntary subordination in the aetiology of affective disorders. Rank theory proposed that depressed mood evolved as a strategy for inhibiting challenge, so that stable social hierarchies could be sustained. Depression is adaptive, Price proposed, because it induces the sufferer to accommodate to low social rank when it has been forced upon him.

Growing acceptance of attachment theory and rank theory has led to suggestions for aetiological classifications of two kinds of depression. Thus, Beck (1983) distinguished between **deprivation depression** (caused by the loss of affiliative opportunities) and **defeat depression** (caused by failure to achieve desired goals). In Beck's view, 'sociotropic' people, to whom affiliative needs are of particular importance, are more prone to develop 'deprivation depression' when their affiliative needs are frustrated, while 'autonomous' people, who are more self-reliant, are more prone to 'defeat depression', when their competitive needs are frustrated. A parallel distinction was made by Blatt (1974) between **anaclitic depression** (Greek, *ana* = upon; *klino* = lean), caused by failure to form lasting attachment bonds, and **introjective depression**, occurring in people with a strict, critical superego, who fail to live up to the high standards they demand of themselves. In addition, Birtchnell (1993) has distinguished between **horizontal depressions**, which result from dissatisfactions in interactions involving 'closeness' and 'separateness', and **vertical depressions**, which result from dissatisfactions in 'upper-to-lower' (rank) interactions.

It is tempting for us to add to this list by introducing the terms **hedonic**

66

depressions and **agonic depressions**, but this would be a contribution of dubious significance. It may well be possible in some cases to distinguish between depressions brought on by loss of attachment figures and those brought on by loss of status, but such distinctions are of little use if both hedonic and agonic forms of depression happen to follow a similar clinical course and show a similar response to treatment. Moreover, both attachment and rank archetypes are simultaneously actualized from the earliest years in view of the fact that the parent–child relationship is a rank relationship as well as one based on attachment. The 'inner working models' (Bowlby, 1969) formed during these years will determine the kind of affective response the adult will make to subsequent experiences of loss or gain of whatever kind.

All that can be said with safety is that both hedonic and agonic considerations may apply in any particular case of manic-depressive disorder, and that the history, rather than the clinical presentation, may establish which has made the greater contribution.

ATTACHMENT THEORY

Attachment behaviour is both instinctive and goal-directed. It results from an inherited predisposition to select salient figures to bond to and also to behave in such a way as to maintain proximity and communication with such figures once the bond has been formed. The affective consequences of this are profound, for attachment is synonymous with love. The formation of a warm, intimate, and lasting relationship with a dependable attachment figure is the basis of human happiness and security. It results in the development of an inner model of the self as capable and worthy of both giving and receiving affection. Any threat to the relationship is experienced as a cause of anxiety, fear, and anger; loss of the loved person results in grief and depression; while restoration of an attachment thought to have been lost results in the experience of joy.

Although these affective consequences of attachment and loss are experienced with particular intensity in early childhood, they nevertheless continue to colour relationships through the entire course of life. The internal working models, or schemata, which the child develops through its experience of intimacy with others, influence his 'relational style' and determine his ability to relate successfully to a wife, children, and relations, and to form alliances with friends and colleagues. Early experiences of defective parenting will result in the formation of defective models and will sensitize the individual to respond to subsequent loss or rejection in a pathological way.

Bowlby's explanation of depression is, therefore, that it is, like grief or mourning, a primary response to attachment loss. Depression as a prolonged and pathological state is particularly liable to occur in individuals who, because of inadequate parenting, have failed to develop a mature

67

capacity to deal with loss. Thus, a woman whose husband deserts her, and whose inner working model is of one who is essentially unlovable, will conclude that there is nothing left to live for and become depressed. 'Death or separation confirms the person's worst expectations and leads to despair as well as anxiety . . . mourning is likely to be characterized by unusually intense anger and/or self-reproach, with depression, and to persist for much longer than normal' (Bowlby, 1979).

Bowlby's contribution was of immense significance. Not only did he introduce ethological concepts into the mainstream of psychiatry, but he stimulated research by proposing his hypotheses in a testable form and he provided insights into the nature and development of attachment bonds which have been of enormous value in the practice of psychotherapy. Evidence supporting his views has come from the consistent finding that patients prone to depression commonly recall lack of parental affection (Parker, 1984). If attachment theory has a defect, it is that it underestimates the role of individual differences (genetic and constitutional) in overcoming traumata suffered in early life. Even gross disturbances in early attachment bonds do not automatically give rise to psychopathology. Nor do the majority of depressed adults have a history of outright parental loss in childhood (Pfohl et al., 1983).

However, there is little doubt that the frustration of attachment needs can be a critical aetiological factor, whether suffered in childhood or in adult life. Brown and Harris's (1978) classic study of depressed women living in inner London demonstrated that adverse life events triggered a depressive response in women in whom a number of vulnerability factors existed: these were the lack of a close confidant, loss of mother before the age of 11, having three or more children under the age of 14 to look after at home, and no employment outside the home. A potent cause of a depressive reaction, it seems, is to have to deal with stress in isolation and without the support of attachment figures to depend on.

As we described in Chapter 3, the strength of the need for attachment is never more apparent than when a young animal or child is separated involuntarily from its mother. The loud protest and dreadful despair which forced separations induce are *primary responses* which are not reducible to other causes: they are due directly to the a priori (phylogenetic) nature of the attachment bond. Evidence concerning the responses of young humans on separation from their mothers has come mostly from observations of children in hospitals and nurseries. These findings were eloquently summarized by Bowlby (1973). The children studied (mostly by James Robertson) were between 15 and 30 months of age. They had been removed from their mothers and familiar environment and placed for a limited period in a residential nursery or hospital ward, where they were cared for by a succession of unfamiliar people. All the children had previously formed secure attachments to their mothers and had never before been separated from them.

From the moment separation began, a predictable sequence of behaviour was observed; it corresponded closely to the sequence reported by Kaufman and Rosenblum (1967) in pigtail monkey infants forcibly separated from their mothers. Bowlby's summary of the stages of the sequence is as follows:

The initial phase, that of **protest**, may begin immediately or may be delayed; it lasts from a few hours to a week or more. During it the young child appears acutely distressed at having lost his mother and seeks to recapture her by the full exercise of his limited resources. He will often cry loudly, shake his cot, throw himself about, and look eagerly towards any sight or sound which might prove to be his missing mother. All his behaviour suggests strong expectation that she will return. Meantime he is apt to reject all alternative figures who offer to do things for him, though some children will cling desperately to a nurse.

During the phase of **despair**, which succeeds protest, the child's preoccupation with his missing mother is still evident, though his behaviour suggests increasing hopelessness. The active physical movements diminish or come to an end, and he may cry monotonously or intermittently. He is withdrawn and inactive, makes no demands on people in the environment, and appears to be in a state of deep mourning. This is a quiet stage, and sometimes, clearly erroneously, is presumed to indicate a diminution of distress.

Because the child shows more interest in his surroundings, the phase of **detachment**, which sooner or later succeeds protest and despair, is often welcomed as a sign of recovery. The child no longer rejects the nurses; he accepts their care and the food and toys they bring, and may even smile and be sociable. To some this change seems satisfactory. When his mother visits, however, it can be seen that all is not well, for there is a striking absence of the behaviour characteristic of the strong attachment normal at this age. So far from greeting his mother he may remain remote and apathetic; instead of tears there is a listless turning away. He seems to have lost all interest in her.

Should his stay in hospital or residential nursery be prolonged and should he, as is usual, have the experience of becoming transiently attached to a series of nurses, each of whom leaves and so repeats for him the experience of the original loss of his mother, he will in time act as if neither mothering nor contact with humans has much significance for him. After a series of upsets at losing several mother-figures to whom in turn he has given some trust and affection, he will gradually commit himself less and less to succeeding figures and in time will stop altogether attaching himself to anyone. He will become increasingly self-centred and, instead of directing his desires and feelings towards people, will become preoccupied with material things such as sweets, toys, and food. A child living in an institution or hospital who has reached this stage will no longer be upset when nurses change or leave. He will cease to show feelings when his parents come and go on visiting day; and it may cause them pain when they realize that, although he has an avid interest in the presents they bring, he has little interest in them as special people. He will appear cheerful and adapted to his unusual situation and apparently unafraid of anyone. But this sociability is superficial: he appears no longer to care for anyone.

(1973, pp. 27–8)

As this distressing description indicates, the depressive reaction of the second stage acts as a means by which a terrible loss becomes acknowledged and accepted and through which the child becomes detached from the most precious asset in his world: his mother. It is possible that Bowlby's description offers a model of all depressive reactions to loss and that to achieve detachment from the lost asset is the primary goal of depression. When detachment has occurred, it is possible to adjust to the new circumstances so that life can go on. In line with this possibility is Wenegrat's (1984) suggestion that agitated depressions, in which psychomotor activity is increased, may well signify protest and yearning, while retarded depressions, in which psychomotor activity is slowed down, could signify despair and hopelessness. These two forms of depression would thus represent the first two stages of Bowlby's triad.

There can be little doubt, therefore, that loss of an attachment figure, either through prolonged separation or death, can be a potent cause of grief, despair, and depression. However, it would be wrong to assume that this is the only cause. In clinical practice it is common to encounter depressions (so-called **endogenous depressions**) which are not readily attributable to any precipitating life event. And of those depressions which are directly attributable to loss (**reactive depressions**), the loss in the majority of cases is not of a loved person but of some other valuable asset, such as a job, status, or financial security. It is difficult, if not impossible, to account for these within the context of Bowlby's attachment theory. Rank theory seems altogether more appropriate to them.

RANK THEORY

Whereas attachment theory proposes that depression is an adaptive response to losing an attachment figure and conceiving of oneself as unlovable, rank theory proposes that depression is an adaptive response to losing rank and conceiving of oneself as a loser. The adaptive function of the depression, according to rank theory, is to facilitate losing and to promote accommodation to the fact that one has lost. In other words, the depressive state evolved to promote the acceptance of the subordinate role and the loss of resources which can only be secured by holding higher rank in the dominance hierarchy. The function of this depressive adaptation is to prevent the loser in a status conflict from suffering further injury and to preserve the stability and competitive efficiency of the group by maintaining social homeostasis.

In circumstances of defeat and enforced subordination, an internal inhibitory process comes into operation which causes the individual to cease competing and reduce his level of aspiration (Gilbert, 1992). This inhibitory process is *involuntary* and results in the loss of energy, depressed mood, sleep disturbance, poor appetite, retarded movements, and loss of confidence which are the typical characteristics of depression.

The selective advantage of an evolved capacity for the recognition and acceptance of rank difference in social groups is that it reduces aggressiveness and establishes precedence in granting rights of access to indispensable resources such as territory, food, and potential mates. It follows that gaining rank is associated with elevated mood and losing rank with depressed mood. The evolutionary advantage of living in groups is the protection it provides from predators. For *Homo sapiens* it also afforded protection from other hominid groups. Living in a group became crucial for safety, for access to resources, for co-operative hunting of large game, and for reproductive success. A sense of belonging has thus become indispensable to our physical and mental security. To be popular and hold rank within a group are immensely desirable accomplishments; to perceive oneself as unpopular and without rank are causes of misery and unhappiness; while to be rejected from the group altogether is one of life's greatest disasters. It is in terms of these factors that joy and sorrow, mania and depression, contentment and anxiety can be most readily understood.

One important contribution of rank theory is that it has proposed a hypothesis of how depression actually evolved: it emerged as the *yielding* component of ritual agonistic conflict. This has been called the **yielding subroutine** (Price and Sloman, 1987). The adaptive function of the yielding subroutine is twofold: first, it ensures that the yielder truly yields and does not attempt to make a comeback, and, second, the yielder reassures the winner that yielding has truly taken place, so that the conflict ends, with no further damage to the yielder. Relative social harmony is then restored.

Similarly, we may offer the hypothesis that mania evolved as the winning component of ritual agonistic behaviour: the **winning subroutine**. Here again, the adaptive function is twofold: first, it ensures that the winner truly wins and makes clear that any attempt at a comeback by the yielder will be successfully resisted, and, second, it ensures that should the yielder attempt to reopen the conflict, the winner will have such resources of confidence, determination, strength, and energy that he will force the yielder to yield for good and all.

Both yielding and winning subroutines thus ensure that social change is accomplished relatively quickly without too much disruption of group

71

activities and that once it has occurred it will prove lasting. The object of the losing strategy is *damage limitation*, that of the winning strategy is *status preservation*. Inevitably, such subroutines carry greater significance among group-living species than among those living a solitary existence. A solitary animal fights for possession of a territory. If he loses a contest for one territory, then he must be able to withdraw and move on to fight for another. Yielding should involve only a brief 'disappointment' on the basis that he who fights and runs away lives to fight another day. Group-living individuals, on the other hand, require more prolonged and complex winning and losing subroutines, for a loser may have to give up a position in the hierarchy that he has held for many years. Should he not greatly modify his behaviour he could be expelled from the group. Chance's concept of 're-verted escape' becomes relevant here.

That the incidence of depression is higher and its course longer than hypomania suggests that natural selection has favoured the prolonged yielding subroutine over its winning equivalent. This could reflect the evident fact that in any asymmetrical society there are potentially more losers than winners. It also reflects the fact that few people are ever known to present themselves at psychiatric clinics complaining of 'suffering' from hypomania. Inevitably, the medical services are concerned with losers rather than winners, and whereas the loser in a physical encounter is more likely than the winner to end up in Casualty, so the loser in a *ritual* encounter is more likely than the winner to end up in the Psychiatric Out-Patients Department.

In order to preserve their cohesive stability, groups exert pressure on their members to conform to group mores and to remain within the group. It is not permitted to go off merely because one has been relegated to a lower status: one may be humble but at least all the advantages of group membership are preserved. Did they not exert such coercion, groups would be in constant danger of disintegration, and human beings would perforce revert to the spaced-out, individual territory-owning existence of reptiles, birds, and many mammals, including our close relative, the orang-utan.

When people encounter one another in contemporary social situations, the issue of dominance does not immediately arise, for such encounters are normally conducted in the hedonic mode. Should they be called upon to work together or live in close proximity to one another, this agreeable state of affairs may well continue indefinitely, provided they are well adjusted individuals and they do not have to make too many controversial decisions. If conflicts should arise between them, however, then the hedonic mode may switch into the agonic or agonistic mode. This phenomenon is well recognized in group psychotherapy (Kennedy and McKenzie, 1986), where the collaborative work of therapy may be disrupted by battles between rivals for leadership of the group. This can accentuate rather than relieve depressive and manic reactions in group members, and the unfortunate therapist may experience great difficulty in switching the group back into the hedonic mode.

What the winning and losing subroutines provide, then, are the *templates* for the manic and depressive reactions. These reactions have, in the course of evolution, become susceptible to triggers other than those concerned with the gain or loss of rank, and may be activated by almost any situation in individuals who, for reasons of personal history, are especially sensitive to experience the affective consequences of a gain or a loss of a specific kind. As Allen (1995) puts it: 'it is the depressed mood state that has been selected by evolution, whereas the clinically depressed state is a pathological aberration based on this adaptive emotional mechanism.' In other words, both mania and depression are pathological conditions based on the inappropriate activation of evolved means of adaptation.

VULNERABILITY TO AFFECTIVE DISORDERS

Vulnerability to an affective disorder is a highly complex issue involving contributions from genetics, family history, early attachment experiences, personality development, stressful life events, environmental contexts, and biochemical factors (Akiskal, 1985, 1989), all of which proceed on the basis of innate social propensities shared by us all. Similar factors would appear to be operative in other primates in addition to ourselves. For example, Akiskal and his colleagues were able to induce depressive behaviour in rhesus monkeys either by separating them from their peers or by injecting chemicals into their cerebral vesicles which had the effect of lowering limbic monoamine concentrations. Kraemer and McKinney (1979) found that the depressive response to each of these contributory factors was increased when they were combined. The capacity to become depressed is a universally apparent human characteristic: it is adaptive (that is, it was positively selected), and, in every individual, a threshold must exist for its activation. Genetic and environmental factors determine whether this threshold is high or low in any individual case. A person in whom the threshold is low will be particularly vulnerable to factors releasing a depressive response.

Studies of families with manic-depressive disorder, comparing the vulnerability of their members with the population at large, show that having one parent with bipolar disorder makes one five times as vulnerable, while having two parents with a disorder increases one's vulnerability by a factor of ten. By far the most impressive studies of the genetic contribution to a psychiatric disorder are **adoption studies**, since they can preclude influences derived from growing up in a disturbed family environment. Wender *et al.* (1986) found that the biological relatives of adopted individuals with affective disorder were eight times as likely to develop unipolar depression as controls. There was also a fifteenfold increase in suicide among their biological relatives.

Moreover, **twin studies** indicate beyond all reasonable doubt that high rates among vulnerable families are related to genetic factors. Thus, the concordance of bipolar disorder among monozygotic twins reared together and among those reared apart is approximately the same: 70 per cent. This is much higher than that for dizygotic twins: 23 per cent. Genetic factors are most clearly demonstrable in cases of severe depression; they are less apparent in milder forms. So far, attempts to link inheritance of the disorder to a particular region of the genome have not been successful.

How genetic factors result in pathology is as yet far from clearly understood. There may well be a number of genetic influences that can increase risk of affective disorder as well as psychopathological influences from parents and peers. The probability is that both sets of contributory factors combine to affect the *threshold of tolerance* to stressful life events. There is evidence that the capacity to cope with stress ('coping behaviour') may itself be genetically influenced (Kendler *et al.*, 1991).

The possibility that heredity, inadequate parenting, and early experiences of loss or separation can organize a neurohormonal vulnerability to depression at the limbic level has been suggested by Meyersburg and Post (1979). Once established, this limbic vulnerability may be triggered by any one of a number of factors ranging from severe physical illness, the use of catecholaminergic drugs, and premenstrual or postpartum hormonal changes, to seasonal light fluctuations and such stressful events as bereavement, divorce, job loss, or demotion.

Akiskal (1988) proposed that heredity and developmental factors interact to bring out personality traits rendering some individuals liable to over-react to the stresses of ordinary life. When a depressive episode remits, the traits nevertheless persist, rendering the individual vulnerable to a further relapse when new stresses are encountered.

The role of personality traits in rendering people susceptible to affective disorders has given rise to such categories as **dysthymia**, **cyclothymia**, and **depressive** or **hypomanic personality types**. These are thought to represent some underlying instability or hyperactivity in the limbic affect systems which have been built-in to the personality structure so as to make such individuals both more vulnerable to and less ready to recover from related forms of affective illness. One who has championed an evolutionary approach to the study of personality is Buss (1991), who advocates a classification in terms of a stable and lasting emphasis on specific domains, namely, sociability, nurturance, aggressiveness, dominance, fearfulness, impulsiveness, and so on. These all relate to personal styles or biases that individuals may bring to social situations, particularly those involving affiliation and rank, and they will influence the form that a disorder will take if the threshold for that disorder is crossed.

Beck (1967), like Bowlby, pointed to the way in which the ground may be prepared for the later development of a depressive illness by a pre-morbid constellation of attitudes and assumptions originating from earlier negative experiences. Watson and Clark (1984) have developed a parallel concept of 'negative affectivity': over time the patient develops a negative view of himself and a negative set of responses to the ordinary events of life.

Long term follow-up studies indicate that the chances of **relapse** from major depression are high. Belsher and Costello (1988), reviewing these studies, concluded that within two years of recovery from a unipolar depression, about 50 per cent of patients relapse. Factors which are found to increase the likelihood of relapse are: the absence of social support from family members and a history of previous depressive episodes. Vulnerability to relapse also appears to be related to an individual tendency to evaluate life events in extreme terms (Teasdale, 1988). Of all factors contributing to relapse, suffering repeated criticism from a spouse was the most common. This accords well with the social rank model of depression which would predict that to be on the receiving end of recurrent 'put downs' would increase vulnerability to relapse. On the whole, there is growing agreement that a critical factor governing vulnerability to affective disorder concerns the issues of rank assessment, RHP estimation, and levels of self-esteem.

SELF-ASSESSMENT

The threat display stage of ritual agonistic behaviour involves the use of an **assessor strategy**. This is an algorithmic capacity that is evolutionarily stable and has been in existence since the evolution of fish and reptiles. As we have seen, it enables an individual to assess whether a rival is stronger or weaker and to produce the appropriate response (that is, fight, submission, or flight). This is a refined judgement. It involves monitoring a complex of signals and it is vitally important to the animal's survival that it gets it right. Birtchnell (1994) has proposed that there are centres in the central nervous system, responsible for monitoring, from minute to minute, how close to or how distant or how 'upper' or 'lower' in relation to others he may be. Birtchnell believes these centres must lie deep within the limbic system because they appear to be so closely linked to the emotions. But clearly cortical mechanisms and centres in the reptilian brain must also be involved. In animals, the functional development of this monitoring system is heavily influenced by experiences of success or failure in previous conflicts. It is on the basis of this algorithm that humans form their **internal working models** of self in relation to others.

Mental well-being depends on forming estimates of one's own power and attractiveness which are accurate and stable. In a sense, this is like a national bank running a currency which is a true reflection of its actual worth (in terms of the goods that it can buy). To inflate the economy is to give the currency a paper value in excess of what merchants consider to be its actual worth in the marketplace. To deflate the economy is to give the currency a paper value corresponding to its actual worth or to devalue it to a level below its actual worth. In terms of the psychic economy, an inflated self-appraisal can lead to mania, a devalued self-appraisal to depression. If our self-appraisal is such that we appear strong and attractive to ourselves, and believe that we are strong and attractive to others, the result is good social adjustment – provided the appraisal is accurate. In people with a **hypomanic** or **depressive personality**, and in those prone to **unipolar episodes of mania** or **depression** their self-appraisal will be chronically inflated or deflated, and relatively insensitive to external social cues. In those with a **cyclothymic personality**, and in those with '**mixed**' or **bipolar forms** of affective disorder, their self-appraisal will be unstable and hypersensitive to the vagaries of their own thoughts and the behaviour of other people. Cyclothymic individuals behave and feel as if they have no firm concept of their social attention holding power (SAHP). They are not clear from day to day what their actual social resources may be: their self-appraisal is heavily dependent on outer events, such as the comments of others, as well as inner events, such as fluctuations in serotonin and noradrenaline levels. A kind word can boost their SAHP as readily as an implied criticism can deflate it. In particularly vulnerable individuals, slight set-backs, rebuffs, and the occasional critical word can combine to produce a downward shift in SAHP in the direction of 'negative affectivity', and the onset of a depressive episode. Such self-appraisals are directly linked to neurohormonal mechanisms which evolved to mediate ranking and attachment behaviour patterns. A subjective SAHP assessment which results in a perception of oneself as being both powerless and unattractive will activate that ancient biological mechanism responsible for the yielding subroutine, with all its depressive and behavioural consequences.

THE CRITICAL THRESHOLD

A depressive illness occurs when one estimates that one's SAHP has reached a critically low level. What is this critical threshold and when is it reached? Allen (1995) has suggested that decline in SAHP reaches a critical point when one begins to see oneself as such a hopeless liability that the group would be better off without one and that one is, consequently, in grave danger of being ostracized.

To be ostracized, even in contemporary circumstances, is an extremely disagreeable experience (one feels literally 'beyond the Pale'), but in the ancestral environment it would have been a disaster. Not only would one's chances of reproductive success be reduced to nil, but also one's chances of survival. However, ostracism has costs for the group as well as for shunned individuals, for the group loses the resources they can contribute to its collective tasks, defence, and economy. As a result, the greater the individual's resources, the less the group will be inclined to ostracize him, even if he breaks the rules or fails, from time to time, to pull his weight. The less the individual's resources, however, the less it will cost the group to ostracize him. Indeed, if his resources are very low, it may be to the group's advantage to do so. The critical point for the onset of a depressive reaction comes when an individual's subjective assessment of his SAHP indicates that it has fallen to the level where ostracism will be the result.

Critics of rank theory are fond of pointing out that not all people who are in subordinate positions, or who are low in social resources, suffer from depression, while people in a high social position (such as a head of state) may do so. This is very true, but in no way does it invalidate the theory. What is critical is what people *perceive* their SAHP to be, and what they themselves believe to be the critical level below which their SAHP must not be allowed to fall. Allen's point is that one's subjective perception of one's SAHP can vary dramatically from its socially objective value. People who become depressed are vulnerable to the perception that their SAHP has reached a critically low point.

If the depressed state is adaptive, what, in these circumstances, is its function? The currency analogy is again relevant here. A weak currency which is held in low regard and sold short by speculators is like a group member who is seen to be using up resources to which his perceived levels of RHP and SAHP do not entitle him, and who, consequently, exposes himself to the disapproval of the group. Unless something is done to change the situation, both the value of the currency and the perceived level of SAHP will continue to fall. In the case of the currency, the effective remedy is devaluation: the fall in value which has been induced by outside pressures is actually accelerated from within so as to reduce it to a level at which outsiders no longer see the currency as devalued and can no longer derive profit from selling it. In the case of the level of SAHP, further disapprobation (catathetic behaviour) on the part of other members of the group is pre-empted by an accelerated fall in the level of SAHP from within (the onset of depression). As a result, the SAHP of the depressed individual is no longer seen as too high by the other group members, who respond by ceasing to put him down. In this way, he is saved from total psychological collapse (a fall in SAHP to zero) and banishment from the group. Because he is perceived as being ill, group disapprobation (catathesis) is replaced by nurturance and care (anathesis) and there is what de Waal (1982) calls a conditional reconciliation – the group restores its approval on condition that the individual ceases to assume an entitlement to resources greater than his perceived status would warrant. The function of the devaluation of mood (depression) is thus damage limitation – a strategy to prevent further loss of reputation and to pre-empt the ultimate disaster of banishment.

Because a depressed individual cannot function properly, his helpless condition makes him dependent on the altruism and generosity of the group. The depression indicates that he is disabled and that allowances should be made for him – he cannot be expected to contribute to the group's economy with the same efficiency as if he were well. In closely knit, kin-based bands of 20 to 100 hunter-gatherers, the depressed mood strategy would have been more successful in achieving its goal of SAHP conservation and recovery than in modern conditions, where people can become isolated without risk to their chances of survival. This might explain the increase in the incidence of depression over the past century, which has seen the 'waxing of the individual and the waning of the commons' as Seligman (1975) memorably put it. In these circumstances, the isolated depressive cannot gain resources in the same manner as our ancestors in the EEA, and the depressive reaction can more readily enter a vicious downward spiral of deepening helplessness and despair.

Allen's suggestion fits well with the clinical facts. Depressed patients commonly express the view that they are good for nothing, have nothing left to contribute, that no one will ever want anything to do with them, and that society would be better off without them. It is in this spirit that many commit or attempt suicide. That the majority also suffer from anxiety, often of severe intensity, squares with Allen's belief that they feel themselves to be under threat of ostracism. For if depression is an adaptive response to the perception of grievous loss, then anxiety is the adaptive response to the perception of grave danger. A further advantage of Allen's proposal is that it helps to explain the observation that depressed patients can use their condition to manipulate others in such a way as to conserve or to restore their SAHP.

THE PARADOXICAL POWER OF THE DEPRESSED PATIENT

In the depressed state, the message of the yielding subroutine may be expressed in the metaphor of sickness. The message is conveyed both to rivals and to allies, to adversaries as well as supporters, to family as well as friends. To rival competitors it is as if the depressed individual is saying, 'I am sick and therefore no threat to you,' and to supporters, 'I am sick and therefore out of action; stop pushing me into the arena to fight on your behalf.'

When a competitor switches from a winning to a losing strategy, he has to take his dependants with him, and this presents the difficulty of persuading them to change their attitude from one of active support to acceptance of defeat. Here the metaphor of sickness may be decisive, for it reclassifies capitulation according to a diagnostic scheme. The hypochondria and physical complaints of severe depression, as well as the delusions of serious disease which are characteristic of a depressive psychosis, fit in with this reclassification, and should serve to convince the home team that the situation has altered and allowances have to be made.

Although depressed people become submissive and inhibit their aggression towards individuals further up the hierarchy, they may still be tetchy, demanding, or downright hostile to their subordinates, spouses, and children.

Here again, the intention would be to convert their dependants from providing active agonistic support in competitive situations to providing nurturant support within the home. The social behaviour of a depressed person depends, to some extent, on the social context in which he is seen: it will differ, for example, in the consulting room, the workplace, and the home. The critical variables will be whether the other person is perceived to be superior or inferior in rank, or as an enemy rather than a friend.

WHY IS DEPRESSION COMMONER IN FEMALES?

RAB evolved as a means of settling territorial disputes between males. Later it became a means of settling male disputes about rank and access to resources, especially females in oestrus. The yielding subroutine and the depressive reaction arose as means of finalizing male rank disputes once they had happened. It might seem entirely appropriate, therefore, to classify RAB, as did Moyer (1976), as 'inter-male aggression'. So if rank theory is correct, how is it that depression is twice as common in females as it is in males?

It is likely that both biological and social factors may be responsible for this female preponderance, which is apparent during the reproductive years and not in childhood or later life. From the standpoint of natural selection, a capacity is selected for in both males and females to the point at which its advantages are exactly balanced by its disadvantages for achieving reproductive success. In the case of depression, this balance differs in males and females because of the greater variance in the reproductive success of males. As a result, depression could reduce reproductive success in males more than in females, since the pursuit of the female requires more determination, more energy, and more initiative than the female acceptance of the male. Thus, it could be that depressed males are less likely to reproduce than depressed females.

In other words, selection for depression may be limited by the effect of depression on reproduction. It follows that if depression has twice the effect on male reproductive success that it has on female reproductive success, then depression will be selected in females until it is twice as common as it is in males.

While it is true that RAB initially evolved for settling inter-male territorial disputes, it gradually became both inter-female and male–female. In polygynous species, it has been used by males to dominate females, and our own species is no exception. In marital agonic conflicts, it is the male who more often dominates the female, so that the female is forced to make greater use of the yielding subroutine of RAB and to suffer its emotional consequences.

The Judeo-Christian tradition has led us into the delusory belief that marriage is naturally a monogamous institution. But the fact of our sexual dimorphism (species in which males are bigger than females tend to be polygynous), combined with the observations of the anthropologists, indicate that the great majority of human sexual unions are, and always have been, legally or tacitly polygynous. This would suggest that asymmetry was built into the family unit by sex. It follows that in any polygamous marriage, the wives will be in competition for the attention and resources of the husband. Each wife will also be in competition with her husband, just as each child is in competition with its parents, for she is likely to desire more resources than he is willing or able to give her. In the polygamous family unit, therefore, there exists a social context rife with opportunities for ritual agonistic conflicts, in which wives, rather than husbands, are likely to be the losers.

As if this were not enough to account for a greater female liability to depression, there must be added the burdens of motherhood. A mother suffers more than a father from their children's struggle for parental investment. Even *in utero* the foetus will, in the interests of its own nutrition, raise her blood sugar and her blood pressure to the point where she may develop diabetes or eclampsia. Then there are the demands for milk to contend with, the long years of dependency, and the birth of other children, all indulging in an endless battle for her maternal investment. Moreover, females have less freedom of movement. Males can more easily escape from agonistic conflicts. But wives are more trapped by social and economic pressures as well as by their greater investment in their children and their home. As a result, they may well have to yield repeatedly in conflicts with a dominant husband.

Childbirth itself brings the risk of **maternity blues** (50–60 per cent of mothers become tearful, feel unable to cope, tired, uninterested in food, and cannot sleep; these symptoms, when they occur, peak about the fifth day) and **post-natal depression** (10–15 per cent; the symptoms usually begin after leaving hospital and can prove resistant to antidepressant therapy). Depressions which follow childbirth are not easy to explain in terms of rank theory, since having a baby brings its own kudos as well as a new attachment figure with whom to form the closest of bonds. Common fears expressed at this stage are that one will be a bad mother, unable to meet the child's needs. Mothers can, in fact, feel dominated and 'put down' by the child, for children can confront their parents in a ritual agonistic manner from a very early age. Mother and child may have running battles over such issues as feeding schedules and sleeping times. If the baby wins, the mother becomes subdominant to him, and her sense of losing control of the situation can invoke a yielding subroutine which is then diagnosed as post-natal depression.

Since females are more committed to relationships than males (who, on the whole, are more committed to rank competition, practical activities, and opportunistic sex) it is likely that females would be more prone to **deprivation depression** (following loss or threatened loss of their attachment figures) and males more prone to **defeat depression** (following loss of resources or rank). The necessary research to test this interesting possibility has yet to be done.

Since the time of Moyer's confident classification of RAB as 'inter-male aggression', it has been recognized that inter-female RAB occurs in many species (Kevles, 1986) and that its outcome affects the reproductive success (or failure) of the contestants. In these species, females of low rank may be prevented from copulating, ovulation may be suppressed, implantation may be inhibited, and, should conception nevertheless occur, the progeny run greater risk of abortion or infanticide. The threat display and actual physical combat between females may not be as dramatic as in inter-male RAB, but the consequences of losing are no less decisive.

In human RAB, verbal abuse has come to play a more significant role in determining outcome than physical aggression. This is as true of female–female RAB as it is of male–male and male–female RAB. All these forms are apparent in the work place, in school, and in the family, between husbands and wives, parents and children, and between siblings. Since females tend to do better than males on tests of verbal ability, they are quite possibly superior in their adaptation to this kind of in-fighting. When a wife wins in a marital conflict, it is usually a verbal victory; when a husband wins, it is often because he has indicated his willingness to escalate matters to a physical resolution.

There are impressive reasons, therefore, why rank theory should be able to account for the evolution and greater preponderance of female depression as a biological propensity. Whether or not this propensity is expressed has much to do with prevailing social and economic factors (as Brown's work has shown) as well as early childhood experiences. There is now some evidence that when women are given equal opportunities, the incidence of depression among them ceases to be greater than for men (Wilhelm and Parker, 1989). However, Wilhelm and Parker's findings are so much at variance with the great majority of other studies of male versus female vulnerability to depression, that their conclusions should be treated with caution. Their subjects were student teachers at the beginning of the study and they were followed up for only five years, when they were still in their early twenties, whereas the sex difference in depressive states does not peak until the early thirties. Moreover, the apparent equality in male and female vulnerability over the five-year period was less due to a reduction in the number of females becoming depressed than to an increase in the number of males. As the authors admit, their findings could reflect a recent and more universal trend towards an increasing prevalence of depression in males aged 20 to 40 years. This could be related to the greater competition men are experiencing from women in the job markets of the world. Wilhelm and Parker plan further follow-up studies of this group, and their findings are awaited with interest.

A study whose findings were uninfluenced by recent social changes was that of Loewenthal *et al.* (1995), who also found an equal prevalence of depression between the sexes in a sample of 339 Jews (157 men and 182 women) affiliated to orthodox synagogues in London. They explain these findings, which contrast with so many others, in terms of the cultural milieu inhabited by orthodox Jews, who particularly esteem the central role of women in family management. The men in this sample were also judged to be more ready than Gentiles to acknowledge that they were depressed, and less likely to seek solace in drink or suicide. It may be objected that student teachers and orthodox Jews are special and untypical groups of people, but findings such as these indicate the extent to which evolved strategies for mediating changes in rank are dependent on social variables for their activation.

BASIC COMPONENTS OF THE YIELDING SUBROUTINE

Since it is a function of science to reduce phenomena to more basic levels of explanation, we must aim eventually to account for the yielding subroutine in terms of neurochemistry and psychopharmacology. However, this object-ive may still be premature, and others are more competent to pursue it. A less ambitious but more achievable aim is to reduce the yielding subroutine to its basic *behavioural* components. The work of behavioural ecologists in making mathematical models of fighting behaviour can be of assistance here. Three basic hypothetical constructs have been found to be essential (Krebs and Davies, 1993):

1 **The calculation of relative RHP** This calculation is made by an individual as he assesses whether he is more powerful than a competitor. In humans, RHP assessment has been partially superseded by the capacity to assess social attention holding power (SAHP) – i.e. the ability to attract attention and investment from other members of the group (pp. 73–4). Whereas RHP determines the balance between attack and submission in combat, SAHP determines the balance between self-assertion and self-effacement in competitive social situations. Lowered relative RHP accounts for the reduced self-esteem, inferiority feelings, and other negative forms of self-perception which are major features of depression; and lowered relative SAHP accounts for associated features such as guilt, shame, social anxiety, and self-blame.

2 **The calculation of Resource Value** This is an estimate of the value of what-ever is being fought over. It expresses the degree of an individual's invest-ment in the goals and incentives which would have to be given up by a yielder. To the extent that rewards are dependent on social status, Resource Value reflects the strength of motivation towards all forms of status acqui-sition displayed by a given individual. Reduction in Resource Value in the

depressed patient accounts for the defeatism, apathy and global loss of interest so characteristic of the condition.

3 **Ownership** It is a widespread convention in the animal world that the owner of a territory almost invariably wins a contest and an intruder loses it. In human beings this 'territorial imperative' extends to possessions, and in depression the sense of Ownership is seriously impaired to the extent that some patients feel they have no right to anything – not even existence itself.

The higher an individual perceives these values to be, the more likely he is to attack rather than back off, or to be self-assertive rather than self-effacing. The lower he perceives them to be the more likely he is to display the yielding subroutine and is more liable to become depressed.

There is only one feature of depression that cannot be related directly to a lowering of relative RHP, of reduced Resource Value, or a diminished sense of Ownership and that is *loss of energy*. However, this can be satisfactorily attributed to an *interaction* between estimates of RHP and estimates of Resource Value. RHP represents the 'can' of conflict and Resource Value represents the 'will'. When both 'can' and 'will' are present then the necessary energy is mobilized to become assertive and to attack. If both 'can' and 'will' are absent, then the necessary energy is unavailable. Overall, low self-assessment on these three basic variables can account for the common clinical manifestations of depressive states.

CONCLUSION

Although we have classified affective disorders as disorders of attachment and rank, we have avoided the use of the terms 'hedonic' and 'agonic' to differentiate them because bonding and dominance systems evidently interact and are not separate. Decisive life events, such as bereavement, separation, and divorce, can indeed precipitate a depressive reaction, but it is not helpful to describe such a disorder as due entirely to loss of an attachment figure. Rank is largely dependent on alliances, and to lose someone with whom one has a close alliance has implications for the rank of the individual so bereaved. Such depressions have both 'deprived' and 'defeated' components. They are adaptive because they effect a reduction of RHP in those who have been supported by the lost person, and because they tailor their dominance level to the new situation. The reason why depression is adaptive, is precisely because it promotes adjustment to attachment loss and loss of rank both at the same time.

6

PERSONALITY DISORDERS

Personality is the term used to describe the sum total of those cognitive, emotional, and behavioural characteristics that a person habitually employs in relating to his or her social environment. Inevitably, an element of arbitrariness enters into the selection of which characteristics are considered to be important in establishing a person's personality profile, but research in this area repeatedly draws attention to what are increasingly considered to be five core dimensions:

1 **Surgency**, which includes power, dominance, and extraversion (as opposed to weakness, submissiveness, and introversion);
2 **Agreeableness**, which includes co-operativeness and trustworthiness (as opposed to aggressiveness and suspiciousness);
3 **Conscientiousness**, which includes industriousness and responsibility (as opposed to laziness and irresponsibility);
4 **Emotional stability**, which includes security and stability (as opposed to insecurity and anxiousness); and
5 **Intellect-openness**, which includes intelligence, perspicacity, creativity (as opposed to stupidity, boorishness, and unimaginativeness).

David Buss (1989; 1995), who has made major contributions to personality research, suggests that these five dimensions recur with such frequency because they represent the most important features of the social landscape to which humans have to adapt. Of the five, **surgency** and **agreeableness** persistently appear as the two major axes of interpersonal taxonomies. And, comments Buss, it is not by chance that power and love emerge consistently and cross-culturally as the two most important dimensions of interpersonal behaviour. The personality disorders considered in this section all involve these crucial dimensions.

Different traits naturally vary with respect to their salience in any one individual. They come to be classified as abnormal or disordered when they depart significantly from the statistical norm, in the sense that extreme forms of a trait are less common than the average. Abnormal behaviour, therefore, is that which goes beyond the usual bounds arbitrarily set by society. A behaviour is of concern to psychiatry when it becomes sufficiently abnormal to involve suffering and/or impaired social adjustment in the subject.

Personality disorders are to be distinguished from **neurotic states** because the former are enduring, habitual modes of adjustment, while the latter are usually more transient and tend to occur as a reaction to specific life events.

Because human character traits are so numerous, clinicians have developed a number of different classifications for personality disorders. The American DSM-IV classificatory system and the European ICD 10 system have both attempted to impose some order on this nosological exuberance, and there is considerable agreement between them, though the agreement is not total. As Rutter (1987) has pointed out, both systems are in agreement that personality disorders persist over time without marked remissions or relapses, they constitute a basic aspect of the individual's usual functioning, and they have their onset in childhood or adolescence.

It is often said that no diagnoses in psychiatry are mutually exclusive: patients have an unfortunate tendency to present symptoms which fit into several different diagnostic categories at the same time. Of no category is this more true than personality disorders. Of the ten personality disorders listed in DSM-IV, we shall classify five of them as *disorders of attachment and rank*. These are **antisocial, histrionic, narcissistic, dependent**, and **obsessive-compulsive personality disorders**. We shall add **type A personality disorder** to these. **Borderline** and **schizotypal personality disorder** will be classified as *borderline states*. **Paranoid, schizoid**, and **avoidant personality disorders** will be classified as *spacing disorders*.

We shall consider antisocial and histrionic personality disorders together because we share the view of Harpending and Sobus (1987) that they are genetically linked.

ANTISOCIAL AND HISTRIONIC PERSONALITY DISORDERS

The social strategy at the core of both these disorders is **deceit**. People with **antisocial personality disorder** are also known as **sociopaths** (United States) and **psychopaths** (United Kingdom). Many people with this disorder are in prison at any given time and it has been estimated that they make up to 80 per cent of the criminal population.

Antisocial personality disorder is characterized by a pervasive disregard for the rights of others. There is a chronic failure to conform to the norms of lawful behaviour and a marked tendency to perform acts which are sufficient grounds for arrest. Deceitfulness is apparent in persistent lying, use of aliases, and conning others for personal profit and for emotional or sexual gratification. Such people are impulsive, seldom if ever willing to plan ahead, and they display heightened irritability and aggressiveness to a degree that frequently involves them in fights and being charged with assault. Their reckless disregard for safety – both their own and other people's – results in high mortality from the increased risk of an accident or violent death. Since they are irresponsible in their dealings with others, they rarely honour their financial obligations and seldom remain long in the same job. When confronted with evidence of the hurt or damage they have inflicted on those whom they may have raped, robbed, or battered, they display a complete lack of remorse and tend to rationalize and justify what they have done.

In addition, psychopaths usually give a history of hyperactivity and persistent lying in childhood, of truancy, delinquency and disruptive behaviour at school, of aggressive sexual activity, and of high mating effort without the formation of lasting bonds – a pattern which results in 'spectacular promiscuity' (Cloninger, 1978). Should they marry they tend to abandon their family early on and fail to provide either their spouse or their children with financial or emotional support. They are socially mobile, travelling from place to place, and are frequently 'of no fixed abode'. In the armed forces, they have a record of disciplinary problems, brief service, and, following discharge, tend to abuse their pension or disability rights. They can, however, be charming and possess both considerable charisma and sex appeal, which makes it easy for them to manipulate and exploit the favours of those off whom they sponge.

The incidence of antisocial personality disorder is much higher among males than among females (approximately 20:1) as opposed to histrionic personality disorder, whose incidence is much higher among females than among males.

Histrionic personality disorder (also known as **hysterical personality disorder**) is characterized by pervasive patterns of behaviour such as attention-seeking, self-dramatization, theatrical posturing, and exaggerated expressions of emotion. People with this disorder feel uneasy in social situations where they are not the centre of attention. They are particularly prone to indulge in inappropriate seductive and provocative sexual behaviour. They use dress, make-up, and over-emphatic forms of speech in order to draw attention to themselves, and they are prone to claim closer relationships with socially or sexually desirable people than they enjoy in reality. They also tend to be highly suggestible and are consequently easily influenced by others. Their case notes often record dramatic medical histories, with extensive investigations and no evidence of physical disease, and the occasional manifestation of **conversion symptoms** (physically inexplicable neurological signs and symptoms). Like psychopaths, people with histrionic personality disorder display high mating effort, indulge in promiscuous sexual relationships, and are responsible for disproportionately large numbers of illegitimate offspring. A high incidence of histrionic personality disorder is also found among the female prison population.

Aetiology

While all personality disorders are thought to be the product of genetic and early environmental factors interacting with one another, research interest has focused on antisocial personality disorder because of the severe social problem that it poses.

That genetic factors are involved there can be little doubt. The children of psychopathic parents are more prone to indulge in antisocial behaviour than the children of parents with other kinds of personality, and this holds good even when the children are adopted and brought up by adults other than their biological parents. Moreover, identical twins have a concordance rate of about 60 per cent for criminal behaviour, compared to 15 per cent for dizygotic twins. Although criminal behaviour is not synonymous with psychopathy, the high proportion of psychopaths in the prison population suggests that the high concordance for criminality may reflect the concordance for antisocial personality disorder.

In terms of psychodynamics, it is evident that psychopaths have failed to form a competent **superego**. Superego formation is dependent on early childhood experience of growing up in a warm, intimate, and lasting relationship with parental figures who are reasonably consistent and reliable in their conduct and who share the moral standards of their community. The majority of psychopaths, however, give a history of parental disharmony, separation and loss. Many have suffered physical or sexual abuse as children and have been brought up in various institutions and foster homes. Whatever bonds they may have formed with parental figures have often been broken, with the result that they have developed a detached, 'affectionless' type of character.

For many years it has been apparent that psychopathy is associated with neurophysiological abnormalities. Both the autonomic and the central nervous systems appear to be involved. As early as the 1940s, EEG studies revealed abnormal tracings in about 50 per cent of the individuals examined. These are believed to reflect a chronic under-arousal of the autonomic nervous system, which is a striking characteristic of psychopathic patients. Studies using the psycho-galvanic skin response have confirmed the clinical impression that psychopaths have a high threshold for the experience of fear or anxiety. They tend to maintain a low pulse rate in the sort of stressful situations which cause tachycardia in normal subjects. Psychopaths also perform poorly in aversive learning experiments, a finding consistent with the clinical observation that they seldom learn to control their antisocial behaviour as a result of punishment or treatment. Their sluggish arousal responses would also help to explain why psychopaths are prone to indulge in dangerous, stimulus-seeking behaviour 'just for kicks'. It seems likely that Mednick and Christiansen (1977) are right to conclude that psychopaths find it easy to indulge in antisocial acts because they experience no anxiety when such acts are contemplated or performed.

However, the aetiological factors so far established for personality disorders are unable to explain why antisocial personality disorder is overwhelmingly a male affliction or why histrionic personality disorder tends to occur predominantly in females. It is precisely because it provides a new and highly instructive perspective on this kind of issue that evolutionary theory is of such importance.

THE EVOLUTIONARY PERSPECTIVE

In terms of ranking psychology, psychopaths and hysterics are **free-riders**. 'Free-riders' are individuals who seek to subvert to themselves an undue proportion of the group's resources without first satisfying the usual requirement of achieving appropriate social rank. The capacity to detect and weed out free-riders has been a significant aspect of human evolution, permitting the intensive group life typical of human communities and may allow a degree of group selection to occur. (This issue is discussed at greater length in Chapter 13.) A genetic basis of free-riding probably underlies the occurrence of both antisocial and histrionic personality disorders.

People with these disorders evidently possess a marked tendency to use what they calculate to be the least costly way of achieving their biosocial goals. Many individuals who meet the criteria of these disorders go through life undiagnosed and undetected, and by evolutionary criteria they are successful, i.e., they acquire resources and mates, have offspring, and invest in kin. Criminologists estimate that less than 20 per cent of people who repeatedly indulge in deceptive behaviour, such as fraud or bigamy, are identified and apprehended. As a consequence, as McGuire and Troisi (1998) argue, selection against traits responsible for these disorders is likely to remain weak because of the relatively low probability of detection in people who carry them. Successful deceivers are those who are capable of estimating the costs and benefits of short-term social interactions, reading other people's assessments of them, and successfully disguising their own intentions. Their insensitivity to feelings of anxiety, guilt, and shame enhances their chances of attaining their biosocial goals since they have the audacity to seize opportunities which most people, being reciprocators, would not feel capable of doing. However, as McGuire and Troisi conclude, the possibility that traits responsible for successful deception are adaptive in certain individuals does not render them socially desirable, for they result in other people being victimized. But it does provide an evolutionary explanation for the persistence of these strategies in a proportion of every population. It would also help to account for their notoriously intractable resistance to treatment.

Phylogenetically, the capacity to deceive (as well as the capacity to detect deception) is very old. Predators can lure prey by issuing false scents or colours, while prey can escape predators by using camouflage or feigning death. Humans are no exception. Not only have they designed games like poker which reward accomplishment in the arts of deceit, but, like the cuckoo, they can use deception to promote their reproductive success.

This issue has been addressed by Axelrod (1984) and Axelrod and Hamilton (1981), who have devised computer-simulated studies of two people engaged in a simple social transaction. Each player is given two options: to co-operate or to defect. Every encounter leaves each player with a certain pay-off. The highest joint pay-off is when both co-operate; the highest individual pay-off is when the opponent co-operates and the actor defects. A crucial factor is the number of encounters. When both actor and opponent have frequent encounters, the best strategy for each of them is to co-operate. A highly mobile individual, on the other hand, who engages in few interactions with any single opponent, can enjoy a series of high pay-offs if he is in the habit of defecting. Thus, reciprocity and 'niceness' are sensible strategies (in terms of inclusive fitness) only when there are frequent encounters between actors and opponents who are blessed with good memories and recall how each has behaved on previous occasions. If actors have poor memories, however, and do not recall what an opponent has done in the past, then the best strategy for the opponent is to cheat. Since the human memory is far from infallible, it follows that in a population of predominantly 'nice' reciprocators, there are potentially rich pickings to be had by an endemic subgroup of mobile cheaters – always provided they can 'pass' as 'nice'.

Building on this work by Axelrod and Hamilton, Henry Harpending and J. Sobus, two anthropologists from Pennsylvania State University, have proposed the idea that both psychopathy and hysteria are adaptive strategies. They argue convincingly (1987) that the differing reproductive strategies of males and females require that male and female cheaters should exhibit very different patterns of cheating. A male cheater should be adept at persuading females to copulate with him and at deceiving them about his degree of commitment, control of resources, and willingness to provide for future offspring. A female cheater, on the other hand, should feign lack of interest in copulation so as to lull the male into a false sense of confidence as to his paternity of any offspring that might result from their encounter. She should also exaggerate her need for the male, her relative helplessness and vulnerability, so as to induce him to lavish more resources, love and attention on her than he might otherwise provide. Finally, the female cheater should be willing to abandon her offspring opportunistically – as soon as she perceives their chances of survival have exceeded some critical threshold.

It will be seen at once that these predictions fit the clinical data for psychopathy in males and hysterical disorder in females. Psychopaths are indeed highly mobile, charming and charismatic, sexually hyperactive non-reciprocators. Hysterics are fecund reproducers, who are skilled at exaggerating their needs, especially to males. Although Harpending and Sobus accept that skill at deception is developed through practice and learning, they nevertheless suggest that both psychopathy and hysteria are, at least in part, genetically transmitted conditions, and that hysteria is the expression in females of the same genetic material that leads to psychopathy in males. Their explanation of the 5 per cent of psychopaths who are females is that female psychopathy carries a heavier loading of the genetic material which, in smaller quantities, results in hysteria. In other words, 'hysteria is a mild form of sociopathy.' Thus, Harpending and Sobus believe that there is some underlying quantitative trait that predisposes the bearer to psychopathy and that when the threshold value of this trait is exceeded psychopathy is the result.

Harpending and Sobus's contribution is important not only because they have indicated how psychopathy and hysteria can function as adaptive tactics but because they have been able to account for the striking contrast in the sexual distribution of these two disorders in terms of the different reproductive strategies imposed by natural selection on males and females.

TYPE A PERSONALITY

Though not usually listed as a disorder, people with type A personality are a recognizable group frequently encountered in the modern world, especially in large business corporations. Typically they suffer, and can make others suffer, high levels of stress.

Originally, the concept was specifically correlated with the high incidence of coronary artery disease among ambitious businessmen. Type A personality is of interest to evolutionary psychiatry since it is very evidently a ranking disorder, in that those with this personality constellation are intensely preoccupied with the competitive struggle for status and resources. They tend to be impatient, aggressive, and intolerant of minor frustrations. They are hypersensitive to criticism, while, at the same time, being extremely critical of trivial errors committed by others. They tend to dominate conversations, speak rapidly and under pressure, are poor listeners and prone to interrupt interlocutors in mid-sentence. They display extreme annoyance if kept waiting in traffic, if someone is late for an appointment, or when dealing with incompetent telephone operators, shop assistants, waiters, or bank clerks. Intense competitiveness causes them to perceive work associates as adversaries rather than as colleagues and to belittle their achievements. Their body posture appears uncomfortable and tense, their movements jerky and frequently repetitive (knee jerking, finger tapping, key jiggling), and they indulge in tuneless whistling, humming, expiratory sighing, yawning, and other unconscious behaviours symptomatic of edgy arousal. 'Time urgency' is a very evident characteristic in virtually any situation.

Aetiology

As must be apparent from the above description, 'type As' function persistently in the agonic mode – in whatever social context they may find themselves. Their self-esteem is entirely dependent upon competitive success. Failure or demotion makes them extremely vulnerable to a depressive reaction. Just as they are critical of others, so they can be extremely critical of themselves, thus putting themselves down. This is the equivalent of the psychoanalytic 'anger-in' formulation of depressive aetiology. The failed type A turns his anger in on himself and makes himself feel bad, unworthy, and helpless.

Examination of the history of type As indicates that as children the love they received was not unconditional. Typically, it was highly contingent on living up to the standards set by a demanding, aggressive mother in the absence of an effective or supportive father figure. In many instances, there seems to have been a failure to acknowledge the child as an autonomous individual. This squares with the feeling commonly expressed by type As that their personal well-being depends on being a lovable, respected, worthwhile person, and that their self-esteem is a direct function of their observable, tangible accomplishments (V. Price, 1982).

NARCISSISTIC PERSONALITY DISORDER

As for people with type A personality, narcissists are preoccupied with status to an exaggerated degree. The most striking features of narcissistic personality disorder are a grandiose sense of self-importance, an insatiable hunger for admiration, and a regular indulgence in fantasies of unlimited success, power, brilliance, beauty, or ideal love. Narcissists tend to believe they are unique and 'special' and that they can only be understood by, and should only associate with, other special people of high status. They have a strong sense of entitlement, in the sense that they entertain unreasonable expectations of especially favourable treatment from others and an automatic compliance with their wishes. Their need for approval renders them extremely vulnerable to criticism, frustration or defeat, any of which can cause them painful feelings of humiliation, shame and inferiority, as well as driving them to respond with rage and vindictiveness. Being acutely aware of their own needs, they lack empathy with other people, whose feelings and wishes they ignore, and they commonly demand special favours without assuming any reciprocal responsibilities. Not unexpectedly, they are bad at forming deep or lasting relationships because others experience them as exploitative, demanding, and arrogant.

Aetiology

Kohut's concept of **mirroring** is relevant to the aetiology of narcissistic personality disorder. Although he fails to adopt an evolutionary perspective, Kohut has drawn attention to the way in which parents feed back to the child delight and pride in its activities. Strong parental approval enables the child to form a self-concept as being valued in the eyes of others. Gilbert (1989) suggests that in eliciting positive mirroring from the parents, the child learns to control the attention of others – acquiring the capacity to attract positive attention to the self through the display of talent, skill, and physical appeal. Thus, the parents are the first bestowers of status and SAHP, and it is as if narcissistic personalities have become arrested at this stage of development. Other people are treated as if they were parent figures whose function is to provide a constant and unending bonanza of love, admiration, and praise.

Exhibitionism, which is characteristic of the narcissist, is also a normal constituent of peer group relationships in childhood. The function of parents is not just to enhance self-value but to give a child the confidence to be assertive, to show off, and to take a lead in peer group interactions. Successful passage through this stage leads to the capacity to be socially effective in later adult life.

Narcissistic disorders arise from damage to the emerging self-image at these early stages of development. Parents can, for example, reflect to their children an inflated view of their beauty and accomplishments with the result that their self-esteem receives a series of blows when tested in the harsh market place of peer relations. Damaged individuals compensate by trying to maintain self-esteem through fantasies of power and success while trying to hold in check their feelings of inferiority. Driven by the desire for status and approval, they entertain the painful expectation that others will humiliate rather than praise them, because they do not possess the qualities that others value.

Since their exaggerated need for praise and approval (SAHP) is seldom adequately met, they tend to switch to the agonic mode, to gain and maintain RHP through manipulating and controlling others. The anxiety from which people with narcissistic disorder are trying to escape is the fear of being found out, humiliated, and demoted. Their profoundly self-centred feelings of entitlement mean that they are usually poor reciprocators and, when they sense they can get away with it, are prone to adopt a 'free-rider' strategy in their dealings with others.

DEPENDENT PERSONALITY DISORDER

This is probably the commonest personality disorder encountered in psychiatric practice. The most striking characteristic displayed by these patients is an excessive need to be taken care of. Excessive neediness is associated with submissive or sycophantic behaviour and with feelings of insecurity linked to fears of separation and loss. Extreme difficulty is experienced in assuming responsibility for decisions without first seeking lavish quantities of reassurance and advice from others. Loss of a relationship is felt as a major catastrophe and an alternative source of support is sought for as a matter of urgency. Any disagreement with a friend or acquaintance is experienced as threatening because it leads to fears that the support of that person could be brought into question or lost.

Aetiology

It is people of this type whom Bowlby categorized as manifesting 'anxious attachment', and it can occur as a result of any of the forms of pathogenic parenting described in Chapter 4. The tactic adopted in this disorder is that of a suppliant subdominant care-receiver. The objective is to pre-empt attack or threat from dominant members of the group, and, by displays of need and dependency, to manipulate potential care-givers to provide nurturance, comfort, and support.

OBSESSIONAL PERSONALITY DISORDER

This is characterized by a pervasive preoccupation with orderliness, perfectionism, and the control of mental and interpersonal events, and the preoccupation persists at the expense of flexibility, openness, and efficiency. In the extreme form, people with obsessional personality disorder are miserly, meticulous hoarders: they are tight with their money, overscrupulous, and over-conscientious about details, preoccupied with rules, lists, and schedules, and unable to throw anything away, even when it is worn out and worthless. Not infrequently, they are workaholics and their devotion to their work tends to exclude leisure activities and friendships; while their perfectionism can interfere with completion of tasks in hand because their over-strict standards cannot be met.

The aetiology of obsessional personality disorder will be considered together with that of **obsessional neurosis** in the next chapter.

7

OBSESSIONAL DISORDERS

The difference between **obsessional personality** (which can be an advantage in someone whose job involves routine attention to detail, such as an accountant or laboratory technician), **obsessional personality disorder** (which impairs spontaneity, social relationships, and task completion), and **obsessional neurosis** (in which thoughts, feelings, and compulsive behaviour patterns cannot be controlled by voluntary effort) is largely one of degree. While it is true that obsessional neurosis can develop in people who do not have obsessional personalities, it is, nevertheless, more likely to occur in people with this rather than any other type of personality. Moreover, there is no clear line of distinction between obsessional symptoms and normal experience. Compulsions, such as 'having to' avoid the cracks in the pavement, are extremely common in normal children, and most of us have, from time to time, experienced unwelcome thoughts, images, or tunes that come into the mind unbidden and will not immediately go away. People who seek psychiatric help for obsessional symptoms, however, generally do so only when they have become severely incapacitating.

Feelings of compulsion are the essence of the obsessional state. People complain of feeling that they have 'got to' think certain thoughts or perform certain acts for fear that some disaster will befall them if they do not comply. Recurrent thoughts, impulses, or images are experienced as intrusive and inappropriate, and their persistence causes both anxiety and distress. In addition, repetitive behaviours (such as hand-washing, ordering and checking things) or mental acts (praying, counting, repeating certain stereotyped words or phrases) have to be performed in accordance with rigidly applied sets of rules if some dreaded consequence is to be prevented from occurring. Not uncommonly, these preoccupations, ruminations, and ritual actions take religious or pseudo-religious forms. Sufferers readily acknowledge them to be absurd and irrational but complain that this insight does not possess sufficient power to help them control or stop them.

Confronted with real-life issues, obsessional people commonly fall prey to indecisiveness and 'obsessional doubt'. In extreme forms, this can render them socially paralysed and helpless.

Fears that they may give way to impulses of a sexual or aggressive nature can also be a sore trial – for example, a fear that they may jump in front of a bus or a train, stab their spouse or their child, make an improper suggestion to the vicar or shout something blasphemous in church. Such urges, whenever they arise, are strongly resisted and seldom if ever carried out, but the inner conflict involved can be exhausting and very disturbing.

Understandably, such people appear tense, stressed, and worried. Often they seek to reduce their anxiety by checking that everything is in order and that nothing is likely to cause disaster. For example, when the family retires to bed, they will go round the house making sure that the doors have been locked, windows barred and bolted, gas taps turned off, television sets unplugged, and so on. These details may be performed in an exactly repeated sequence. Eventually, when the ritual has been completed, the patient can go to bed. But, once there, anxious doubts begin to arise that some detail may have been omitted, and so the whole process may have to be repeated, often a set number of times, before the obsessive worrier can eventually go to bed and fall into a fitful sleep.

Another common fear is of disease or infective contamination. This can lead to compulsive washing – of hands, hair, clothes, kitchen surfaces, utensils and knives, anything which it is feared could have come into contact with a noxious, disease-carrying agent.

The purpose of all such compulsive actions is to allay anxiety that a real or imagined catastrophe will occur if the necessary steps to avoid it are not taken. If the feared catastrophe is specific – that one will be instrumental in bringing about the infection or death of someone important or loved – then the remedy is to clean and sterilize everything that could possibly be implicated. If, on the other hand, the feared catastrophe is vaguely recognized or unknown, then compulsive rituals of a more religious and 'propitiatory' nature will be performed which are designed to keep the gods or 'powers that be', in good humour and thus less likely to cast thunderbolts in one's direction. Afflicted by vague anxieties, obsessionals may take refuge in compulsive orderliness on the principle that anything at any time can cause trouble, and that the more things one can keep in order, the less chance there is that they will go wrong. Such behaviour is often frankly superstitious – it may arise from the quasi-magical idea that if one counts every step to an appointment and touches every third lamp-post on the way, nothing untoward will happen when one arrives.

Aetiology

The overriding affliction of the obsessional state is the fear that things will get out of control and that catastrophe will ensue. Obsessional symptoms and compulsive behaviours arise as means to prevent this from happening.

What is the precise nature of the catastrophe that obsessionals constantly seek to avoid? In therapy, they commonly express a number of fears, but the commonest relate to a sense that life is essentially a precarious undertaking, and that, at any time, they might do or say something – or not do or say something – that could result in criticism from authority figures, unbearable feelings of guilt, shame, or worthlessness, loss of the love and goodwill of their attachment figures, loss of the respect of their acquaintances, and – the ultimate disaster – being rejected as totally unacceptable and cast 'beyond the Pale'.

It is in order to prevent these dreaded consequences that *obsessionals make exaggerated use of the normal procedures of control* – namely, attention to detail, anticipation of things that might go wrong, taking preventive measures (including prayer and religious rituals to propitiate the gods), checking that everything is in order, and so on. Subjectively, obsessionals feel driven to perform all their tasks to the point where they place themselves beyond attack and beyond reproach. Only when they reach the heights of sheer perfection in all spheres of activity can they hope to be truly safe, but, such are the conditions of human existence, they never arrive at their goal. Theirs is the struggle of Sisyphus.

In his book *Anxiety and Neurosis*, Charles Rycroft (1970) describes the attitude obsessionals adopt to their own emotional life and that of people around them as reminiscent of a colonial governor ruling an alien and potentially rebellious population, or like an animal in possession of a territory over which it has incompletely established power and mastery. All spontaneous tendencies, all uncensored emotions, are treated as if they were dangerous and subversive invaders. They have to be attacked so as to expel them or to force them into submission.

When the intruder is an alienated part of the self, the attack is recognized by analysts as repression. Because sexual or aggressive impulses are experienced as particularly threatening by obsessional patients, they have to be ruthlessly beaten into submission for fear that they might otherwise get out of control. Obsessionals thus use willpower as a dominating and repressive force to exert agonistic control over the more primitive parts of the personality, which are disciplined like subordinates in need of strict supervision.

The evolution of **checking** and **cleaning** behaviour provides an interesting area for conjecture. Checking probably arose in relation to the acquisition and defence of resources – food, territory, and mates. Hunting and warfare require careful strategic and logistic planning, involving the checking of weapons, hunting materials, food supplies, etc., ensuring that all is in order and nothing has been overlooked. There may indeed be an overall cognitive module for checking, verifying, and getting things 'right', and this aspect of 'obsessional' behaviour could well become of interest to cognitive science. The existence of some such propensity would appear indispensable to success in all scientific, economic, academic, and technological endeavours, as well as in hunting and military expeditions.

When human communities began to store surplus food and to make tools, weapons, and utensils these valuable possessions had to be protected from those who may have wished to appropriate them. Security arrangements had to be frequently and thoroughly checked to ensure that they were in effective operation. Since security checking is a comparatively recent evolutionary development, it must have wide genetic variation, and will still be under active selection. Genes responsible for excessive checking in sexually inhibited obsessionals will be lost to the gene pool as will genes responsible for inadequate checking in those who perish through an inability to protect their stores. In this way a balance exists between those who check too much and those who check too little: too much checking may be diagnosed as obsessive-compulsive behaviour; too little carries no diagnostic label but comes under the general heading of 'carelessness'.

Washing and cleaning behaviour evolved as a defence against micro-organisms. Since germs cannot be seen or easily conceptualized, notions such as 'contamination' and 'purification' emerged to organize the appropriate defensive behaviour: those who clean too much may become obsessional neurotics, while those who clean too little may suffer higher mortality from infection.

Similarly, the **morbid jealousy** displayed by some obsessionals towards their spouses can be understood as an exaggeration of normal jealousy which evolved to maintain the fidelity of a sexual partner and prevent extramarital conceptions. However, the reproductive advantage of mutual jealousy for the fitness of both partners has to be balanced against the danger of pair-bond disruption if jealousy is too intense.

A related issue concerns the religious propensities of human beings. Freud famously described religion as the universal obsessional neurosis of mankind. We might reverse this definition and see obsessional neurosis as the private religion of the individual. All societies known to anthropology possess religious beliefs and practices which employ ritualized behaviour to placate and manipulate the gods with such objectives as guaranteeing rainfall, promoting the fertility of the soil and the size of the harvest, as well as preserving the faithful from natural disasters, providing for the expiation of guilt, and fulfilling the quest for salvation or redemption. The compulsive rituals practised by people with an obsessional neurosis bear a close resemblance to the religious rituals practised all over the world and performed with similar objectives. Obsessive-compulsive disorder might, therefore, be classified as a disorder of the religious archetype or module.

The evolutionary perspective thus makes sense of the complex behaviour patterns of obsessive-compulsive states which were previously viewed as bizarre, pathological, and largely inexplicable.

8

ANXIETY AND PHOBIC DISORDERS

Anxiety is a heightened state of vigilance associated with an awareness of threatened danger. It is so universal a phenomenon, that everyone has experienced it, from time to time, as a normal and inescapable part of life. Anxiety becomes a diagnosable disorder when it becomes excessive, inappropriate, persistent, and incapacitating. DSM-IV and ICD 10 differ in their attempts to classify different types of anxiety disorder, but most authorities agree in distinguishing three of them: **generalized anxiety disorder**, **phobic disorders**, and **panic disorder**. We shall follow the DSM-IV classification.

GENERALIZED ANXIETY DISORDER (300.02)

DSM-IV describes the essential feature of generalized anxiety disorder as excessive anxiety and worry, occurring more days than not for a period of at least six months, about a number of events or activities. People with the disorder find it difficult to control their worries, which are accompanied by additional symptoms, such as restlessness, fatigue, difficulty in concentrating, irritability, increased muscle tension, and disturbed sleep. The anxiety is generalized and 'free floating', in that it is not triggered by any specific object or situation as it is in **panic** or **phobic disorders**. The frequency, intensity, or duration of the anxiety is far out of proportion to the actual likelihood or impact of any feared event. People with the disorder tend to worry about the ordinary routines of daily life, such as job responsibilities, finances, household chores, car repairs, the health of family members, being late for appointments, and so on. Somatic symptoms are common: these include trembling limbs, twitching muscles, clammy hands, dry mouth, sweating, nausea or diarrhoea, urinary frequency, and an exaggerated startle response. Depressive symptoms are also common.

Most people with generalized anxiety disorder report that they have felt anxious most of their lives. Although over half of those presenting for treatment report onset in childhood or adolescence, onset occurring after the age of 20 is not uncommon. The course is chronic but fluctuating and often worsens during times of stress.

PHOBIC DISORDERS

Phobic disorders produce the same disagreeable symptoms as generalized anxiety disorder but they occur in association with something specific such as heights, crowds, or spiders. DSM-IV makes an elaborate distinction between **specific phobia (300.29)**, **agoraphobia without history of panic disorder (300.22)**, **social phobia (300.23)**, **panic disorder without agoraphobia (300.01)** and **panic disorder with agoraphobia (300.21)**. The traditional psychiatric practice, by contrast, has been to lump all phobias together, specifying the stimulus to which a particular phobia is linked. Whether or not the object or situation causes the sufferer to panic is dependent on the intensity of the fear that the stimulus evokes. Panic attacks can occur, however, without the sufferer being aware of any definite cause for them.

PANIC DISORDER

DSM-IV describes a panic attack as a discrete period of intense fear which has a sudden onset and rapidly builds up to a peak. It is often accompanied by a sense of imminent danger or impending doom and an overwhelming urge to escape. It is associated with a number of somatic or cognitive symptoms, such as palpitations, sweating, trembling, shortness of breath, choking, chest pain, nausea or abdominal distress, lightheadedness, feelings of unreality (**derealization**) or feeling detached from oneself (**depersonalization**), fear of losing control or going mad, fear of dying, numbness, tingling sensations, chills or hot flushes.

A **panic disorder** is diagnosed when panic attacks recur unexpectedly and are associated with persistent concern about the possibility of having additional attacks. The symptoms are episodic but not linked to specific circumstances.

Aetiology

As all textbooks acknowledge, the aetiology of the anxiety and phobic disorders is imperfectly understood. A genetic factor has been thought to be important because the concordance for these disorders is greater among monozygotic than dizygotic twins. But this could well be because anxiety, a natural, adaptive attribute, is **normally distributed** throughout the population, with the result that some individuals (especially close relatives) have brisk autonomic responses associated with feeling anxious while in others they are more sluggish. As with depression, there is a much greater vulnerability to anxiety and phobic disorders among women, and the reasons for this sex difference may be similar in both cases (see Chapter 7). Phobias are common in children and, while most disappear with time, some may persist into adulthood. Bowlby and his followers have implicated anxiety about the availability of attachment figures in the production of these disorders. Aversive conditioning is also thought to be a factor, as when a phobia of dogs follows an occasion when a person was attacked and bitten by a Rottweiler. In many instances, no specific cause can be identified.

The taxonomy of fear has long been a subject of interest to psychiatrists, who have delighted in compiling lists of phobias and calling them by Greek names in the hope that, like 'proper doctors', they were describing disease entities. This has proved a popular activity, because being able to label a common fear with a scientific term couched in a dead language confers a certain spurious authority on the diagnostician. Unfortunately, it does not throw much additional light on the nature and cause of the condition so elegantly described, and it is not much help to the patient.

THE EVOLUTIONARY PERSPECTIVE

Psychiatric emphasis on anxiety as a classifiable 'illness' has given rise to the erroneous belief, current through most of this century, that anxiety is 'neurotic' and that no well-adjusted person should expect to suffer from it. In fact, the capacity to experience anxiety is indispensable to survival and reproductive success. An animal incapable of fear is a dead animal. The Dodo died because throughout the existence of its species it had inhabited an environment without predators and it knew no fear. But when humans arrived, bringing predators with them, this tame, fearless creature rapidly succumbed to them and became extinct.

It was through the study of anxiety that the idea first entered psychiatry that a mental symptom could have a biological basis. In his essay 'A phylogenetic fantasy', Freud suggested that certain states of mind, such as paranoia and anxiety, were remnants of responses which were biologically adaptive in human beings up to the time of the Ice Age. Jung also believed that such states possessed an evolutionary basis which predated the family conflicts which figured so extensively in the psychoanalytic literature of human ontogeny.

Anxiety is a form of vigilance which enables an organism to be alert to environmental changes so that it can be prepared to meet whatever emergencies may arise. W.B. Cannon (1929) linked this state of vigilant alertness to the neurophysiological state of **arousal** which, he demonstrated, was mobilized in response to a perceived threat by hypothalamic structures in the limbic system, acting through the sympathetic division of the autonomic nervous system and its connections with the endocrine glands. Arousal prepares the body for violent action. The heart rate increases, the blood pressure goes up, adrenaline is secreted, energy stores are mobilized in the liver and released into the bloodstream, blood is redistributed from the internal organs so as to carry oxygen and energy to the muscles and the brain. At the same time, the thyroid gland is stimulated to increase the efficiency of body metabolism. Laboured breathing occurs, and the large muscles used in violent action are brought to peak efficiency. Red corpuscles are liberated from the spleen to increase the oxygen-carrying capacity of the blood. Small muscles at the base of the hair follicles contract causing the hair to stand on end, the sweat glands secrete profusely, and so on. All these changes have the effect of preparing the organism to respond in a number of characteristic ways, such as fighting, fleeing, freezing, or submitting.

Since Cannon's time a wealth of laboratory and clinical evidence has accumulated to prove that the **limbic system** is the anatomical core of the arousal state associated with patterns of fight and flight. The neurophysiological components of anxiety, fear, and panic are broadly similar, whether cued by snakes, spiders, darkness, thunderstorms, or social scrutiny. They constitute a general systemic response to a wide variety of potentially dangerous situations. Anxiety disorders are thus to be understood as exaggerated or inappropriate forms of adaptive strategies.

As has already been noted, Bowlby's ethological approach to attachment threw light on the biology of **separation anxiety** and **anxious attachment**, when a subject experiences emotional distress on separation or threatened loss of a loved figure. The biological significance of anxiety for ranking behaviour was first elucidated by Marks (1969) and Rycroft (1970), and this work has been extended by Nesse (1987). All agree that the physiological and psychological components of anxiety, fear, and panic galvanize an organism to adaptive action.

A promising neuro-evolutionary theory of **panic disorder** has been advanced by Klein (1993). Panic attacks occur, according to Klein, when a 'suffocation monitor' signals (erroneously) that there is a lack of oxygen. This sets off an evolved 'suffocation alarm system', which would account for the dyspnoea (panting for breath) so apparent in a panic attack. The physiological mechanism responsible for detecting potential suffocation raises levels of CO_2 and lactate in the blood, causing a reflex increase in the respiratory rate. In addition to explaining the respiratory correlates of panic, Klein's hypothesis would also account for the observed absence of panic in circumstances where blood CO_2 is lowered (e.g., during pregnancy and delivery), and the increased incidence of panic in circumstances when blood CO_2 is raised (e.g., during the premenstrual period, during sleep, and in patients suffering from respiratory insufficiency).

It has been suggested that panic may represent an adaptation, not just to the possible threat of suffocation, but to any situation from which it is appropriate to take energetic flight (Nesse, 1987). As Stein and Bouwer (1997) argue in an important review of the literature on the neuro-evolutionary approach to anxiety disorders, it is likely that various triggers, including separation, bereavement, and other kinds of loss, as well as a history of traumatic suffocation, have the effect of lowering the threshold for the panic response.

ANXIETY AND THE IMMUNE SYSTEM

Nesse draws an instructive parallel between anxiety and the immune system, which has both general and specific defensive functions. The general responses of the immune system involve pain, fever, inflammation, and lymphocyte mobilization, while its specific functions include the production of immunoglobulins (in response to invasion by bacteria), interferon (in response to viruses), eosinophils (in response to parasites), and natural killer cells (to attack cancer). So it is with anxiety. General threats release general anxiety, which promotes physiological arousal in preparation for flight or fight, 'freezing' or submission. Predators promote flight, weaker challengers release attack, high places cause 'freezing', and stronger challengers stimulate submission. Moreover, just as the immune system can over-react (anaphylaxis), under-react (immune deficiency), respond to the wrong cue (allergy), or wrong pathogen (autoimmune disease), so anxiety can be excessive (panic), deficient (hypophobia), or a response to a situation which is not dangerous (a phobia of harmless grass snakes).

Nesse goes on to indicate two ways in which domain-specific anxiety resembles the body's response to invasion by foreign material: *anxiety which promotes avoidance or escape*, which results in removing the individual from a source of threat, just as disgust, vomiting, diarrhoea, coughing and sneezing will separate him physically from a pathogen; and *anxiety which promotes aggressive defence*, which motivates the individual to attack the source of danger (such as biting, striking, clawing, spraying with noxious substances), just as the immune system will attack and destroy bacteria.

Nesse concludes that subtypes of anxiety exist which give rise to specialized responses to specific kinds of threat, and that these subtypes are subsumed under a more generalized anxiety response. This would explain the clinical observation that while some patients experience general 'free-floating' anxiety, others suffer intense anxiety only in specific situations (phobic anxiety).

Nesse might be right. Just as it is easy to make lists of phobias with Greek names, it is not hard to think of adaptive responses which could be linked with them. For example, fear of heights (**acrophobia**) promotes *freezing* rather than escape (thus rendering one less likely to fall); fear of blood (**haemophobia**) causes *fainting* with its associated bradycardia and rapid drop in blood pressure (thus rendering one less likely to bleed to death); fear of open or public spaces (**agoraphobia**, *lit.* 'fear of the market place') causes one to stay at home (thus rendering one less likely to be mugged or raped); while fear of flying (**aerophobia**) keeps one on the ground (thus making it impossible for one to be killed in an air crash). However, it does not automatically follow that the anxiety experienced in each of these situations must be specifically linked to an adaptively appropriate response. After all, fear of spiders, fear of snakes, and fear of animals in general (**arachnaphobia**, **ophidiophobia**, and **zoophobia**) results in *avoidance, freezing, escape,* or *attack* (according to one's appraisal of the situation). All that can be said with certainty is that an organism responds to threat with anxiety and arousal. Once the nature of the threat is perceived and assessed, behaviour is released which is judged to be appropriate to the circumstances. The anxiety is a necessary preliminary and it helps to energize the subsequent behaviour. But such behaviour is not an automatic subroutine of the anxiety experienced; an element of choice occurs at some higher level of appraisal.

To be in the grip of a phobia is to realize the power of an autonomous complex operating at an ancient and unconscious level of the brain. One may realize how absurdly irrational one's terror of a little spider in the bath may be, but one's higher, recently evolved cerebral capacities are incapable of doing anything to control it. One just has to withdraw and leave somebody else to deal with the spider. This is the usual way of coping with a phobia: one does everything possible to avoid proximity to the source of the fear. Being quite unable to control it, one has no option but to keep away from everything associated with it. For it seems that situations are assessed at different levels of the brain and that conflicts can arise between these levels as to which strategy to adopt. At the conscious level, one may tell oneself not to be silly, that it's only a harmless little spider, and that one should swat it with the loofah and stop making a fuss. Instead, one finds oneself running out of the bathroom, screaming for help. Clearly one has been 'taken over' by a defensive response, which is beyond voluntary control because it is located, beyond the reach of consciousness, in the limbic processing system.

FEARS, ANCIENT AND MODERN

Anxiety disorders are of the utmost interest to evolutionary psychiatrists, for when the various phobias suffered by modern men and women are examined in detail, there is nothing modern about them. They are all exaggerated fears of objects, animals, or situations that were potentially life threatening in the environment of evolutionary adaptedness. This vital point is invariably overlooked in textbooks of psychiatry.

Anxiety and fear are adaptive responses to the kind of dangers humans have been exposed to in the course of their evolution. This is why we fear ancient dangers such as snakes, spiders, high or open places, and not modern dangers such as cars, guns, cigarettes, whiskey, and saturated fats, which kill off our contemporaries in far greater numbers. Modern phobias, such as going to school or to the dentist, or of contracting AIDS, are contemporary versions of adaptive fears of going off the home range, getting hurt, or of getting infected. Some modern phobias are a composite of ancestral fears: fear of flying, for example, has been *prepared* by the primordial dangers of heights, falling, loud noise, and being trapped in a small, enclosed place from which there is no exit.

One universal fear which is manifested throughout the world community in infants, starting at about six months of age, is fear of strangers (**xenophobia**). This begins as shyness or slight wariness of unfamiliar people, and by twelve months it has become a very evident fear. It is during this period that young children delight in crawling off in exploratory forays away from their mother, using her as a 'secure base', thus rendering themselves vulnerable to the attention of strangers. There can be little doubt about the adaptiveness of infant xenophobia. Infanticide by strangers is so common among primate species as to constitute a strong selective force, and, as we have already noted, human infants are more likely to be abused or killed by non-kin to whom they have not become emotionally attached than by those to whom they are genetically (and emotionally) related (Daly and Wilson, 1989).

The archetypal mechanisms with which the human organism is endowed function in the manner of Ernst Mayr's 'open programmes': they serve as *biases to learn* certain cues and responses rather than others, so as to adapt appropriately to environmental variations. Archetypes are thus *prepared* (by evolution) to become active in response to certain environmental stimuli in accordance with certain built-in rules. These biases facilitate swift responses with a minimum of previous experience. Snakes rapidly come to evoke fear, dominant conspecifics to evoke submission, bad food to evoke nausea. That we rapidly learn the actual cues betokening danger is because selection has prepared us to encounter them. The behaviour of parents and peers promotes this rapid learning. For example, when a young child is approached by a strange person or animal, it characteristically looks at its mother to monitor her responses. If she smiles it is reassured; if she shows alarm, this releases and augments the child's fear.

Parents have always helped children to learn anxiety through admonition and the recital of fairy tales, as well as by example. In the modern world, films and television may have the same effect. The ready elicitation of fear by the mere description or representation of frightening situations – particularly archetypal ones – permits learning to occur without having to undergo the dangerous experience itself. Many children replay these homilies and representations in their dreams and nightmares, thus actually suffering the association between the feared object or situation and the sense of panic that it induces. However, 'prepared' fears are much more rapidly acquired than unprepared ones; and this helps to explain why parents have difficulty in conditioning their children to fear evolutionarily recent dangers such as knives, plastic bags, matches, and electric sockets. It might also explain why behaviour therapists treating alcoholics with aversion found induced nausea a more effective aversive stimulus than electric shocks.

Often enough, the conditions that give rise to flight, withdrawal, or other demonstrations of fear, both in animals and in humans, are not necessarily dangerous in themselves; but, on examination, it becomes clear that they are related, if only indirectly, to situations that actually are a hazard to life or limb. As Bowlby (1973) put it:

> In a wide array of animal species including man, a principle condition that elicits alarm and retreat is mere strangeness. Others are noise, and objects that rapidly expand or approach; and also, for animals of some species though not for others, darkness. Yet another is isolation.
>
> Now it is obvious that none of these stimulus situations is in itself dangerous. Yet, when looked at through evolutionary spectacles, their role in promoting survival is not difficult to see. Noise, strangeness, rapid approach, isolation, and for many species darkness too – all are conditions statistically associated with an increased risk of danger.

The tendency to react with fear to such common stimulus situations, then, is due to genetic biases that possess survival value, in the sense that they prepare individuals to meet real dangers. This is why fear can be aroused in a variety of situations that are not, in fact, dangerous. Thus, to show panic fear in response to finding oneself in an enclosed space like a lift or a tube train, to react with terror in response to the perception of height, or to the realization that one is entirely alone in the dark, may seem absurd to a normally adjusted person, but viewed from a biological standpoint, these reactions are understandable as manifestations of ancient response patterns. What the individual is responding to are the natural cues, or **sign stimuli**, commonly associated with danger in the ancestral environment. Often these cues do not signify any menace at all, but the fact remains that they *could* do. It is not altogether inappropriate, therefore, for the individual to respond to them with wariness or fear, if only on the principle that it is better to be safe than sorry. From the 'ultimate' point of view of survival and repro-ductive success, it is better to respond with anxiety or arousal to a thousand false alarms than to risk a single failure to respond when the danger is real. What has happened in the phobic patient is that this natural response system has become both over-sensitive and hyper-reactive.

PHOBIAS, SOCIAL AND NON-SOCIAL

Many contemporary phobias reflect ancient response mechanisms which protected our ancestors from physical dangers; but most modern phobias reflect social anxieties that are no less ancient. As with depressive responses, anxiety is released by almost any situation perceived as constituting a threat to one's RHP or SAHP. **Agoraphobia** is made up of both social and non-social anxieties. Agoraphobic patients are fearful when they are away from home: on the one hand, they fear open or crowded spaces; on the other hand, they fear social situations which they may not be able to handle and from which they may not be able to escape without embarrassment.

Agoraphobia can also be understood as an innate fear of straying from the home base. Most animals are territorial. Once they have established a territory, they defend it vigorously against all comers, and are usually victorious. Some species have a home range which they patrol and share with conspecifics. But few seem happy to leave their home range. Irven De Vore (1965) describes how an attempt was made to drive a troop of olive baboons over the boundary of their range: they fell to the ground manifesting extreme degrees of anxiety and panic. Other species, like wildebeest, forage over large distances, while others again, like birds, are strictly territorial at certain times of the year yet, at other times, have the capacity to make long migrations. But on the whole, animals are 'stay-at-homes', and it is the ability to leave home *without* anxiety that is exceptional and which requires explanation.

In the case of humans, one possibility is that selection has occurred for wanderers: it was these who trekked into Asia, Oceania, Australasia, the Americas, and the northern wastes after the Ice Ages, spreading across the globe in an adaptive radiation which effectively multiplied the genes of those who made the journey and survived to reproduce. In addition, the hunting mode of existence made it necessary for males to travel far from their home base. That agoraphobia is much commoner in females than in males could be linked to this. When the males were away hunting, it would have been a foolish woman who strayed far from camp on her gathering expeditions: not only were there wild beasts to fear but young men from neighbouring groups collecting scalps as part of their initiation ordeals.

Staying close to home in times of male absence was not incompatible with going on the long treks required of women belonging to nomadic groups when the males were in attendance. This fits with the observation that agoraphobic women may display considerable mobility once they are removed from their local area. One agoraphobic girl, for example, was able to enjoy a long continental tour on the back of her boyfriend's motor-bike.

When treating patients with agoraphobia, it is helpful to bear in mind the association that exists in the majority of animal species between ownership and RHP: the owner of a territory displays confidence, the intruder does not. A rise in self-esteem can increase the range of an agoraphobic patient: it is as if she feels she has a right to patrol a larger area and, as a result, her sense of being an intruder when she strays off her home ground is reduced. As Leary and Downs (1995) have shown, a rise in self-esteem lowers both subjective anxiety and physiological arousal. Thus, to boost the self-esteem of an agoraphobic patient may be a more effective remedy than attempting to 'decondition' her anxiety by taking her into those places she most fears –

an heroic therapy which can result in a reinforcement of her conditioned aversion. Another therapeutic measure is to encourage good relations with neighbours, so as to transform alien territory (which the patient expects to be agonistically defended) into a home range (which can be hedonically shared). It can also be helpful for a patient to be reassured that there is nothing absurd about preferring to remain safely at home instead of going out shopping on her own. After all, there were no supermarkets in the EEA, and 'gathering' was almost certainly done in the reassuring intimacy of familiar groups of women.

In **social phobia**, the fear is unequivocally one of exposing oneself to situations where one might be subjected to the criticism of others. DSM-IV describes social phobia (300.23) as 'a marked and persistent fear of social or performance situations in which embarrassment may occur.' Exposure to any such situation invariably results in symptoms indistinguishable from those described under **generalized anxiety disorder**. As a result, all situations in which one may find oneself open to scrutiny are strenuously avoided – these include parties, seminars, meetings, canteens, and any gathering where one may be called upon to speak or express an opinion. The underlying fear seems always to be that one will be negatively judged – as inadequate, stupid, unattractive, weak, and unworthy to be a member of the group. This is an exaggeration of normally adaptive anxieties about conforming to group customs of dress, speech, manners, conventions, and laws so as to be an acceptable and valued member of the community.

Stein and Bouwer (1997) have advanced the hypothesis that social phobia results from the pathological triggering of an appeasement display, which is often characterized by blushing. The lowered eyelids, averted gaze, nervous grin, and reddening of the face, have the effect of mitigating the negative reactions of others: it is as if appearing embarrassed substitutes for an apology. The authors cite data supporting the notion that patients with social phobia misperceive signals from others which could indicate the need for appeasement, in that they have an exaggerated sense of their own lowly status in comparison with the supposed high status of other people, and are consequently over-sensitive to the possibility of coming under social threat.

The capacities for embarrassment, shame, and guilt are necessary, as we have already noted, to ensure social harmony and group cohesiveness. When exaggerated they can result in disorders other than social phobia: these include **avoidant personality disorder**, uncontrollable blushing or sweating in social situations, fear of looking or smelling abnormal (**dysmorphophobia**), fear that others might hear one urinating or defecating (**sphincteric phobias**), and so on. In all these instances, the basic fear is that of losing SAHP as a result of being judged unworthy or unacceptable. Such fears are commonly associated with **anxious attachment**, **separation anxiety**, and fears of losing one's partner to a rival. These can in turn lead to **pathological jealousy**, and, in obsessional people, to morbid rumination and ritual checking on the partner's suspected infidelities.

CONCLUSIONS

Emotions are adaptive responses that we have acquired through natural selection. Their profound influence affects our bodies, our behaviour, and our minds. Different emotions relate to different adaptive strategies. Anxiety is the emotion one feels after the cues associated with a possible danger have been perceived and before the nature of the danger has been fully recognized (Rycroft, 1970). It is how one feels on arrival at an examination hall before one has read the questions, and how one feels after the results are published but before one has found one's name on the list. For our ancestors living in the EEA, perception of cues indicating the approach of a potential enemy or dangerous animal, would have resulted in anxious vigilance which persisted until the intruder's intentions had been confirmed. Should the intruder indicate he was about to attack, fear would energize the appropriate response, whether it be to fight, or run away, or climb up a tree.

Panic strikes when something dangerous happens which is totally unexpected and, in the absence of all promonitory cues, evokes no preparatory vigilance or anxiety. Such experiences, once they have occurred, are viewed by psychiatrists as potentially **traumatic**. The concept of trauma is derived from general medicine, where it signifies the infliction of physical injury through external violence. Psychological trauma can result in such conditions as **post-traumatic stress disorder** (309.81), which follows 'exposure to an extreme traumatic stressor involving direct personal experience of an event that involves actual or threatened death or serious injury' (DSM-IV). The person's response to the event will have involved intense fear, helplessness, or horror. Characteristic symptoms include persistent re-experiencing of the traumatic event, avoidance of stimuli associated with the trauma, and persistent symptoms of increased arousal. The adaptive function of such an extreme and enduring reaction is presumably to discourage the victim from ever again exposing himself to a comparable danger. For a soldier, fire-fighter, or steeplejack such avoidance may be incompatible with continuation of his professional role. Classification of the condition as a disorder, requiring early retirement on medical grounds, can be a face-saving solution, as well as providing a therapeutic and economically satisfactory outcome.

Anxiety, as we have suggested, is probably a normally distributed trait throughout the whole population. Most of us experience enough anxiety to function efficiently. Some of us experience too little or too much. As with other biological variables, a **homeostatic** mechanism appears to regulate defensive responses so as to tune them, in the majority of people, to an intensity which is appropriate to the circumstances. People who suffer excessive pain are disabled and cannot live a normal life. People who lack the capacity to feel pain may die young because they do not avoid injury with sufficient alacrity. So it is with anxiety. Too much anxiety can keep one housebound on a diet of tranquillizers; too little can lead to death or social ostracism. Students who experience no anxiety at the thought of impending exams may fail them through lack of knowledge, while those who experience too much may fail them through lack of concentration.

This biphasic function, in which moderate amounts of anxiety promote adaptive efficiency, while excessive or inadequate amounts militate against it, has been formulated in the Yerkes/Dodson Law (Yerkes and Dodson, 1908). This states that with mounting arousal, performance at first increases and then gradually falls off. Hans Selye (1974) made similar observations on the function of stress. An organism performs most efficiently, he discovered, when it is subjected to moderate amounts of stress. Too much or too little stress results in impaired performance. That psychiatric textbooks contain no section on **hypophobias** is not because these do not occur, but because fearless people do not present themselves for treatment. If they come to the attention of a psychiatrist, it is because of some other disorder associated with an incapacity to experience fear. The most common of these, and the most disastrous in its consequences, is **anti-social personality disorder**.

9

EATING DISORDERS

Our justification for including eating disorders in this section derives from our view that, in order to compensate for feelings of personal inadequacy in forming attachment bonds and attaining status, these patients misapply adaptive mechanisms which evolved to enable our ancestors to adjust to fluctuations in the food supply in the EEA.

While there is general agreement that **anorexia nervosa** and **bulimia nervosa** are psychiatric disorders, there are major differences of opinion about **obesity**. Obesity is included in ICD 10 as a general medical condition but excluded from DSM-IV 'because it has not been established that it is consistently associated with a psychological or behavioural syndrome.' Obesity is conventionally described as having many causes: genetic, physiological, and cultural. The causal factors involved in eating disorders which will be of primary concern to us are phylogenetic and psychosocial.

ANOREXIA NERVOSA (307.1)

This bizarre and paradoxical condition of self-starvation, which predominantly afflicts young females from affluent families, was first described by Richard Morton in 1689. It was given its present name by William Gull in an address at Oxford in 1868. Though Gull stressed its psychogenetic nature, it was to be confused for many years with **hypopituitarism (Simmond's Disease)**, until Sheehan and Summers (1949) established that emaciation is not a characteristic feature of hypopituitarism and that anorexia nervosa must be regarded as a separate condition. Many psychiatrists, however, continued to view anorexia nervosa as a variant of other psychiatric syndromes, such as **depression, obsessive-compulsive disorder**, and **schizophrenia**, and it was not until the late 1960s that a clear consensus about the condition began to emerge. Bruch (1965), for example, described it as 'a relentless pursuit of thinness', Crisp (1967) as 'weight phobia', and Russell (1970) as 'a morbid fear of becoming fat'. Many pointed out that 'anorexia' was not an accurate term to describe the condition, since it is not due to 'loss of appetite' but to an *excess of control* over what is eaten, so as to induce loss of weight.

The overwhelming majority of sufferers are female (over 90 per cent) with a peak onset in late adolescence. It is rare in women over 40. Girls from well-off families are at least four times more likely to develop the condition than girls from working-class families (who, conversely, are more prone to become obese).

The main clinical features of anorexia nervosa are an intense wish to be thin, an equally intense fear of being fat, a low body weight (associated with a distorted body image as being still 'too fat'), and amenorrhoea. Typically, the condition begins with normal dieting in a previously slightly overweight adolescent, which progresses to a relentless effort to achieve and maintain an abnormally low body weight. A distorted attitude to weight, shape, and fatness is associated with a fastidious avoidance of all foods thought to be 'fattening'. A proportion of sufferers eventually resort to self-induced vomiting, as well as the use of laxatives, purgatives, diuretics, and appetite-suppressing drugs.

There is disagreement about how emaciated a patient needs to be to qualify for the diagnosis of anorexia nervosa, but a weight of less than 75–85 per cent of the average population weight for height is generally accepted as sufficient. Substantial weight loss is usually followed by amenorrhoea, and it is characteristic that this is usually accepted with indifference by anorexic patients. In girls whose illness begins before puberty, primary amenorrhoea occurs and may present as a diagnostic problem. The equivalent of amenorrhoea in the anorexic male is diminished sexual interest and potency.

Other clinical features are evident. People tend to become reclusive and secretive, and obsessive-compulsive behaviour is common, associated with the extreme need to exercise rigid control over what is eaten. Since fear of losing control is an ever-present threat, vigilance is exercised over every calorie consumed. An obsessive preoccupation with the issues of food and weight may be associated with ritual weighing many times a day, measuring body parts, and repeatedly using mirrors to examine buttocks, hips, thighs, or any parts which are considered 'too fat'. The longer the condition persists the more liable patients are to become mean and to begin hoarding and stealing food. Family relationships come increasingly under strain as attempts to coax, bully, or bribe the patient to eat more are met with implacable opposition and a staunch refusal to acknowledge that any problem exists. Some will use their condition like a 'hunger-striker' in prison in order to control the behaviour of others by threatening to starve themselves still further if people will not co-operate and allow the patient to manage her diet as she wishes. Social and sexual contacts are avoided and anorexics may withdraw into long and arduous periods of private study. Mood changes are common, patients tending to become depressed if they gain weight and elated if they regain control.

BULIMIA NERVOSA (307.51)

Although this disorder may occur as a chronic phase of anorexia nervosa, it can also occur without preceding anorexia and is thus regarded as a syndrome in its own right. The term **bulimia** refers to episodes of uncontrollable and excessive 'binge' eating. This is one component of the syndrome. A second component consists of behaviour designed to prevent weight gain – namely, severe dietary restriction, self-induced vomiting, the abuse of purgatives, laxatives, and appetite-suppressing drugs, as well as excessive exercising. Patients will often delay eating for as long as possible before they lose control and over-eat. More than 50 per cent binge eat and vomit at least daily. To meet the strict diagnostic criteria of DSM-IV, binge eating and the inappropriate compensatory behaviours must occur, on average, at least twice a week for three months.

As with anorexia nervosa, people with bulimia nervosa are excessively preoccupied with their appearance, have a distorted and exaggerated image of their shape and weight, harbour morbid fears of becoming fat, and an intense desire to be slim. They are also highly sensitive to changes in their weight, and a gain of one or two pounds is regarded as a major disaster. They react by renewed dieting, depression, feelings of guilt and worthlessness, and social withdrawal.

Unlike people with anorexia nervosa, however, bulimics are unable to maintain rigid control over their appetite for long periods, with the result that their body weight tends to remain within the normal range for their height, and their menses, though they may be irregular, are not lost. Another important difference is that whereas anorexics feel in control of their appetite and therefore do not want treatment, bulimics have lost control of their appetite and therefore do. They are, nevertheless, slow to come forward because they feel ashamed and guilty about their behaviour and fear that nothing can be done to help them. People with bulimia nervosa also tend to be more extraverted, socially competent and sexually experienced. However, they are equally status conscious, achievement orientated, and industrious.

Binges typically occur in response to hunger pangs after a period of dietary restraint. They may also be triggered by a stressful incident or by a dysphoric mood state ('comfort eating'). But the reduction of dysphoria is transient because it is accompanied by self-disparagement and feelings of disgust for having lost self-control. When a patient starts on a binge, she will usually continue until she is uncomfortably, or even painfully, full. At the neuropsychic level, a conflict prevails between a (lower level) urge to eat and a (higher level) determination not to eat. First one side wins, and then the other. When the 'lower level' desire takes over, it may be accompanied by feelings of dissociation. Between 30 and 50 per cent of patients with bulimia nervosa have personality features that meet the criteria of one or more **personality disorder(s)** (most frequently **borderline personality disorder**).

Stealing is not uncommon in these patients, especially the shop-lifting of food because, as often as not, they cannot afford the considerable outlay required to finance their binges.

Self-induced vomiting, using fingers to stimulate the gag reflex, is the commonest compensatory technique (80–90 per cent), followed by the use of laxatives (30–40 per cent). What determines the differential diagnosis is whether binge eating and vomiting occur within the context of anorexia nervosa (malnutrition + amenorrhoea) or whether bulimia nervosa is primary (normal weight range and menstruation usually present, if somewhat irregular). As with anorexics, over 90 per cent of bulimics are female.

Aetiology

Eating disorders are more prevalent in developed (rather than developing) nations, where an abundance of food is associated with a strong cultural emphasis that to be beautiful is to be thin. Adolescence is a critical period for the development of self-esteem: it is a time of identity crisis and of extreme sensitivity to the opinion of one's peers, especially members of the opposite sex. Teasing about being fat, or any physical abnormality, can have a devastating effect at a time of emerging sexual awareness and growing independence from parental influences.

Surveys among teenage schoolgirls in North America and in Europe have regularly found that a high proportion of them are conscious of their weight and their diet. The class relationship is also well established. In the United Kingdom, for example, girls at private schools are five times more likely to develop anorexia nervosa than girls at state comprehensive schools. A significant number of patients who develop eating disorders come from families with a greater than normal incidence of obesity and depressive disorder. Children who were overweight from an early age are particularly at risk. It is as if the appetite regulating mechanism in the hypothalamus has been set to 'advance', with the consequence that these patients continue to feel hungry after they have eaten sufficient to maintain a normal body weight. **Obesity** at adolescence, associated with peer reaction to the condition, can result in feelings of profound self-loathing and disgust. Yet, hypothalamic dysfunction and hypercellular adipose tissue make it extremely difficult for them to initiate and maintain a programme of weight reduction, and it seems likely that such people are particularly vulnerable to develop bulimia nervosa.

Psychoanalytic discussion of these disorders has focused on the struggle for control so evident in anorexic and bulimic patients, the adolescent's need to achieve a valid sense of identity, and to experience feelings of competence and effectiveness. The families of anorexics, it is argued, have failed to give their child a sense of her own autonomy, competence and self-value. Typically, parents are over-controlling, seeking always to impose their own wishes, thus impairing their daughter's capacity to know and respond to her own judgement and desires. The anorexic strategy is designed to escape from an ineffectual role and to establish a subjective sense of power and authority. Her whole self-worth then becomes identified with the idea of thinness. It has also been suggested that those anorexics who have grown up in homes with excessively controlling parents are provided with a parental model for the exercise of control. By usurping this controlling function and applying it to their own bodies they fashion an effective weapon for subverting parental authority, thus satisfying the desire evident in many over-controlled children to rebel and take the law into their own hands.

Another theoretical approach that has proved influential is that of Crisp (1967), who maintains that anorexia nervosa represents a retreat from the overwhelming problems of adolescence and a psychobiological regression to childhood. Through systematic self-starvation, a girl keeps herself physically and psychologically in the pre-pubertal state. Hence the typical absence of secondary sexual characteristics (well-formed breasts, buttocks, and hips), the amenorrhoea, and the 24-hour LH/FSH secretion pattern, which resembles that of girls who have not yet reached puberty.

THE EVOLUTIONARY PERSPECTIVE

While all authorities agree that anorexia nervosa and bulimia nervosa arise from social pressure on women in our society to be slim, few, if any, of them, seem curious as to why this pressure should exist in the first place. For evolutionary psychiatry this is the crucial issue, for it sees human adiposity and its variations to be fundamentally related to (1) biological mechanisms whose evolved function is to contend with fluctuations in the food supply, (2) the present and anticipated availability of resources in the environment, (3) the display of social status, (4) the capacity of individuals to 'cheat' by assuming the attributes of higher status than they know themselves to possess, and (5) the evolved capacity of females to respond to fluctuations in variables (2) and (3) by altering the timing of reproduction.

It is most unlikely that, in the pre-agricultural conditions prevailing in the EEA, food supplies would have been constant, regular, and adequate for the daily needs of a hunter-gatherer population throughout the year. Even a highly sophisticated agricultural society, like that of ancient Egypt, had to be prepared for times of deprivation, as Joseph's Biblical interpretation of Pharaoh's dream demonstrates: the seven fat kine represented seven fat years during which supplies must be hoarded; the seven lean kine represented seven years of famine which the supplies had to be adequate to meet. In the absence of barns and silos, our pre-agricultural ancestors had no option but to conserve resources in their adipose tissues during the good times and to metabolize them sparingly when bad times struck and adequate nourishment was unavailable.

Binge eating would, therefore, have been adaptive in the EEA, on the ancient principle of 'Eat, drink and be merry, for tomorrow we die.' The adaptive programme would decree: 'If it is there, eat it – especially if it is sweet, fatty, or tastes of salt' (all relatively rare but vital commodities in the ancestral environment). Not only would it have been advantageous in these conditions to eat plenty when the food was available, but also to control appetite and be indifferent to hunger pangs when it was not. Our ancestors would probably have been called upon to use these adaptive strategies in the course of a year. In the modern world they are obsolete, except among the very poor and among those with eating disorders: the bulimic makes use of both strategies in the course of a day; the anorexic makes use of the second strategy all the year round. The hoarding and stealing often observed in these conditions reveals how much they have to do with the laying up and rationing of resources.

An adaptive propensity to eat regularly and well when resources are available is particularly important for the female, who must be adequately nourished in order to conceive, to bring her child to term, and to feed it when it is born. In line with this supposition is the finding of one study of American college students that 79 per cent of females and 49 per cent of males admitted to episodes of 'uncontrolled excessive eating' (Hawkins and Clement, 1980).

From the viewpoint of ranking theory, obesity, anorexia nervosa, and bulimia nervosa can all be regarded as side-effects of the 'class struggle.' For most of our existence as a species, obesity has probably functioned as a status symbol. Its symbolic significance is determined by cultural attitudes and by the availability of food. When food is scarce, 'fatness' symbolizes high social status, and human cultures still survive in which desirable women are too fat to stand up. In these cultures, 'thinness' symbolizes low RHP and, therefore, indicates low social standing.

In cultures where food is consistently abundant, however, low ranking individuals can acquire sufficient resources to become as fat as persons of high rank, and 'fatness' loses its status appeal. As a result, the symbolism is reversed, and it becomes a symbol of high rank to be thin. When this reversal occurs, a new factor is introduced into the situation: to keep thin in the presence of abundant supplies demands the acquisition and maintenance of *self-control*. This would help to explain why it is affluent families which place great store on diet, health, fitness, appearance, and self-presentation, and why the education of rich children is so much more demanding (and unpleasant) than that of poor children. The traditional boarding school regimes of cold showers, long-distance runs, team games, bad food, and long absences from home, are all designed to inculcate self-control and tolerance for adversity. The anorexic is one who learns these 'virtues' too well.

The element of *cheating* becomes apparent in bulimia nervosa, when patients seek to maintain their high social status of 'thinness' while secretly gorging themselves and putting fingers down their throats in the locked seclusion of the bathroom. Both bulimics and anorexics suffer from feelings of low self-esteem and are guilty about the subterfuges to which they have to resort in order to achieve the degree of thinness that they desire. It is because they are aware of cheating that they are secretive and ashamed, and fearful of being found out. In her own way, the anorexic deals with this more effectively than the bulimic, and this makes her more difficult to treat. For, as Gilbert (1992) has pointed out, she transforms her fears of being shamed and humiliated into *pride*. She achieves this through self-starvation. Her ability to tolerate hunger pangs, and to go on tolerating them indefinitely, becomes a source of triumph in self-conquest. Anorexics, for all their feelings of personal inadequacy, can be extremely competitive with other women. As the Duchess of Windsor observed: 'A woman can never be too rich or too thin.' In a society that values thinness as highly as ours, the anorexic can achieve high status in her own estimation by becoming superthin. All fat women are despised, their gross condition being equated with public humiliation, a sign that they are socially worthless. It is this that makes treatment of the condition so hard. The therapist is trying to deprive the patient of the only thing she feels proud of, the one truly valuable quality that she can recognize in herself: her ability to conquer her appetite and stay thin. It is the bulimic's failure to achieve this goal that causes her to acknowledge defeat and seek treatment.

One of the most striking features of anorexia nervosa is the apparent inability to stop dieting when a reasonable degree of slimness has been achieved. Why do severely anorexic girls have to go on to the point of extreme emaciation and even death? It seems that once weight falls beyond a certain point mental and physiological changes occur which turn the discipline of dieting into a form of addiction. At this point, according to Ploog and Pirke (1987), the hunger-regulating centres become linked to the reward systems in the CNS, and this, they maintain, would account for the inability to halt weight-reduction once it has been carried beyond a certain point. Cerebral reward systems may also be implicated in the patient's satisfaction in exercising control over her body and her social status. The consequences of this satisfaction for increased self-esteem and for the treatment of the disorder are considered in Chapter 20 (pp. 251–53).

A further evolutionary perspective has been suggested by Surbey (1987), who proposes that anorexia nervosa is a reflection of the female ability to alter the rate at which reproductive functions are permitted to mature in response to prevailing environmental conditions. Surbey makes use of Wasser and Barash's (1983) 'reproductive suppression model', which they summarize as follows: 'females can optimize their lifetime reproductive success by suppressing reproduction when future conditions for the survival of offspring are likely to be sufficiently better than present ones as to exceed the cost of suppression itself.' The model is based on the observation that puberty is delayed or reproduction suppressed in female mammals of a number of different species when they are subjected to stress or are in a poor physical condition. The ability to delay reproduction is adaptive because it enables a female to avoid giving birth when conditions are not conducive to her offspring's survival. This seems to square with the facts of anorexia nervosa. Since amenorrhoea occurs in all typical cases, reproduction is effectively suspended. The endocrine profile remains pre-pubertal in nature, and only exhibits the adult form after normal weight has been restored. Anorexia nervosa thus alters a girl's developmental trajectory from that of an early maturer to that of a late maturer, and this does not appear to have any deleterious effect on fitness.

From a phylogenetic standpoint, however, anorexia is too modern a condition to be viewed as a direct result of selection, as Surbey readily admits. Rather, anorexia is a disordered variant of the adaptive ability of females to alter the timing of reproduction. Feeling unready to assume the emotional, biological, and socio-economic responsibilities of womanhood, the anorexic puts them off until such time, if ever, that she feels she can. For these emaciated young women, it is not the environment that seems inauspicious but their subjective assessment of their own ability to meet the normal demands of human life.

Part III
BORDERLINE STATES

10

THE BORDERLINE STATE

The story of the development of the borderline concept has been well told by Gordon Claridge (1985) and our own view of borderline states has been enriched by his excellent *Origins of Mental Illness*. The borderline concept arose because many people with psychiatric disorders cannot be conveniently pigeon-holed into the neat categories devised for them by the diagnosticians. In practice, one may often encounter individuals presenting such a complex clinical picture that it is not easy to decide whether they are mildly psychotic, severely neurotic, or suffering from a long-standing personality disorder. Originally introduced by psychoanalysts to describe a group of patients who proved resistant to therapy, or indeed were made worse by it, the borderline concept has come to be applied to individuals whose abnormal personalities seem to combine features of neurotic and psychotic symptomatology. Before proceeding any further, therefore, we should briefly examine these diagnostic categories.

NEUROSIS AND PSYCHOSIS

Certain basic classificatory distinctions made by psychiatrists in the nineteenth century have continued to exercise their influence up to the present time. Most fundamental of these was the distinction between disorders which were associated with organic pathology and those which were not. The **organic** group of psychiatric disorders, which have been classified in terms of their physical aetiology, are not dealt with in this book because evolutionary psychiatry has, in our view, a more urgent contribution to make to our understanding of the second group, the so-called **functional** disorders. It is these that have traditionally been subdivided into two subgroups: the neuroses and the psychoses. The **neuroses** have included the **obsessional disorders, anxiety** and **phobic disorders, hysterical** and **conversion disorders, non-psychotic affective disorders,** and **eating disorders**, while the **functional psychoses** cover **schizophrenia** (including **paranoid disorders**) and **manic-depressive psychosis**. The **personality disorders, reproductive disorders,** and **addictive disorders** are usually classified as separate groups in their own right.

121

The distinction between the neuroses and psychoses has long been based on such criteria as the degree to which insight is retained, the personality involved, social adaptation maintained, contact with reality preserved, and the severity of the condition. Crucial criteria are the presence or absence of delusions or hallucinations. These distinctions are set out in Table 4.

Table 4 Criteria for the distinction between neurosis and psychosis

Criteria	Neurosis	Psychosis
Insight	Retained	Lost
Personality	Partly involved	Wholly involved
Social adaptation	Fair	Very poor
Contact with reality	Retained	Lost
Severity	Mild	Severe
Delusions	Absent	Present
Hallucinations	Absent	Present

Neurosis and psychosis are useful descriptive terms which are still in general use, though they have been dropped from classificatory systems such as DSM-IV and ICD 10. As many critics have pointed out, the division between the two groups of disorders is far from watertight. Thus, some schizophrenics, especially young and intelligent ones, realize that they are mentally ill, while some hysterics do not. In severe obsessional neurosis, the personality may be profoundly implicated, while in some manic-depressives and in some schizophrenics in remission, the personality may be relatively intact. The social adaptation of some neurotics, especially those with severe generalized anxiety or with agoraphobia, may be so poor that they cannot go out to work, while that of some paranoid schizophrenics is relatively unimpaired and they can. While it may be true that most psychotic disorders are more severely incapacitating than most neurotic disorders, exceptions are commonly encountered. Nevertheless, neurosis remains a convenient term for a group of psychiatric disorders which, however severe, do not involve hallucinations, delusions, or loss of insight; while psychosis still finds currency as a broad term to cover those severe disorders in which hallucinations and delusions do occur in people with relatively poor insight into their condition.

When someone develops a psychiatric disorder, what determines whether they become neurotic or psychotic? And, if they are driven over the borderline from the former to the latter, what determines the form that the psychosis takes? The answer that psychiatrists invariably give is that combinations of factors are involved, including genetics, early conditioning, traumatic precipitating events, and the premorbid character structure of the individual. One possibility has been suggested by Claridge (1985; 1987), namely, that susceptibility to psychotic thinking is distributed throughout the population and exists independently of any susceptibility to a particular form of psychiatric illness such as affective disorders, schizophrenia, or alcoholism. This might help to explain how it is that some people may be depressed or hypomanic or have a schizoid personality without becoming psychotic, while others with these conditions do.

Another suggestion, advanced by Brant Wenegrat (1984), is that a psychosis is in many ways like a **fever**. Just as fever assumes different forms according to the underlying disease process (in, for example, malaria, lobar pneumonia, or tuberculosis), so psychosis assumes different forms according to the psychopathology of the individual. Schizophrenia, manic-depressive psychosis, psychotic depression, and paranoid psychosis, can each be conceptualized as the supervention of a psychosis on an underlying personality or affective disorder. Thus each major psychotic illness has a non-psychotic counterpart (see Table 5).

Table 5 Some psychotic illnesses and their non-psychotic counterparts

Psychotic	Non-psychotic
Schizophrenia	Schizotypal personality disorder
Manic-depression	Cyclothymic personality disorder
Psychotic depression	Non-psychotic depression
Paranoid psychosis	Paranoid personality disorder

In all these instances there is an evident genetic loading.

Like fevers, different psychoses share common psychological and physiological features. Psychologically, psychoses resemble one another in producing delusions, hallucinations, disorganized thinking and speech, resulting in social maladjustment and dysfunction, while physiologically, psychoses resemble one another in their excessive dopamine activity (which is not specific to schizophrenia as was previously thought), raised serum creatine phosphokinase levels, neuromuscular dysfunction, and diminished skeletal muscle and platelet mono-amine oxidase. It is also significant that dopamine blocking agents have the capacity to alleviate psychotic symptoms non-specifically, irrespective of their diagnostic category. Moreover, psychosis may develop in essentially normal people following physiological or psychological stresses, such as amphetamine, LSD, or alcohol abuse, and extreme social or emotional loss or rejection. Acute schizophrenia can occur in patients who have little or no schizotypal genetic loading and who achieve relatively normal readjustment on recovery. It is possible that this kind of acute, single-episode schizophrenia occurs in young people who are genetically predisposed to respond to stress with psychosis, and the good prognosis could mean that they are not really schizophrenic at all. Wenegrat suggests that 'low threshold psychosis' could be a better term for their condition and that 'schizophrenia' should be reserved for *process* schizophrenia, which has a bad prognosis and becomes chronic.

Differential diagnosis between psychotic categories is, nevertheless, possible, as the existence of DSM-IV demonstrates, as a result of careful clinical examination of their psychological and physiological characteristics. Hans Eysenck (Eysenck and Eysenck, 1976) is one who has argued that what determines whether an individual manifests a schizophrenic or an affective disorder is the premorbid character structure. What he labels as 'psychoticism' is a *general* dimension of personality, which predisposes certain individuals to psychotic breakdown of whatever kind. What determines the form the psychosis takes is the individual's weighting on another personality dimension, namely, introversion–extraversion: when psychoticism is combined with introversion, the result is schizophrenia; when psychoticism is combined with extraversion, the result is manic-depressive psychosis. Since the introvert–extravert dimension is a continuum, it follows that many combinations are possible and can either give rise to the distinctive clinical picture of schizophrenia or manic-depression or to mixed forms deriving their symptomatology from both psychotic disorders.

Certainly, borderline states can appear as precursors of full-blown psychotic disorders of either type. One critical factor, we believe, is whether the individual still experiences himself as socially engaged or whether he feels socially detached, alienated, and 'beyond the Pale'. The type of psychosis manifested may well reflect a deeper, inherent personality structure, which inclines to one or other end of the introversion–extraversion continuum. The extraverted psychotic is more likely to retain some sense of group membership (and develop a psychotic depression) while the introvert is more likely to feel completely detached from the group (and become schizophrenic).

In sum, we can agree with Stone's (1980) suggestion that three frames of reference are involved in borderline states:

1 **the constitutional element**: this consists of the hereditary factors which predispose to a major clinical syndrome like schizophrenia or manic-depression;
2 **the adaptation level**: this reflects the degree of personality integration (or disintegration) which ranges from the neurotic, through the borderline, to the psychotic; and
3 **the personality type**: this contributes to the behaviour and the psychological 'style' of the borderline patient.

As psychiatrists everywhere increasingly acknowledge, a number of their patients cannot readily be assigned to either neurotic or psychotic categories, such is the complexity and inconsistency of the clinical picture they present. It is these who straddle the borderline. While neurotics remain realistically involved with their social group, psychotics become alienated from it: people on the borderline alternate between these social and asocial conditions.

Claridge (1985) quotes a seventeenth-century physician, who summed it up well: 'All is caprice,' he wrote. 'They love without measure those whom they will soon hate without reason.' Theirs is both a linking and a spacing disorder.

LINKING VERSUS SPACING

When dealing with an assortment of facts or observations, the natural tendency of the human mind is to dichotomize. We have already encountered many instances of this, the dual existence of the hedonic and agonic modes being a prime example. In addition to analysing populations in terms of their propensity to affiliate or compete (Empodocles' love and strife), we may also understand them in terms of their tendency either to concentrate within a confined area or to spread out over a large one. As Gardner (1988) put it, 'two basic messages are conveyed by all intraspecific communications: conspecifics tend to link themselves or space themselves in optimal ways in space and time.'

Social gregariousness was first systematically investigated by Sir Francis Galton (1822–1911). He concluded that patterns of gregariousness evolved through natural selection for the reason that individuals who formed aggregates would be less at risk from predators than those who lived in solitude. But there were critical limits of degree. Too close gregariousness would result in overcrowding and in destructive disputes over territory and mates, while groups becoming too widely scattered would not provide each other with adequate defence. This balance between **affiliation** (which is too close) and **isolation** (which is too great) is one that all individuals, and all groups, continuously strive to maintain.

It would seem that a fundamental dialectic between **individuality** and **relatedness** has proceeded throughout the course of evolution. Guisinger and Blatt (1994) relate this dichotomy to many similar distinctions that have been suggested in the latter half of this century, including autonomy and surrender (Angyal, 1951), agency and communion (Bakan, 1966), individuality and togetherness (Bowen, 1966), separation and attachment (Bowlby, 1969), power and affiliation, achievement and intimacy (McAdams, 1980; McClelland, 1980), individualistic and mutualistic urges (Slavin and Kriegman, 1992). Although selection pressures push in divergent directions (that is towards self-development and relatedness), Guisinger and Blatt (1994) suggest that a dialectical system operates between them, so that self-development is contingent on the development of interpersonal relationships and that mature relationships are contingent on the development of a mature self-identity. At adolescence these two lines of development become integrated to some extent in the formation of what Erikson (1959) called *identity*, but a dialectical tension persists between them throughout the life-cycle.

Beck's (1983) distinction between **autonomous** and **sociotropic personality types** has already been noted: 'Just as the autonomous type relies on distancing to facilitate his goals, so the sociotropic person seeks closeness.' These contrasting tendencies closely resemble Jung's distinction between **introverts** and **extraverts**, and when they are developed to an exaggerated degree they can become implicated in the aetiology of psychiatric disorders. For example, Beck argues that a fear of closeness in autonomous types may be expressed in the psychiatric illness of **claustrophobia**, while fear of distancing in sociotropic types may be at the basis of **agoraphobia**. There is also an association between fear of closeness and **schizoid personality** and **schizophrenia** in autonomous types, and between fear of distancing and **depression** in sociotropic types. But in people of whatever type, the 'dialectical tension' between opposing tendencies towards linking and spacing can result in serious disorders. This inherent conflict in social living was of particular interest to the late R.D. Laing (1960), who held it responsible for the induction of **psychosis** – the individual's fear of 'engulfment' driving him over the borderline into psychotic isolation. We shall consider these spacing disorders in Part IV. But first we must turn our attention to the curious personality characteristics of those who languish on the frontier between neurosis (and membership of the group) and psychosis (and alienation from it).

11

BORDERLINE PERSONALITY DISORDERS

On the whole, psychoanalysts have proved more tolerant than psychiatrists of the idea that there is no clear dividing line between the neuroses and psychoses, and, because psychoanalysis has influenced American psychiatry so much more than psychiatry in Britain, it is in the United States that most of the research on borderline conditions has been done. Many have gone along with the psychoanalytic assertion that borderline disorders constitute a halfway stage in the disintegration of the personality in the course of its decline into schizophrenia.

The close proximity of these disorders to schizophrenia was recognized by the nomenclature that was applied to them from the start. Such diagnostic terms as 'pseudoneurotic schizophrenia', and 'borderline schizophrenia' were used to describe individuals who were emotionally unstable and unpredictable, displayed a poor sense of identity, indulged in a rich and somewhat bizarre fantasy life, and who made use of the ego-defence mechanism known as 'splitting', whereby contrary feelings towards others, such as love and hate, could be sustained without fragmentation of the personality. While many were socially isolated, lonely and depressed, others managed to form personal relationships, though these characteristically tended to be of a dependent rather than a reciprocal nature. Usually they were more socially and sexually active than schizophrenics, though their work and educational records tended to be similar. Moreover, some were observed to have occasional, if brief, episodes of psychosis, and many displayed other 'schizophreniform' characteristics such as anhedonia (the inability to experience pleasure), episodic distortions of cognition, and odd or bizarre patterns of thought.

If borderline patients lived in a no man's land between neurosis and psychosis, many also seemed to inhabit the territory between schizophrenia and manic-depression. Mood instability is common among them, and many authorities have noted a clinical affinity between borderline states and affective disorders as well as with schizophrenia. Genetic studies have also found that borderline states occur with greater than chance expectancy among the biological relatives of manic-depressive as well as schizophrenic patients (Siever and Gunderson, 1979). Furthermore, it has been claimed that borderline patients treated with drugs regularly show a more satisfactory therapeutic response to antidepressants than to the major tranquillizers effective in treating schizophrenia. Psychiatrists increasingly acknowledge a lack of that *discontinuity* between the clinical pictures of schizophrenic and affective disorders which would justify their classification as entirely separate and distinct disease entities. 'Schizo-affective states' have long been recognized, where a mixture of schizophrenic and affective symptoms occur in the same patient.

Refinement of the borderline concept came with the work of Spitzer *et al.* (1979), who conducted a nationwide survey of the diagnostic practices of American psychiatrists in their use of the term 'borderline personality disorder'. On the basis of this survey, they felt they could distinguish two major forms of usage: one which emphasized attenuated schizophrenic characteristics, such as cognitive distortions, and disordered thought patterns; and one which stressed signs of emotional instability, such as impulsiveness, hostility, and self-injury. Having devised rating scales, distributed them widely and analysed the results, Spitzer and his colleagues finally designated two categories of disorder which are now recognized by the DSM-IV classification as **schizotypal personality disorder** and **borderline personality disorder**.

While acknowledging that these classifications cut through the jungle of terminology surrounding borderline states, Claridge (1985) questioned whether Spitzer's two categories are truly distinct kinds of disorder or whether they merely represent different manifestations of a common, underlying 'borderline personality structure'. He concluded that they probably were distinct and that they represented mild manifestations or *formes frustes* of the disposition to one or other of the two major forms of psychotic illness.

Borderline personality disorder will be described in this chapter, whereas schizotypal personality disorder will be discussed in the next. The reason for this reorganization of the DSM-IV classification is that, in our view, the individual with the borderline personality disorder is still operating within the boundaries of the group, whereas the individual with a schizotypal personality disorder has crossed the boundary and is, as a consequence, suffering from a spacing disorder.

BORDERLINE PERSONALITY DISORDER (301.83)

The essential feature of borderline personality disorder, states DSM-IV, is a pervasive pattern of instability of interpersonal relationships, self-image, and affects, together with marked impulsiveness, which begins in early adulthood and is present in a variety of contexts.

The criteria for establishing the diagnosis are met if five or more of the following features are present:

1 frantic efforts to avoid real or imagined abandonment;
2 a pattern of unstable and intense interpersonal relationships, alternating between extremes of idealization and devaluation;
3 identity disturbance: a marked and persistently unstable sense of personal identity;
4 impulsiveness in at least two areas that are potentially self-damaging (e.g., over-spending, unsafe sex, substance abuse, reckless driving, binge eating);
5 recurrent suicidal behaviour, gestures, or threats, or self-mutilating behaviour;
6 affective instability (e.g., intense episodic dysphoria, irritability, or anxiety usually lasting a few hours and only rarely more than a few days);
7 chronic feelings of emptiness;
8 inappropriate, intense anger or difficulty in controlling anger (e.g., frequent displays of temper, recurrent physical fights); and
9 transient, stress-related paranoid ideas or severe dissociative symptoms.

Aetiology

This disorder represents an extreme form of Bowlby's **anxious attachment**. There is commonly a history of insecure parental attachments in childhood, pathological parenting (see p. 46), and a failure to form 'basic trust'. People with this disorder may be understood as having embarked on a life-long quest for reliable figures (or parent substitutes) to provide the love, care, stability, and security that their own family failed to provide. With each new encounter they feel they may have found what they are looking for, and gross over-idealization of the new acquaintance may occur as early as the first or second meeting. But as soon as it is realized that the new person is unable to lavish all the loving care that is longed for, the initial feelings of love and admiration rapidly turn into anger, resentment, and despair, as well as an indulgence in self-damaging behaviour. Their inability to form stable relationships and to hold on to a job means that they are often forced to endure low social status, and this serves to increase their feelings of bitterness and frustration.

There is considerable variability in the course of borderline personality disorder. The most common pattern is one of chronic instability in early adulthood, with episodes of serious affective disorder and impulsiveness, together with a heavy reliance on medical and psychiatric services. The disorder is at its most severe during the early adult years, and tends to improve with advancing age. Provided the disturbed behaviour of people with the disorder has not resulted in ostracism, incarceration, or early death, they may achieve greater stability in their relationships by the time they are in their forties and even settle into steady employment. This brings them a measure of emotional reassurance and a degree of social status which may serve to strengthen a valid sense of personal identity. Therapy in these cases is largely a matter of providing support and encouragement during the stormy decades which precede mid-life.

Part IV

SPACING DISORDERS

12

SPACING PERSONALITY DISORDERS

The disorders included in this chapter are **avoidant, paranoid, schizoid**, and **schizotypal**. We have chosen to classify these personality disorders, together with **schizophrenia**, as spacing disorders because they have a major characteristic in common: people with these conditions all have difficulties in forming and maintaining personal relationships and in functioning appropriately as members of a social group. In addition, they tend to deal with these social difficulties by adopting a strategy of withdrawal. Withdrawal effectively removes them from the common social arena of linked interpersonal transactions and puts them in an alternative space of their own making. This alternative, private space may have a geographical location (such as a hermitage, a desert island, a cave, or a monastic cell) or it may have a psychological location – a 'walled citadel', so to speak, within themselves. It is true to say, therefore, that people with these disorders have crossed the social boundary which contains all other members of their group, and have moved into 'outer' (or 'inner') space.

AVOIDANT PERSONALITY DISORDER (301.82)

DSM-IV describes people with avoidant personality disorder as displaying a pervasive pattern of social inhibition, feelings of inadequacy, and hypersensitivity to negative evaluation, beginning by early adulthood and present in a variety of contexts, as indicated by four (or more) of the following:

1 they avoid occupational activities that involve significant interpersonal contact, because of fears of criticism, disapproval, or rejection;
2 they are unwilling to get involved with people unless they are certain of being liked;
3 they show restraint within intimate relationships because of the fear of being shamed or ridiculed;
4 they are preoccupied with being criticized or rejected in social situations;
5 they are inhibited in new interpersonal situations because of feelings of inadequacy;

6 they view themselves as socially inept, personally unappealing, or inferior to others; and

7 they are usually reluctant to take personal risks or to engage in any new activities because they may suffer embarrassment.

People with avoidant personality disorder are often vigilant in their appraisal of the behaviour and facial expressions of those with whom they come into contact. Their tense, fearful demeanour may elicit ridicule from others, which only serves to confirm their self-doubt. Others describe them as shy, timid, lonely, and isolated. The major problems associated with this disorder occur in social and occupational settings. Their relative isolation means that they lack a social support network to help them to weather crises, and their avoidant behaviour can seriously impair their prospects for employment or promotion.

Aetiology

The prevalence of avoidant personality disorder in the general population is about 1 per cent. It is reported to be present in about 10 per cent of outpatients seen at psychiatric clinics.

People with avoidant personality disorder, like those with **dependent personality disorder**, have often endured the kind of parenting and peer relationships in childhood which induce chronically low levels of self-esteem. However, they adopt different strategies for survival. As was noted in Chapter 6, dependent types tend to assume the role of suppliant care-receiver and attempt to pre-empt attack from higher-ranking members of the group through submissive behaviour. Avoidant types, by contrast, tend to contract out of close relationships altogether. The striking feature of avoidant personality disorder is withdrawal in order to avoid humiliation and rejection rather than seeking out people on whom to depend and by whom to be taken care of. They resemble Murray Parkes' patients who showed 'compulsive self-reliance' (1973). Much as people with avoidant personality disorder would like to enjoy intimacy and social rank (and may enjoy both in fantasy), their low self-assessment convinces them that they can expect neither in reality, and must be prepared to 'go it alone'.

PARANOID PERSONALITY DISORDER (301.0)

DSM-IV describes people with paranoid personality disorder as having a pervasive distrust and suspiciousness of others such that their motives are interpreted as malevolent, beginning in early adulthood and present in a variety of contexts, as indicated by four (or more) of the following:

1 they suspect, without sufficient basis, that others are exploiting, harming, or deceiving them;

2 they are preoccupied with unjustified doubts about the loyalty or trust-worthiness of friends or associates;
3 they are reluctant to confide in others because of unwarranted fears that the information will be used maliciously against them;
4 they read hidden meanings (demeaning or threatening) into benign re-marks or events;
5 they persistently bear grudges, i.e., they are unforgiving of insults, injuries, or slights;
6 they perceive attacks on their character or reputation that are not apparent to others and are quick to react angrily or to counter-attack; and
7 they have recurrent suspicions, without justification, regarding the fidelity of their spouse or sexual partner.

Not surprisingly, people with paranoid personality disorder do not make the easiest of companions or workmates, and, as a consequence, they tend to have major problems with personal relationships. Because they are hyper-sensitive to real or imagined insults, they are prone to suspect that their reputation is under attack, and to react with anger or extreme hostility. Not uncommonly, such behaviour elicits a hostile response from others, and this is taken as confirmation of the original suspicions held against them. Dis-putes with neighbours, municipal authorities, and officials of all kinds are extremely common, and people with the disorder can be highly litigious. At the same time as feeling generally in a state of siege, they may entertain grandiose fantasies of possessing exceptional authority, power, and rank. These tend to be associated with the creation of negative stereotypes of other groups, which may be seen as living personifications of the enemy archetype. As a result, people with the disorder are sometimes perceived as 'fanatics', and may form cults round themselves, made up of people who share their beliefs.

Under stress, people with paranoid personality disorder may experience brief episodes of psychosis or may proceed to the development of **schizo-phrenia** or a full **paranoid delusional disorder**. Occasionally the condition may be associated with **obsessive-compulsive disorder**, **agoraphobia**, or **major depressive disorder**.

Aetiology

The prevalence of paranoid personality disorder has been estimated as 0.5 to 2.5 per cent of the general population. It occurs in between 2 and 10 per cent of those attending psychiatric clinics. There is some evidence of an increased prevalence of the disorder in relatives of patients with chronic schizophrenia and, more specifically, of patients with **delusional disorder, persecutory type**.

While there may evidently be a genetic predisposition to the disorder, a substantial number of people with this type of personality report inadequate parenting in childhood, especially a lack of loving intimacy, and the use of frequent criticism and punishment to induce feelings of inferiority and guilt as means to enforce discipline.

THE EVOLUTIONARY PERSPECTIVE

As with anxiety, fear and depression, we all share, in some degree, the paranoid disposition. Evolution has prepared us to be wary about things as they happen, to be vigilant, anxious, suspicious. In the environment of evolutionary adaptedness, such responses were entirely appropriate. Life on this planet has, in effect, 'taught' us as a species to expect trouble. Trouble is in the natural order of human existence. If you want to survive you have to realize that trouble is never far away. You have to look out for it. It is not pathological, therefore, to assume that there is more going on behind the scenes than meets the eye. There usually is!

For most of us, what keeps our perceptions and beliefs within the bounds of sanity is our relationship with other people and the feed-back that such relatedness brings. For the isolated individual there is no social feed-back, no way in which to test the reality of his perceptions. In a world where there is no affirmation or contradiction of what one sees, hears, or thinks, the ground is fertile for the growth of bizarre misconceptions. We shall return to these considerations in the next chapter, where we shall also examine the role of persecutory feelings in causing groups to split and subgroups to migrate to new and 'promised' lands.

People with paranoid disorders possess in strong measure the capacity to recognize deceit. Both the capacities to deceive and to detect deception are phylogenetically very old, as we saw in our earlier discussion of **anti-social** and **histrionic personality disorders**, where the work of Axelrod (1984) was mentioned (see p. 89 above). Human social interactions are based on trust. In Axelrod's terminology, the highest joint pay-off when two individuals interact is for both to co-operate and not to deceive one another. However, a 'free-riding' individual can enjoy a higher pay-off if he is in the habit of cheating and moving on, before his deceit is recognized and held against him. This, we suggested (following Harpending and Sobus, 1987), was the strategy adopted by psychopaths and hysterics. The paranoid type, by contrast, is not interested in quick pay-offs but in detecting cheats before they can deceive him. Accordingly, he distrusts everybody, and this creates a widening gulf between himself and others. Not only does this serve to increase his social isolation, but, lacking the reassurance of friendly alliances, he is also more likely to read deception into the ordinary actions of everyone. His chronic suspicion of other people's good intentions then becomes a self-fulfilling prophecy.

SCHIZOID PERSONALITY DISORDER (301.20)

DSM-IV describes people with schizoid personality disorder as exhibiting a pervasive pattern of detachment from social relationships and a restricted range of expression of emotions in interpersonal settings, beginning by early adulthood and present in a variety of contexts, as indicated by four (or more) of the following:

1 they neither desire nor enjoy close relationships, including being part of a family;
2 they almost always choose solitary activities;
3 they have little, if any, interest in having sexual experiences with another person;
4 they take pleasure in few, if any, activities;
5 they lack close friends or confidants other than first-degree relatives;
6 they appear indifferent to the praise or criticism of others;
7 they show emotional coldness, detachment, or flattened affectivity.

The essential characteristic of people with this disorder is their social and emotional detachment. They are quintessential 'loners', who are seen by others to be cold, aloof, and withdrawn. Their indifference to what others may think of them marks them off from people with **avoidant personality disorder**. Oblivious to the normal subtleties of social interaction, they respond inappropriately to social cues, and present a 'bland' exterior that gives little or nothing away as to their inner thoughts and feelings. Although they may not function well in a work situation that requires co-operation with others, schizoid types may do outstanding and original work in conditions of social seclusion. Under stress, people with this disorder may experience brief psychotic episodes, lasting minutes or hours. In some individuals, schizoid personality disorder may occur as a pre-morbid antecedent to **schizophrenia** and occasionally to **manic-depressive psychosis**.

Aetiology

The concept of a schizoid personality was first formulated at the Burghölzli Hospital in Zurich, soon after Eugen Bleuler (1911) had introduced the term schizophrenia into psychiatry. The Burghölzli team attempted to define the latent or pre-schizophrenic personality structure. Following up his father's work, Manfred Bleuler found that at least 50 per cent of his schizophrenic patients had shown schizoid traits before the onset of their psychosis. Rather than representing a specific genetic defect, Bleuler believed that a broad underlying hereditary tendency towards schizoid character structure manifests itself in different ways: in some people it results in characteristics which are compatible with healthy adjustment; in others it may result in

137

maladaptive or even psychotic behaviour when the characteristics are assembled in certain 'disharmonious' combinations.

Whatever the nature of the genetic contribution, a factor which is known to predispose an individual to develop this personality disorder is the loss of, or prolonged separation from, the mother in early childhood. This was certainly true of two of the most important and original thinkers in the history of Western civilization, Isaac Newton and René Descartes, both of whom were schizoid personalities and both of whom lost their mothers in infancy (Storr, 1972; Stevens, 1995). Abandoning hope of achieving emotional fulfilment in the outer world of human relationships, both turned inwards to construct intellectual worlds of such ingenuity and brilliance that they made the scientific age possible. In this way, it seems that schizoid (and schizotypal) individuals, may protect themselves from psychotic breakdown by developing their personal resources of intellect, personality, and charisma. These efforts can enable them to capitalize on their unusual states of mind. A sizeable proportion are less successful, however, and instead of achieving cultural distinction, they either potter on in their besieged state of schizoid seclusion, or descend into the as yet unredeemed hell of schizophrenia.

SCHIZOTYPAL PERSONALITY DISORDER (302.22)

DSM-IV describes schizotypal personality disorder as 'a pervasive pattern of social and interpersonal deficits marked by acute discomfort with, and reduced capacity for, close relationships as well as by cognitive or perceptual distortions and eccentricities of behaviour'. As with borderline personality disorder the pattern has begun by early adulthood and is present in a variety of contexts.

The criteria for establishing the diagnosis are met if five or more of the following features are present:

1 ideas of reference (i.e., incorrect interpretations of external events as having a particular meaning specifically for the person concerned);
2 odd beliefs or magical thinking that influences behaviour and is inconsistent with subcultural norms (e.g., superstitiousness, belief in clairvoyance, telepathy, or 'sixth sense'; in children and adolescents, bizarre fantasies or preoccupations);
3 unusual perceptual experiences, including bodily illusions;
4 odd thinking and speech (e.g., vague, circumstantial, metaphorical, over-elaborate, or stereotyped);
5 suspiciousness or paranoid ideas;
6 inappropriate or constricted affect;
7 behaviour or appearance that is odd, eccentric, or peculiar;
8 lack of close friends or confidants other than first-degree relatives; and

9 excessive social anxiety that does not diminish with familiarity and tends to be associated with paranoid fears rather than negative judgements about the self.

Aetiology

This kind of disorder is clearly much closer to the frontier with schizophrenia than borderline personality disorder. Sometimes people with schizotypal personality disorder give the impression that they have actually crossed it. For example, they may believe that they have special powers to predict events before they happen, that they can read others' thoughts, or exercise magical control over them. Perceptual alterations may also occur, in that they may sense that other people are present and may hear voices murmuring their names. The disorder is distinguished from schizophrenia, however, by the absence of persistent psychotic symptoms, especially delusions and hallucinations.

Genetic factors, combined with forms of parenting that undermine the development of self-esteem and confidence in the ability to form personal relationships, provide the most likely aetiological contributions. Although people with the disorder may express regret at their lack of relationships, they give the impression of having withdrawn into an inner world of thoughts and fantasies. When obliged to interact with others, they tend to do so in an inappropriate, stiff or constricted manner, and they are usually unable to join in friendly chatter or banter at work. As a result, they are left alone with their thoughts, and are regarded as odd and eccentric. Not uncommonly, they may become the butt of jokes, and this can drive them further into a sense of isolation.

However, schizotypal personality disorder generally follows a reasonably stable course, with a relatively small proportion of individuals developing schizophrenia. The majority survive by adopting a strategy of detachment – detachment from the need for emotional support, and detachment from the need for status. It is as if the outer world ceases to be of much account and the inner world comes to supplant it, but without crossing the brink of psychosis. For the schizotypal personality, the borderline is a tightrope, along which the individual walks with relative impunity, by dint of keeping himself very much to himself.

THE EVOLUTIONARY PERSPECTIVE

Like people with schizoid personality disorder, those with schizotypal personality disorder often reveal a greater propensity for original and creative, albeit sometimes bizarre, patterns of thought. They may not only be brilliant mathematicians like the Nobel laureate, John Nash, Jr, but may become the charismatic leaders of religious cults. Success in such activities can serve to draw them back into a sense of group membership which may result in reduction in the severity of their symptoms and act as a preventive factor against the development of a full-blown schizophreniform psychosis – or promote recovery from such a psychosis after its onset. The implications of this finding for the genetics of spacing disorders as well as for the phenomenon of group splitting are described in the chapters on **schizophrenia** and **research** (see particularly pp. 146–57 and 264–68).

13

SCHIZOPHRENIA

This terrible and catastrophic condition persists as the great unresolved mystery of psychiatry. Why does it continue to afflict 1 in every 100 human beings in the course of their lifetime in every corner of the world, when schizophrenics themselves have a much lower fertility rate than average? Indeed, why does schizophrenia exist at all? What is it? And why did it come into existence in the first place? We shall return to these issues later in this chapter, but first we will examine the clinical nature of the condition.

THE CLINICAL PICTURE

As DSM-IV acknowledges, no single symptom is pathognomonic of schizophrenia; the diagnosis is based on recognition of a constellation of signs and symptoms together with a history of impaired occupational or social functioning.

Characteristic symptoms may be conceptualized as falling into two broad categories – positive and negative. The positive symptoms appear to reflect an excess or distortion of normal functions, whereas the negative symptoms appear to reflect a diminution or loss of normal functions. The **positive symptoms** include distortions or exaggerations of inferential thinking (delusions), perception (hallucinations), language and communication (disorganized speech), and behaviour (grossly disorganized or catatonic behaviour). These positive symptoms may comprise two distinct dimensions, which may in turn be related to different underlying neural mechanisms and clinical correlations: the 'psychotic dimension' includes delusions and hallucinations, whereas the 'disorganization dimension' includes disorganized speech and behaviour. **Negative symptoms** include restrictions in the range and intensity of emotional expression (affective flattening), in the fluency and productivity of thought and speech (alogia), and in the initiation of goal-directed behaviour (avolition).

DSM-IV lists the following **diagnostic criteria for schizophrenia**:

A *Characteristic symptoms*. Two (or more) of the following, each present for a significant portion of time during a one-month period (or less if success-fully treated):

1 delusions;
2 hallucinations;
3 disorganized speech (e.g., frequent derailment or incoherence);
4 grossly disorganized or catatonic behaviour; and
5 negative symptoms, i.e., affective flattening, alogia, or avolition.

Note: Only one Criterion A symptom is required if delusions are bizarre or hallucinations consist of a voice keeping up a running commentary on the person's behaviour or thoughts, or two or more voices conversing with each other.

B *Social/occupational dysfunction*. For a significant portion of the time since the onset of the disturbance, one or more major areas of functioning such as work, interpersonal relations, or self-care are markedly below the level achieved prior to the onset (or when the onset is in childhood or ado-lescence, failure to achieve the expected level of interpersonal, academic, or occupational achievement).

C *Duration*. Continuous signs of the disturbance persist for at least six months. This six-month period must include at least one month of symp-toms (or less if successfully treated) that meet Criterion A (that is, active-phase symptoms) and may include periods of prodromal (preliminary/advance) or residual symptoms. During these prodromal or residual periods, the signs of the disturbance may be manifested by only negative symptoms or two or more symptoms listed in Criterion A present in an attenuated form (such as odd beliefs, unusual perceptual experiences).

The list of criteria goes on specifically to exclude schizo-affective and mood disorders, substance and general medical disorders, and pervasive de-velopmental disorders.

The median age of onset for the first psychotic episode of schizophrenia is in the early to mid-twenties for men and in the late-twenties for women. The onset may be abrupt or insidious, but the majority of individuals display some type of prodromal phase manifested by the slow and gradual devel-opment of a variety of signs and symptoms (such as, social withdrawal, loss of interest in school or work, deterioration in hygiene and grooming, un-usual behaviour, outbursts of anger). Eventually, the appearance of some active-phase symptom marks the disturbance as schizophrenia.

The course and outcome in schizophrenia are variable. Some individuals display exacerbations and remissions, while others remain chronically ill. Complete remission (a return to full premorbid functioning) is not common. Of those who remain ill, some appear to have a relatively stable course, whereas others show a progressive worsening, associated with severe disability. Because positive symptoms are particularly responsive to treatment, they typically diminish, but in many individuals negative symptoms persist between episodes of psychotic breakdown.

Numerous studies have indicated a group of factors that are associated with a better prognosis. These include good premorbid adjustment, acute onset, later age at onset, being female, the existence of precipitating events, an associated mood disturbance, brief duration of active-phase symptoms, good inter-episode functioning, minimal residual symptoms, absence of structural brain abnormalities, normal neurological functioning, a family history of mood disorder, and no family history of schizophrenia.

SCHIZOPHRENIA SUBTYPES

DSM-IV distinguishes five subtypes of the condition. These are paranoid, disorganized, catatonic, undifferentiated, and residual subtypes. We will summarize each of these in turn.

Paranoid type (295.30). The essential feature of this type is the presence of prominent delusions of a persecutory nature and/or auditory hallucinations while cognitive functioning and affect remain relatively unaffected. The delusions may be multiple, but are usually organized round a coherent theme. The hallucinations, typically, are related to the content of the delusions. The individual may adopt a superior and patronizing manner, and the combination of persecutory delusions with powerful feelings of injustice and anger may predispose him or her to violence. Onset tends to be later in life than the other types of schizophrenia and the prognosis may be considerably better, particularly with regard to occupational functioning and the capacity for independent living.

Disorganized type (295.10). The essential features of this type are disorganized speech, disorganized behaviour, and flat or inappropriate affect. Behavioural disorganization may lead to severe disruption of the ability to perform the activities of daily life (showering, dressing, or preparing meals). Criteria for the catatonic type are not met and the delusions and hallucinations, if present, are fragmentary and not organized into a coherent theme. Associated features include grimacing, mannerisms, and other oddities of behaviour. Impaired performance may be noted on a variety of neuro-psychological and cognitive tests. The subtype is also associated with poor premorbid personality, early and insidious onset, and a continuous course without significant remissions. Historically, and in other classificatory systems than DSM-IV, this type is termed **hebephrenic**.

Catatonic type (295.20). The essential feature of this type is a marked psychomotor disturbance which may involve either complete immobility or excessive activity, extreme negativism, mutism, peculiarities of voluntary movement, and echolalia or echopraxia (repetition or mimicry of another person's words and actions). During severe catatonic stupor or excitement, the patient may need careful supervision to avoid self-harm or danger to others. There are potential risks of malnutrition, exhaustion, hyperpyrexia, or self-inflicted injury.

Undifferentiated type (295.90). The essential feature of this type is the presence of symptoms that meet Criterion A of schizophrenia, but which do not meet criteria for the paranoid, disorganized, or catatonic type.

Residual type (295.60). This type is diagnosed when there has been at least one episode of schizophrenia, but the current clinical picture is without prominent positive psychotic symptoms (such as delusions, hallucinations, disorganized speech or behaviour). Continuing evidence of the disturbance is indicated by the presence of negative symptoms (such as flat affect, poverty of speech, or avolition) or two or more attenuated symptoms (for example, eccentric behaviour, mildly disorganized speech, or odd beliefs). If delusions or hallucinations are present, they are not prominent and are not accompanied by strong affect. The course of the residual type may be limited in time and may represent a transition between a full-blown episode and complete remission. However, it may also be continuously present for many years, with or without acute exacerbations.

Aetiology

Numerous studies have confirmed beyond all reasonable doubt that a genetic factor contributes to vulnerability to the disorder. While estimates vary to some extent, there is, nevertheless, agreement that schizophrenia is more common in the families of schizophrenic patients than in the population at large, where the lifetime risk is in the region of 1 per cent. For second-degree relatives (grandchildren, nephews, nieces) of a known schizophrenic the risk increases to 3–5 per cent, for siblings 10–15 per cent, and for children of two schizophrenic parents 37–45 per cent. Twin studies have established that monozygotic twins are more concordant for schizophrenia than dizygotic twins. If one twin of a monozygotic pair is schizophrenic there is a 45–50 per cent chance of the other twin becoming schizophrenic. For dizygotic twins the figure is 15–17 per cent.

Studies of adopted children brought up away from their biological parents from an early age lend impressive weight to the importance of genetic influences. A pioneer study by Heston (1966) compared two groups of fostered children. The mothers of one group were schizophrenic, while those of the other had no psychiatric diagnosis. None of the latter group developed schizophrenia, but 17 per cent of the former did. Moreover, they also showed a higher incidence of other disorders, especially personality disorders. Another interesting finding was that in members of the former group, who had schizophrenic mothers but were themselves free of psychopathology, a greater number took up artistic or creative professions. In the last thirty years, a considerable amount of confirmatory evidence has been gathered in a number of developed countries.

What form does the inheritance take? Is it monogenic (caused by a single gene), polygenic (caused by the cumulative effect of several genes), or heterogeneous (caused by a number of genes which express themselves in different aspects of the disorder)? Despite all the research devoted to these questions, we still do not know the answer. One theory that has received favourable attention is that of Gottesman and Shields (1982), who proposed a 'multifactorial-polygenic-threshold' model. This holds that the genes responsible for the predisposition to schizophrenia are widely dispersed, in varying degrees, throughout the general population. In order to develop clinical schizophrenia, an individual has to cross a threshold, beyond which the genetic predisposition becomes manifest. The critical point at which the threshold is fixed is determined by the genetic loading that an individual carries, combined with his or her accumulated life experience. This model deservedly commands respect, for it has been applied successfully to physical diseases, such as diabetes mellitus.

Should the predisposition to schizophrenia indeed prove to be inherited in a graded fashion, then it should be possible, as Claridge (1985) suggested, to find a counterpart in the behaviour of normal individuals. We shall return to this suggestion in discussing our **group-splitting hypothesis** later in this chapter.

Apart from genetics, research effort has increasingly focused on what is assumed to be the *cause* of schizophrenia, which is thought to be some anatomical or neurophysiological abnormality. The history, signs, symptoms, and course of the condition will, it is believed, once the putative cause has been found, then be shown to be mere epiphenomena of a purely organic pathology.

Advances in this direction have already been made. There is evidence that some schizophrenic patients have brain abnormalities. These include enlargement of the cerebral ventricles, decreased temporal and hippocampal size, and increase in the size of the basal ganglia. Imaging techniques have indicated that some patients have abnormal cerebral blood flow and glucose metabolism in the prefrontal cortex. The shrinkage of the temporal lobes is thought to be due to an agent acting on the foetus before birth. That schizophrenia is more common among people born during the winter could be explained by greater maternal risk of viral infection during the winter months, and this might account for the temporal lobe abnormalities. Some neurological deficit is also suggested by the 'soft signs' found in schizophrenic patients on neurological examination: these may be poor performance on co-ordination tests, left/right confusion, and so on.

This kind of research, combined with biochemical investigations and research in molecular genetics, will doubtless yield more insight into the organic changes associated with this erstwhile 'functional' disease. However, psychological and social factors will continue to exercise their influence. Even among monozygotic twins, half the siblings do not develop schizophrenia. Stressful events shortly before onset have been shown to be important precipitating factors. Chronic family stress is more likely to provoke relapses once the condition is established, especially when 'high emotional expression' is usual between family members.

While all these findings are important, what is of primary interest to evolutionary psychiatry is why in every human population so many people are born with a susceptibility to the condition. If there is such a thing as a *schizophrenic gene*, or a polygenic disposition to schizophrenia, what can be its selective advantage?

THE EVOLUTIONARY PERSPECTIVE

Schizophrenia presents a major challenge to the explanatory powers of evolutionary psychiatry. How can the bizarre qualities so typical of the disorder be derived from underlying characteristics to be found in normal biology and psychology? How is it that the genetic predisposition which results in schizophrenia in some people can result in adaptive traits in others? For adaptive the predisposition must be, otherwise it could no longer be with us. Far from eliminating it, natural selection has fixed it as an enduring component of the human genome.

When the genetic contribution to schizophrenia has been established, the media will doubtless herald the discovery of 'the schizophrenic gene'. But this would be misleading. For it seems probable that the genetic material responsible will be found in a much larger proportion of the population than the mere 1 per cent unfortunate enough to express it as a psychotic disease. Schizophrenia may well be the exorbitant price that some of us pay for humanity's possession of a valuable adaptive asset – in the same way that diabetes mellitus is the price paid by some people today for an adaptive mechanism which enabled our ancestors to survive in food-scarce environments in the past. What was once advantageous for the many, has now become disadvantageous for the few in an environment where sugar products abound. In a sense, schizotypal genes are like the genes responsible for sickle-cell anaemia, which enhance the well-being of carriers by protecting them from malaria while impairing those with greater genetic loading by afflicting them with anaemia. Parallels are to be drawn from psychiatric disorders where adaptive traits inherited by all human beings – for example, anxiety, phobias, depression, jealousy, excitement – may become maladaptive in certain individuals.

If, then, the predisposition that may result in schizophrenia is inherited in graded form, it could account for the kinds of personality organization which lie on a continuum between normality and psychosis – the schizoid, schizotypal and paranoid personality types. In both schizotypal and schizophrenic people similar perceptual aberrations occur, together with highly eccentric patterns of thinking, speech, and belief, the same self-referential sensitivity to outer events, and a heightened awareness of unusual ideas and images emanating from their minds. These features have often been subsumed under the term **schizophrenia spectrum disorder**. What possible advantages can such oddness bring?

The group-splitting hypothesis of schizophrenia

We believe that the predisposition to schizotypal thinking and behaviour has evolved in close association with other adaptations which together have resulted in the threefold enlargement of the human brain in the course of the past 3 million years. If mood disorders are the result of strategies that evolved much earlier in the context of competition between individuals, then schizoid disorders are the result of strategies that evolved more recently in the context of competition between groups. Whereas the ultimate function of the manic-depressive diathesis is to promote stability within the group, the ultimate function of the schizoid diathesis is to split the group into two incompatible subgroups when the original group has become too large.

Human groups, like all groups of social animals, possess an inherent dynamic to thrive and multiply until they reach a critical size at which the resources at their disposal are no longer adequate for their needs. At this point they become unstable, and split. When the split occurs, the group divides into two opposing factions, and all the mechanisms which previously served to promote group solidarity are put into reverse so as to drive the two subgroups apart. At this point, the issue of leadership becomes crucial for survival, because the leader has to inspire the departing group with its sense of mission and purpose, its need to unite against all odds, its belief that it can win through and find its own 'promised land'. Such a leader needs the sort of charisma traditionally granted by divine will and maintained through direct communion with the gods. It is when called upon to fulfil this exalted role that the schizoid genotype comes into its own.

This fissive process, repeated again and again wherever human groups have taken up residence, has had an adaptive function in spreading out human communities over the surface of the planet in a quest for new resources.

It is difficult, if not impossible, to know what our forebears must have gone through as a hunter-gatherer band grew beyond its critical size of 40–60 members and suffered the social tensions, the personal rivalries and conflicts, which paved the way for the eventual split. How would the decision to separate be taken? Who would leave and who would stay? Would there be a rational political decision, or would half the community suddenly get up and leave, like starlings abruptly setting off on their migration south? Would there be a preliminary polarization into two potential units, like an amoeba preparing to divide and reproduce itself? How much verbal and physical hostility would be generated between them? Would the subgroup that remained behind be in possession of the principal resources, and would the disaffected subgroup leave because these were denied them? How would they plan their departure? How would they know where to go and what to do when they got there? Could they possibly have risked the separation without a leader to inspire and guide them?

Answers to some of these questions may be gleaned from contemporary studies of disaffected groups which separate from their host community and set off in quest of some promised land. These studies indicate that having a charismatic leader is indispensable to the survival of such groups. Especially relevant to our argument is the finding that virtually all such leaders seem to be borderline or schizotypal personalities. In a brilliant investigation of charismatic leadership, Charles Lindholm (1990) describes how figures like Adolf Hitler, Jim Jones, and Charles Manson inspire incredible loyalty in the followers who gather round them. Yet to others unaffected by their personalities, they appear half mad, 'driven by violent rages and fears that would seem to make them repellent rather than attractive, while their messages look, from the perspective of the outsider, to be absurd melanges of half-digested ideas, personal fantasies and paranoid delusions.'

The relationship between charismatic leaders and the followers who gather round them has long been a subject for systematic scrutiny, and many have contributed valuable insights and terminologies to describe them: Weber's 'epileptic prophets', Durkheim's 'collective effervescence', Mesmer's 'animal magnetism' invested in the person of the hypnotist, Nietzsche's 'superman', Eliade's (1964) shamanic 'technicians of the sacred', the millennial cults of medieval Europe so vividly described by Norman Cohn (1970), and Le Bon's 'inspired leader' recruited from 'the ranks of those morbidly nervous, excitable, half-deranged persons who are bordering on madness' (Le Bon, 1952). When this information is collated, it throws valuable light on the fate of disaffected groups once they have selected and granted allegiance to a leader. The data can be summarized under five headings:

1 the personal qualities displayed by charismatic leaders;
2 the social conditions in which people turn to them;
3 the sanctification of the relationship of group members with each other and with the leader through religious forms and rituals;
4 the paranoid 'pseudospeciation' and genocide of other groups; and
5 the outcome: either the establishment of a new culture or the annihilation of the group.

1 **Charismatic leaders**. Nearly all are men, though history records some outstanding female examples, such as Joan of Arc. Of those for whom personal details exist, most would readily satisfy the DSM-IV criteria for **borderline, schizotypal**, or **paranoid personality disorder**. The most striking

thing about them is their *shamanic* quality. The Tungus noun *saman* means 'one who is excited, moved, raised.' As a verb, it means 'to know in an ecstatic manner.' Ethnological studies of shamans in Siberia, Africa, and North America reveal them to be close to the borderline but not over it: they are schizotypal, not schizophrenic (Price and Stevens, 1998). As with all charismatic leaders, their influence arises from the uncanny, hypnotic power of their personalities, the force of their rapidly shifting emotions, the bizarre manner of their speech, their capacity to enter a state of dissociation and to leave it at will, and their apparent ability to put themselves in close touch with the unconscious and to articulate its archetypal contents, in a way that convinces their followers that they are divinely inspired.

2 **Social conditions**. The social conditions from which charismatic leaders characteristically arise are similar to those which would have prevailed in an ancestral group that had outgrown its available resources – deprivation, mutual suspicion and hostility, lack of cohesion, the decay of traditional authority and values, desperation, an intensifying sense of crisis. All this induces paranoia and feelings of wounded narcissism among the alienated individuals of the disaffected group and renders them susceptible to the paranoid, 'borderline' utterances of the charismatic. In Germany, for example, all these circumstances were in place before the advent of Adolf Hitler – the social fragmentation and internal hostility following the defeat of the First World War, rocketing inflation followed by the great depression of 1929, millions out of work and on the breadline, government locked between the numerous parties of the left and the right, the sense of being victims of 'encirclement' by hostile neighbours, of being 'stabbed in the back by the traitors of 1918', and so on. A society in this chaotic state is ripe for domination by a borderline personality to reflect its misery and to empower it with a vision of salvation.

3 **Religious forms and rituals**. Central to the charismatic experience is the ecstatic merger of leader and led in a form of *participation mystique* which assumes religious intensity. The inspired figure is always one who stands apart, completely focused on his inner vision. This sets him on a level above that of ordinary humanity. It means that he speaks with the conviction of 'higher authority', which puts the followers in awe of him. They adore him and long to place themselves under his influence, for he can heal their fears of separation by giving them direction and welcoming them into the arms of a charismatic group. With time, this union, even in the most secular charismatic movement, assumes an unmistakably religious form, as the new group is bound together in its faith and rituals. Thus Nazism had its Messiah (Hitler), its Holy Book (*Mein Kampf*), its cross (the swastika), its religious processions (the Nuremberg Rally), its rituals (the Beer Hall Putsch remembrance parade), its anointed elite (the SS), its hymn (the Horst Wessel Lied), excommunication and death for heretics (the concentration camps), its devils (the Jews), its millennial promise (the Thousand Year Reich), and

its Promised Land (the East). The shamanic utterances of Hitler were legion: 'I'm now and then aware that it is not *I* who is speaking, but that something speaks through me.' 'I go the way Providence dictates with the assurance of a sleepwalker.' He claimed that he heard voices like those which inspired Joan of Arc: they told him to rescue the Fatherland from the Jews. He also claimed that he had a vision of Wotan pointing to the East above the heads of the cheering crowds at the time of the Austrian Anschluss. Again and again he declared that he and Germany were mystically merged: 'I know that everything that you are, you are through me, and everything I am, I am through you alone!'

4 **Paranoia and genocide**. As the group coalesces round its leader and celebrates its sense of being extraordinary, unparalleled, 'chosen', and unique, so it becomes increasingly hostile to all other groups. This is fuelled by a shared paranoia between leader and led. The actual nature of the paranoid belief system is usually 'revealed' to and by the leader with all the certainty of a delusional conviction: once formed it is unshakeable and all other beliefs centre round it. For Hitler, with his obsessions about disease, germs, and contamination, the elimination of the Jewish and Slavic peoples was an act of public hygiene indispensable for the purification of the world in preparation for the millennial rule of the Master Race. Erik Erikson introduced the term *pseudospeciation* to describe the way in which one human group can come to identify and treat members of other groups as if they were lower forms of animal life and not human at all. It then becomes possible to exterminate them without feelings of guilt. Hitler commonly referred to Jews as *Untermenschen* (subhumans). Charles Manson taught his white, middle-class dropouts that blacks were debased and unacceptable and, eventually, vilified all outsiders, excluding them from the territory of his 'family'. But Hitler was, in this evil particular, the charismatic leader par excellence: instead of leading a subgroup, he took over the host group, completely displacing the old guard, and then proceeded to mastermind the split in German society between the Aryans and the Jews. Having pseudospeciated the Jews he expelled those who could leave and began the extermination of those who could not, before leading his own people off into the promised land of the East.

5 **The outcome**. The tendency for charismatic movements to end in violence and bloodshed is as evident from recent history as it is in the history of the distant past. Hitler's paranoid vision inspired a civilized nation to fight the most destructive war and to commit the most massive genocide of a hideously strife-torn century, Jim Jones led nearly a thousand men, women and children of his Temple into a remote region of Guyana and told them to take cyanide (which they did willingly in the belief that they would accompany him to heaven), while Charles Manson, having convinced his disciples that he was Christ incarnate, led them in the apparently senseless killing of ten people.

*

How are we to understand these catastrophic outcomes in terms of the dynamics of group splitting? In the ancestral environment they must have been a common enough occurrence, when the number of populations had reached a balance with the available territorial resources. For the number of groups to remain constant once all spare land had been occupied, it would mean that as groups split to form new groups, an equal rate of group elimination would have to occur. Part of this elimination would have been due to natural causes such as starvation and disease, but the remainder would have been carried out by other groups in the form of genocidal warfare. Radcliffe-Brown's (1922) observations of conflict between tribesmen in the Andaman Islands lends support to this view. After some years of skirmishing with an enemy tribe, the elders would assemble beneath a banyan tree to lament the loss of their sons in battle and the destruction of their tribe's economy by the necessity of keeping it on a war footing. Eventually, a consensus would emerge that the time had come to wage a 'war to end all wars' so as to remove the menace for good and guarantee that their children and grandchildren could live in peace for ever. A massive effort would then be made to achieve the total destruction of the neighbouring group. Such was the thinking behind the Roman destruction of Carthage and the European destruction of the Amerindians.

Should the environment prove more hospitable and 'the Promised Land' be found and occupied, inaugurating a period of peace and prosperity, then the leader with his followers will create a new culture with new truths, new gods and, ultimately, a new language. For this achievement, schizotypal genes could prove indispensable.

Schizotypy and charisma

A number of schizotypal characteristics, especially in their *strong* form as manifested in an acute schizophrenic episode, lend themselves to the charismatic leadership of a split-off and migrating group. These include the cognitive dissonance, the preoccupation with religious themes and belief in the occult, the disordered language and use of neologisms, the mood changes, the delusions and hallucinations which typify the condition. These peculiarities could well make it possible for a single individual to detach himself sufficiently from the prevailing culture of his group to develop an entirely new, arbitrary belief system, which could be held with such conviction as readily to influence others when they were themselves in a disturbed or disaffected state. We shall examine each of the above characteristics in the light of this possibility.

Cognitive dissonance. Since the beliefs propounded by the prophet are likely to be incompatible with reality, there must be some means of reconciling the followers to these disparities when they occur. An example of this is the way in which the Jehovah's Witnesses periodically proclaim the date of Armageddon, only to have to revise it when the day arrives and passes with no sign of the predicted cataclysm. (This difficulty has led to the recent somewhat uncharismatic decision to abandon precise predictions in favour of the bland assertion that it will happen 'at some time in the future'.) The cognitive dissonance of schizotypy would not only permit the prophet to ignore this embarrassment but to demonstrate to his flock that his faith is in no way affected by it. A Maori prophet, Rua, who prophesied that King Edward VII would arrive in New Zealand on a date in June, 1906, with a gift of £3 million to enable Rua to buy back the Maori lands from the whites, gathered a group of approximately a thousand people around him. When both King and money failed to materialize, more than half his followers loyally accompanied him on a long march into the Urawera Mountains, where they established a farming community. Rua had many children, and remained the respected leader of the commune, preaching a religion based on the Old Testament. The settlement flourished until it was attacked and overwhelmed by the police in 1916 (Webster, 1979). Festinger (1957), who infiltrated a millennial cult, found that the non-occurrence of the leader's prediction of the world's end actually intensified the loyalty of his group. It was Hitler's cognitive dissonance that enabled him to go on talking of victory as the Russians approached the suburbs of Berlin in 1945 and to move divisions about on his war map that had long ceased to exist. Without this fatal schizotypal characteristic, the war may have ended somewhat earlier.

Religious preoccupations. The belief systems, moral values, and ruling ideology of the great majority of human communities have been rooted in religion. The religious tenets to which a group subscribes, and which differentiate it from all other groups, are held to have been 'revealed' to the founding fathers by the gods at the beginning of time. Such revelations commonly come in the form of visions, dreams, or supernatural voices. The probability is that those responsible for receiving these divine messages were well endowed with schizotypal genes. Revelations of this kind could have been of crucial importance to a disaffected group splitting off from its parent community and setting out on the perilous journey to the Promised Land.

The English psychologist Peter Chadwick (1997) has given a graphic account from his personal experience which illustrates the potential for religious leadership in the mildly schizophrenic state. Writing of his own schizophrenic illness he says he reached a point where he came to feel that he was in touch with 'a presence' – 'an awe-inspiring force, which existed, now, as if behind a thin membrane. Any sense of ego or identity was gone, I was a vehicle, a *channel*, my existence was "vehicular". Psychosis this was not, at least not yet. For example, there was no Messiah delusion: "A Christ could be said to *accompany* the world, but not a Borderliner," I penned. But there was none the less a sense of unearthly knowledge and of joy that pervaded me at this time – objectivity and ecstasy were now fused. My religiosity, such as it was, magnified a thousandfold. The Lord's Prayer resonated and thundered through my mind. I felt I had been given a spiritual mission of the utmost importance. I could "see to infinity", I had reached a zone where "the life system" was strangely making contact, through me, with "the not-of-this-life system" – as indeed maybe it was.'

The records of the Alister Hardy Research Centre in Oxford provide many examples of experiences which might be classified as psychotic or religious depending on their context (Jackson, 1997). In some, but of course not all, cases, the schizotypal or schizophrenic state appears to recruit an archetypal experience of being the channel between a transcendent entity and mankind. Such experiences are common among those who become prophets, less so among their followers. Followers may be prone to see apparitions, have out-of-body experiences, extrasensory perceptions, sleep paralysis, and contacts with the dead (McClennon, 1997), for such phenomena are reported by a larger percentage of the population than the kind of mystical experience described by Claridge (Hufford, 1992). People susceptible to paranormal experiences are also found to be more suggestible than average and have a greater capacity for dissociation (Schumaker, 1995); they are such stuff as cults are made on.

Disordered language. Language is both a uniter and a divider, in that it is fundamental to ingroup/outgroup distinctions. All geographically separated populations develop their own language on the basis of the 'language acquisition device' and 'deep structures' implicit in the human brain (Chomsky, 1965; Pinker, 1994). Even within the same nation, or tribal affiliation, dialects develop which strengthen ingroup loyalty and outgroup discrimination. Class distinctions, age group differences, subcultural affiliations (punks, drug addicts, bikers), professional identities (doctors, lawyers, soldiers, oil rig operatives) are all served by the use of special accents, terminologies, slang, acronyms, and tones of voice. As Aldous Huxley once observed, language is more effective at separating people than in keeping them together. 'The Americans and the English have everything in common,' said Oscar Wilde, 'except, of course, the language.' The speed with which a new group begins to assert its identity through the invention of new linguistic forms can be very rapid, and this probably played a significant role in group splitting, especially if it took place along generational lines. The schizotypal penchant for the production of idiosyncratic language, speech patterns and neologisms would have promoted this. The charismatic leaders' verbal mannerisms would be adopted by the subgroup and this would further vitiate relations with the old, parent group, thus facilitating the split.

Mood changes. The mercurial mood changes of the schizotypal personality are part of his 'uncanny' charismatic appeal to his followers. When depressed, the prophet sits brooding on the iniquities of his enemies, biding his time. When elated, the spirit enters into him, he proclaims his message, recruits supporters, and finds the necessary energy to lead them out of 'bondage' into the Promised Land.

Delusions and hallucinations. What is outstandingly abnormal about schizotypy is the failure to adjust to the consensual reality of the ingroup. Moreover, when paranoid ideation supervenes matters are made considerably worse by the 'perception' that ingroup members are in fact hostile members of an outgroup. Should a schizotypal leader succeed in communicating his paranoid ideas to a substantial portion of the ingroup, as, for example, Hitler succeeded in doing, then the situation becomes ripe for schism.

That paranoia is a natural accompaniment of group separation can be observed among immigrants and the authorities who deal with them. People from different ethnic backgrounds, as well as those who are political or economic refugees, commonly become suspicious and defensive in responding to the new surroundings, the rules and regulations, the new language, and the perceived indifference of the host society. This in turn generates fury and frustration among the immigration officials, and a vicious circle of mutual distrust is brought into being. While this does not constitute a diagnosable disorder, it nevertheless illustrates the function of paranoia in sowing dissension between subgroups and driving them apart.

Since group solidarity is maintained by a communality of belief, it is clear that a new group, if it is to split off, must create a new consensus which is at odds with the old. It is here that the schizotypal leader, with his genius for delusional and hallucinatory originality, can become indispensable. Delusions characteristically arrive in the mind intact and with the force of a revelatory insight. Once established, they are unshakeable. Held with absolute conviction, they are impervious to all rational argument. This intransigence can be impressive, especially to people who feel disaffected, bitter and uncertain about what to think or do. We are all to some extent both sceptical and credulous, and whether we embrace or dismiss a new idea depends very much on our state of mind when we encounter it. People who join cults usually do so when they have become alienated from their friends and families and have fallen into a state of pessimism and despair. The bizarre belief system of a new cult holds out to them the promise of salvation, and, if they can make the necessary cognitive leap, they may experience an ecstatic transcendence of their previously miserable existence. They find the light and the way. Marc Galanter (1989), who has studied this phenomenon, discovered that the more bizarre the belief, the more cohesive the group and the more elevated the mood of its members. This squares with the anthropological finding that every human population subscribes to a belief system, which appears arbitrary and irrational to outsiders, and which differentiates it from all other groups.

Delusions are commonly reinforced by auditory hallucinations. The prophet's 'voices', composed from elements of his unconscious mind, provide him with an inner reference group with which to test and confirm his convictions. Voices carry tremendous force when, as in the case of Joan of Arc, they are believed to be direct expressions of the Will of God. They are of particular importance to the charismatic when he is in a state of isolated withdrawal before any followers have gathered round him. Even for the schizotype, it is difficult, without at least one close confidant, to maintain an intact belief system in opposition to the majority view. In the absence of outer companions, voices may compensate by providing the necessary support.

Though our emphasis is primarily on the ultimate (evolutionary) causes of schizophrenia spectrum disorder rather than the proximate (individual) causes, we certainly do not wish to minimize the importance of neuropathology in the aetiology of the condition. For example, Frith (1994) has suggested that schizophrenic delusions and hallucinations are due to deficient self-monitoring. When we think, speak, or make some movement, there are 'corollary discharges' in the central nervous system that inform us that these thoughts, words and actions are, in fact, our own. When we move our eyes, for instance, a perceived object shifts its position on the retina, yet, subjectively, we experience the object as remaining in the same place. If, however, the eye muscles are experimentally paralysed with curare, an attempt to shift the gaze results in a subjective sense of the room spinning round. In schizophrenia, Frith argues, there is a central nervous abnormality which prevents these corollary discharges from getting through to their appropriate receptors, so that our subliminal speech is heard in the form of hallucinatory voices, and our actions appear to be directed from outside. Such a failure in self-monitoring could well be a component of the 'spontaneous mazeway resynthesis' (Wallace, 1956) or 'hierophantic realization' (Eliade, 1958) characteristic of the schizotypal prophet. His new ideas and beliefs would then seem to come from outside and would be attributed to the direct intervention of God.

SCHIZOTYPY, SCHIZOPHRENIA, AND RANK

The question as to why some people with a genetic loading for schizotypy become charismatic leaders while others become schizophrenic patients can be partially answered in terms of, first, the weight of the genetic load and, second, the social context.

The better prognosis of schizophrenics living in traditional, cognitively coherent, non-industrial societies would suggest that the breakdown of

community bonds and the loss of a cognitive consensus may act synergistic-
ally with genetic factors to produce the higher incidence and worse prognosis of schizophrenia in industrial societies. In line with this reasoning is
the finding of an increased incidence of schizophrenia among immigrants to
Western countries and among populations living in recently industrialized
areas of the Third World.

Schizotypal traits typically come to medical attention at about the time
when young people are in the process of disengaging from their families of
origin and when their primary preoccupations are with acceptance by and
membership of their peer group and with fears of being rejected or excluded. In pre-industrial societies, the difference between the family milieu
and the social milieu was less great and initiation rituals facilitated the transition. But Western society provides no such assistance and young people
who combine a schizotypal predisposition with low self-esteem and with a
lack of emotional support are at greater risk. The poor educational and
vocational performance typical of those liable to develop schizophrenia
means that they must endure low social status, and this forces them into a
strategy of either submissiveness or withdrawal.

The situation begins to look brighter, however, if the oddly withdrawn
and aloof individual is perceived as having charismatic qualities, especially
if the peer group is in need of a charismatic leader to enable it to split off
from the parent group and to migrate. Then the power of the schizotype's
inner vision, previously experienced in solitary seclusion, may begin to
influence others, transforming its originator from subdominant to dominant status, and granting him a new and significant identity, boosted by the
adulation of his supporters. In this way a collective crisis can provide the
necessary circumstances to divert the schizotypal individual from a
schizophrenic career by granting him a highly valued, socially integrated
role. Thus, although the charismatic leader may well possess the underlying neuro-psychic predisposition to become schizophrenic, he is protected from psychosis by the adulation, affirmation and authority conferred on him by his group. It follows that if for any reason his charismatic career should be cut short, the resultant loss of status could induce
a breakdown, whether schizophrenic, schizo-affective, or purely depressive
in nature.

The 'ideas of reference', the exquisite self-consciousness, and the fears of
being stared at so characteristic of people with a schizotypal disposition are
also related to considerations of social rank and SAHP. The fear of being
stared at is the fear of being attacked. Interestingly, the eye is one of the
most common features of schizotypal art. How are we to relate this phenomenon to our evolutionary heritage? Ethological studies have shown that
staring and visual attention are very important among all social mammals.
The higher a dominant animal ranks in the social hierarchy, the more the
less-dominant members of the society stare at and attend to him. Dominant

animals accept such attention as rightfully due to them and are unperturbed by it, but if a subdominant animal is stared at by a dominant animal, the subdominant experiences it as frightening and intimidating. A dominant animal's stare is usually one of reproof and is aggressive in intent.

The same is true in human communities. Kings, queens, presidents, prime ministers, television personalities, and pop stars all thrive on being looked at and attended to. Their self-esteem usually glories in such regard. But a person of low status who is stared at, or one with feelings of low self-esteem, experiences it as threatening and a cause for alarm. A schizotypal person with low self-esteem is, therefore, manifesting a normal mammalian response in his or her dislike of being the subject of visual scrutiny.

Schizoid withdrawal is, after all, associated with feelings of being different from all other people and with a dread of attracting notice and receiving the attention of others. Fear of being 'seen through' and recognized as 'odd' or as an 'outsider' induces stress, and confirms the defensive strategy of social avoidance. Isolation leads to a failure to edit thoughts, speech and behaviour in line with what is perceived by other group members to be appropriate, and to a perpetuation of conceptual errors and deviant behaviour patterns despite consensual disapproval (so called 'cognitive slippage'). This opens up the route to psychosis. Driven further into himself, the besieged individual falls victim to his inner voices, idiosyncratic ideas and disordered thought processes. No longer certain about the distinction between inner and outer reality, he becomes confused about all interpersonal boundaries and inundated with feelings of influence and persecution. There is now nothing left between him and schizophrenia.

GROUP SPLITTING AND GROUP SELECTION

To summarize the position developed so far: we have suggested that the schizotypal genotype is an adaptation whose function is to facilitate group splitting, and that this is achieved by the formation of a subgroup or cult under the influence of a charismatic leader, who is enabled by his borderline psychotic thinking to separate himself from the dogma and ideals of the main group, and to persuade his followers that he is uniquely qualified to lead them to salvation in a promised land.

Up to this point, we have been concerned with the relation between group splitting and individual psychopathology. However, it is important that we should also place the phenomenon of group splitting in its wider biological context. Among animals living in groups, group splitting is a necessary preliminary to *dispersal*. In many animal species two classes of phenotype are apparent: the maintenance phenotype and the dispersal phenotype (Geist, 1978, 1994). The *maintenance phenotype* is best adapted to the existing habitat. The *dispersal phenotype* is adapted to facilitate movement to a new habitat and ensure survival in conditions which differ from those prevailing in the natal environment. Accordingly, the schizotypal personality could be viewed as a form of dispersal phenotype. It constitutes a high-risk strategy, for most dispersal phenotypes perish. But should they prove adaptive in a new environment, they may promote the 'adaptive radiation' of new dynasties.

Thus, the schizotypal personality has the capacity for creating a new community with a new world view; but most individuals with this personality disorder achieve little or nothing; and those who become psychotic tend to end up forming a 'pseudocommunity' of delusional referents in a long-stay ward or community 'rest home' (Lemert, 1967). However, a small number become founders of new communities in reality, and it is the enhanced reproductive success of these privileged individuals that compensates for the reduced fertility of schizophrenic patients.

A further theoretical possibility is that the schizotypal personality may facilitate group selection for altruistic characteristics. In any group there will be free-riders as well as altruists. If a particular group is to be selected in preference to other competing groups, it is essential that altruists should substantially outnumber free-riders. It is therefore important that group splitting should occur rapidly enough to prevent the number of free-riders achieving numerical superiority over altruists. Consequently, it follows that any factor that promotes the rate at which groups split will make the possibility of group selection more likely. The emergence of schizotypal personalities in groups could constitute such a factor, providing the conditions necessary for group selection to occur. Since this is an unfashionable position to adopt, it requires some justification.

The concept of group selection has had a bumpy ride. Early geneticists, such as R.A. Fisher (1930), J.B.S. Haldane (1955) and S. Wright (1931; 1948; 1980), believed group selection to be possible in theory but unlikely in practice. On the whole, it was thought that free-riding individuals would reproduce more rapidly than altruistic individuals prepared to sacrifice selfish interests for the good of the group, and that, as a consequence, group selection would be unlikely to occur.

However, the idea once more became a subject of interest in the 1950s as a result of the work of V.C. Wynne-Edwards (1962; 1965). He suggested that if populations were not to outgrow their food supply and become extinct, they would have to regulate their numbers, and that such regulation would require certain individuals to refrain from reproduction. The only way in which such unselfish behaviour could evolve, Wynne-Edwards argued, was through group selection. But the triumph of the 'selfish gene' theory in the 1970s put an end to such speculation by establishing to most people's satisfaction that altruistic behaviour can be accounted for by kin selection leading to higher inclusive fitness. Since then the idea of group selection has been in abeyance, supported only by a few stalwart mavericks like Irenäus Eibl-Eibesfeldt (1995), David Sloan Wilson (1997), and Sober and Wilson

(1998), and like Stephen Jay Gould (1992), who holds that selection proceeds at several levels simultaneously – that is, at the levels of genes, organisms, local populations and species.

Our own equating of the schizotypal genotype with group splitting has persuaded us to look again at the phenomenon of group selection, and to ask whether this might not be a unique human adaptation, just as schizophrenia is a unique human disease. The argument against group selection is not only that free-riders would multiply too quickly but that there is too much genetic transfer between groups for group selection to be either feasible or necessary. In addition, it is argued that groups do not split frequently enough nor do they sufficiently often become extinct for group selection to occur. But these arguments do not take into consideration the major change in the form of social competition which has occurred over the last few million years. Those who argue against group selection may seriously underestimate the rate at which human groups split and the frequency with which numbers of them became extinct under the conditions prevailing in ancestral environments.

Attention has already been drawn (see p. 51) to the way in which competition by attraction (hedonic competition) has evolved alongside agonistic competition, and to the fact that success in hedonic competition serves to raise a component of individual self-esteem that Gilbert has called social attention holding power (SAHP). Both sociologists (for example, Kemper, 1984; 1990) and anthropologists (for example, Barkow, 1980) have stressed the importance of voluntarily bestowed status and prestige in human social relations. Since the capacity for agonistic competition still resides in human beings, virtually all communities have sanctions against it, so as to permit hedonic competition to prevail. These sanctions, which have been described under the heading of 'counter-dominance' by Boehm (1993), effectively prevent powerful individuals from forcibly wresting leadership from whoever has been appointed by the will of the group. Even our own society is reasonably successful at eliminating agonistic behaviour from the main forums of social competition, confining it to places where sanctions have little influence, such as the school playground and the prison cell.

In hedonic competition, two rivals display, not to each other (as in agonistic competition) but to the group as a whole, presenting their attractive qualities in an effort to elicit group approbation. The group members' response (either approbation or disapprobation) differentially raises or lowers the self-esteem of those who are displaying, and at the same time confers on them differential prestige (which is the systemic correlate of SAHP). This evaluative process is extended to all members of the group, with the result that a rank order is established, with each group member having a rating on the prestige scale. The criteria of evaluation differ according to the status competed for: high-ranking individuals are evaluated for qualities of leadership, while low-rankers may be evaluated for whether they merit membership of the group at all. In the Kurelu people of New Guinea, for example, the prestige scale extends from the 'Big Man' at the top down to the lowly *kepu* (which literally means 'pubic hair') at the bottom (Matthiessen, 1962). But at all social levels, an important component of evaluation concerns the willingness of the individual to sacrifice personal interests to those of the group.

The extended childhood of human beings allows the community plenty of time to evaluate new members long before they reach the age of reproduction. It would be extremely difficult for a free-rider to pass this long scrutiny, to say nothing of the testing ordeals of painful and demanding rites of initiation, without betraying his selfish tendencies. Should any free-rider reach marriageable age without being ejected, he will find his opportunities limited by the strict rules of the group. Marriages are commonly arranged by members of the older generation, who are well aware of everyone's reputation. If a free-rider fails to win a bride, he can, of course, try for an extramarital impregnation. But with unmarried girls this is likely to end in abortion or infanticide, and with married women he will be up against their jealous husbands and their fear of acquiring a reputation as a 'whore'. It is unlikely, therefore, that the genes of selfish individuals can enjoy such an overwhelmingly easy ride in human communities as many geneticists assume.

That competition by attraction has come very largely to replace competition by intimidation has been facilitated by the parallel development of the human capacity to communicate through speech. That group members can discuss one another, means that they can readily allocate favourable or unfavourable reputations, granting high rank to those who are competent and public spirited as well as identifying and eliminating free-riders. The ability to detect free-riding qualities has led to such concepts as the 'cad', 'bounder', or psychopath. The charismatic leader, with his paranoid traits, may be expected to excel at such detection.

Language could contribute to the group selection process in a number of significant ways:

1 It promotes group splitting by enabling the charismatic leader to transmit his message of salvation to his disciples and mobilize their departure from the parent group.
2 It permits the detection of free-riders, enabling group members to give them a bad reputation and to eliminate them from the marriage market.
3 It enables group members to discuss the criteria by which prestige is to be allocated, and to pass these criteria on to subsequent generations, celebrating them in heroic myths, legends and songs.
4 It promotes the extinction of neighbouring groups by labelling them as 'subhuman' and therefore meriting elimination.
5 It reduces genetic transfer between neighbouring groups by maintaining their independent and separate existence through differences in accent and

dialect. It also allows laws to be passed against miscegenation as the Nazis did with their notorious 'Blood Protection Law' in Nuremberg on 15 September 1935, which forbade marriage and any sexual contact between Aryans and Jews.

In addition to the use of language to pseudospeciate neighbours, the human psyche has other capacities which seem all too well adapted to the successful extermination of competing groups. These include the tendency of every group to see itself as 'chosen' to be the centre of the universe and everyone else as barbarians; the ready mobilization of patriotic fervour when the group is insulted and threatened from outside; the willingness of young men to be heroes, to go off and die for their nation, and the willingness of their families to encourage them to go; the belief that the tribal gods are the only true gods and that all mankind should be made to submit to them or die, to name but a few (Stevens, 1989).

We can, therefore, visualize human groups going through different functional phases. First, there is a growth phase when numbers increase to the carrying capacity of the habitat. Then, if there is a hostile neighbour, a war phase may intervene, with gradual escalation of hostilities until the other group is eliminated. This is followed by a further growth phase to replace the members lost in the war. When the carrying capacity of the habitat is again reached, there being no longer a hostile neighbour, the process of group splitting occurs. Part of the group departs, possibly under the leadership of a charismatic figure, to occupy new territory – perhaps that which previously belonged to the group which has been destroyed. The two groups then become established as separate entities, with their own emerging dialect and beliefs, and, as their numbers multiply, become enemies in their turn. In this manner the process of group selection could proceed.

CONCLUSION

Hedonic competition represents a new and specifically human form of intrasexual selection. For the first time in evolutionary history, competition between rivals is decided, not by physical conflict between the rivals themselves, but through evaluation by third parties. This represents a revolutionary change in the whole selection process, because the *criteria* for selection (that is, the criteria on which the third party evaluation is based) are *culturally* determined. This allows new criteria for selection to emerge, for when groups with different criteria go to war with one another, it will lead to rapid selection of those criteria sets which promote greater group efficiency. This new form of selection, which may be called **externally mediated sexual selection**, represents the most radical development in the evolutionary process since sexual selection itself emerged partially to replace natural selection as the main evolutionary agent.

Furthermore, **mate selection** has also become externally mediated in groups where marriages are arranged for young people by their elders – a common procedure in traditional and primordial societies. This introduces to human sexual relations a form of **artificial selection** such as that so effectively employed by breeders of animals and plants.

These changes, we believe, contributed to the explosive increase in brain capacity over the past 3 million years and to the complexities of human psychology and society as they have developed up to the present time. In particular, we believe that the genetic tendency to schizophrenia evolved in the context of a runaway process which involved rapid group splitting, rapid group elimination, externally mediated sexual selection, and gives rise to the possiblity of selection between groups. The whole process was facilitated by and contributed to the evolution of language.

Part V

REPRODUCTIVE DISORDERS

14

REPRODUCTIVE SUCCESS AND FAILURE

It is not the business of evolutionary psychiatry to adopt moralistic attitudes to the phenomena it describes, but to make human behaviour, and its disturbances, comprehensible in evolutionary terms. In the past, psychiatrists have discussed reproductive disorders under such headings as **sexual perversions** or **sexual deviations**, using a tone of clipped disapproval to indicate that they, like their readers, will find the whole subject distasteful and one to be passed over as quickly as possible. Evolutionary psychiatry cannot indulge in such cursory condescension, since it regards reproductive success as the ultimate goal of human behaviour. Variations in reproductive behaviour must, therefore, be a primary focus of our study.

Instead of the pejorative terms applied by traditional psychiatry, DSM-IV prefers to classify alternatives to 'normal' sexual behaviour as **paraphilias** ('parallel forms of loving', from the Greek *para* = beside, and *philia* = love).

In our view, paraphilias merit consideration as psychiatric disorders only when, first, they preclude sexual reproduction, and, second, they are a source of distress, guilt, or shame to the individual attracted by them. Paraphilias become a psychiatric problem only if society disapproves of them. When social attitudes change – as they have, for example, in the case of homosexuality – the psychiatric prognosis for those who experience their sexual orientation as burdensome is immeasurably improved.

HUMAN REPRODUCTIVE TASKS

The achievement of reproductive success makes such demands on the individual that it is not surprising that so many aspects of the human ethogram are implicated. These have been summarized by Buss (1991) as follows:

1 To compete with members of one's own sex to attract mates.
2 To select a mate possessing the greatest reproductive value available.
3 To achieve conception.
4 To retain one's mate once selected.
5 To form reciprocal alliances.

6 To build coalitions and participate in co-operative groups.
7 To ensure the survival and reproductive success of offspring.
8 To invest in kin other than offspring.

Although the human mind-brain evidently contains a large number of strategies which have evolved to achieve specific adaptive tasks (which happen incidentally to promote inclusive fitness), fitness is to be conceived as an ultimate goal not a proximate motivation. Reproduction is the overriding biological objective of sexuality, but it is seldom experienced as such, since few, apart from the devoutly religious, mix sexual enjoyment with the conscious intention of producing children. Sexuality is concerned as much with pleasure and with bonding as with procreation. But it provides the necessary alchemy to draw men and women together in a committed relationship of sufficient duration to produce and rear their progeny.

Sexuality is thus more than a mere 'drive' or amorphous 'instinct'; it is better conceived as an archetypal system because of its typical behavioural expressions, its universality and its power. Bonding with a sexual partner is a matter of far greater significance than the mere gratification of lust.

MALE AND FEMALE STRATEGIES

Both males and females approach marriage with a different set of conscious assumptions and unconscious motives. Biology can make certain practical observations and theoretical predictions as to what these assumptions and motives will be. 'In the most distinct classes of the animal kingdom,' wrote Charles Darwin (1871), 'with mammals, birds, reptiles, fishes, insects, and even crustaceans, the differences between the sexes follow almost exactly the same rules; the males are almost always the wooers. . . .'

The female, Darwin observed, is far less eager than the male. She is coy and altogether more selective. Her reticence leaves males with no other choice than to compete with one another for her favours. This explains why males of many species have evolved special weapons, such as horns and large canine teeth, the better to fight one another when females come into oestrus. While human males possess no such specialized equipment, human females are no less choosy than their mammalian sisters in preferring a male of good strong, healthy physique with adequate status, sincerity and commitment to guarantee that he will stand by her till her offspring have reached sexual maturity. For their part, males are looking for a young, healthy female, with ample mammary glands and broad hips, capable of bearing them many children.

George Williams (1966) was the first to draw attention to the unequal *sacrifices* that males and females have to make in order to achieve reproductive success. For mammalian males, the necessary sacrifice is virtually zero in terms of energy and resource expenditure: their essential role ends with copulation. For females, on the other hand, copulation is only the beginning. And in terms of sexual economics it is hard to escape the feeling that natural selection has been grossly unfair. The relative cost to the mother in time, effort, calories, energy, and pain, is so much greater than to the father that it confirms one's impression that nature can have no sense of justice at all. Yet the father's genes benefit equally with those of the mother. It is in the female's genetic interest, therefore, to assume the burdens of reproduction only when the social and economic circumstances are propitious and when she has taken great care to select the fittest available male.

Williams characterized male courtship behaviour as an advertising campaign by which a man seeks to persuade a potential female partner of just how splendidly fit he is. But if the female is not to be short-changed, it is essential that she should be able to detect false advertising when she sees it. There is psychological evidence that human females are particularly gifted in such detection.

Responding to Williams's ideas, Robert Trivers (1972) proposed that *sacrifice* should be replaced by the idea of *investment*. While females inevitably make the higher investment in offspring, the actual degree of imbalance between maternal and paternal investment is less great in humans than in many other species. Human fathers invest far more time, attention, guidance, and love in their offspring, for example, than male chimpanzees. However, the disparity exists, and Trivers argued that the degree of disparity in any given species would be correlated with certain behaviours, such as the extent to which males would be eager to copulate and females prudent to select, the proneness of either sex to be faithful or unfaithful, and so on. Thus it would be predicted that human males, relative to females, would be more promiscuous, less discerning, more prone to casual, anonymous sex and to the use of prostitutes and pornography. Many independent studies have established that this is indeed the case for men across a variety of different cultures.

The ease with which males can get their genes into the next generation is apparent from the simple fact that men produce infinitely more sperms than women do ova. In the course of her reproductive lifetime a woman will produce little more than 400 eggs, while a man produces between 100 million and 200 million individual sperms, each containing a unique combination of his genes, every time he ejaculates. It follows that one man could, given the opportunity, inseminate and fertilize large numbers of women, and this disparity is reflected in the psychology of the two sexes. The relative promiscuity of the male makes opportune sex far more appealing to him than it does to the female, with her need for masculine commitment; and anthropology has established that polygyny seems to be the natural state for humanity, in the sense that men, given the chance of taking more than one wife, are strongly inclined to do so. Of the 1,154 societies for which anthropologists have data, no less than 980 of them (and that includes practically all known hunter-gatherer societies) have allowed a man to have two or more wives.

It is reasonable to conclude, therefore, that if males evolved to compete for scarce female eggs, then females evolved to compete for scarce male investment (Wright, 1994), and marriage evolved for the protection of women and children by adding social coercion to reinforce the strength of the man's commitment to them. When marriage is weakened as an institution and divorce made easy, it is women and children who suffer more than men. Moreover, men are much more likely than women to marry after a divorce, for they tend to marry younger women who are often marrying for the first time. This is a further example of a disparity between the sexes, reflecting different biological imperatives. When David Buss (1989) examined the marital statistics of 37 different cultures, he found that in every one of them males preferred younger females as partners (the younger the woman the more children she can bear) and females preferred older males (on the whole, they enjoyed higher status and more resources than younger males). Asked why they want younger wives, men do not, of course, explain their preference in reproductive terms but in terms of physical attractiveness. But beauty is the external sign of youth and fertility.

SEX AND GENDER

The sex of a new individual is determined at the moment of conception by the presence or absence of a Y chromosome. All foetuses develop along female lines unless at least one Y chromosome is present. The effect of a Y chromosome is to cause testes to form in the sixth week after fertilization. From that moment onwards the foetus manufactures its own male hormones (the androgens) and it begins to follow a distinctively male, as opposed to female, ground plan. The radical influence of male hormone secretion on foetal development is due to the fact that the testes become productive *before* the formation of the external genitalia and the brain. This means that the neurophysiological foundations for the later development of personality, cognitive function, social and sexual behaviour are laid under the powerful influence of steadily increasing quantities of androgen.

While the normal male carries one X and one Y chromosome, the normal female carries two X chromosomes. The presence of two X chromosomes means that the gonads are differentiated later, and the two ovaries are not formed until the sixth month. For the first six weeks of life, therefore, the embryo is hermaphroditic, in the sense that the foetus has the same physical structure whether it is male or female.

The physical consequences of possession of a Y chromosome for early gender distinctions are so obvious that there can be little dispute about them. Male foetuses grow faster than females, and at birth male infants are

168

both heavier and longer. Thereafter, from infancy to old age, males have larger and more powerful muscles; their hearts are bigger and stronger; their lungs have greater vital capacity; and their basal metabolic rate is higher. They make better athletes in that they can run faster, jump higher and put shots further; their pectoral girdle makes overarm throwing stronger and more accurate; and their hand grip is, on average, twice as strong as women's. The cardiovascular system of men is better able to adapt to stress and physical exertion, and one function of the male hormone, testosterone, is to promote the formation of red blood cells, with the result that, after puberty, male blood has more haemoglobin than female blood and can carry more oxygen. Males are also more efficient at eliminating metabolites like lactic acid, which are the by-products of muscular activity. The most striking female differences, on the other hand, become apparent after puberty, with the development of a larger pelvis, wider hips, and capacious breasts.

From the behavioural standpoint, men engage in more risk-taking activities than women, especially between the ages of 16 and 24, the peak period for mate competition (Wilson and Daly, 1985). Women show superior object memory and spatial-location memory compared with men (a possible adaptation to gathering edible fruit, berries, and vegetables), while men show greater spatial-rotation ability compared with women (a possible adaptation to hunting) (Silverman and Eals, 1992).

It is clear that in the course of evolution males have adapted more than females to a mode of existence which is physically demanding. This is evidently the biological basis of the **division of labour** between the sexes that is characteristic of the great majority of societies known to anthropology, where child-rearing is almost invariably the responsibility of women and hunting and warfare the responsibility of men. These differences have less to do with cultural stereotypes than some fashionable contemporary notions would have us believe. Yet the unsustainable idea that gender differences are due entirely to culture and have nothing to do with biology still enjoys wide currency in our society, even though it rests on the discredited **tabula rasa theory** of human ontogeny. Research in child development, initiated by Bowlby and by Ainsworth (1964) in the 1950s and continued over the last forty years, has corroborated their view that the human infant is no blank slate, passively submitting to the inscription of life's lessons, but an active participant in the developmental process. While there can be no doubt that environmental factors exert an enormous influence over an individual's psychological development, what these factors influence are the evolved predispositions with which all children are born.

Like every other major behavioural system, sexuality is present a priori as an archetypal component which manifests itself in the course of development. Freud drew attention to certain 'component instincts' of adult sexuality, such as clasping and pelvic thrust, as being present from a surprisingly early age and provided striking behavioural evidence for the existence of what he called, to the horror of his contemporaries, **infantile sexuality**.

The gender differences which are already apparent at birth become more evident as the child grows towards puberty. A child's awareness of its gender is established by as early as 18 months of age, and the bond to the father is important if this is to be satisfactorily achieved. Studies of children reared without fathers have indicated that they are more likely to experience difficulty in defining their gender identity than children whose fathers are present during the first years of life. It is probable that a reliable father-figure is particularly important if a boy is to actualize, both in consciousness and behaviour, his own masculine potential. Many studies confirm the relatively high incidence of sex-role confusion in boys who grow up without fathers, and the relative absence of such confusion in fatherless girls. As gender-consciousness emerges, a boy comes to recognize that his bond to his father is based on shared *identity*, while the girl comes to appreciate that it is based on *difference* (that is, the father presents her with her first profound experience of the essential 'otherness' of the male).

Although a father is not crucial to the development of a girl's gender-identity, he can nevertheless significantly influence the way in which she *experiences* her femininity in relation to a man. Girls who grow up without fathers may have little doubt that they are women, but when it comes to living with a man as his partner they can feel badly confused and unprepared. It is as if they lack the necessary psychic vocabulary.

Fathers and mothers are important, therefore, in enabling their children not only to establish a sense of gender but also in assuring their capacity to make good relationships with members of the opposite sex. Once established, gender and contrasexual awareness are refined through interaction with the peer group, especially in play. Many of the gender roles and attitudes adopted by children in play are, of course, culturally related, based on mimicry of the parents and other significant adults in the community. But, as we have already noted, these cultural influences proceed on the basis of an archetypal design, determined by the evolutionary history of our species. Patterns of playful activity have been studied in numerous human and animal communities. Young male rhesus monkeys, for example, characteristically indulge in rowdy forms of rough-and-tumble play, while young females prefer to pass their time in more gentle activities such as mutual grooming. The innate basis for this difference has been demonstrated experimentally: deprived of all opportunity to learn through imitation, rhesus infants reared in isolation from birth will nevertheless manifest the behaviours typical of their sex when given the chance to do so on introduction to their peers.

Similar differences are apparent in the play patterns of human young in a variety of different cultures. Throughout childhood, girls tend to be more **affiliative** than boys in that they are more prone to seek the proximity of others and to display pleasure in doing so. Boys, on the other hand, are less interested in social interaction for its own sake and prefer to spend their time in some form of **physical activity**, such as running, chasing, and playing with large, movable toys. One study investigated the behaviour of boys and girls in six cultures – India, Okinowa, the Philippines, Mexico, Kenya, and New England – and found essentially similar patterns of male and female behaviour in all of them. In all cases, girls were found to be more nurturant and affiliative, boys more physically active and aggressive (Whiting, 1963).

In another study, Low (1989) examined child-rearing practices in 93 different cultures and found that boys are consistently trained to show greater fortitude, aggression, and self-reliance than girls, while girls are consistently trained to be more responsible, obedient, and sexually restrained than boys. Low also noted that the more polygynous the society, the more intensely competitive the boys were trained to be. These findings are in accordance with predictions based on evolutionary theory.

For both sexes, adolescence is a time of heightened interest in sexual activity, increased pleasure in sexual fantasy, heightened self-consciousness, and greater sensitivity to peer group opinion. For males, it is also a time of increased risk-taking and of intense competition with other males for status and access to females. School, which tends to facilitate the emergence of these gender-related components of the personality, represents a modern extension of the trials, ordeals, and rituals incorporated in ancient puberty initiation rites: sexually segregated schools strengthen the identity of children with their own sex, while sexually mixed schools enable their pupils to fill out their a priori assumptions about the qualities and characteristics of the opposite sex. Whatever the academic environment, however, peer play between the sexes is an important preliminary to later success in courtship and marriage.

SUMMARY

The consequences of intrauterine and extrauterine influences on the development of gender-related patterns of behaviour are evident in virtually all human societies, and they may be summarized as follows:

1 The greater strength, size and aggressiveness of males equips them to compete with each other for rank and female partners, to patrol and hunt over a large territorial range, and to compete with neighbouring groups for environmental resources.
2 The highly developed spatial ability of males equips them to explore the physical environment and to maintain an accurate sense of orientation when away on the hunt, while their efficient co-ordination of large muscle groups enables them to use weapons and throw projectiles effectively.

3 The widespread occurrence of male puberty initiation rites serves to test and validate masculine hunting and warrior skills, to cement bonds between males of the same cadre, and to eliminate 'free-riders' from the group.

4 The evolved sexual strategies for males prompt them to be lustful, novelty-seeking, susceptible to visually arousing erotic stimuli, and interested in casual sex.

5 The extended family configuration of small human groups develops the qualities of nurturance, loyalty and devotion in females so that they function effectively as mothers, educating their offspring and protecting them up to the age of puberty.

6 The highly developed communication skills of females (language, feelings, intuitions) equip them to maintain close attachment bonds with their children, husbands, and kin.

7 Female puberty initiation rites, where they occur, affirm a female's status in the community as a mature woman capable of fulfilling her reproductive functions.

8 The evolved sexual strategies for females prompt them to be selective and to seek to confine sexual relations to the context of a secure and lasting relationship.

MARITAL PROBLEMS

The facts of sexual dimorphism as well as the different reproductive strategies followed by males and females have, since time immemorial, provided rich soil for the seeds of marital conflict to take root and fructify. For all their inherent differences, however, both males and females want a mate to be attractive, sincere, loving, and faithful.

Female fidelity reassures a man that in caring for his wife and her offspring he is fostering the reproductive future of his own genes, while male fidelity reassures a woman that enough food and protection will be available for her children to grow up and produce her grandchildren. Such ubiquitous human torments as **jealousy**, **anxiety**, and **fear** of losing one's partner, can therefore be seen as adaptive mechanisms designed to maintain fidelity. Because these emotions are so powerful and so potentially disturbing, they commonly have psychiatric consequences. Fears about remaining healthy, strong, attractive and young in order to keep one's mate have been a ready source of anxiety to countless generations of people, especially wives. What will happen if she loses her desirable attributes? This preoccupation has become particularly prevalent in a world where divorce has become easy and promiscuity less frowned upon. Marriage is evidently more adaptive than promiscuity and probably more conducive to psychological well-being. Promiscuity, it is true, gives males more access to more females and grants females immediate access to resources, but without long-term commitment of the male to the female the chances for offspring (and gene) survival are greatly reduced.

The major threat to a marriage is, of course, the fear that one partner will defect and seek an alternative partner elsewhere. Both partners are to varying degrees vigilant to this possibility and quick to experience jealousy at the prospect of it occurring. The focus of jealous concern is different for the two sexes: male jealousy is focused primarily on whether sexual penetration has occurred or not, while female jealousy is concerned with losing the exclusive commitment of the husband. Similarly, when adultery does occur, the motives differ along gender lines: for a male, the motive is often sexual novelty, erotic satisfaction having become jaded through over familiarity with the same partner; for a woman, the motive is usually the perception that another man is superior to her husband in status, integrity, and loyalty.

When sexual differences arise within the marriage, these too are commonly related to underlying conflicts determined by evolutionary forces. Males are more readily aroused than females and more easily satisfied. This makes biological sense. A man who reaches orgasm only very slowly may well be able to please his partner by bringing her to orgasm before him. But, being satisfied, she may decline to continue, with the result that his genes will not achieve their goal. Equally, a woman who reaches orgasm quickly and stops intercourse before her partner has ejaculated, will not enjoy the same reproductive success as women whose sexual appetites are less eager. It can be difficult, therefore, for marital partners to synchronize their sexual responses to the point of mutual satisfaction.

Moreover, it has been estimated that a third of women never achieve orgasm during intercourse and that another third do so only occasionally. This points up a further difference between male and female strategies. In males, the reproductive significance of orgasm is crucial, for it coincides with ejaculation. For women, however, orgasm is of little or no biological importance, since they are just as likely to become pregnant whether they have an orgasm or not. But a woman's desire to experience orgasm and a husband's inability to give her one before he is spent and ready for sleep may be a cause of considerable frustration and discontent.

In view of the apparent biological irrelevance of orgasm in females, the question arises as to how and why women have orgasms at all. One interesting suggestion has been made by Donald Symons (1979): that the neurophysiological mechanisms responsible for orgasm are present in both males and females even though they are of reproductive importance only to the male. This is because the genetic blueprints for males and females have, in the interests of functional simplicity, remained basically similar throughout the course of evolution. Yet the blueprint is capable of modification to serve the reproductive needs of each sex in the course of personal development. Support for Symons' theory comes from the discovery that a woman's sexual readiness and her capacity to experience orgasm are both increased if she is given male hormone (Kane *et al.*, 1969).

These differences in evolved strategies help to account for the complaints that bring patients to sexual problem clinics. Surveys consistently reveal that while men complain principally of problems with genital response such as premature ejaculation, women complain predominantly of lack of sexual interest and enjoyment, lack of sufficient foreplay on the part of their husbands, and insufficient attention from them when love-making is over. To evolutionary theorists the disparity in these complaints confirms expectation: males are easily aroused because it serves gene proliferation, while quick arousal would be disadvantageous for women as being incompatible with their strategy of careful mate appraisal. As Wilson (1989) has suggested, understanding the differing response cycles of men and women, as well as appreciating the biological basis of this difference, can be fundamental to success in sex therapy.

Marital dysfunction is a major cause of unhappiness and psychiatric morbidity in our society. In one study of self-poisoning, for example, 68 per cent of the married men and 60 per cent of the married women reported marital disharmony as the cause of their attempted suicide (Kessel, 1965). Another study of parasuicide revealed an even higher proportion of men and women blaming marital problems for their actions (Bancroft *et al.*, 1977). Usually there had been a serious row a few days before the attempt; and half the men confessed to an extramarital affair in the previous twelve months. Marital discord, separation, and divorce seem to be increasing as social attitudes change from seeing marriage as a social *institution* to conceiving it as a personal *relationship* (Dominian, 1980). In this transformation, the issues of rank and attachment become increasingly salient: the self-esteem of both partners as well as their capacity to give and receive affection is of even greater importance to a union that has to stand on its own feet and survive on its own terms without the traditional underpinning of a social or religious obligation. Learning how to form and sustain emotional bonds occurs in childhood through growing up in a stable and loving family, where the parents are as committed to each other as they are to the welfare of their children. As more families disintegrate, more children grow up without these indispensable experiences, and the less capable they are of forming stable marital bonds themselves. This fact represents the most serious, and potentially the most disastrous, departure of our society from the satisfaction of the basic archetypal needs of growing children.

Evolutionary psychiatry has no ready solution to offer to this enormous problem. What it can do is draw attention to the central importance of stable family bonds for the healthy development of young people and reveal the nature of the underlying reproductive strategies that human families, whether monogamous, polygamous, or polyandrous, have everywhere sought to contain and satisfy. The adoption of the transpersonal perspective that evolutionary psychology can bring should be of assistance to psychiatrists, psychotherapists, and counsellors, who have to tackle these issues at first hand, as well as guiding legislators and their advisors in framing policies to cope with what threatens to become a major social catastrophe.

15

HOMOSEXUALITY

Homosexuality is the desire to have sexual relations, either in fantasy or in fact, with a member of one's own sex rather than a member of the opposite sex. It is an habitual pattern of sexual behaviour which, by its very nature, precludes reproduction, and it is, therefore, appropriate to discuss it in this section. This in no sense implies a negative moral judgement. Indeed, it is possible to argue, on the contrary, that any mode of adjustment which brings sexual fulfilment *without* procreation is to be welcomed in an over-populated world. A common condition of great cultural significance, homosexuality constitutes a major puzzle for evolutionary psychology: how is it possible to account for the inclusive fitness of genes which predispose people to homosexual behaviour? Clearly such genes must possess some adaptive advantage otherwise they would have disappeared from the genome. What can this be?

MALE AND FEMALE HOMOSEXUALITY

Homosexual behaviour is of particular interest to evolutionary psychology because it provides an opportunity to study male and female sexuality 'in pure culture', so to speak; for homosexual men and women are free to express their sexual proclivities without having to take into account the demands, wishes or needs of the opposite sex.

Male homosexuals are sexually more active than lesbians and, before the AIDS epidemic, they were much more promiscuous. In 1981, Bell *et al.* estimated that 25 per cent of male homosexuals had sex with more than a thousand partners. Lesbians, on the other hand, show no greater tendency to promiscuity than heterosexual women, their median number of partners being only three in the course of their lifetime (Loney, 1974). While some homosexual males seek and find a lasting sexual bond with one partner, they are an exception. Close and lasting relationships are much commoner among lesbians. These findings are completely in accordance with the differential sexual strategies for males and females described in the last chapter.

As with all other paraphilias, the incidence of homosexuality is far higher among males than among females. This reflects the male propensity to seek sexual *variety* as a primary goal (Symons, 1979). In many instances this is adaptive because it prompts males to have sex with different partners, thus leading to their greater reproductive success. However, the masculine yen for sexual novelty can result in less adaptive sexual interests, such as fetishism and sex with other males.

Aetiology

That genetic factors are involved in the aetiology of homosexuality is apparent from twin and adoption studies. When pairs of twins are reared apart, monozygotic twins consistently show a greater concordance for homosexuality than dizygotic twins. There is also a greater correlation for homosexuality with biological relatives than with adoptive relatives, and a higher incidence among the brothers of homosexuals than among the brothers of heterosexuals. The fact that a higher incidence of homosexual family members is found among maternal relations than among paternal relations lends support to the contention that a region of the X chromosome may predispose individuals to become homosexual. However, this suggestion has not been confirmed.

Neurophysiological research has established that the centres responsible for sexual orientation (whether an individual prefers same-sex or opposite-sex relations) are separate from the centres responsible for typical gender-related attitudes and behaviours. Both areas are situated in and around the hypothalamus, which is closely related to the pituitary gland. These are:

1 The INAH3 region of the medial pre-optic area: this controls sexual orientation, and is reported in homosexual males to be only one-third to one-half of the size of the same area in heterosexual males.
2 The pre-optic anterior nucleus: this controls male mounting behaviour in mammals, including primates, and is twice as large in males as in females.
3 The ventro-medial nucleus: this is responsible for the cyclic release of sex hormones in females.
4 The anterior nucleus: this organizes female receptivity to male mounting behaviour.

One theory of homosexual development holds that the specialized nuclei which are involved in the establishment of heterosexual preferences escape exposure to circulating male hormone in otherwise normal XY individuals, with the result that although the body becomes masculine, sexual preferences remain those of a female (Feldman and MacCullough, 1971). Less commonly, in XX individuals, the sex preference area is accidentally masculinized with the result that a constitutional female develops a lesbian orientation. A more recent view is that female hormones, especially luteinizing hormone (LH), are also implicated in the development of foetal gender identity and sexual preference. But the idea persists that the separate areas of the brain, one concerned with sexual orientation and the other with sex-typical behaviour, develop in opposite directions in those destined to become homosexual.

Summarizing the evidence, Glenn Wilson (1989) concludes that sex orientation is fixed relatively early in pregnancy (during the third and fourth months) whereas sex-role behaviours are determined later (during the fifth and sixth months). The influence of genetic factors in triggering hormonal changes during these critical phases of foetal development has yet to be worked out, but it is known that both endogenous and exogenous hormonal fluctuations can be decisive at these times. Exposure of the mother to stress, for example, can interfere with testosterone production in the male foetus, while the use of drugs which block or augment the effects of androgens can also be decisive in the development of male and female babies.

Development of a male foetus is, as was noted in the previous chapter, a more elaborate process than development of a female foetus, for it involves the added complexity of converting a standard female embryo into a sexually competent male. As a consequence, there are more things to go wrong. This may help to explain why male homosexuality is so much more common than lesbianism. But another, equally important, explanation, examined later in this chapter, depends on the evolved determinants of male ranking behaviour, which become salient during the second (fifth to sixth month) phase of brain masculinization (Wilson, 1989).

Although genetic factors are clearly implicated in the development of a homosexual orientation, they are not necessarily decisive in all cases. As is apparent in a large number of medical and psychiatric conditions, people with the same genotypes can develop different phenotypes as a result of different environmental influences, such as hormonal fluctuations *in utero*, parental influences in childhood, peer group experiences, and so on, to say nothing of cultural influences operating independently of genes, hormones, and parents. Weak or absent fathers, emotionally demanding mothers, being an only child and subject to parental pampering, have all been blamed by psychotherapists of different schools, but carefully controlled studies of homosexual and heterosexual men and women, together with their family histories, have failed to substantiate these contentions. Neither paternal nor maternal personality traits or parental relationships, sibling constellations or early experiences of many kinds have been shown to be significantly different between the two groups. Virtually the only significant predictor of later homosexual preference was gender nonconformity in childhood, namely effeminacy in boys and tomboyishness in girls (Bell *et al.*, 1981). In line with this finding, as many as 65 per cent of male homosexuals acknowledge that they may have been effeminate in childhood, compared with only a very small percentage of heterosexual men (Saghir and Robins, 1973). Green's (1987) longitudinal study has confirmed this association. Green conducted a fifteen-year comparison between two groups of boys aged between 4 and 12 years at the beginning of the study: the boys were allocated to 'effeminate' and 'masculine' groups on the basis of objective criteria and tests. Of the 30 boys in the 'effeminate' group, no less than 24 developed a homosexual orientation, while only 1 of the 25 'masculine' controls became predominantly homosexual as an adult. Boys in the first group scored higher on psychological dimensions such as 'nurturance' and were more likely to want to be actors. Boys in the second group were more interested in sports and were more likely to want to be athletes, engineers, or pilots.

While other studies have confirmed that homosexuals are more likely to have been effeminate as boys, it must be clearly acknowledged that there are many homosexual men who give no signs of effeminacy in childhood. However, Weinrich *et al.* (quoted by Werner, 1995) found that homosexuals who had been effeminate boys were more likely to adopt a passive role in homoerotic relations.

CULTURAL FACTORS

Phenomena which are due entirely to cultural influences show wide variations in incidence and form. The more universal, stable, and consistent a behaviour appears across cultures, the more likely it is to be genetically determined. Although homosexuals are regarded differently and treated differently by different societies, valued or tolerated by some, despised or persecuted by others, there are striking cross-cultural similarities in the ways that homosexual behaviours are manifested. These manifestations are sufficiently consistent to permit classification, and Dennis Werner (1995) has distinguished four main types which he calls adolescent, age-grade, transvestite, and gay types respectively:

1 **The adolescent type** is found among a number of Oceanic, African, and South American cultures as well as in European boarding schools. In this type, homosexual relations are confined to adolescents and disappear after marriage.
2 **The age-grade type** is the master/apprentice, mentor/pupil system in which older men have sexual relations with younger men. It prevailed in ancient Greece and the Middle East as well as among Tibetan monks and Japanese samurai. Some cultures hold that sex between older and younger males is indispensable for normal masculine development. The Sambia and the Etoro, for example, are convinced that boys cannot become men unless they receive semen from their elders. Among these peoples, heterosexual unions are taboo for most of the year, but sex between men and boys is considered to be good at all times. Interestingly, the Etoro have no special term for 'homosexuality', presumably because they view it as a normal and indispensable part of masculine life.

3 **The transvestite type**. This is by far the commonest type, in which exclusive homosexuals (often effeminate in their behaviour) have sexual relations with men who are normally heterosexual. This type occurs among such diverse peoples as Southern Europeans and their descendants (for example, Brazilians), North American Indians, native South American societies, Far Eastern and Asian cultures, among whom it is acceptable that a predominant homosexual will have sexual relations with predominantly heterosexual men.

4 **The gay type**. In this type, men whose orientation is predominantly homosexual have sexual relations primarily with other homosexuals. This is the least common type, but the one that predominates among Northern Europeans and their descendants and is probably spreading to other cultures. Werner (1995) suggests that individualism and the Protestant work ethic, combined with the competitive, capitalist economy, have caused men to renounce the more flexible, easy-going attitude of their forebears to same-sex relations, with the result that exclusive homosexuals have been driven into ghettos where they are confined to sexual relations with each other.

One or more of these types may coexist in the same society. Before liberalization of the laws against homosexuals, for example, all four existed among various groups in our own society. Greater public awareness of homosexuality has probably resulted in a diminution of types (1), (2), and (3), and an increase in type (4). Countries where type (3) predominates make a clear distinction between those who adopt the active and passive roles in homosexual relations. Those who adopt the passive role are classified as homosexual, while those who adopt the active role are regarded as normal, and usually marry and have children. This has probably always been the prevailing pattern. There are numerous instances of heterosexual men gratifying their lust with men happy to adopt the passive role when females are unavailable (in prison, on board ship, in barracks and boarding schools, in traditional communities where female virginity is highly prized and strictly protected). When females are plentifully available, however, homosexual men have recourse to each other.

THE EVOLUTIONARY PERSPECTIVE

How is it possible for the homosexual orientation to recur, generation after generation, when the logic of natural selection would dictate that the propensity should be eliminated from the human genome? Since the propensity has survived and is widely distributed as a human behaviour pattern, it must in some way reflect an adaptive mechanism. What could this be?

The probability is that no gene is specifically responsible for 'homosexuality' as such but rather that genes exist which may confer inclusive fitness advantages on heterosexual individuals who carry a lower genetic load – in

180

the same way that sickle-cell anaemia genes protect heterozygotic individuals from malaria (see p. 146). A dominant gene for exclusive homosexuality could not be passed on to future generations; but a non-dominant gene could be passed on through the relatives of an exclusive homosexual, either because the homosexual helps his relatives to raise more children (**the kin selection hypothesis**) or because the non-dominant gene itself provides reproductive advantages when combined with other genes in heterosexual individuals (**the heterozygous hypothesis**).

One possibility would be that degrees of *social* dominance/submission are determined by combinations of genes, and that some individuals are born with a heavier genetic loading for dominance behaviour and others with a heavier loading for submissive behaviour. Such loading is probably normally distributed. After all, only one individual is ever at the top of the dominance hierarchy, with a few at the bottom: the majority are somewhere in between and will be called upon to display dominance to their inferiors and submission to their betters. Those with a predominantly submissive loading have less chance of competing successfully in ritual agonistic conflicts and will, therefore, be less likely to mate and reproduce. Dominant males, as we have repeatedly observed, are polygynous and their dominance grants them access to several females, which inevitably leaves fewer females to go round. A number of subdominant males will, therefore, be unable to find female partners. Development of a homosexual orientation, in these circumstances, would afford a solution.

Thus the genetic contribution to homosexuality may not be sexual at all, but may be such as to render a male less able to compete for rank, either agonically or hedonically. Equally, his pre-natal masculinization may have been incomplete, causing similar competitive disadvantages. Another factor could be a fear of rejection by potential female partners, either because of earlier painful experiences with female peers or because he has been made to feel incompetent and unattractive. Such factors could cause males to give up the unequal struggle with other males for heterosexual partners and turn them in the direction of homosexuality.

This has been called the **dominance failure theory** and it would help to account for the fact that not only are there more male homosexuals than lesbians but also that virtually all reproductive paraphilias are more common in men. As is well recognized, defeat in RAB, causing lower RHP and lower self-esteem, has sexual as well as depressive consequences. Fearing further defeat, a male will turn to substitute gratifications such as masturbation, use of pornographic material, **voyeurism, fetishism, sadomasochism**, or **paedophilia**. It is but another solution to the problem of failure in inter-male competition to opt out of the masculine rat race altogether and assume a female role or identity (**transvestism**, or **transsexualism**).

Finally, the influence of social and religious taboos against homosexuality must be taken into account. In traditional Jewish, Christian, Islamic, and

Hindu societies such taboos were extremely powerful and the pressure on individuals to get married commonly forced people with homosexual preferences to suppress them, and to marry and produce children. Many men whose tastes are primarily for members of their own sex are nevertheless capable of heterosexual intercourse (though this may require the use of homosexual fantasies during the act). Consequently, coercion could have accounted for the persistence of an inherited homosexual predisposition in these societies. This possibility gives rise to an interesting paradox: the disappearance of ancient sexual taboos from our own society, which enables homosexuals to enjoy sex freely with each other, avoid marriage, and cease to produce offspring, could result in a gradual decline in the number of homosexual genes in the population and in the number of people displaying a homosexual orientation.

ANIMAL PARALLELS

Sommer's (1990) study of homosexuality and evolution presents many examples of animal parallels to homosexuality, from the lowly parasitic worm (*Moniliformis dubius*), the 'transvestite' bluegill sunfish, and the female-scented Manitoba garter snake, to the penchant for anal intercourse displayed by male macaques and gorillas. Among primates, most sexual behaviour between males involves the display of dominance and submission.

The study of animal homologues is particularly important because it provides clues to the evolution and structure of human homosexual behaviour. Numerous male primates (including baboons, orang-utans, chimpanzees, and bonobos) demonstrate their dominance by mounting a subdominant male as if he were a female. Others (such as squirrel monkeys) display dominance by mounting and anal penetration, while still others (Japanese macaques, rhesus macaques, and gorillas) mount, penetrate, and ejaculate. Although same-sex sexual behaviours have been most commonly observed in primates, in connection with dominance/submission behaviour, they also frequently occur among adolescent animals at play and between mature males who demonstrate a special affective interest in one another. Such behaviour serves to promote the benevolent interactions characteristic of the hedonic mode. For example, mutual masturbation has been observed among stump-tailed macaques and genital to genital contacts between male bonobos. Some male rhesus macaques have actually demonstrated a preference for homosexual over heterosexual partners, though such a preference is rare throughout the animal kingdom generally (Werner, 1995).

In the great majority of primate societies, the 'courtesies of rank' are commonly expressed in gestures which, to the unbiased eye, are clearly sexual in nature. The dominant animal demonstrates his superiority by adopting a masculine heterosexual posture while the subdominant adopts a feminine posture of sexual presentation. It is as if the subdominant is saying to the dominant, 'I am no more of a threat to you than if I were a female'.

Interestingly, as is often the case with human homosexual partners, roles are sometimes reversed in primates. Thus, among squirrel monkeys, a dominant animal may present his anus to a subdominant, or a dominant howler monkey may sniff and lick a subdominant's genitals; but it is much more usual for the dominant to take the active sexual role. Homologues also exist in primate dominance behaviour for the exhibitionism and 'water sport' activities of human paraphilias. For example, a dominant squirrel monkey will open his thighs and display his erect penis to a subdominant and then squirt urine in his face. Exposure to the urine of a dominant male has the effect of lowering the testosterone level of subdominant male mouse lemurs, with a consequent reduction in their sexual activity (Stoddard, 1990). The consequences of this quaint assortment of sociosexual activities are always to defuse encounters which might otherwise become violent and thus to promote social homeostasis. All such behaviours have been selected because of their contribution to maintaining the basic asymmetry of the vast majority of primate social and sexual interactions. Among free-ranging rhesus monkeys, for example, it is the dominant 20 per cent of males who perform 80 per cent of the copulations. At least 50 per cent of rhesus males never copulate at all. A similar asymmetry is observed among polygamous tribes such as the Yanomamo in the Amazon (Freedman, 1979). In Western society, which is theoretically monogamous, the disparity is not so great, but a sizeable number of men fail to mate, while rich, successful and eminent men may marry several times over as well as having mistresses and casual affairs. Before the use of contraception, particularly in rural or preliterate populations, the great majority of women, on the other hand, mated and produced offspring.

Wilson (1989) adopts a group selectionist standpoint in reviewing these facts, arguing that polygynous groups have a selective advantage over monogamous groups because in the former there is continuous selection for superior males – it is the healthy, strong, skilful, and intelligent males who sire the greater proportion of the next generation. It can be no biological accident that polygyny is the prevailing mating system throughout mammalian, primate, and human populations. As Wilson points out, the removal of some males from the breeding pool does not materially effect group survival, if all the females are impregnated by the other males. On the contrary, it could enhance a population's effectiveness – and ultimately the effectiveness of the species – precisely because it entrusts reproduction to dominant males of high 'stud value'. Indeed, the severe male initiation rituals practised by warlike tribes, such as some Indian tribes in North America, went a long way to ensure this. So great were the ordeals decreed by these rites that some young braves perished, while others failed. Any young man who failed yet survived was either expelled (which would have meant virtually certain death) or permitted to continue living within the tribal group on condition that he became a *berdache*. Berdaches, who were believed to have magical or shamanic powers, had to dress and behave as women and could only enjoy sexual relations with a man. In other words, the berdache was rejected by the group as a male, but tolerated as a 'female' – like a subdominant or marginalized non-human primate.

KIN SELECTION AND HUMAN ADAPTABILITY

William Hamilton, who proposed his theory of kin selection in 1963, can justly be regarded as the father of neo-Darwinism, which sees selection as occurring not at the level of the group, the family, or even the individual, but at the level of the gene. Kin selection is thought to work in this way: if a gene emerges that happens to make an individual behave in a manner that promotes the reproductive success of other individuals who are likely to carry a copy of that gene, then the gene may thrive, even if the reproductive prospects of the individual who carries it are diminished in the process. For example, an animal that emits a warning cry when a predator approaches may call attention to itself and perish. But as a result of its public-spirited action, its kin may all survive through heeding the warning and by escaping to their shared burrow, taking copies of the hero's genes with them to safety. What matters in terms of the neo-Darwinian paradigm, is not the survival of the individual, but the survival of the gene.

The theory of kin selection not only explains altruistic behaviour like that displayed by the individual who dies in order to save his kin, but also an anomaly like the existence of sterile ants, which devote their lives to serving the welfare of their fertile relatives. Could the same principle apply to homosexuality? Are homosexuals adopting a similar strategy? Do they, like sterile ants, decline responsibility for having direct offspring of their own, but nevertheless succeed in getting copies of their genes into the next generation by contributing to the survival of their nephews, nieces and cousins? On the face of it, probably not. In our society, homosexuals are not noted for staying close to their siblings so as to help rear their children. On the contrary, most seem to escape from their families of origin to large cities so as to be free to enjoy the social support and sexual opportunities available in their own subculture. In the ancestral environment, however, no such cultural alternative existed, and those individuals with a predominantly homosexual orientation would have had either to contribute to the survival of the group (their kin) or risk ostracism and death. Moreover, wealthy homosexuals sometimes shock their friends by leaving the bulk of their estate, not to their sexual partner, but to some nephew or niece whom they may not have seen for years. When a man decides to pass on his worldly resources to those who carry 25 per cent of his genes, rather than to a life-long companion who carries none, it begins to look a little like kin selection in action.

It is not unusual for homosexuals to out-achieve their siblings education-ally and economically, perhaps because they have more time and fewer en-cumbrances, and, as a result, many are in a position to promote the welfare of their siblings' offspring, should they wish to do so. This could be a fruitful area of research. But whether or not kin selection can help account for homosexual behaviour in contemporary circumstances, it should not be forgotten that such behaviour may have been adaptive in the ancestral en-vironment, where everyone in the same group was kin. The masculine ideal after which many homosexual men are questing (certainly in traditional communities of the 'transvestite' type) is undeniably one that carries a high degree of fitness (handsome, muscular, sexy, strong). Such ideal figures when found (considered 'bisexual' in our society, but 'normal' in traditional soci-eties) usually marry and have children. Is the homosexual who finds him, loves him, and supports him in fact serving his lover's genes (which in an ancestral kinship group would certainly contain replicas of his own)?

At present we cannot be sure. But, however we seek to explain the genetic processes underlying the homosexual condition, the fact remains that an evolved behavioural system which releases courtship, mating and repro-ductive behaviour in most men in the presence of a responsive female, re-leases similar behaviour in a minority of men in the presence of a responsive male. In the latter instance, it is as if the behavioural system has allowed itself to be deceived so that it permits the individual to mate with a person of biologically inappropriate gender. Such is the flexibility of human nature, that, once natural selection has created a form of behaviour, it can be ad-apted to other uses. For example, a childless couple may so 'invest' in their pets, that the sudden death of a loved dog or cat in a road accident can be as devastating as the loss of a child. Similarly, a soldier may risk his life for his 'brothers in arms', though they are not his brothers at all and his heroism does nothing for his genes. Yet in ancestral conditions, they would at least have been cousins, since his fellow warriors would all have been members of his clan.

It is in the nature of evolved mentalities and archetypal systems that they are primed to become active in certain typical situations; but it does not follow that they will inevitably be activated by those figures for whom they were planned. A baby becomes attached to the maternal figure who cares for it, whether she be its biological mother or not. In the EEA, those individuals who inspired empathy, compassion, and love were likely to be kin; in the modern world this is unlikely to be the case. But, whatever the genetic ex-planation may be, the evolved capacity is present and available wherever circumstances may seem propitious for its expression. As Robert Wright (1994) has said: 'That some people's sexual impulses get diverted from typ-ical channels is just another tribute to the malleability of the human mind.'

While it is unlikely that genes have been selected specifically because they lead to exclusive homosexuality, there can be no doubt that the capacity for homosexual behaviour is of extremely ancient lineage and that its contribution to social harmony in primate communities in resolving rank disputes, forging alliances, relieving agonic tensions, and promoting friendliness and co-operation has, on the whole, been beneficent rather than inimical. With such powerful evolutionary back-up, those who share this orientation have little cause for shame and every reason to emphasize through their own lives the contribution they can make to the hedonic well-being of society.

16

SADOMASOCHISM

The problem of how to explain sadomasochism has tormented psychiatrists, appropriately enough, ever since Krafft-Ebing drew attention to the phenomenon in his widely influential *Psychopathia Sexualis* (1885; 1965). Sadism (so named after the notorious Marquis de Sade, 1740–1814) Krafft-Ebing described as the experience of pleasurable sexual sensations produced by acts of cruelty and bodily punishment, which reflected 'an innate desire to humiliate, hurt, wound or even destroy others in order thereby to create sexual pleasure in one's self'. By contrast, masochism (named after the novelist and historian Leopold von Sacher-Masoch, 1836–1895) represented 'a peculiar perversion' in which the affected individual is controlled, both in sexual feeling and in thought, by 'the idea of being completely and unconditionally subject to the will of the opposite sex; of being treated by this person as by a master, humiliated and abused. This idea is coloured by lustful feeling; the masochist lives in fancies, in which he creates situations of this kind and often attempts to realize them.'

The question of how it is that painful and humiliating activities can be experienced as sexually pleasurable has generated a huge literature but has never really been solved. The majority of theoretical accounts so far advanced, whether they be psychoanalytic, psychiatric, or psychosocial, have suffered from similar drawbacks: they are, by and large, untested and unproven, all too often they reflect moralistic, condemnatory attitudes rather than scientific objectivity, and they usually restrict themselves to the context of psychopathology. Although numerous case studies have been published which go some way towards accounting for the genesis of sadomasochism in individuals, no satisfactory explanation has so far been offered for the phenomenon as a whole, nor has there been any adequate description of how such behaviour could have evolved *as a possibility* for individual human beings to adopt in the first place.

The solution proposed in this chapter is that sadomasochism results from the ontological fusion of two phylogenetic propensities – sexuality with dominance and submission.

SADOMASOCHISM IN FANTASY AND PRACTICE

The DSM-IV classification makes a distinction between **sexual masochism** (302.83) and **sexual sadism** (302.84), though most authorities consider sadism and masochism to be two aspects of the same disorder. The diagnosis is applicable if there are present 'over a period of at least 6 months, recurrent, intense sexually arousing fantasies, sexual urges, or behaviours involving the act (real, not simulated) (1) of being humiliated, beaten, bound, or otherwise made to suffer [masochism],' or (2) 'in which the psychological or physical suffering (including humiliation) of the victim is sexually exciting to the person [sadism].' It is appropriate to consider either of these conditions as a disorder, according to DSM-IV, if 'the fantasies, sexual urges, or behaviours cause clinically significant distress or impairment in social, occupational, or other important areas of functioning.'

The **Manual** states that sadistic or masochistic fantasies have usually been present since childhood and the age at which sadomasochistic practices begin with partners is variable, but generally happens by early adulthood. The course of the condition is chronic, in the sense that the person tends to derive sexual enjoyment from repeating the same sadistic or masochistic acts over periods of many years, without increasing the potential injuriousness of the behaviour involved. In some cases, however, the severity of the pain inflicted or endured can increase over time. In a small number of cases the activities can be so serious as to result in the death of the victim.

Most sadomasochists seek consenting partners with whom to act out their fantasies, and 'S&M' clubs and contact magazines exist in many large cities for the purpose of assisting those so inclined to find a partner willing to satisfy their needs. Unfortunately, a small number of sexual sadists, particularly those with an associated antisocial personality disorder, are prone to act on their sadistic urges using unwilling victims, and may seriously injure or even kill them.

The masochistic acts which may be sought with a partner include restraint ('bondage'), blindfolding, spanking, caning, whipping, 'pinning and piercing', and humiliation (for example, being urinated or defecated upon, being forced to crawl or bark like a dog, or being subjected to verbal abuse).

Sadistic fantasies or acts may involve activities which indicate the dominance of the sadist over the victim (for example, using any of the techniques, listed above, that masochists wish to suffer).

INCIDENCE

As with other paraphilias, the proportion of the population that entertains sadomasochistic desires or fantasies is impossible to determine with any degree of accuracy, but it is certainly very large. Kinsey's finding that more pornographic literature is devoted to sadomasochism than to any other form of sexual activity has been confirmed by other researchers. Kinsey also reported that one in eight females and one in five males were aroused by sadomasochistic stories (Gebhard, 1969). The success of films and literature dealing with sadomasochistic themes, as well as the space devoted by the popular press to such matters, testifies to their power to arouse interest in very large numbers of people. In recent years, the fashion industry has made sadomasochistic symbolism its own, with the result that shaved heads, studded wrist straps, pierced ears and noses, tattoos, heavy boots, leather garments festooned with chains and thongs, have been all the rage. The line between what is to be regarded as normal and abnormal is, therefore, extremely hard to draw.

The psychiatric view of sadomasochism, encapsulated in the DSM-IV description, has been determined by that self-selected and unrepresentative sample of individuals who have felt a need to present themselves for treatment. These are the ones who feel guilty, isolated, and ashamed of the fantasies that otherwise bring them so much pleasure. The likelihood is, however, that the majority of sadomasochists do not experience their proclivities as an affliction and do not consider them as requiring psychiatric attention. Sociological studies based on questionnaires and interviews with advertisers in contact magazines, with members of SM clubs, customers of leather and rubber stores, and so on, have established that, as with other sexual orientations, the gratification derived from indulging in favourite fantasies and scenes is too great for the subject to wish to change them. On the whole, sadomasochists seem doubtful that a visit to a psychiatrist would be of any use to them, arguing that anyone feeling guilty or isolated on account of their desires would do better to join a club of like-minded individuals or employ the services of a prostitute.

THEORETICAL PERSPECTIVES AND THEIR LIMITATIONS

Sadomasochism has been extensively studied by sexologists, psychoanalysts, and sociologists and each of these groups has attempted to account for sadomasochistic fantasies and practices within the theoretical framework of its own discipline. The most influential theoretical formulations have been those of psychoanalysis, but these, like the rest, have been of limited value because of their lack of an epistemological foundation in human phylogeny.

To Freud, masochism proved a major problem from the start. How could he account for this bizarre phenomenon when he had already asserted the psychoanalytic dogma that all mental processes were governed by the pleasure principle and the avoidance of pain? In terms of Freud's original model of psychic functioning the masochist's desires and behaviour were totally incomprehensible. Sadism, on the other hand, was easier to explain as 'an aggressive component of the [male] sexual instinct which has become exaggerated.' The exaggeration Freud attributed to the trauma of having witnessed 'the primal scene' (the parents having sexual intercourse) which the child had interpreted as 'some sort of ill-treatment or act of subjugation.' This contributed to 'a predisposition to a subsequent sadistic displacement of the sexual aim' (*Three Essays on the Theory of Sexuality*, 1905). Masochism, Freud could accept as a normal component of the female sexual instinct because of the biological necessity for the woman to submit to penetration in the sexual act. But in a man, Freud held that masochism was invariably perverse and that it could only be explained as a turning of sadistic impulses against the self.

In *Beyond the Pleasure Principle* (1920), however, Freud abandoned his earlier formulations and explained sadomasochistic phenomena as being a fusion between (sexual) libido and aggressiveness. He postulated two primary instincts: *Eros*, the life instinct, linked to sex, and *Thanatos*, the death instinct, linked to aggression. Where he had previously held that masochism, at least in men, was never primary and could only occur when sadism was turned against the self, Freud now accepted that primary masochism did indeed exist in all men and women as a universal propensity to self-destruction. In this, we can now see with hindsight, Freud may have been groping towards a recognition of the hedonic and agonic modes as innate psychosocial propensities; but his formulation of these psychosocial adaptations in terms of instinctive drives was a simplistic misrepresentation of the complex archetypal structures involved.

A more satisfactory attempt to reconcile the facts of masochism with Freud's pleasure principle was made by Theodor Reik (1941), who realized that the instinctual goal of masochism is not pain but *pleasure*: 'The urge for pleasure is so powerful that anxiety and the idea of punishment themselves are drawn into its sphere.' Anxiety was clearly an aspect of masochism, but, Reik suggested, 'In place of pleasure accompanied by anxiety, there steps anxiety-producing pleasure, resulting in *an osmosis of pleasure and anxiety*' (our italics). The question for psychoanalysis to answer was how pain and anxiety could become pleasurable in the first place.

An explanation which achieved wide currency in the 1970s was Paul Gebhard's (1969) notion that masochism constituted a pleasurable expiation of guilt:

> During childhood, puberty, and part of adolescence, sexual behaviour is punished and it is easy to form an association between sexual pleasure and punishment. The masochist has a nice guilt-relieving system – he gets his punishment simultaneously with his sexual pleasure or else is entitled to his pleasure by first enduring the punishment.

Equally, Gebhard continued, the masochistic bondage enthusiast 'enjoys not only the restraint itself but the guilt-relieving knowledge that if anything sexual occurs it is not his or her fault'.

Gebhard was also one of the first theorists to make a connection between

190

human sadomasochism and the behaviour of other mammalian species in which coitus is preceded by apparently aggressive behaviour. Moreover, he noted that, from a phylogenetic viewpoint, it was no surprise to find sadomasochistic behaviour in human beings: 'Animal and human social organization,' he wrote, 'is generally based on a dominance-submissiveness relationship, a peck-order.' Unfortunately, he failed to recognize this social organization as being archetypally structured, preferring to see it as a form of culturally induced behaviour peculiar to Western society. This led him into the usual cultural relativism typical of psychoanalytic writing: 'When one couples the difficulties of sexual gratification with the problems involved in living in a peck-order society, one has an endless source of frustration which lends itself to expression in pathological combinations of sex and violence.' Although Plains Indians and Aztecs indulged in bloodshed and torture, they were not, Gebhard asserted, sadomasochistic in a sexual sense: 'A society must be extremely complex and heavily reliant on symbolism before the inescapable repressions and frustrations of life in such a society can be expressed symbolically in sadomasochism.' Thus, although Gebhard sketched out possible phylogenetic preconditions for the development of sadomasochism, his formulations remained culture-bound and tied to the traditional psychoanalytic demonisms of repression, frustration, and guilt.

The contribution of sociology to this area has been important, less for its theoretical input than for its collection of data relating to the actual behaviour, beliefs, values, and social circumstances of sadomasochists, viewed as ordinary citizens rather than psychiatric patients. An excellent series of essays, edited by Thomas Weinberg and G.W. Levi Kamel (in Weinberg and Kamel, 1983) provides a cornucopia of such information and presents a melange of different theoretical orientations. But, here again, little or no significance is attributed to the evolutionary perspective. 'Among the theoretical points of view utilized by our contributors,' wrote Kamel in a chapter entitled 'Toward a sexology of sadomasochism', 'are symbolic interaction theory, frame analysis, dramaturgical sociology, phenomenal sociology, and structural functionalism'. This 'variety of sociological and socio-psychological perspectives' betrays such a blindness to the flash of Occam's razor ('Entities must not be multiplied beyond necessity') as to put one in mind of Polonius's list of dramas of a visiting troupe of players ('pastoral-comical, historical-pastoral, tragical-historical, tragical-comical-historical-pastoral')! Such disciplinary profusion indicates not so much a clear theoretical orientation as an abundance of research funds, combined with a lack of a unifying vision of the type that the evolutionary perspective could provide. As Kamel himself frankly admits, 'one of the most absorbing questions about sadomasochism remains to be answered. This is the mystery that has baffled observers for centuries – the question of the origins of sadomasochism. No satisfactory theory yet exists.' It is the intention in this chapter to show that such a thing does exist.

The drawback of all theories hitherto advanced is, as Kamel says, partly due to their inability to explain the presence of sadomasochism among otherwise unremarkable individuals who often exist within widely different societies. 'It is this universality of S&M that is perhaps most interesting, because the forms it assumes, though sometimes different, have elements that are surprisingly similar.'

To do justice to Weinberg and Kamel, they raise all the right issues. But they stop short of finding the common denominator underlying them. Indeed, they are pessimistic about the possibility of finding it: 'It does not seem likely that the experts will arrive at any type of agreement in the near future,' writes Kamel in his otherwise excellent concluding chapter. He suffers from the frustration and pessimism afflicting all social scientists who feel compelled to discount the incisive contribution that Darwinian theory could make towards establishing a firm foundation on which their ever-multiplying disciplines might be based.

HETEROSEXUAL AND HOMOSEXUAL SADOMASOCHISM

Sociological studies have established important epidemiological differences in sadomasochistic interests and practices between men and women and between people of both sexes whose adjustment is heterosexual or homosexual.

In the first place, practically all authorities agree that the great majority of sadomasochists are men, among whom masochists are much commoner than sadists. Numerous studies endorse Kamel's (1983) impression that 'participants prefer the passive role by approximately 3:1' (Spengler, 1977; Patrias, 1978; Gosselin and Wilson, 1980; Moser and Levitt, 1987), and that 'most of the erotic literature is intentionally written to titillate slave fantasies.' There is also general agreement that 'SM is the prerogative of high status, educated, middle-class people' (Thompson, 1994).

Kamel's conclusion that 'women are rarely interested in S&M in either role, when compared to the much greater interest of men', echoes Spengler's (1977) finding that 'it is almost impossible to question sadomasochistically oriented women in the subculture; there are hardly any nonprostitute ads and very few women in the clubs.' More recently, however, Thompson (1994) reports that some lesbians have started setting up a small number of SM clubs and contact magazines (one such is *Mistress – For the Modern Mistress and Her Household*, catering for the 'upsurge in the number of girls wanting to give themselves in voluntary service to dominant ladies, and of ladies wishing to receive such service') and that some heterosexual women are beginning to show more interest than hitherto. But reviewing the literature as a whole, the impression persists that it is men who are excited by SM and that, when they take the initiative, some women are prepared to play along with them. Female sadists are particularly rare and it seems that of those who do exist the majority are prostitutes who are willing to play the sadistic role to gratify male clients purely for commercial reasons.

Role-playing, fantasy, and theatricality form the very essence of all sado-masochistic activities. Both sadists and masochists pool their fantasy resources, work out many of the details of what will happen, and set limits to how far things may be allowed to go. Sociologists, such as Weinberg, refer to this as 'consensual sexual violence'. Often, 'it is the masochist who controls the interaction in a sadomasochistic episode. That is, he sets the limits by key-ing this activity as make-believe, something that is to be understood as not the "real thing"' (Weinberger and Kamel, 1983). As Gebhard (1969) comments, the sadist is often not truly in charge but is really *servicing* the masochist.

Freud's view that women are sexually masochistic by nature is certainly not borne out by the virtual absence of 'submissive' female advertisements for 'dominant' males in SM contact magazines. Indeed, 'it is commonly the case that sadistic men cannot find a masochistic female partner' (Pengelley, 1978). It is far commoner for submissive men to advertise for dominant women, and for dominant women (usually prostitutes) to advertise for sub-missive men. This is an interesting reversal of the usual biological and stereotypical roles, and has to be accounted for. As Weinberg observed, 'Men who are submissive would appear to be able to reconcile these needs with the social pressures on males to be active, dominant, and superordinate to women by donning a special role within an S&M episode.' Weinberg continues, 'it is the actor as a "child" ("slave", "female maid", "dog", etc.) who is being beaten, degraded, humiliated, and so forth, and not the person in his "actual social identity" as an adult male.' While this may explain how a man may segregate the make-believe fantasy scene from his everyday life, so preserving his self-esteem, it does not explain why the need to indulge in such a profound role reversal should arise.

Another form of role reversal, where a sadist will adopt the masochistic role, or vice versa, is also commonly noted. 'A sadist is simultaneously a masochist,' wrote Freud (1938), 'though either the active or the passive side of the perversion may be more strongly developed in him and thus represent his preponderant sexual activity.' Havelock Ellis (1926) adopted much the same perspective: '"Sadism" and "masochism" are simply convenient clinical terms for classes of manifestations which quite commonly occur in the same person.' There is little doubt, however, that most sadomasochists have a preference for one role or the other. As noted above, most of them (3:1) prefer the masochistic role, and, if they play the sadistic role, it is often on the *faute de mieux* principle that somebody has to do it when a natural sadist is not in the vicinity – rather in the way that women will dance together at a party when there are not enough men to go round.

This form of role reversal is probably more common among homosexual than heterosexual sadomasochists. Indeed, the homosexual SM scene is al-together more sophisticated, less covert, and more efficiently organized than its heterosexual equivalent, as is apparent from the excellent studies of Kamel (1983) and Thompson (1994). In an invaluable essay *Leathersex: Meaningful Aspects of Gay Sadomasochism*, Kamel emphasizes that 'leathersex' is less about the infliction and suffering of pain than about dominance and submission. On the basis of an analysis of an impressive amount of data, Kamel demonstrates that gay SM involves four basic elements: **masculinity** (as expressed by leather, uniform, industrial clothing, heavy boots, and toughness), **humiliation** (through derogatory speech, physical degradation, 'water sports'), **fear** (via threats of violent punishment), and **restraint** (via shackles and bondage).

Leathermen see their activities as being entirely masculine. To them submission has nothing to do with adopting a female role either in fantasy or reality. 'Gay masochists', maintains Kamel, 'have fewer identity difficulties than their straight counterparts,' because, 'maleness is understood not always in terms of dominance; it can be submissive, too.' The significance of this is apparent when the meaning of social rank and status is considered in the context of evolutionary theory.

EVOLUTIONARY HYPOTHESIS

The explanation that evolutionary theory has to offer to explain the behaviour of sadomasochists – the dominance and submission, the infliction and the suffering of injury, the respect and the humiliation, the freedom of the master and the bondage of the slave, all experienced in the interests of sexual stimulation – is that two ancient and closely linked phylogenetic systems, one concerned with **reproduction**, the other concerned with **social rank**, have become fused in the course of ontological development to form a new integrated behavioural system whose goal is no longer high social rank or reproductive success but sexual pleasure.

SADOMASOCHISM AND RITUAL AGONISTIC BEHAVIOUR

Human societies have, of course, developed many other ways of regulating asymmetry between members of the same sex in addition to ritual agonistic behaviour (RAB) – through social class, caste barriers, guild membership, professional organizations, educational distinctions, titles, military ranks, and so on. But the capacity for ritual agonistic conflict persists in us all as a primitive 'reptilian' mechanism underlying the consequences of more recent evolution, such as the mammalian affiliative structures of the limbic system responsible for parent–child attachments, pair-bonding and alliances, as well as the complex capacities for culture creation possessed by the higher centres of the human brain. Such is the complexity that confronts the investigator that it is easy to miss the basic components unless one is alerted to look out for what they may be. The value of comparative ethology is that it orients our faculties to perceive what might be present, not as mere cultural arte-facts, but as specific patterns of behaviour with archetypal determinants deeply embedded in the vertebrate genome.

To shine the light of ethology on the phenomena which form the subject matter of this chapter is to make one truth vividly clear: *if the innate cap-acity for RAB were not encoded in the human brain, sadomasochistic be-haviour could not exist as a sexual possibility.* All the components of RAB – apart from sexual excitement, which has to be added – are implicit in every sadomasochistic scenario. The most important of these components is the ability to use **anathetic** ('putting up') and **catathetic** ('putting down') signals (gestures, behaviour, language) which have evolved in order to maintain the 'gap' in relative RHP between dominant and subdominant individuals once it has been established through ritual agonistic conflict (Price, 1988).

RHP is a measure of an individual's capacity to threaten and fight suc-cessfully in any potential conflict with a conspecific. Signals of RHP are common across species: as early as 1872, Darwin pointed out that threat and appeasement, dominance and submission, are based on the same antithetical principles in both animals and man. A threatening animal does everything to make itself appear bigger and stronger, while a submitting animal makes itself appear smaller and weaker. These biological truths have become ritual-ized in human societies – as, for example, when monarchs assume an erect bearing as they pass among their bowing and curtsying subjects.

While signals of absolute RHP are constant across species, the actual form that RAB takes is species-specific, for each species has evolved its own kinds of combat – the head-charging of bison, the antler-locking of deer, the gill-erection of Siamese fighting-fish, the vertical threat displays of male sticklebacks, and the tail-bashing of crocodiles. As well as being able to use such indicators of high RHP as superior size, strength, erect posture, elegant plumage, and other 'status symbols', human beings are unique in the animal kingdom in being able to verbalize their signals of high relative RHP. Con-sequently, although human ritual agonistic encounters can certainly come to blows, they commonly take the form of 'slanging matches' through which one contestant implies his own high RHP (boasting) while he draws atten-tion to the implied low RHP of his adversary (sarcasm, disparagement, and insult). Escalated catathetic signals involve physical contact, such as hitting, scratching, biting, caning, flogging, and so on. Most sadomasochistic fan-tasies and scenes follow this progression: from the use of verbal catathetic signals (humiliation and abuse), through the use of threats and intimidation, to the actual infliction of punishment or pain. The progression is generally associated with mounting sexual excitement, which culminates in orgasm, and the end of the scene.

Within the established hierarchies of social animals, a dominant will monitor the gap in resource holding power between himself and a sub-dominant to ensure that it remains sufficiently wide. If it becomes too narrow for comfort, down-hierarchy catathetic signals are directed at the subordinate in order to lower his RHP. Once the gap has been restored to the dominant's satisfaction, the catathetic signalling ceases. The corresponding strategy for the subordinate is to signal his low RHP and send anathetic signals up the hierarchy to ensure that the dominant perceives an adequate RHP gap (that the subordinate knows his place and is keeping in it).

In asymmetrical human relationships, the RHP gap is maintained by conventions of speech, tone of voice, general manner or demeanour, direction of visual regard, and facial expression. The dominant may signal his high RHP by addressing a subordinate by his surname, giving him orders (asking him to do things without saying 'please'), adopting a haughty or condescending manner, using a 'posh' voice, staring at him, and so on. Meanwhile the subdominant may signal his relatively low RHP by addressing the dominant as 'sir', doffing his cap, pulling his forelock, standing to attention, saluting, adopting a 'respectful' manner, being compliant and obedient, dropping his gaze and looking towards the ground, and so on. Organizations such as the army have ritualized some of these gestures so that a series of asymmetrical relationships can exist within the context of a hierarchy which is stable because it is formal and institutionalized. In sadomasochistic scenarios any of these forms of RHP signalling can be eroticized and put to the purposes of sexual stimulation.

The factor of ritual is of great importance and needs to be emphasized, for dominance–submissive behaviour is an expression of *ritual* agonistic behaviour; and catathetic signals achieve a *ritual* lowering of RHP in the subordinate individual to whom they are directed. This is the ritualized equivalent of a more direct, more brutal lowering of RHP which results from non-ritualized fighting and the actual infliction of physical wounds. Moreover, the pain sense has *itself* become ritualized in the course of evolution. Physical pain, which first evolved to protect the organism from physical (non-social) insult, became ritualized through the receipt of catathetic RHP-lowering signals and through further selection pressure to become mental pain, which is suffered in response to criticism, reproof, or verbal humiliation. A similar process involving the assimilation and ritualization of sexual excitement together with relative RHP signalling has evidently occurred in sadomasochism.

DEVELOPMENTAL CONSIDERATIONS

How does a sadomasochistic orientation develop? Somehow, through the association of sexual excitement with the powerful emotions of guilt, shame, and lowered self-esteem, *psychic pain is transformed into sexual pleasure*. The ontological timing of this transformation must be important, for it usually occurs in relation to parental or pedagogical disciplinary procedures experienced in childhood. The traditional British practice of segregating adolescent boys in all-male boarding schools, where all forms of sexual behaviour were prohibited, while at the same time, exposing them to the regular spectacle and experience of canings on the buttocks, is a case in point. The partiality of ex-public school masochists for the cane has been frequently noted by prostitutes who have been interviewed by sociologists or who have published their memoirs (for example, Cynthia Payne, in Bailey, 1982).

Some families, like some societies, are more agonistic than others; and some parents relate to their children more through power than love: they are more prone to dominate them and control them through threats and punishment, the induction of guilt and shame, and by assaults on their self-esteem. Clinical experience indicates that it is children with this kind of family background who are particularly prone to ameliorate their chronic feelings of humiliation by eroticizing them. This can result in a lasting masochistic adjustment or, when they grow up, they themselves may become sadistically inclined. As Bowlby (1979), observed: 'Each of us is apt to do unto others as we *have been* done by. The bullying adult is the bullied child grown bigger.' 'Sadomasochism is an adaptive response to the sado-masochism of a parent,' wrote Susanne Schad-Somers (1982). 'The price paid for maintaining the illusion of a mother's love is *introjection* (psychic incorporation of the sadistic parent).' This is one of the more satisfactory psychoanalytic formulations which should stand the test of time, for it un-doubtedly describes one route by which individuals may enter the sado-masochistic arena. It also provides an insight into how agonistic experience can be transformed into hedonic satisfaction through the intervention of Eros. But the route is not always as direct. In practice, one encounters people who have developed a sadomasochistic orientation despite a family background in which loving permissiveness has reigned. For these, the agon-istic tensions of school life came as a nasty shock; and experiences of being rebuked, disciplined, and punished were more bitter and more humiliating through being unprepared for and entirely unexpected. Here again, the means used to hedonize them has been erotic.

The biological truth of the matter is that agonistic competition is a fact of human life and cannot be eradicated by love alone, as two thousand years of Christianity have amply demonstrated. Agonistic behaviour has been pres-ent and evolving for over 300 million years, and is deeply embedded in the genome and in our brains; whereas hedonic affiliation has been in existence for only one-thirtieth of that time. Sadomasochistic experience straddles both modes of existence. While abiding by the hedonic rules of conventional life in a modern democracy, sadomasochists keep their erotic agonism hidden 'underground'. Within the privacy of the 'games room', they prepare their equipment, don their fetishistic gear, and descend into the darker, more ancient strata of the psyche, to reawaken the reptilian life that lurks there. Then, their atavistic rites complete, they reascend through more recent mammalian and primate cerebral accretions to re-emerge, blinking but satisfied, in the hedonic light of democratic day.

The role of schooling in the genesis of sadomasochism is important because of its influence over the course of adolescent development. Schools represent a modern extension of the extremely ancient institution of **puberty initiation rites**. These emerged to deal with the threat that young men, their aggressiveness and sexuality stimulated by the sudden, dramatic increase in the quantities of male hormone circulating in their blood, presented to the established male hierarchy. All successful societies in the history of our species have had to develop means of disciplining the young and coercing their energies into the service of the social system. Theoretically, there are any number of ways in which such constraints might be applied, but in fact the variety is small, for our innate propensities impose upon us a relatively simple social vocabulary. Thus, although the initiation procedures used in different cultures may vary to a certain extent, a number of standard elements prevail. In all of them:

1 initiation is primarily an all-male concern;
2 the young initiates are removed from all contact with females;
3 they are subjected to ordeals and trials of endurance by the older males, they are hazed and humiliated, sometimes beaten and homosexually assaulted, and physically mutilated, usually in the genital region (e.g., circumcision or subincision), but sometimes by tattooing or knocking out teeth;
4 they are instructed in tribal lore, myths and traditions;
5 they are ritually 'slain' and brought back to life; and
6 everything is done in the name of tradition, hallowed by the tribal gods.

Describing these procedures, the anthropologists Lionel Tiger and Robin Fox (1972) wrote:

> Without a knowledge of male secrets and male rituals and taboos, a boy could not be a man. This was the trick. One could not simply *become* a man, one had to *know how* to become a man. The first schools, in the technical sense, were initiation schools. Their overt function was to pass on knowledge and to make men; their covert function was to preserve the ascendancy of the elders.

Having been initiated, however, the young males achieve the crucial advantage of being admitted to a place in the hierarchy: they are now part of the organization of male dominance patterns that exists to regulate mating, hunting, and defence. In terms of attachment theory, initiation may be understood as a means of facilitating the transfer of attachment from mother and immediate family to the male group and the tribal gods, and, once a bride has been wooed and married, to the new family unit. In sadomasochistic development, this too has become sexualized, particularly in homosexual sadomasochism, whose erotic practices involve a clear re-enactment of ancient initiatory procedures.

HOMOSEXUAL AND HETEROSEXUAL SADOMASOCHISM RECONSIDERED

We are now in a position to relate the details of sadomasochistic fantasies and practices to the archaic agonistic behaviour patterns on which they are based. As Kamel's (1983) descriptions make clear, homosexual sado-masochistic scenarios are erotic parodies of the usual primate dominance hierarchy and its practices replicate, as we have seen, the traditional rites of masculine initiation. What the homosexual sadomasochist is turned on by is *maleness per se*. It is as if ranking and the accoutrements of rank are taken as symbolic of the quintessence of masculinity: *ranking is what men do*. So, if a man wishes to immerse himself sexually in the essence of maleness, he plays at rank. Even to be a low subdominant is still essentially male, because to adopt such a role is to be accepted into the male dominance hierarchy and to find a place there. In other words, the sadomasochistic encounter is itself experienced as an initiation, a *rite d'entrée* into maleness, for it is a set of erotic variations on the basic archetypal themes of masculine initiation. It is practised and experienced with the intensity of a religious ritual.

The supreme significance of masculine rank and rank differentials is em-phasized by the ritual use of uniform, intimidation, and fear. The fetishistic value placed on leather, military uniform, boots, and so on, reflects their connotations of macho toughness. Worn by the master they epitomize his authoritarian dominance as well as his extreme masculinity. Humiliation and intimidation are key ingredients because of their crude and blatant demonstration of the wide gulf in status existing between the participants: 'Masochists are in the act of being slaves and sadists are being masters, when performing acts of humiliation,' comments Kamel (1983). Verbal abuse, urination, and the use of humiliating postures (crawling, boot-licking, and so on) are all designed to 'degrade the slave and "exalt" the master'. Thus the peak of sexual excitement is achieved by doing everything possible to exaggerate and indeed to revel in widening the 'RHP gap'.

Kamel stresses that the use of pain is not the primary objective of these 'scenes'. 'The pain of S&M is defined differently because it is the method by which partners maintain their dominant and submissive roles.' The whip in the master's hand is his symbol of authority, it signifies who is boss. When he uses it, it is not so much from a wish to harm, injure, or hurt the maso-chist as to dominate him. Pain is an added means by which both celebrate masculine rank differentials: the sadist demonstrates his masculine authority by threatening pain or inflicting it; the masochist demonstrates his mascu-line submission by proving he 'can take it'.

The many forms of bondage and physical restraint commonly employed in sadomasochistic scenarios are similarly used to establish roles of widely differing status by rendering the slave helpless and putting him completely in the power of his master. Many sadomasochists eschew such obvious controls as ropes, chains, and manacles, preferring to replace them with psychological controls exercised through rank and extensive disciplinary powers. The slave 'is made to feel that any attempt to leave the presence of his master would be in vain, and would only elicit more punishment.' In this, we have a direct replica of the 'reverted escape' behaviour observed by Chance in subdominant baboons (see p. 49).

One interesting and important observation made by Kamel is that 'off-the-scene' relations between men who adopt dominant and submissive roles for sexual gratification are usually friendly and egalitarian. 'Dominance and submission for most leathermen is not so real that they lose sight of a more genuine mutual respect. Likewise, their sense of self-esteem remains intact, unharmed by their activities.' Moreover, after orgasm, demonstrations of mutual warmth and affection are common. These are reminiscent of the 'reconciliation behaviour' (hugging, patting, kissing) observed by de Waal (1988) to occur following status conflicts among chimpanzees.

Kamel (1983) concludes that lasting SM partnerships are not uncommon and 'appear to be among the most stable arrangements in the gay community, bound by considerable emotional and personal investment, and not simply by ropes.'

By comparison, heterosexual SM is a more complex, more convoluted phenomenon, because behaviour which evolved to permit males to dominate other males in the interests of social cohesion has become inverted and translocated to permit males to be dominated by females in the interests of sexual pleasure. The relative reluctance of females to participate in such activities is also a factor requiring explanation.

The aetiological significance of the parent–child bond is more apparent in heterosexual than homosexual SM. When a man is humiliated and beaten by a woman, social metaphors are invoked which are acted out in the SM scenario – nursemaid/child, mistress/pupil, and so on. Prostitutes who specialize in playing the role of 'dominatrix' remark on how frequently their clients want to adopt child-like roles.

Many masochists, as we have noted, hold positions of social, political, and economic importance, functioning effectively in society in a manner indistinguishable from normally adjusted, 'initiated' males. Yet once they enter their favoured SM scenario with a 'mistress' they revert to the pre-initiation status of a naughty boy and permit themselves, within the limits of fantasy and theatrical play-acting, to be dominated, humiliated, and punished by a strict maternal figure. In homosexual masochism, something more is involved, for the masochist is being dominated, humiliated, and punished not merely by a paternal figure, but by a 'master of initiation', so as to experience himself as a man. What has happened in the case of heterosexual sadomasochism is that an archetypally masculine social pattern of dominance has assimilated a female into its hierarchical structure *by virtue of the subject's heterosexuality*. This serves partly to explain why women do not, on the whole, initiate or particularly wish to participate in sadomasochistic activities with a male partner, unless begged (or paid) to do so.

That males are more prone to sadomasochism, and indeed to all paraphilias, than women is due to the greater lability of the male sexual response, which makes them more susceptible to conditioning by specific erotic experiences at crucial stages of development. Although women can be just as status conscious as men, and increasingly compete with them for status in the workplace, making effective use of both anathetic and catathetic signals to maintain their rank in the pecking order, they do not, on the whole, eroticize their triumphs and humiliations with the same frequency and apparent facility as their masculine competitors and colleagues.

ARCHETYPAL FUSION

If the hypothesis is correct, that sadomasochism is the product of a fusion between two phylogenetic propensities, one concerned with reproduction and the other with social rank, then we have to ask how it is that these two systems can become 'fused'. It is now evident that we all inherit the propensities for sexual and ranking behaviour and that salient incidents at critical periods in childhood can activate these propensities in conjunction with one another so as to produce sadomasochistic fantasies and behaviour. Though it is possible that certain individuals may be genetically predisposed to make this fusion more readily than others, the probability is that the ranking system can become integrated with the sexual system in anyone given the necessary childhood conditioning.

In addition to the psychoanalytic and sociological theories reviewed in an earlier part of this chapter, a number of attempts have been made to provide neurophysiological explanations of the phenomena involved. The most persuasive of these include theories of 'general arousal', 'excitation transfer', and 'endorphin liberation'. Here each of these theories is taken in turn. (They are reviewed in greater detail by Thompson (1994), but not from the evolutionary perspective.)

As has already been seen, **arousal** is a state of neurophysiological excitation whose biological function is to prepare an animal to take effective action in an emergency – to flee from a predator, to stalk and attack prey, or to fight with lethal determination when its essential interests are threatened. Inevitably, such a state of excitation is associated with powerful emotions. The neurophysiological characteristics of arousal are similar in all intense emotional states whether they be sex, anger, fear, physical threat, or aggression. The neurophysiological substrate for a fusion between sexual and dominance systems probably exists, therefore, at the limbic level, where connections between crucial limbic centres would permit the arousal associated with dominance or submission to acquire sexual connotations.

One of the first attempts to explain sadomasochism in terms of general arousal was made by Havelock Ellis (1926) in his *Studies in the Psychology of Sex* published between 1896 and 1928. Unfortunately, Ellis was under the impression, shared by Krafft-Ebing and Freud, that sadomasochism was primarily about the sexual enjoyment of pain rather than dominance or submission, and his formulation suffers from this limitation. 'Pain acts as a sexual stimulant,' he declared, 'because it is the most powerful of all methods of arousing the emotions.' Sadomasochists, he argued, were people whose sex drive was 'weak' and who, *faute de mieux*, had recourse to anger and fear, whose emotive energy they transformed into sexual excitement. The trouble with this suggestion was that he could give no satisfactory account of how the transformation occurred. Nor did his theory square with the observation that sadomasochists, far from having a weak sexual drive, have an extremely active sex life, which often takes place in fantasy, where the stimuli capable of activating fear or anger are absent.

A more satisfactory attempt to account for the link posited by Havelock Ellis between painful and erotic stimuli is that of Dolf Zillman (1984) who has produced a theory of **excitation transfer**. The capacity for mutual facilitation lies in the sympathetic nervous system and, according to Zillman's idea, the poor degree of differentiation at the sympathetic level between activities associated with sex and aggression would help to explain the cross-cultural finding that apparently aggressive acts such as biting and slapping are commonly associated with human love-making. Similarly, 'rough-housing, pinching, biting, and beating' can emerge in monogamous unions as a means of combating 'physical habituation', the relative boredom that can occur as the result of having sex year-in and year-out with the same partner. Pain, Zillman points out, unlike sex, is extremely resistant to habituation. However, for it to work as an effective stimulant, pain must remain *secondary* to sexual excitement. The moment it becomes primary, sexual pleasure is lost.

Zillman argues that excitation transfer can occur between any of the emotional reactions associated with sympathetic activity. Thus, anxiety and fear can facilitate sexual responsiveness as well as pain, provided they are not of sufficient intensity to suppress erotic excitement. This would go some way to account for the common experience that pleasure in love-making is enhanced when indulged in as a means of 'making-up' after a quarrel. The generalized sympathetic arousal ensures that vasocongestion of the genitals, resulting in penile erection and vaginal readiness, is more likely to occur.

An explanation of how the experience of having the buttocks slapped might come to be sexually arousing was that of Eugene Levitt (1971) who drew attention to the fact that buttocks, like breasts, are secondary sexual characteristics which are arousing in themselves and that, unlike breasts,

they are innervated by the same third and fourth sacral nerves which innerv-
ate the genitalia.

The discovery of opiate-like substances, called **endorphins**, which are produced and released in the brain and the entire central nervous system in
response to noxious stimulation, has provided a further explanation of the
mysterious link between pleasure and pain. Endorphins, like their manu-
factured analogues heroin and morphine, greatly reduce the intensity of
physical and mental suffering and promote a heightened sense of well-being.
The experience of threats, fear, humiliation, and physical punishment results
in endorphin release which, when combined with sexual excitement, could
well enhance the victim's feelings of satisfaction.

These theoretical contributions are all helpful as far as they go, but they
do not take sufficient account of the primary role of fantasy in the sexual
experience of sadomasochists. As Thompson (1994) says, 'fantasy is far
more important to SM than the acting-out of any painful experience, and
reveals how one's imagination is vital in setting up, controlling and determining the reaction to events.' It is of interest that D. Patrias (1978; quoted
by Thompson) found that memories of the earliest sadomasochistic feelings
reported by his respondents involved being sexually aroused by scenes in
horror and pirate films and by fantasies of being made to submit to an
authority figure, such as a parent, teacher, or summer camp leader. It was
only much later, Patrias's informants reported, that they began to seek partners with whom to realize their fantasies. By this time, their sexual responses
had become organized round the usual archetypal themes of dominance,
submission, humiliation, and punishment.

In sadomasochistic scenarios, it is true, painful and anxiety-arousing
stimuli are deliberately and imaginatively used to stimulate sexual arousal,
but these stimuli are also deliberately put to the same use in masturbation
fantasies. That excitation transfer and endorphin release may occur in physical actuality is understandable enough, given the facts of sympathetic in-
nervation, but to account for excitation transfer and endorphin release on
the symbolic plane of fantasy requires a different order of explanation. That
fantasy reigns supreme in SM is too readily overlooked by behaviourists like
Zillman who have traditionally left fantasy out of their reckoning. Theories
of the 'excitation transfer' and 'endorphin-liberating' type would provide a
more satisfactory account of sadomasochistic phenomena if practice invariably preceded fantasy in the genesis of the condition. But they do not. The
psychic inducement of sexual arousal through the imagined infliction or
suffering of pain, humiliation, anxiety and fear occurs repeatedly on many
occasions and over long periods of time before the necessary partner is
found with whom to try them out in reality.

What excitation transfer and endorphin release can help to explain is the
way in which masochists, once they have found a partner, may engage
in progressively 'heavier' scenes, exposing themselves to the experience of

painful and anxiety-evoking stimuli of ever greater intensity in the search for greater sexual enjoyment. What they cannot explain is the genesis of the condition in the first place – except, perhaps, in those relatively rare cases where the original erotic interest can be traced to a spanking in childhood. In most cases, what seems to have become eroticized in childhood fantasy is the *psychic* pain of humiliation and the *imagined* pain of physical punishment, rather than the experience of *actual* pain suffered in physical reality. If sadomasochism is due to excitation transfer, endorphin release, or the integration of sex and dominance centres in the limbic system, then these neurophysiological processes must be susceptible to activation at the psychic as well as the physical level. Fantasy, it seems, is the great integrator.

One possibility that would correspond with the facts is that individuals who, from early childhood, have been particularly gifted with a rich fantasy life, are more susceptible to develop paraphilias than those whose mental life is more closely geared to external reality. Evidence that would tend to support this view comes from Eysenck's finding that introverts are more likely to develop sexual deviations than extraverts because their relatively poor social skills, doubts about their sexual attractiveness, feelings of low self-esteem, and fears of rejection, make it hard for them to establish intimate relationships with a sexual partner (Eysenck and Eysenck, 1976). In addition, Eysenck believes that the cerebral cortex of introverts is maintained in a higher state of arousal (being solitary, they live more in their thoughts and fantasies than extraverts) and this is conducive to the development of fixed ideas, fetishistic obsessions, bizarre sexual practices, and the experience of guilt. This is an intriguing possibility that deserves closer scrutiny. If Eysenck is right, a correlation should be found between being an only child, being deprived of peer play, having an introverted disposition, and a proneness to develop sadomasochistic fantasies or other paraphilias.

Once the phylogenetic dimension is acknowledged as playing a crucial role in determining the form assumed by common paraphilias, it becomes possible to propose precise and relevant hypotheses which can be put to the scientific test.

TREATMENT

When people with paraphilias seek psychiatric help it is usually not because they want their sexual tastes changed but because they are guilty about them and fear falling foul of society. This is just as well, for psychotherapy can relieve guilt and anxiety, but can do little to change a sadomasochistic orientation once it is established. It seems that once the responsible archetypal centres have become 'fused' at the limbic level, they possess an adhesive power of such magnitude that it is not possible for any known therapeutic procedure to prise them apart.

In seeking to relieve the anxiety and guilt suffered by some paraphiliacs, the moral attitude of the psychiatrist is no less important than that of society and the law. A therapist who strongly disapproves of sado-masochistic practices is likely to make matters worse rather than better, because it is fear of disapproval that will have caused the symptoms for which the person seeks help. For the 'distress' required by DSM-IV to satisfy its criterion for the classification of sadism or masochism as a 'disorder' is inflicted by society and not by the disorder. Clearly, society must have an interest in protecting its members from cold-blooded sadists who would humiliate and harm them against their will. But in a liberal society, it should be possible for freely consenting adults to participate in their preferred sexual activities without incurring the disapproval of their psychiatrist or the wrath of the law. What cannot be tolerated is the infliction of anguish on unwilling victims, and the alleviation of guilt in sadists who wish to do such things (always assuming that they are capable of experiencing guilt) should never be a goal of psychiatric treatment. People should be helped to realize that to have reached sexual maturity with a paraphilia is a major responsibility, and the aim of therapy should be to enable them to live with their orientation without guilt but in such a way that no harm will accrue to their partners.

As with all other conditions, a positive approach is essential on the part of the therapist. There are usually possibilities for growth and better adjustment inherent in most functional disorders. Sadomasochists are not merely people still in the grip of parent–child conflicts which have been eroticized; they are motivated to actualize archetypal systems, and, in the process, to experience a sense of fulfilment. Archetypal actualization brings its own satisfaction, and the combined fulfilment of dominance or submission with sex is no exception. In homosexual sadomasochism there is the added factor of actualizing *masculinity* through repetition in an erotic context of the rites of male initiation. Far from being destructive, therefore, sadomasochistic partnerships can be seen as a form of creative bonding through which each seeks in his or her own way to contribute to the happiness and fulfilment of the other. In furthering such a therapeutic attitude to the condition, however, membership of the SM subculture can often be of more assistance than psychiatry.

17

PAEDOPHILIA

Paedophilia is the desire to have sexual relations, either in fantasy or in fact, with a prepubescent child. In common usage, the term paedophile has come to be applied to all individuals who desire to have sexual relations with young people below the age of consent. The precise term for those desiring sex with under-age adolescents is *ephebophiles* (from the Greek *ephebe* = adolescent) but it is not often used. The great majority of paedophiles are male and they vary in the degree to which they can sublimate or feel compelled to act out their desires. Some, possibly a majority, are able to find a measure of fulfilment in committing themselves to a mentoring role, such as school teacher, sports coach, scout master, or child care worker, while successfully inhibiting physical expression of their erotic desires; others may limit their amorous propensities to touching or fondling children, occasionally sharing sexual innuendoes or erotic jokes with them. Others again may go so far as to manipulate the child's genitals or perform fellatio or cunnilingus; while others may go further still and actually penetrate the child's vagina, mouth or anus with their fingers or penis, using various degrees of force or coercion to do so. Except in cases where the disorder is associated with sexual sadism, the paedophile may be genuinely attentive to the child's needs, either out of love and affection, or a wish to retain his or her loyalty so as to make it unlikely that the child will reveal to others the erotic nature of the relationship. While some paedophiles prefer boys, others prefer girls, and some are aroused by both. The course of the condition is usually chronic, especially in those attracted to boys. Among convicted paedophiles, the recidivism rate is approximately twice as high for those who prefer boys to girls. The great majority of homosexual males are not, however, paedophiles.

INCIDENCE

From the concentrated attention given to this subject both by the social sciences and the popular media, one might feel justified in concluding that contemporary Western society has for the last two decades been in the grip of a pandemic of child sexual abuse. Yet historical research would indicate that sexual contacts between children or adolescents and adults are less frequent at the present time than they were in the past (Bullough, 1990). Until comparatively recently, in many parts of the world, marriages between adult males and prepubescent females were not uncommon, though consummation did not usually occur until after the child had attained menarche. Famous examples of such betrothals are provided by St Augustine (AD 354–439), Mohammed (AD 570–632), the Indian mathematical genius, Srinivasa Ramanujan (1887–1919), and Mahatma Gandhi (1869–1948). Throughout Europe in the eighteenth and nineteenth centuries child prostitution was widespread. In England the law permitted a child of twelve to consent to sexual behaviour with an adult, while children under twelve, though nominally protected, could be seduced with relative impunity. It was only after a number of well-publicized scandals in the late nineteenth century that laws were tightened and the age of consent raised to thirteen in 1875 and to sixteen in 1885.

Interestingly, an ethological parallel exists to human child betrothal as conducted by St Augustine and Mahatma Gandhi. Among Hamadryas baboons it is common for a young adult male to adopt and care for a sexually immature female years before she becomes reproductively competent. The male's behaviour remains 'parental' rather than sexual during the female's 'minority', but becomes overtly sexual with her transition to sexual maturity. This indicates a degree of 'functional proximity' (Feierman, 1990) between these two motivational states, the parental and the sexual. We shall return to this observation when considering the evolutionary perspective on paedophilia.

Since sexual contacts between adults and children are less common than hitherto, the rapid expansion of the literature on child sexual abuse in recent decades is something of a puzzle. A number of factors may explain it. Judeo-Christian societies have tended to be censorious about all forms of non-procreative sex. Until the 1960s, homosexuality came in for the most intense condemnation. Then, with the liberalization of legal and social attitudes to homosexuals, men whose sexual interests were invested in children and adolescents became the primary targets of moral obloquy. This may have been fuelled by feminist rhetoric, the emergence of 'victimology' as a fashionable subject of discourse, and the literature inspired by it. Reviewing this literature, Paul Okami (1990) concluded that much of it was generated by factors other than a concern for the actual consequences for children of having sexual contacts with adults. The social-activist posture adopted by many professionals, together with their endorsement of specific sexual–political ideologies, have, declared Okami, engendered a body of literature that could be more properly described as social criticism than as social science.

Another factor stimulating interest in child sexual abuse has been the plentiful availability of research funds. Responding to media agitation, the Child Abuse and Treatment Act, signed by President Nixon in January 1974, provided $86 million to be spent over a three-and-a-half-year period, mostly on research. Substantial appropriations continued into the 1990s. The consequent mountain of research publications on the subject amply bears out the truth of the sociological law stated by Bullough (1990) that if there is research money available, research in the field will escalate.

Yet, despite this abundance of research activity, it is still difficult to be certain about the size of the problem that the sexual abuse of children represents. So profound is public hostility to those afflicted with paedophilic desires, that very few paedophiles ask for help before they have been apprehended and sent to prison. This inevitably means that the bulk of research findings from studies into the condition are derived from individuals who have actually been convicted of sexual offences with children. There is no means of knowing how many more paedophiles there may be in the community whose activities or desires go undetected. Moreover, estimates of the number of children and adolescents who have actually had sexual relations with adults differ widely according to the viewpoint of the investigator and the definition of sexual abuse that is employed.

Such estimates are further compromised by the bitter controversies surrounding the 'false memory syndrome', the dubious results of police trawls for evidence against people suspected of paedophilia which may have encouraged some previous inmates of children's homes (particularly those with a history of antisocial personality disorder) to make false accusations in the hope of being awarded considerable sums in compensation (Webster, 1998), and the extravagant assertions about the prevalence of child sexual and 'Satanic' abuse by certain sections of the media. Adult/child sexual behaviour is such an emotive issue, so shrouded in guilt and moral hyperbole, that it is unlikely that many adults or juveniles uninvolved in criminal proceedings will talk openly to researchers about sexual adventures they may have had with one another in the past. As a result, estimates of the incidence of paedophilic behaviour in the community remain largely conjectural.

AETIOLOGY

Discussion of the causes of the paedophilic orientation have typically focused on psychological and social factors and have left phylogenetic considerations out of account. The most commonly accepted view is that adults who sexually abuse children were themselves sexually abused in childhood. This is known as the 'abused/abuser hypothesis' (Garland and Daugher, 1990). A number of clinical reports have been published which would seem to support this hypothesis. However, it does not hold up when large numbers of cases are subjected to careful scrutiny. Thus, when men convicted of sexual offences against children and adolescents are questioned, no more than 30 per cent of them report having experienced sexual contact with an adult during their own childhood or adolescence. This is no higher than the incidence reported by non-sexual offenders and by sexual offenders not involved with children or adolescents. Moreover, approximately 25 per cent of adult females report that they were sexually involved with an adult when they were children or adolescents, yet women account for less than 10 per cent of sexual offenders with children or adolescents.

The abused/abuser hypothesis is, therefore, inadequate to account for the data. If sex between adults and juveniles contributes to the intergenerational transmission of such behaviour then it must be just one factor operating in conjunction with others. Even among those individuals who have had sex with adults in childhood only a minority grow up to be paedophiles. Why should this be? One possibility is suggested by the 'entrapment hypothesis' postulated by Money (1990), namely, that a child who experienced himself as entrapped in a sexual relationship with an adult is more likely to become a paedophile himself in comparison with an individual who *freely* indulged in such a relationship while a child. The 'entrapped' child Money describes as caught up in a 'Catch-22 dilemma': this, he says, is likely to happen in a taboo activity such as sex between a child and an adult in that 'you are damned if you reveal it, and you are damned if you don't'. The juvenile entrapped in a sexual relationship with an adult cannot escape from it without suffering the trauma of disclosure and cannot remain in it without suffering the consequences of sexual exploitation. This kind of childhood dilemma is not infrequently reported as having been experienced by adult paedophiles, but not by the majority. In cultures such as the Sambia and the Etoro (see p. 179 above), however, where sexual contact between adult and juvenile males is accepted as a norm, there is no evidence to suggest that these juveniles are unable to mate and reproduce when they attain the status of marriageable adults (Schiefenhövel, 1990). In traditional Hawaiian society all forms of sexual behaviour were valued as positive and pleasurable. Sexual interaction between adults and juveniles was no exception, though it was seen as being beneficial to the juvenile rather than gratifying to the adult. Adult erotic interest in juveniles, whether homosexual or heterosexual, was accepted as natural; and an adult who regularly expressed an erotic prefer-ence for young people was regarded as eccentric rather than bad (Diamond, 1990).

Although Money's 'entrapment hypothesis' may account successfully for a number of cases of paedophilia, many authorities are agreed that it is certainly not essential that an individual should have felt victimized by a relationship with an older man or have experienced it as traumatic. Indeed, there is much evidence to suggest that a later paedophilic orientation may in some measure be the result of experiencing such a relationship in childhood as supportive and highly gratifying (e.g., Seghorn *et al.*, 1987; Storr, 1964;

Summit, 1983). Through the mechanism of identification with the older partner, the boy may become predisposed himself to be sexually involved with boys when he is an adult. He may then identify with his young Ganymedes as being the recipients of affection (Money, 1990).

However, these aetiological possibilities do not account for the 70 per cent of convicted adult paedophiles who maintain that they had no sexual encounters with adults when they were children. Evidently, other factors are involved. What light, if any, can evolutionary biology throw on the problem?

THE EVOLUTIONARY PERSPECTIVE

We would entertain the hypothesis proposed separately by Eibl-Eibesfeldt (1990) and by Money (1990) that two innate biosocial propensities – care-giving and sex-mating – have become fused in the course of ontogeny in those who display the paedophilic orientation. As Money states it: 'The pedophile's attachment to a child represents a merger of parental and erotic love.' The terms he adopts for 'archetypes' or 'biosocial propensities' are 'phylogenetic building blocks' or 'phylisms', maintaining that in the course of individual sexual development these phylisms are capable of being diverted from their usual mode of expression. In those who become paedo-philes, the phylism of parent/child bonding becomes diverted and eroticized into lover/lover pairbonding.

What, then, prevents the great majority of parents and children from finding each other sexually attractive? The answer is the **Westermarck effect**, which de-eroticizes individuals who are close and familiar to a child as it grows up (hence brothers and sisters and children reared in kibbutzim rarely fancy one another). Thus, a parent who raises a child from infancy to ado-lescence is so familiar with the child, and the child so familiar with the parent, that they develop 'familial bonding' (Erikson, 1993) and an aversion to sexual relations. Absence of the Westermarck effect would account for the finding that surrogate parents are so much more liable than biological parents to abuse their charges (Daly and Wilson, 1989). Moreover, because the incest-avoidance mechanisms (which prevent children and parents from becoming sexually attracted to each other) do not operate between teachers and their students, there is always a possibility that such mentoring types of relationship may become sexual in susceptible individuals.

Money proposes that in people destined to become paedophiles the mer-ger between the care-giving phylism and the sexual mating phylism occurs during the developmental period when what he terms the 'lovemap' is dif-ferentiating. By 'lovemap' he designates 'a developmental representation' in the mind/brain depicting the idealized lover and the idealized programme of desired sexual activity. The sensitive period when the lovemap is differentiat-ing is the stage of 'juvenile sexual rehearsal play' within the peer group. This stage is apparent in other species of primate as well as the human. Erotic

210

incidents – or the absence of them – experienced during this stage may decisively influence the dynamic configuration of the lovemap, so as to result in enduring patterns of paraphiliac responsiveness, including paedophilia among others. If the development of the lovemap subsequently fails to progress in synchrony with chronological age, then the individual will remain psychosexually juvenile and possibly attracted to juveniles himself. The sex of the original playmate, suggests Money, probably determines whether the subsequent paedophilic attraction is heterosexual or homosexual.

The importance of sexual play among juvenile peers is evident in studies of the sexual development of nonhuman primates. Rhesus monkeys reared in isolation and deprived of juvenile sexual rehearsal play do not develop competent copulatory behaviour as adults and do not reproduce. Similarly, the puritanical attitudes to sexual behaviour characteristic of northern European and American societies has encouraged negative parental and paedagogical interventions in playful sexual experiments among children. The consequent distortion of the developing 'lovemap' might help to account for the large number and variety of paraphilias reported in these societies.

Important insights into the aetiology of adult male sexual interest in children is provided by the phylogeny of **sexual dimorphism**, which results in the different physical dimensions and characteristics of human males and females (Medicus and Hopf, 1990). Paedophiles regularly report feelings of social inadequacy in relation to their peers. When these individuals contemplate sexual relations with adult partners they suffer from anxiety and this effectively deters many of them from taking initiatives in that direction. Fear and sexual desire are functionally incompatible states in human males, who are usually incapable of physical arousal if they feel inferior to or intimidated by a sexual partner (unless, of course, they are masochists). Unlike mature females, however, children do not arouse feelings of inferiority or anxiety in these men because of the small stature of children, their lack of sexual experience, and their own feelings of social insecurity. The substitution of a juvenile for a mature woman as 'sexual object' is also facilitated by the points of resemblance that are apparent between children and nubile females – the smaller physical dimensions in comparison to the male, the absence of body hair, the small mouth, delicate features, and 'unbroken' voice, as well as the 'babydoll' child schema that many heterosexual men find attractive.

It must be acknowledged, however, that not all men who are primarily attracted to children or adolescents are incapable of sexual relations with mature women. A proportion of them – it is not known how many – do marry and produce children of their own, as do a proportion of men whose primary sexual orientation is directed towards other men. They adopt this course either as a result of conventional social pressures or as a disguise for their true proclivities, but their underlying preferences persist as a result of the factors discussed in this chapter and in Chapter 15. Paedophiles, like homosexuals, only come to the attention of psychiatrists when they run foul of society or suffer from psychiatric sequelae directly related to their sexual orientation.

Further insight into the contribution of erotic substitution to the aetiology of paedophilia comes from the study of sexual behaviour in cultures other than our own. The 'age-grade' pattern of 'master/apprentice' homosexual relations was, as already described (p. 179 above), prevalent in classical Greece and the Middle East, among Tibetan monks and Japanese samurai, as well as the Sambia and Etoro peoples. There is a widespread belief among tribal units in Papua New Guinea that adult semen must be administered to boys if they are to grow into men. Among the Etoro, for example, boys are required to drink adult semen during acts of oral intercourse; among the Kaluli, anal intercourse is the preferred method; while among the Onobasulu the adult male masturbates over the boy and rubs semen into his skin. Evidently, belief in the maturational powers of semen provides a cultural sanction for these acts: it adds philanthropic satisfaction to sexual gratification for the men, and makes boys eager to avail themselves of the scarce and valuable resource which they consider indispensable to the full flowering of their manhood. A parallel belief might hold that semen is necessary for the development of puberty in girls and would provide a cultural justification for gynaephilic paedosexual behaviour, but we are unaware of any anthropological record of such a custom.

Male and female worlds in Melanesia have traditionally been rigidly separated, and this separation has been associated with a male fear of female genitals and menstrual blood (Schiefenhövel, 1990). Preferential female infanticide has also been practised in this region, with the result that there were typically more males than females (among the Sambia, for example, the ratio was 3:2). In these societies homosexual relations between younger and older males have become ritualized and institutionalized. 'Men are expected to plan, work, fight, and sometimes die together', writes Schiefenhövel. 'The necessary altruistic behavior and effective co-operation of the warriors as well as the acceptance of a male hierarchy would have been fostered by the institution of prescribed homosexuality.' Here, as with many Western paedophiles, fear of the mature female has been associated with a substitution of erotic interest in juveniles, which has in turn been put to paedagogic purposes.

Another consequence of the smaller stature and lower social status of children is that adults are automatically put in a position of dominance over them. As Eibl-Eibesfeldt (1990) has argued, males who are aroused by the 'lust of submission' may be stimulated when they find themselves in authority over children and young adolescents. The phylogeny of human sexual behaviour reveals two major components: the agonic, dominance/submission behaviour characteristic of reptilian sexuality and the hedonic, affiliative relations which have evolved independently in birds and mammals. 'Vestiges of a sexuality based on dominance-and-submission relations without love are still present in some human behaviours', says Eibl-Eibesfeldt. In this more 'reptilian' mode of sexuality, the roles adopted by the participants (whether dominant or submissive) are more important than the personal identity of the individuals performing these roles. As a result, paraphilic lust for juveniles based on dominance-and-submission is experienced as impersonal and is likely to be engaged in with numerous partners. In traditional British public schools, organized on strictly hierarchical lines, where older boys dominated younger boys and masters dominated all boys, the reptilian component of paedophilia could easily be activated, especially when caning on ritually 'presented' buttocks (a form of displaced or symbolic intercourse) was a daily, and often public, occurrence.

However, the erotic relationships which developed in public schools often had a powerfully hedonic component as well. The more recently acquired form of sexual behaviour characterized by affiliation is superimposed on the agonic reptilian heritage. But affiliative erotic love, as Eibl-Eibesfeldt points out, itself evolved in birds and mammals together with the development of parental care-giving behaviour. 'Since human adult/adult romantic love is derived by phylogeny from parent care-giving behaviour,' asserts Eibl-Eibesfeldt, 'it is easily seen how, in some adult humans, the feeling of love toward children has been retained and eroticised, which is the true meaning of the term "pedophilia".'

Eibl-Eibesfeldt also advances the important argument that the vulnerability of humans to behavioural disorders is due to the rapid evolution of our species. That humans are particularly prone to behavioural disorders is, he suggests, because human social behaviour is safeguarded to a lesser degree by phylogenetic adaptations than is the social behaviour of other species. The rapid evolution of the brain did not allow for all the fine-tuning needed for such behaviour-controlling safeguards, while providing the necessary neuronal equipment for behaviour which is more plastic and flexible and more influenced by learning and personal experience than in other primate species.

THE JUVENILE CONTRIBUTUION

An aspect of sexual relations between adults and children or adolescents which is commonly overlooked is the contribution made by children and adolescents themselves. Authorities dealing with paedophiles invariably attribute responsibility entirely to the adult and exonerate the juvenile from playing any part in initiating or sustaining any sexual relationship that may have developed. That paedophiles commonly report their under-age partners as actively welcoming their attentions is discounted as a rationalization and a disgraceful attempt to excuse their behaviour. While this may often be the case, it is undeniable that many children in our society – especially those in boarding schools and childrens' homes – suffer from 'parent hunger'. They are what Mia Kellmer-Pringle has called 'touch-hungry children'. It is possible that the care-eliciting 'phylism' in these children may become eroticized just as the care-giving phylism may be eroticized in adult paedophiles. Thus, children starved of parental affection may compete for the love and attention of adults in their environment by using erotic solicitation as a strategy for survival. To suggest this possibility is not to excuse adults who exploit the emotional needs of children for their personal gratification but to provide an evolutionary explanation as to how and why erotic bonds between adults and juveniles may occur. We would propose that both care-eliciting and care-giving phylisms can be eroticized. But when this leads to a sexual relationship between an adult and a child or adolescent, then it is the adult who must bear the greater moral responsibility for initiating the relationship and for its consequences for the child.

TREATMENT

Treatment of those individuals who have a paedophilic orientation is profoundly complicated by the social horror that the condition engenders. Practically all jurisdictions in the United States have 'reporting laws' which make it the mandatory duty of any professional, such as a physician, clinical psychologist, social worker, counsellor, teacher or religious minister to report any self-confessed paedophile who may come to their attention. As a result, it is understandably rare for paedophiles to present themselves for treatment unless they have already been apprehended by the law. The danger of being 'turned in' is too great (Feierman, 1990).

In prison, paedophiles are treated very much as other criminals and rarely offered any psychological or medical help. When they are released, this state of affairs continues, not least because of the tremendous liability borne by therapists responsible for the treatment of such patients should they re-offend. 'In the United States', says Feierman, 'self-help groups such as Sexaholics Anonymous, which are based on the principles of Alcoholics Anonymous, are distinguished by the relative absence of pedophiles and ephebophiles' (those attracted by adolescents).

In Britain, a similar lack of psychological and social support is compounded by the use of paedophile registers and the necessity for a convicted paedophile to inform the police when he takes up residence in a given locality. This ensures that the demonization, ostracism, and loathing with which the general public responds to the condition persists.

Having had extensive clinical experience with convicted paedophiles, Feierman believes that, given adequate psychotherapeutic support prior to their offence, many of them could have lived with the knowledge of their paedophilia without feeling compelled to act out their desires. Instead of ostracism, isolation, and persecution, these individuals need support and encouragement to contain their desires and to find socially productive ways of sublimating them. Individual psychotherapy can go some way towards achieving this, but supportive groups organized along the lines of Sexaholics Anonymous can go much further. Paedophiles are, after all, only one of several categories of male for whom the desired sex object is not legally or morally available (e.g., the man who covets his neighbour's wife). Unfortunately, in the present climate of opinion, the creation of paedophile support groups would run the risk of hostile investigation on the suspicion that they were 'paedophile vice rings' rather than psychotherapeutic initiatives to assist individuals to deal with their sexuality and to protect vulnerable children with whom they may come into contact.

Unless the attitude of society, law enforcement officers, and therapists changes, the outlook for these unfortunate individuals will continue to be grim.

Part VI

DREAMS, TREATMENT, RESEARCH, AND THE FUTURE

18

SLEEP AND DREAMS

If sleeping and dreaming do not perform vital biological functions, then they must represent nature's most stupid blunder and most colossal waste of time. When an animal is asleep it cannot protect itself from predators, cannot forage for food, cannot procreate, or defend its territory or its young. Yet for over 130 million years, despite enormous evolutionary changes, sleeping and dreaming have persisted in large numbers of species.

During each 24-hour period, all animals display circadian rhythms of activity and rest. Some animals, such as owls, bats, and rodents are active at night and rest in the daytime, while others, like humans, chimpanzees, and dogs, go about their business in daylight and rest when it is dark. The biological advantages of sleep are that it helps conserve energy while, at the same time, enforcing immobility and keeping the animal out of danger in its burrow, nest, or home.

Non-dreaming sleep evolved about 180 million years ago, when warm-blooded mammals evolved from their cold-blooded reptilian ancestors, whereas REM sleep ('rapid eye movement' dreaming sleep) evolved about 50 million years later. Until then, the early mammals, known as monotremes, reproduced by laying eggs in the same way as reptiles and birds. REM sleep appeared on the evolutionary scene when mammals began to reproduce *viviparously* (their offspring were born directly from the womb, not hatched out of eggs). Why should these evolutionary developments coincide, in the first instance, with quiet non-REM sleep and, second, with the innovation of active dreaming sleep?

The most likely explanation arises from the differing metabolic needs of reptiles and mammals and the greater immaturity (and learning capacity) of viviparous young. Being cold-blooded, reptiles have a ready source of energy in the sun, but this is not available to them at night, when they are particularly vulnerable to attack. Warm-blooded mammals, on the other hand, are less at the mercy of the weather and the time of day because they have acquired the homeostatic capacity to maintain their own constant body temperature. However, to sustain this, mammals have to seek more energy in the form of food so as to stoke the boilers of their metabolism, and, as a consequence, an efficient method of energy conservation, such as that provided by longish periods of sleep, is an adaptive survival mechanism of obvious significance for them.

But what of dreaming sleep? Here the explanation probably has to do with the greater vulnerability of viviparous offspring. Whereas birds and lizards are reasonably well-developed when they break out of their eggs, viviparous young are relatively helpless, and have to accomplish much learning and growth, particularly of the brain, before they are capable of independent survival. REM sleep is thought to play an important role in developing the infant brain and in activating those neural programmes responsible for basic and characteristic patterns of behaviour, such as those involved in maternal bonding, in environmental exploration, and in play.

Certainly, the presence of REM sleep in so many species and its persistence through so many millions of years can only indicate that dreams perform a crucial survival function in all mammals. This realization has stimulated intense study of mammalian sleep in the belief that it can reveal the meaning, purpose, and function of dreams.

ANIMAL DREAMS

In the light of all the evidence amassed during the past forty years, no one but the most fanatically anthropocentric behaviourist would seek to deny that animals have dreams. But can we ever hope to know what it is that they dream about? The answer is that we can, and that we almost certainly do. The evidence comes from direct observations of the behaviour of intact and surgically deprived animals during REM sleep, and from inferences based on EEG recordings taken from wide-awake animals as they perform activities essential for their survival. We owe this evidence to Michel Jouvet of the University of Lyon and to Jonathan Winson of Rockefeller University.

Jouvet (1975) has made two outstandingly important observations: first, that dreams arise from bursts of activity in biologically ancient parts of the brain, and, second, that both animals and humans get up and act out their dreams when the brain centres responsible for inhibiting movements during sleep are incapacitated. For example, dreaming cats (whose descending neural fibres responsible for inhibiting movement during REM sleep have been cut) will, in their sleep, get up and 'stalk' hallucinated prey, 'pounce' upon it, 'kill' it, and start to 'eat' it.

Winson's research interest has been primarily focused on the relationship between REM sleep and memory (1990). The neural basis for memory storage has been traced to the hippocampal region of the limbic system and to its connections with the neocortex of the brain. In 1954, John D. Green and Arnaldo A. Arduini of the University of California at Los Angeles recorded a regular rhythm of six cycles per second in the hippocampus of apprehensive rabbits. They named the signal *theta* rhythm.

Further observations on other awake animals, including tree shrews, moles, rats, and cats, detected theta rhythm when they were behaving in ways most crucial to their survival. Thus predatory behaviour in the cat, prey behaviour in the rabbit, and exploration in the rat were most reliably associated with theta rhythm and it is precisely these behaviours that are, respectively, most important for their survival. For example, a starving rat will always carry out a preliminary exploration of the environment before it settles down to eat the food placed in front of it.

Finally, in 1969, these observations were supplemented by a report from Case H. Vanderwolf of the University of Western Ontario that there was one behaviour during which all the animals he studied consistently revealed hippocampal theta rhythm, and that was REM sleep.

It was clear, therefore, that theta rhythm was involved in dreaming, in memory storage, and in the performance of crucial survival behaviours, and this led Winson to a highly significant conclusion – namely, that '*theta rhythm reflected a neural process whereby information essential to the survival of a species – gathered during the day – was reprocessed into memory during REM sleep*' (Winson, 1990; italics added).

On the whole, Winson's suggestion was enthusiastically received, for it made persuasive sense of the data. Dreams, it was widely agreed, could be the means by which animals update their strategies for survival by re-evaluating current experience in the light of strategies formed and tested in the past. This is done when the animal is asleep because it is only during sleep that the brain is free of its outer preoccupations and able to perform this vital activity – rather like bank clerks doing their sums after the public is locked out and the blinds drawn down.

HUMAN DREAMS

Winson believes that what is true of lower mammals could also apply to primates, including humans: 'Dreams may reflect a memory-processing mechanism inherited from lower species, in which information important for survival is reprocessed during REM sleep. *This information may constitute the core of the unconscious*' (*ibid*; italics added). The association between dreaming and remembering is apparent in experiments on both animal and human subjects: REM sleep deprivation impairs the capacity to remember tasks from one day to the next.

For all its billions of cells, the neocortex is of finite size, and if all events and experiences were placed on permanent record in the long-term memory, the brain would need to be much bigger than it is. Winson conjectures that it would be so large that we should need a wheelbarrow to carry it about in. Clearly some sorting process must be at work, selecting what is important and 'memorable' from what is insignificant and to be discarded. Could dreams be implicated in this procedure? Crick and Mitchison (1983) are not the only researchers to think they are, though these authors have chosen to emphasize the discarding 'unlearning' aspect of the dream rather than the aspect concerned with selecting and recording. In fact, most dream researchers are now of the opinion that dreams are involved in the selection and retention of memories significant to the individual. The crucial question concerns the criteria on which the selection is based: what decides whether an experience is sufficiently important to be built into the permanent repertoire of memories available to a mammal as it goes about its daily life? Winson's answer is that it is the collective 'phyletic memory' of the species. In other words, dreaming is a *selective processing device* which constantly monitors and evaluates recent memories against a store of coded information in the central nervous system which has been painstakingly assembled during millions of years of evolution and which provides an indispensable set of rules for determining what is significant for a member of a given species and what is not.

In support of his argument about brain size, memory storage, and the function of dreaming, Winson cites the example of one of the last surviving monotremes, an anteater known as the echidna – an egg-laying mammal that emerged from the reptiles about 180 million years ago. From our point of view the most important facts about the echidna are that, although a small animal, it has a relatively enormous neocortex (as large as ours, in fact) and it does not have REM sleep. Since it does not dream, the echidna needs a much larger cerebral cortex to hold all the information it gathers in a lifetime of monotreme existence.

For millions of years it would seem that evolution stopped right there. But then, with the emergence of viviparous mammals, an extraordinary innovation occurred. This happened because there was a limit to the size to which heads could expand (to accommodate an ever-increasing cerebral cortex) if the newborn infant could hope to pass through its mother's pelvis and survive. The problem of how to reconcile restricted head size with cerebral efficiency was one that took nature a long time to solve, but the solution was one of startling originality: REM sleep.

A comparison of what we know about animals' dreams with what we know of our own yields one important difference, and that concerns the nature and complexity of what is dreamt, for animal dreams appear to be linked more directly to phyletic considerations than human dreams. While it is true that our dreams can present us with the great archetypal themes of human life, this is by no means invariably the case. When animals get up and act out their dreams, however, they seem always to involve the major survival issues of the species concerned. This must reflect evolutionary developments that have occurred since we parted company with our mammalian ancestors – our acquisition of language and the use of symbols, for example. As a result of these developments, human consciousness is less tightly strapped down to the archetypal wagon on which it rides, and we are able to assess present information in the light of past personal experience, without having constantly to refer back to ancient phyletic programmes in the 'collective unconscious'. This has enabled ontogenetic learning to proceed with greater efficiency in humans than in other primates and mammals, and it is not unreasonable to expect such an advantage to be reflected as much in our dreams as in our cultural behaviour.

Identifying his 'memory processing device' with the unconscious, Winson concluded that Freud was right in viewing dreams as meaningful and as constituting the Royal Road to the unconscious, but that he was wrong in considering the unconscious to be a seething cauldron of various lusts, and wrong again in interpreting dreams as disguised versions of these lusts. However, Winson made little reference to Jung, and this was a serious omission. For what is so fascinating about the hypotheses of both Winson and Jouvet is that they exactly parallel Jung's idea, proposed much earlier this century, that dreams compensate for one-sided attitudes of the conscious ego by mobilizing archetypal components from the collective unconscious in order to promote the individual's better adaptation to life. In fact, *their hypotheses are Jungian theory in modern biological dress*. Yet the irony is that while Winson praises Freud for having got it partially right, neither he nor Jouvet give much credit to Jung, who seems to have got it wholly right.

As is now well established, the dreaming state of REM sleep is quite different from any other psychophysical state. Typically associated with a low-voltage, desynchronized pattern of electrical activity arising from the cerebral cortex, REM sleep is also characterized by rapid conjugate movements of the eyes, and sporadic activity in certain groups of small muscles together with an absence of tone in the large anti-gravity muscles of the legs, back, and neck. The pulse and respiration are irregular, the penis becomes erect, and the blood pressure, brain temperature, and metabolic rate are all raised. When subjects are awakened from this state dreams are reliably reported on 70–90 per cent of occasions.

Periods of REM sleep regularly occur about every ninety minutes throughout the night, each episode persisting for a longer period of time, ranging from approximately five minutes to forty minutes. This cyclic regularity would suggest that dreaming is not dependent upon outside influences and this has been confirmed by the failure to induce REM periods experimentally by application of external stimuli – a finding compatible with Freud's assertion that the content of dreams is determined not by extrinsic stimulation but by programmes intrinsic to the dreamer's own mind. Equally, it has not proved easy to manipulate the content of dreams by exposing subjects to films, stories, and happenings immediately before sleep or by the application of stimuli after sleep has begun. Thus, in the dreaming state, the subject is on the whole refractory to events proceeding in the environment.

The hierarchical structure of the brain is reflected in the way it builds behaviour patterns out of what ethologists call *fixed acts*. These are stereotyped motor sequences which are the building blocks of behaviours necessary for survival and reproduction, and they are as apparent in typical dream sequences as they are in patterns of behaviour. For example, defensive behaviour, such as fleeing from threat, is apparent in the classic chase dream, attack behaviour in dreams of physical combat, and appetitive behaviour in dreams of a frankly erotic nature. The basic four F's of fixed action are feeding, fighting, fleeing, and fornication. If REM is indeed a 'genetically determined behavioural rehearsal', then the vital significance of dreams is that they enable the animal to respond appropriately to eating, aggressive, attacking, or sexual opportunities even before the gustatory, threatening, or erotic stimuli have been encountered in reality: the neural programme for behavioural acts must be in place before any particular behaviour is demanded.

In his invaluable book *The Dreaming Brain*, J. Allan Hobson (1988) maintains that this is as true of humans as of other mammals.

> Since any form of behaviour is a complex sequence of reflex acts, the difference between this and the previous level of organization is only one of degree. Even in the fully developed human animal, when behaviour is (more or less) under voluntary control, particular behaviour has the quality of a fixed act when adequately triggered and permitted to run its course.

And Hobson concludes:

> Our dreams tell us clearly that the repertoires for these 'instinctual' acts are indeed represented within the central nervous system. The extraordinary plasticity of the dream experience includes a rich over-representation of significant behaviours: fear, aggression, defence, and attack; approach-avoidance; and sex. At the level of our psychological experience, we find evidence of the whole repertoire.

Hobson's conclusion is in line with Hall and Nordby's (1972) demonstration of the universal occurrence of typical dreams involving aggression, being pursued, sex, and so on. That phylogenetically ancient structures must play an important role in human dreams may be deduced from one study of the common dreams reported by college students in which the following themes were reported in descending order of frequency: falling, being pursued or attacked, repeated attempts at performing a task, experiences connected with academic work, and sex (Sagan, 1977). All these types of dreams, with the exception of those concerned with academic work, have fairly evident phylogenetic links. It is not surprising, for example, that a creature which in earlier stages of its evolution spent much of its life in trees, should experience anxiety dreams of falling. Similarly, **nightmares** of being pursued or attacked are to be expected in a species whose primordial conflicts have involved hunting, fighting, and striving for dominance. Furthermore, the vital need to master changes in the environment, to acquire physical skills, perform religious and social rituals, require repeated attempts to learn and perform such tasks. Finally, the contribution of sexual behaviour to the survival of the species requires no comment.

THE TWO BASIC ARCHETYPAL MODES: SMILING AND FROWNING AT THE ANGELS

In confirmation of Chance's claim (1988) to have defined two basic archetypal modes, cross-cultural evidence indicates that certain facial expressions involved in hedonic and agonic relations, such as smiling, frowning, and disdain, are genetically determined. What is so fascinating about these behaviours is that their early ontological development seems to be linked with the REM state. Thus, REM-state smiling, sometimes referred to as 'smiling at the angels', appears in human infants before the development of social smiling in wakefulness. Similarly, complex expressions normally associated with anger, perplexity, and disdain also first appear in the REM state. In other words, these behaviours rehearse and anticipate those social capacities which will appear in wakefulness some weeks later. It was precisely such findings as these that led Michel Jouvet (1967) to conclude that the REM state plays a crucial role in the maturation of species-specific instinctual behaviour. There is also a similar and highly instructive correlation between dreaming and playing in the development of capacities crucial to survival.

ARCHETYPAL DREAMS IN EARLY CHILDHOOD

One question inevitably arises: If foetuses and neonates spend all or most of their time dreaming, what on earth can they be dreaming about? Presumably, these dreams must, in Jung's terminology, be entirely archetypal. As brain structures develop, the basic forms of psychological ideation and imagery associated with them are assuming their first dimly perceived forms. Support for this supposition comes from the dreams of young children which are found on examination to be full of archetypal implications. Indeed, Jung's belief that there is an archetypal foundation to dreams came from his early realization that his childhood dreams contained transpersonal elements which could not have been derived from his own experience.

The common childhood fears – of the dark, of strangers, of rapidly approaching objects – can all be understood as 'early warning' devices put there by evolution because of the constant dangers in the ancestral environment. The dreams of childhood are full of 'Things' and monsters that threaten to attack. That this seems so much worse in the dark is because humans have bad night vision and because the great cats hunt during the hours of darkness. This built-in awareness of the ever present 'Thing' that might attack makes children sensitive to cues that might naturally be associated with it. Thus, the predator archetype is evident in many child-hood fears and nightmares. For example, Susan Isaacs gives an account (in Klein *et al.* (1952)) of a one-and-a-half year old child who was so terrified by the broken and flapping sole of her mother's shoe that the shoe had to be hidden away. When she saw it again 15 months later she was able to say 'I thought that it could eat me right up.'

ARCHETYPES AND NEUROSCIENCE

We are left with the conclusion that modern neuroscientific findings, to-gether with the theoretical constructs placed upon them, are all remarkably compatible with Jung's theory of archetypes, originally formulated in the early part of this century. Although Paul MacLean proposed his concept of the triune brain several years after Jung's death, Jung had already suggested that dreams about mammals or reptiles could relate to phylogenetically an-cient mammalian and reptilian structures in the brain and that they were to be understood as expressions of the deeper intentions of nature itself:

> The evolutionary stratification of the psyche is more clearly discernible in the dream than in the conscious mind. In the dream the psyche speaks in images, and gives expression to instincts, which derive from the most primitive levels of nature. Therefore, through the assimilation of unconscious contents, the momentary life of consciousness can once more be brought into harmony with the law of nature from which it all too easily departs, and the patient can be led back to the natural law of his own being.
>
> (CW16, para. 351)

At the time, this was little more than a hunch, but he had the courage to back it. On its basis, he built his understanding of human psychopathology and devised a treatment for its cure. In Jung's view, our major difficulties, whether neurotic, psychotic, psychopathic, or political, come from losing contact with 'the age old unforgotten wisdom stored up in us'. If we wished to re-establish contact with this great reservoir of human potential then there was only one way open to us: we must pay close attention to our dreams.

Animal dreams abound in analytic practice. For example, *a rather timid woman, who was scared of her difficult and demanding boss, dreamt of a large black dog that stood in its kennel staring at her. A voice said: 'He's stubborn but he's as good as gold if you treat him right.'* Working on the dream herself, she thought at first that the dog represented her boss, but, at her next ana-lytic session, she realized that it was a stubborn, potentially aggressive part of herself that she wasn't using. The value of this insight was apparent in the weeks that followed, for she was able to make good use of the dog image in her working life: it gave her the courage to be stubborn and aggressive herself when her boss failed to 'treat her right'. This is an example of a compensatory dream making available to the dreamer potential that she did not realize she possessed. That she discovered her own stubbornness and aggression in mammalian form might indicate that it was still not sufficiently assimilated into her conscious personality to appear in her dreams as human.

NEUROPHYSIOLOGICAL THEORIES OF DREAMING

It would be wrong, however, to imply that all researchers agree that dreams are meaningful psychological events. As Freud wrote at the end of the last century:

> Dreaming has often been compared with the 'ten fingers of a man who knows nothing of music wandering over the keys of a piano' . . . and this simile shows as well as anything the sort of opinion that is usually held of dreaming by representatives of the exact sciences. On this view a dream is something wholly and completely incapable of interpretation; for how could the ten fingers of an unmusical player produce a piece of music?

(1900; 1976)

This materialistic, anti-psychological attitude has persisted right up to the present time, fuelled by the current enthusiasm for computer analogies of the brain. For example, in 1977 J. Allan Hobson and his Harvard colleague Robert McCarley proposed an entirely neurophysiological theory of dreaming which they called the 'activation-synthesis' hypothesis. According to this theory, dreams are evoked by a 'dream state generator' which is 'switched on' in the brain stem during REM sleep and bombards the forebrain with randomly synthesized misinformation. Dreams are the result of the cerebral cortex making whatever sense it can out of the nonsense with which it is presented. 'In other words, the forebrain may be making the best of a bad job in producing even partially coherent imagery from the relatively noisy signals sent up by the brain stem. . . . The brain, in the dreaming sleep state, is thus likened to a computer searching its addresses for key words.' Essentially, dreams were, in their view, merely the senseless, random accompaniments of autonomous electrical activity in the sleeping central nervous system, and the question as to whether or not dreams had a meaning was a red herring.

Another computer analogy was advanced by the British psychologist, Christopher Evans, in his book *Landscapes of the Night: How and Why We Dream* (1983), where he proposed that dreaming represents the brain-computer's 'off-line' time, when it processes information gathered during the previous day and updates its programmes in anticipation of the morrow.

The 'reverse learning' theory of dreaming proposed in 1983 by Francis

Crick and Graeme Mitchison held that dreaming is merely a means of dumping redundant information, of 'removing parasitic modes which arise after the [cortical] system has been disturbed either by growth of the brain (when new connections are constantly being made) or by the modifications produced by experience.' What was happening during REM sleep, they asserted, was 'an active process which is, loosely speaking, the opposite of learning. We call this "reverse learning" or "unlearning". In other words: "we dream in order to forget."'

Crick and Mitchison's hypothesis received so much attention that one might have thought that it was something startlingly new, but one would have been misguided. A very similar idea was proposed as long ago as the 1880s by Robert, who described the dream as 'a somatic process of excretion.' 'A man deprived of the capacity of dreaming,' Robert wrote, 'would in course of time become mentally deranged, because a great mass of uncompleted, unworked-out thoughts and superficial impressions would accumulate in his brain and would be bound by their bulk to smother the thoughts that should be assimilated into his memory as completed wholes.' This view, as Freud commented, reduced dreams to the lowly status of mere 'scavengers of the mind' (Freud 1900; 1976).

The trouble is that researchers so often become powerfully attached to their own theories, and so hostile to those who adopt others, that they forget they are all partially sighted observers examining different aspects of the same elephant in the dark, each believing that the particular bit of trunk, foot, or tail they are grasping represents the whole beast. Freud was evidently grasping its private parts.

Infinitely preferable to this groping in the dark would be a holistic attitude to dreaming, enabling the hermeneutic (interpretive) and scientific (experimental) approaches to complement and correct one another to the mutual advantage of both. The best of the contemporary dream researchers, such as J. Allan Hobson, have come to recognize this. In place of the purely physiological approach which he originally adopted, Hobson has come round to the view that dreams are not without psychological meaning:

> I differ from Freud in that I think that most dreams are neither obscure nor bowdlerized, but rather that they are transparent and unedited. They reveal clearly meaningful, undisguised, and often highly conflictual themes worthy of note by the dreamer (and any interpretive assistant). My position echoes Jung's notion of dreams as transparently meaningful and does away with any distinction between manifest and latent content.

> (1988, p. 12)

Hobson even mentions with approval the Senoi-Malaysian people who discuss their dreams every morning and consider them to be guides to their current concerns and actions: 'like the Senoi,' adds Hobson, 'I regard

228

dreaming as indicative of my internal state and take its data into account in my day-to-day self-assessment.' This is precisely the same exercise that Jung practised on a daily basis for most of his life after his break with Freud.

Another important dream researcher, Kleitman's pupil William C. Dement, to whom we owe the term 'REM sleep', also came to appreciate that dreams are rich in meaning and can carry enormous transformative power. One of his own dreams demonstrates this:

> *Some years ago I was a heavy cigarette smoker – up to two packs a day. Then one night I had an exceptionally vivid and realistic dream in which I had inoperable cancer of the lung. I remember as though it were yester-day looking at the ominous shadow in my chest X-ray and realizing that the entire right lung was infiltrated. The subsequent physical examination in which a colleague detected widespread metastases in my axillary and inguinal lymph nodes was equally vivid. Finally, I experienced the incred-ible anguish of knowing my life was soon to end, that I would never see my children grow up, and that none of this would have happened if I had quit cigarettes when I first learned of their carcinogenic potential. I will never forget the surprise, joy, and exquisite relief of waking up. I felt I was reborn. Needless to say, the experience was sufficient to induce an immediate cessation of my cigarette habit. This dream had both antici-pated the problem, and solved it in a way that may be a dream's unique privilege.*
>
> *Only the dream can allow us to experience a future alternative as if it were real, and thereby to provide a supremely enlightened motivation to act upon this knowledge.*
>
> (quoted by LaBerge, 1985, p. 192)

This is a good example of the superior wisdom that dreams can access to the dreamer as well as the therapeutic influence they can exert by correcting potentially self-destructive attitudes of ego-consciousness. To dismiss dreams of this order as mere 'activation-synthesis' or 'reverse learning' does them less than justice. Nor do these reductive, neurologically based theories give a useful account of how dreaming evolved, why it has persisted, and what its psychobiological functions could be.

DREAMS AND MENTAL ILLNESS

Many authorities have compared the phenomena of dreaming with the signs and symptoms of psychotic illnesses. Immanuel Kant's observation that 'the madman is a waking dreamer' was echoed by Krauss's (1859) state-ment, quoted by Freud (1900; 1976), that 'insanity is a dream dreamt while the senses are awake.' Schopenhauer (1862) described dreams as a brief madness and madness as a long dream, while Wilhelm Wundt (1874) wrote:

'We ourselves, in fact, can experience in dreams almost all the phenomena to be met with in insane asylums'. No less an authority than Bleuler considered the secondary symptoms of schizophrenia (such as hallucinations, delusions, negativism, and stupor) were identical with dreaming. One of his brightest pupils, C.G. Jung, agreed, arguing that if a dreamer were to walk about and act as if he were awake, then he would present a clinical condition closely resembling **dementia praecox** (schizophrenia). 'Find out about dreams,' maintained Hughlings Jackson, 'and you will find out about insanity' (Feierman, 1982). Contemporary researchers, such as Hobson (1988), have reaffirmed that dreams and psychoses are closely related.

Hobson describes five cardinal characteristics of dreams and shows how they are mimicked in mental illness. These are (1) the illogical content and organization of dreams which defy natural laws as well as the unities of time, place, and person; (2) the intense emotions which are capable of disturbing the mental state of the dreamer (as in nightmares and anxiety dreams); (3) the experience of fully formed sensory impressions in the absence of outer stimuli; (4) the uncritical acceptance of the curious and bizarre things which are seen, heard, and felt; and (5) the difficulty of remembering the dream when it is over. Hobson draws clear parallels between these characteristics and the disorientation, bizarre thought patterns, powerful affective states, delusions, hallucinations, and amnesias experienced by psychotic patients.

Viewed from the standpoint of normal consciousness, the most striking feature of both psychosis and dreaming is *loss of insight*: fantastic events seem absolutely real – so much so that awakening from a dream is like recovering from a psychotic episode at the moment the realization dawns that one has been deluded and hallucinated: 'Thank God! It was only a dream!'

The discontinuities, incongruities, improbabilities, illogicalities, uncertainties, mythical constructions, and non sequiturs so typical of dreams are very like the 'thought disorder' regularly observed in schizophrenic patients since the time of Emil Kraepelin (1856–1926), while schizophrenic 'loss of volition' resembles the common dream experience of lethargy, dragging feet, not being able to get done what has to be done. The ghastly sense of helplessness or paralysis suffered in **nightmares** and **night terrors** has parallels in the rigidity of **catatonic schizophrenia** and the 'tonic immobility', or 'freezing in horror', seen across the evolutionary spectrum as an extreme response to severe stress. The powerful emotions of excitement and fear which can influence the mental state in dreams are also apparent in the clinical conditions of **mania** and **phobic anxiety**. In dreams we also experience amnesia (we remember little or nothing about our waking state) and we confabulate – facts which have persuaded some researchers to compare dreaming with **Korsakoff's psychosis**, in which memory loss is associated with confabulation (the invention of events in considerable detail in order to compensate and disguise the memory loss). In addition, dreaming closely resembles clinical delirium; and, interestingly enough, the EEG pattern characteristic of **delirium** is similar to that recorded from subjects in REM sleep.

Thus, it is not far-fetched to consider dreaming to be a form of licensed madness occurring in the asylum of sleep, and this conclusion has highly significant implications for psychopathology. No less an authority than Aristotle suggested that the hallucinations and delusions of the insane, the illusions of normal waking life, and the fantastic experiences of the dream world are not merely similar, but may actually share a common origin. Similarly, Hobson argues that dreaming could well be the mental product of the same *kind* of psychobiological process that appears to be deranged in mental illness. 'This conclusion gives the scientific study of the dream process implications beyond the realm of dreaming itself: since all the major signs of mental illness can be imitated by normal minds in the normal state of dreaming. The study of dreams is the study of a model of mental illness' (1988, p. 9).

If this is so, how is it possible to maintain that dreams have an adaptive or creative function? If dreams are a form of temporary madness how on earth can they be thought to enhance our lives? The answer is that it depends on the attitude one adopts to mental illness. If one regards all psychiatric symptoms as simply the tragic and meaningless consequences of psychopathology then it is hard to see how dreams, inasmuch as they resemble such symptoms, can have a beneficial influence. But if, on the other hand, one regards psychiatric symptoms as meaningful responses to major problems encountered by individuals in their lives, and as attempts to adapt to these problems, then the parallel with symptom formation becomes less dire in its implications for dreaming.

Mental illness, like dreaming, can be conceived as a meaningful response to the total life situation. Instead of stigmatizing psychiatric symptoms as pathological entities, they can be approached, like dreams, as symbolic communications from the unconscious indicating where the patient has become embroiled in the fundamental problems of life and showing how he is attempting to achieve some kind of resolution of them. Thus, the discovery of parallels between dreams and the symptoms of mental illness does not require one to adopt a pessimistic or pathological view of dreaming. Freud was correct in seeing a relationship between dreams and psychiatric symptoms, not because dreams are pathological phenomena, but because dreams and symptoms are similar attempts at adaptive adjustment and derived from the same intrapsychic source. 'Symptoms', wrote Jung, 'are always justified and serve a purpose.'

THE NOCTURNAL THEORY OF SCHIZOPHRENIA

One interesting attempt to link the dreaming brain to the clinical phenomena of schizophrenia is that of Jay R. Feierman (1982; 1994). Adapting Bleuler's and Jung's insights that a schizophrenic is a dreamer in a world awake, Feierman proposed that the schizophrenic brain is operating in P mode (processing information and transferring short-term memories into the long-term memory which normally occurs during sleep, especially in REM sleep) while the person is awake. The specific abnormality carried by the schizophrenic, maintains Feierman, is a genetic variant for nocturnal activity. But instead of being allowed to live a nocturnal existence, schizophrenics are coerced by normal social expectations into a life of activity during daylight or under conditions of artificial lighting, with the result that they persist in processing information in wakefulness using a brain which continues to function as if it were asleep.

This peculiarity is genetically determined. The non-genetic factor which is responsible for the induction of schizophrenia, according to Feierman, is quite simply the presence of light. A nocturnal animal hides itself away from daylight and uses the daylight hours for sleep and P mode processing, performing its waking activities during the hours of darkness. Thus the life of a nocturnal animal is spent almost entirely in the absence of light.

In support of his theory, Feierman pointed to the fact that some surviving primate species are nocturnal and that this indicates that a genetic determinant for nocturnal, dark-adapted activity must at some stage have entered the primate gene pool from which our own species originated. Moreover, there are no recorded instances of schizophrenia in people blind from birth, while the incidence of schizophrenia among totally deaf people is similar to that of the population at large. Unlike non-schizophrenic people, schizophrenic patients fail to suppress muscle tension during REM sleep and catatonic schizophrenics tend to be more active during sleep than during wakefulness. The solitariness of schizophrenics also squares with Feierman's theory, since the great majority of nocturnal species live a solitary existence.

The advantage of Feierman's theory is that it is testable. For example, if schizophrenic patients in the acute phase of the illness were permitted to live an entirely nocturnal, dark-adapted existence, exposed only to light at the red end of the spectrum, their illness should remit. Moreover, post-mortem examination of the eyes of people with a history of schizophrenia might reveal that their retinas approximate more closely than those of controls to the retinas of nocturnal animals (that is they should be more richly supplied with rods relative to cones). To our knowledge, neither of these research projects has been undertaken.

Should the nocturnal theory of schizophrenia be supported by research evidence, it would in no way conflict with our own group-splitting hypothesis. Indeed, it would be compatible with it, since, as described in Chapter

13, charismatic leaders, gurus, shamans, and visionaries almost invariably possess access to the liminal state, in that they can be in touch with normally unconscious processes while in a condition of apparent wakefulness.

SUMMARY AND CONCLUSIONS

The findings of dream science are compatible with the insight expressed by the British sexologist Havelock Ellis (1899) that dreams represent 'an archaic world of vast emotions and imperfect thoughts', the study of which might reveal to us primitive stages in the evolution of mental life. As Freud's colleague, Sandor Ferenczi, said, 'Dreaming itself is the workshop of evolution.' At night, it seems, we enter an archetypal world where we participate in the phylogenetic programme of our species and share with it our mite of the day's experiences. Let us summarize the evidence:

1 The emergence of dream sleep 130 million years ago and its persistence across a wide range of species demonstrates that it is a neuropsychic activity of the greatest biological significance.
2 EEG records in sleeping decorticate cats and in humans with gross cerebral lesions reveal that the low voltage fast waves of REM sleep originate in evolutionarily ancient centres in the brain stem.
3 In addition, the paleo-mammalian structures of the mid-brain are active in REM sleep, as may be deduced from the associated changes which occur in pulse and respiratory rates, blood pressure, penile dimensions, vaginal blood flow, emotional state, temperature regulation, and so on.
4 When brain centres responsible for maintaining the relatively immobile state of REM sleep are removed or inhibited, animals 'act out' patterns of behaviour which are typical of their species and crucial for their survival.
5 These observations, which clearly demonstrate that brain structures possessing an extremely long evolutionary pedigree are involved in dreaming, give impressive support for two hypotheses: (a) that neuronal complexes crucial to the human ethogram (the Jungian 'archetypes') are located in these regions, and (b) that a phylogenetic continuity exists for essential archetypal patterns which extends from reptilian through mammalian to human forms of behaviour and experience.
6 The findings that EEG theta rhythm, originating from a specific part of the paleo-mammalian brain, namely, the hippocampus, is associated with the performance of crucial survival behaviours and with memory storage as well as with REM sleep lends weight to the additional hypothesis that in dreaming sleep an animal, including the human animal, is updating strategies for survival in the light of its own experience and in the light of all the potential for experience specific to the species.
7 The close parallels between the phenomena of dreams and psychosis suggest that investigation of the cerebral processes associated with both these

conditions could be of the greatest significance for the future of psychiatric theory and practice.

Dreams, then, are predictable episodic phenomena, associated with cyclic functions in the central nervous system, and have their basis in biology. As Hobson (1988) has put it, dreams are the product of a 'genetically determined, functionally dynamic blue-print' in the brain, whose function is '*to construct* and *to test* the brain circuits that underlie our behavior – including cognition and meaning attribution'. While he believes this test programme to be essential to normal mind/brain functioning, Hobson does not consider that one has necessarily to remember its products in order to reap its benefits. On his own admission, however, he has found these benefits to be enhanced when he makes the effort to remember them. One can only endorse Ernest Rossi's (1972) succinct conclusions that dreaming is 'an endogenous process of psychological growth, change and transformation', and that dreams themselves constitute 'a laboratory for experimenting with changes in our psychic life.'

Yet, for all the outstanding contributions to dream psychology made by such pioneers as Freud, Jung, and many others, dreams remain an underutilized resource whose enormous therapeutic potential is ignored by the majority of psychiatrists and therapists.

NOTE

Much of the information used in this chapter appears in *Private Myths: Dreams and Dreaming* by Anthony Stevens (Hamish Hamilton, 1995), where the arguments here presented are examined and discussed in greater depth.

19

CLASSIFICATION

At the start of this project, the authors were sceptical of current psychiatric nosology, believing it possible to produce a biological basis for a classification of mental disorders which would be more satisfactory than that embodied in DSM-IV or ICD 10. However, when our analysis was complete, we found ourselves to be in agreement with many aspects of the current scheme. On the whole, there are good biological reasons for upholding the distinctions between the schizophrenic and affective psychoses, between neurotic (reactive), and psychotic (endogenous) forms of depression, and between three categories of personality disorder.

DISTINCTION BETWEEN SCHIZOPHRENIC AND MOOD DISORDERS

We believe that these two groups of disorder reflect two major emergent properties which are linked to the life-cycle of human groups. For part of their existence, groups manifest a strong tendency to integration and cohesiveness, while at another stage they display an equally strong propensity to split into daughter groups. These two stages are broadly analogous to the phases of integration and division which characterize the life-cycle of unicellular organisms.

We had already identified affective disorders as adaptive mechanisms responsible for maintaining group integration by sacrificing the mental health of individuals to the stability of the group. We subsequently became interested in the possiblity that schizophrenia, in terms of both face validity and construct validity, was related to group splitting: the alienation so characteristic of the schizotypal or schizophrenic patient was a clinical parallel to the alienation of a daughter group from the main group and from other daughter groups. We concluded, therefore, that the two major groups of 'functional' psychosis were a clinical reflection of two fundamentally different, in fact opposite, group functions. Should our intuition prove to be correct, it will serve greatly to strengthen the epistemological foundations of psychiatry as a branch of medical science. What could be more validating of

235

Kraepelin's original distinction between manic-depression and dementia praecox? And what more supportive of the classifications that have persisted through the past century to be enshrined in the present edition of the *Diagnostic and Statistical Manual of Mental Disorders*?

On the other hand, we found no evolutionary indications for the subdivisions of schizophrenia listed in ICD 10 and DSM-IV. It seems likely that the genotypical susceptibility to schizophrenia manifests itself in a diffuse manner consonant with the concept of **schizophrenic spectrum disorder**. This manifests itself in the qualities of stubbornness, eccentricity and frank bloody-mindedness linked to the capacity to conceptualize new belief systems and to adhere to them with a degree of conviction seldom available to those who do not share the schizotypal disposition.

We should, perhaps, make it clear that our concept of splitting is distinct from Bleuler's (1911) concept of schizophrenia (literally, 'split-diaphragm' – that is, a division in the seat of the soul). For Bleuler, the most striking feature of the condition was the split between thinking and emotion which resulted in the characteristic 'incongruity of affect' which could allow a patient to emit a loud guffaw while predicting the end of the world, or to weep when announcing triumph in the National Lottery. Bleuler's usage is, therefore, entirely different from our own and should not be confused with it.

MOOD DISORDERS

The basic classificatory distinction between manic and depressive forms of affective disorder is entirely compatible with our view that they reflect mechanisms in the reptilian brain which access the alternative strategies of escalation and de-escalation in status conflicts. While these mechanisms operate adaptively in most cases, in some individuals they may become disconnected from environmental influences and act autonomously, thus giving rise to endogenous forms of manic-depressive psychosis.

With regard to depression, we maintain that all manifestations of the disorder may be understood as direct consequences of an involuntary subordinate or low self-esteem strategy. This de-escalating strategy, mediated by the reptilian brain, may manifest itself in one of three clinical forms:

1 as a life-long trait, which may be diagnosed as a **depressive personality disorder**;
2 in individuals with low self-esteem who, in congenial circumstances may appear relatively normal, but who, when adversity strikes, may develop a **neurotic** or **reactive depression**; or
3 in individuals who adopt a relatively high self-esteem strategy and who, when severe adversity strikes, are plunged into a state of low self-esteem quite at variance with their usual self-concept and develop a **psychotic depression**.

The symptoms of both the second and third forms may overlap in many particulars, but there are two significant ways in which they differ: one concerns the degree to which the patient's personality is observed to change, and the other concerns the patient's own assessment of past achievements. Thus, the friends and relatives of people afflicted by a psychotic depression commonly remark on the radical personality alteration that has occurred: 'He's a totally different person', they say, or 'She's just not the woman I married.' By contrast, friends of people who develop a neurotic depression tend to say 'He's much as he's always been, but more so.'

The second distinction is even more striking. Whereas all depressive patients have a depressed view of themselves, the world, and the future (Beck's cognitive triad), only psychotic depressives have a depressed view of the past. They are often deluded about their former rank and personality, flatly denying that they have ever possessed social status or resources. Their past achievements appear to them a hollow sham. This is the yielding subroutine at its most incisive: since these people deny they ever held social rank, it follows that there can be no former rank for them to regain. This has the adaptive function of accommodating them to their reduced circumstances.

The difference between the two types of depression is not unlike the difference between the reaction of an animal suddenly demoted in its social hierarchy and the behaviour of an unfortunate creature that has been kept in a subordinate position for the whole of its adult life (Price, 1969). This does not mean that the two types of depression are necessarily homologous in human and non-human primates but reflects the fact that any animal living in a social hierarchy is likely to possess different strategies for dealing with subordination – one for individuals who have always been subordinate and one for those who are accustomed to dominance. It is clear that the latter will demand a more radical and potentially more traumatic process of adaptation on the principle that 'the higher they climb, the harder they fall.'

PERSONALITY DISORDERS

Our initial scepticism about the current classification of personality disorders was modified when our analysis yielded support for three main groups or clusters. Though these do not precisely coincide with Cluster A, B, and C personality disorders as described in DSM-IV, there are, nevertheless, considerable overlaps. The main personality disorders classified by DSM-IV are as follows (disorders that we have translocated are put in brackets):

Cluster A: paranoid, schizoid, schizotypal;
Cluster B: antisocial [borderline], histrionic, narcissistic;
Cluster C: [avoidant], dependent, obsessive-compulsive.

Our own classification is compatible with this scheme except for three particulars:

1 we believe that **borderline personality disorder** warrants classification on its own;
2 we consider that avoidant personality disorder should be classified as a **spacing disorder**, along with the paranoid, schizoid and schizotypal disorders of Cluster A.
3 we maintain that Cluster B and C disorders represent subgroups of what we have termed **personality disorders of attachment and rank**.

Our own classification may be summarized as follows:

Spacing personality disorders: avoidant, paranoid, schizoid, and schizotypal.
Borderline personality disorder.
Attachment/rank personality disorders:
   Subgroup (a):   antisocial, histrionic, narcissistic
   Subgroup (b):   type A, dependent, obsessive-compulsive.

In our classification, **spacing personality disorders** reflect the genetic potential for behaviour implicated in group splitting and in the clinical manifestations of schizophrenic spectrum disorder.

Borderline personality disorder occurs in those individuals with low self-esteem who experience themselves as teetering on the brink between insider and outsider status.

Attachment/rank personality disorders of **subgroup (a)** are found in individuals who are non-reciprocating free-riders, while those of **subgroup (b)** occur in people who are reciprocators and who endeavour to adapt to group pressures either by dominating (type As), by being submissive supplicants (dependent types) or by striving to be 'perfect' and above reproach (obsessive-compulsives). People with attachment/rank personality disorders of either group experience themselves as contending for survival in the context of the group.

CONCLUSION

We have been surprised and gratified to discover the extent to which our evolutionary analysis of mental disorders would seem to be in accord with current diagnostic categories. While the schemes incorporated in ICD 10 and DSM-IV publications are both empirical and inductive, our own evolutionary reasoning is essentially deductive (Wilson, 1993), working, as we have, from the laws of evolution and genetics. That these two paths should coincide and lead us to the same destination was contrary to our expectation. What the evolutionary perspective adds is a more comprehensive understanding of psychiatric conditions as expressions of normal, adaptive patterns of behaviour which, for one reason or another, have become exaggerated or distorted. We are optimistic that an awareness of the biological bases of the various forms of psychopathology will prove fruitful not only for psychiatric epistemology but for finding future innovations in treatment and research.

20

TREATMENT

A NEW ORIENTATION

What the evolutionary dimension brings to the treatment of psychiatric disorders is a new perspective, a new orientation. Although psychiatry has long since abandoned the concept of demonic possession to account for the symptoms it endeavours to treat, it still approaches mental illness as if it were an enemy to be fought and overcome. The patient is expected to go through the rituals of consultation, 'mental state' examination and diagnosis, to collude with the psychiatrist in becoming detached and objective about his condition, and to place himself in the capable hands of the doctor and his team. The patient's only responsibility in the matter is then to 'keep taking the pills'. Many patients prefer it this way, finding it hard to accept responsibility for their circumstances, preferring to blame life events and other people for the way they feel, and to adopt a passive or dependent attitude to the psychiatrist who is willing to offer them treatment. For their part, psychiatrists, reliant as they are on the medical model, have encouraged this, because, like their patients, they can see little that is positive or meaningful in their clinical condition, only suffering, hopelessness and pain.

Evolutionary psychiatry, on the other hand, adopts a transpersonal view of the patient's situation. Instead of seeing his illness purely as the product of his familial and social circumstances, it examines it in the context of the evolved goals, needs and strategies that have determined human behaviour since our species came into existence on the African savannah. From the evolutionary standpoint, a psychiatric disorder is not a medical disaster like cancer or a stroke but an ancient adaptive response which for some contemporary reason has become maladaptive to the detriment of the patient's emotional and social life.

While evolutionary psychiatry endorses the traditional approach of taking a careful history in order to elicit signs and symptoms and paint a detailed clinical picture, it regards a compulsive preoccupation with forcing symptoms into precisely numbered diagnostic categories as misguided, since it thrusts all the inessential features of the patient's condition into the foreground while giving inadequate attention to the evolved strategies on which the condition is based. The patient's history has to be taken beyond his purely personal predicament and related to the story of humankind. For what psychiatry has traditionally classified as 'illness' is often a consequence of a potentially healthy organism struggling to meet the exigencies of life: symptom formation is itself an adaptive process. To consider symptoms as the products of a hypothetical disease entity does not necessarily make their meaning clear: viewed in an evolutionary context they are more likely to be comprehensible. This is an important point. Understanding symptom formation as a creative and adaptive act can be of the highest value, providing that precious commodity, **therapeutic optimism** – both in the doctor and the patient. Instead of forms of futile suffering, symptoms can be seen as the growing pains of people struggling to adjust to the demands that life puts on them.

Therapeutic optimism is further encouraged by the evolutionary view that every human being is richly endowed with the archetypal potential of the species. This means that, however disordered, one-sided or constricted individual psychological development may be, the *potential* for further growth and better adaptation is still *there*, implicit in the psychophysical structure of the organism. As a result, patients may be helped to *grow beyond* the defective or inadequate form of adjustment that their personal circumstances have hitherto allowed.

The evolutionary perspective thus brings with it a change in the traditional attitude to the 'patient'. Whether we like it or not, we are all in the human zoo together, and patients should be regarded as fellow inmates – not as sick victims but as candidates for the development of a better adaptation. Instead of passively accepting medicine and support, they are to be encouraged to participate in their suffering so as to confront its *meaning*, the therapeutic objective being to develop a creative relationship to their symptoms and to the adaptations underlying them.

More important still, the evolutionary perspective grants an expanded view of the self – that it is not just the sum total of the life experiences of one's personal history but the product of many millions of years of development. What evolution proposes, man or woman disposes. Within each one of us the vast potential of humanity is contained. Few of us ever make more than fractional use of that amazing capacity, and this failure can itself result in impaired function and efficiency. 'The vast majority die without realizing more than a fraction of their powers', wrote A.R. Orage. 'Born millionaires, they live and die in poverty.'

What Jung called **individuation** (the process of becoming as complete a human being as it is possible, given one's circumstances, to become) is about integrating ontogeny with phylogeny, uniting one's personal existence with the potential existence of humanity. It means using the mentalities with which natural selection has endowed us and bringing them to fulfilment in our lives. When a patient enters the consulting room, he brings with him, in a manner of speaking, a crowd of people from his past. That psychiatry has always known. What evolutionary psychiatry has recognized is that he also brings the hunter-gatherers, anteaters, and reptiles from his ancestral past. By the end of a consultation, the room is crammed with this menagerie, each member of which has a right to be listened to, and, if possible, to have his needs fulfilled. It is, says Gilbert (1989), like training a football team, encouraging each individual player to develop his skills and to integrate them with the skills of the other players, so that they come to the point where they play most effectively as a *team* rather than a set of competing individuals.

Success in this endeavour will depend on the therapist's skill in releasing the unused creative potential in the patient's personality. A model for this is provided by classical Jungian analysis, which seeks to mobilize archetypal components of the phylogenetic psyche by encouraging patients to dream, to fantasize, to paint, to open themselves to relationships with new friends and to find new ways of relating to old ones, as well as becoming conscious of the strategies and conflicts that have been controlling their lives in the past. To make headway in such demanding work, therapists have to develop their own personality and creative abilities if they hope to do much more than patch up their patients and enable them to go on existing. But this can make the life of a committed therapist rewarding, challenging, and immensely worthwhile.

We will consider the use of these principles in the treatment of depression, anxiety and phobic disorders, and anorexia nervosa.

DEPRESSION

Albert Squires, a hospital porter, had been off sick for three months before his general practitioner referred him to the psychiatric out-patients clinic of the hospital where he worked. He presented with the signs and symptoms of a major depression – depressed mood, weeping, anhedonia, loss of interest and sexual libido, impaired sleep and appetite.

A decent, reliable and conscientious man, with no previous psychiatric history, he had come to work at the hospital nine months earlier, having served for a number of years before that as a merchant seaman. All had gone well with this new job until, at the end of his first six months, the head porter sent for him and rebuked him for not taking any sick leave! Mr Squires explained that he would certainly take sick leave if he became ill, but since he was in good health this would not be necessary. 'You're missing the point', said the head porter. 'I don't care whether you're ill or not. When a man is off sick, the rest of us get paid overtime. So if you don't take your sick leave, you're letting the side down. You're cheating us out of money we're entitled to.'

To Mr Squires this was an important moral issue. Being an honest sort of chap, he didn't see how he could possibly stay off work and send in a sick note when he was feeling perfectly well. So he declined to go along with the head porter's scheme. Gradually the atmosphere at work changed: his previously happy relationship with his work mates turned sour as they avoided him and showed their disapproval of his 'unco-operative' attitude. He felt shunned and increasingly isolated, with the result that his slide into depression began. Eventually, unable to face going to work any longer, he was forced to go off sick. He brooded on the injustice of his position, but the irony did not escape him that his colleagues were drawing their overtime pay despite the moral stand he had taken on the issue.

What light does evolutionary theory throw on this case? How are we to understand the social situation in which Mr Squires's depression had occurred? What evolved strategies were being used at different levels of the triune brain? What helpful advice could we give to the patient?

Porters in a large hospital constitute a small tribal group with its own hierarchy, values, rituals and modes of functioning. As with all such groups, membership depends on acceptance by other members of the group and the allocation of status within the group. Acceptance and status depend, in turn, on conformity to the group's ethos. Once membership has been granted on these terms, an individual's self-esteem (RHP and SAHP) as well as his sense of personal health and well-being become dependent upon the continued good opinion of the group. The realization that one has offended the group, lost status, and been threatened with ostracism, can, as was suggested in Chapter 5, result in a depressive disorder. A depression is particularly likely to result if the individual is forced into an *involuntary* use of the yielding subroutine, as was the case with Mr Squires.

We have drawn attention to two fundamental vertebrate strategies for dealing with adversity: one is to attack, to escalate the action, to 'go for it' with the determination to 'win at all costs' (**the escalating** or **winning strategy**); the other is to yield, to back off or submit, to de-escalate, to 'cut one's losses' (**the de-escalating** or **losing strategy**). The phylogeny of social competition has decreed that the decision to escalate or de-escalate should be taken *at all three levels of the triune brain.*

Each of the 'three central processing assemblies' of the triune brain (MacLean, 1985) has the autonomous power to select either a winning or a losing strategy:

1 At the highest (neocortical) level a conscious assessment of the threat is made and the decision whether to fight or yield is taken in full awareness of the circumstances.
2 At the middle (limbic, paleo-mammalian) level a semi-conscious, emotionally loaded assessment of the threat is made and the selection of the

winning strategy of anger or the losing strategy of 'feeling chastened' proceeds with much less awareness of the circumstances.

3 At the lowest (reptilian) level an unconscious, instinctive assessment of the threat is made and the winning strategy (in the form of elevated mood) or losing strategy (in the form of depressed mood) is selected at a level beyond all awareness of the social circumstances involved.

How does the existence of these three strategic levels of operation help us to understand Mr Squires's depression? Careful examination of his thoughts and feelings about his predicament made it apparent that his highest (neo-cortical) and middle (limbic) levels had selected the winning strategy, while his lowest (reptilian) level had selected the losing strategy. At the highest level, he was sticking to his moral principles and refusing to collaborate with the head porter's dishonest scheme. At the middle level he was sustained by powerful feelings of self-righteousness, disapproval of the head porter's chicanery, resentment at his colleagues' unfriendliness and fury at the injustice of it all. But the lowest level had, without any voluntary participation on the part of consciousness, gone for the losing strategy and dragged him down into depression, effectively sabotaging all attempts by the higher centres to stand by correct moral principles and 'fight the good fight' to the point of victory.

If these are the neuropsychic facts of the situation, how do they enable us to help him? First of all, they can give him some insight into what has been happening to him. That, in turn, might provide him with the data necessary to take action to resolve the conflict holding him in its grip. In view of his background, it was felt that a nautical analogy would advance his understanding.

He was asked to imagine a cargo ship sailing through icy waters. The Captain is an extremely conscientious man, with a tight schedule to keep. He could make a wide detour south so as to avoid the ice, but since he hates being late and could not think of letting his Company down, he decides to risk ploughing on through the ice-floes and keep on course.

The helmsman, who knows nothing of the Captain's schedule, though he can see the ice-floes ahead, decides the Captain must know best and holds his course, as ordered.

The Chief Engineer down in the engine room knows nothing of all this, however, and busies himself maintaining the engine revs in accordance with the commands from the bridge.

Soon the ship begins to take a battering from the ice. The Captain, though anxious, refuses to alter course, while the helmsman, who is partially deaf, is aware of little apart from the Captain's instructions. However, the Chief Engineer not only hears the ice clanging against the plates of the hull, but sees water spurting through the joints between them, and judges the situation too dangerous to proceed. On his own initiative, therefore, he throws the engines into reverse.

When this parable was put to him, Mr Squires at once saw that his conscious mind was like the Captain who had decided that virtue must prevail and that he must stick to his course at all costs. Mr Squires also conceded that his emotions had been like the helmsman, who could see only part of the picture, but carried on regardless, loyally convinced he was doing the right thing. It was the deepest level that Mr Squires had most difficulty in understanding – the profound alteration of mood that had completely paralysed his capacity for effective action – but slowly he came to appreciate that, at this unconscious level, his mind had indeed behaved like the Chief Engineer. It was as if it had decided that the psychological damage and the emotional pain he suffered each day at work was too great to be endured, so that the engine room in his brain had refused to provide the energy to keep him on the course he had taken and had 'gone into reverse' so as to pull him out of the intolerable situation.

Having understood this much, what – as Mr Squires himself was quick to ask – should he do about it? From the 'ultimate' standpoint of evolutionary processes, it does not matter whether a protagonist in a conflict wins or loses but that the conflict should be settled one way or the other. Then damage to both parties is minimized: both go their own way, and both live to fight another day. In selecting the winning or losing strategy, what matters from the individual combatant's point of view is that all three levels of the brain should agree in adopting the same strategy. If there is a fundamental disagreement between them, one level selecting one strategy while the others select the opposite strategy, then the likelihood of an affective disorder is greatly increased. As far as the individual's mental health is concerned, therefore, it is unimportant which strategy is adopted provided that all three 'central processing assemblies' are *pulling together towards the same objective*, enabling him either to win decisively or to make a total withdrawal from the conflict.

It follows that Mr Squires can adopt one of two courses:

1 If he decides to adopt a winning strategy and go on to the attack, he can, with the full backing of the psychiatric department, report his predicament to the District Health Authority and request suspension on full pay while his allegations are investigated. His objective will be to expose the irregularities of the portering department, have the head porter sacked, and perhaps take over the post himself. This tactic, backed up with the threat of a civil suit against the Health Authority for negligence in failing to deal with a flagrant misuse of the sick leave system and for allowing the patient's health to suffer through bullying by the head porter should be sufficient to galvanize the Authority into immediate action.
2 If he decides to adopt a losing strategy, however, he could come round to the head porter's point of view. He could bring himself to appreciate that the sick leave racket was a quasi-legitimate way of getting the porters more

money. In fact, the Health Authority wished to pay the porters more but were prevented from doing so by the national guidelines. They consequently turned a blind eye to the routine abuse of the sick pay system, accepting that each porter would benefit by an extra two weeks' holiday a year and receive overtime pay as a bonus when their colleagues were on leave. Having come to see the essential fairness of this irregular arrangement, Mr Squires could then write a letter of apology to the head porter, acknowledging the error of his ways and promising to be more co-operative in future. The probability is that his anger against his colleagues will then subside and that in future he will share their disapproval of any new porter who tries to buck the system.

Though Mr Squires gave his enthusiastic consent for us to describe his case, in the hope that it might be of some help to others, he was not willing to permit us to divulge which of these alternative courses of action he chose to adopt. But, as far as the therapeutic outcome is concerned, the choice is immaterial. Winning and losing are both healthy activities: evolution has seen to that. It is in helping the patient to integrate the decision-making activities of all three levels of his brain that the therapeutic challenge lies.

The alternative strategies and their levels of operation are summarized in Table 6.

Table 6 Alternative strategies for social competition at three brain levels

| | Alternative strategies | |
Brain level	Winning (escalating)	Losing (de-escalating)
CORTEX (reason)	Fight to win	Actively submit
LIMBIC (emotion)	Get angry	Feel chastened
REPTILIAN (mood)	Mood elevation	Depression

People develop a depressive illness when the losing strategy of the lowest (reptilian) level is activated in conjunction with an inappropriate adoption of the winning strategy at the highest (cortical) level and/or the middle (limbic) level. What keeps the patient depressed is the failure to resolve the situation by yielding at the higher levels. Since the reptilian depressive strategy is beyond the reach of conscious intervention, it cannot be changed by an act of will. Yet it continues to sabotage the patient's capacity to win. If the depression prevails and the patient is eventually forced, despite himself, to give up at the higher levels and adopt a unifying losing strategy at all three levels of the brain, then the depression remits, its object achieved.

We may thus reformulate the depressive predicament as one of *blocked higher level losing*. The block to voluntary yielding may occur either in the patient (where it may be due to an elevated moral sense or to pride or stubbornness) or to a third party (who may refuse to accept that the loser has yielded). In primate society, giving way is very easy. A monkey has merely to make a submissive gesture indicating that he has no intention of behaving in a dominant way. But in human society it can be much more complicated. The loser has to *obey* the winner, which may be difficult or impossible for a number of reasons. For example, a winner may demand something that a loser cannot provide. A dominant husband may insist that his subdominant wife should produce a more enthusiastic sexual response, or that she should lose weight, or give up a nervous tic that irritates him. The unfortunate wife's failure to comply may be construed by her husband as stubbornness (a winning strategy at the highest level) and he may continue his attacks. This may result in depression, which, by taking away both the wife's willpower (the cortical level) and resentment (the limbic level) brings all three levels into a united adoption of the losing strategy. However, in this instance, the depression will not remit as long as the husband keeps up his attack. The wife's depression will only lift if she convinces him that she has done everything in her power to obey him.

In a marriage of this kind, the submissive partner is in a no-win situation comparable to that of the victim of a mugging who cannot convince his assailant that he really has no money on his person, or the torture victim who cannot persuade his torturer that he truly does not possess the information required. If such victims become depressed, it is a depression of the 'learned helplessness' kind described by Seligman (1975). Children in a similar situation, with insatiably critical parents may, as we saw in Chapter 16, escape depression by eroticizing their enforced submission and becoming sexual masochists.

Some of the most intractable depressions occur when the dominant party is such a bully that even complete yielding is not accepted. Such spouses may keep their partners depressed as a deliberate policy of coercion so as to prevent them from doing what they might do if they were less depressed – e.g., spend more money, invite family and friends to the house, make sexual demands, or even seek sexual satisfaction elsewhere. Such a husband will take care to maintain a wide 'RHP gap' by issuing frequent catathetic signals so as to keep his wife 'in her place'. Wives subjected to this sort of treatment understandably become depressed and are difficult to help since their husbands deny all responsibility and refuse to participate in any programme of treatment.

In most cases where a depression is induced by a third party, however, it is often due less to systematic bullying than to ignorance or misunderstanding on the part of the victor. It may be due to a breakdown in communication, the winner failing to tell the loser what is required. This happened to Mrs Robinson, who was referred to psychiatric out-patients with a depression. When her two children were old enough, she had decided to go back to work. Her husband, it subsequently became clear, was ambivalent about this. On the one hand, he was glad of the extra money; but on the other, he was not at all happy about the extra freedom it gave her. He had heard all about working wives having illicit liaisons at the office, but he was quite unable to bring himself to tell his wife about his jealous fears. As a result, he did not confront her over the work issue, but started to put her down in various ways, implying that she was ugly, stupid and lazy, which made Mrs Robinson both angry and miserable, for she had no idea how to respond. Her attempts to defend herself against his attacks were futile because her beauty, intelligence, and character were not really the point at issue. Eventually, Mrs Robinson became too depressed to work and had to give up her job, thus giving her husband what he wanted. It was a Pyrrhic victory, since he had to forgo the advantages of an additional salary coming into the house. But as his catathetic behaviour subsided, so Mrs Robinson's depression improved.

When planning treatment, it is important to determine whether a depression is following an adaptive course – i.e., it is inducing the patient to give in, accept loss or defeat, and adopt a higher (cortical and/or limbic) losing strategy – or whether it is following a maladaptive course – i.e., the depression is making matters worse, as in the case of the wife whose dominant husband demanded a more enthusiastic sexual response but whose consequent depression only served to render her completely frigid. When a depression is maladaptive, the appropriate course is to treat it quickly with antidepressants, but when it is adaptive it is more important to use psychotherapy to help the patient to an awareness of his or her total situation.

As we saw in the case of Albert Squires, the winning strategy of the middle (limbic) level is characterized by the emotion of anger. The phylogenetic point of this is that *it is extremely difficult to give way if one is angry*. Anger is the emotion of *attack*. It facilitates winning by providing an uprush of energy. The outcome leads to mood change. If the circumstances are propitious and the anger results in victory then there is an elevation of mood. If the circumstances are unpropitious and the anger has to be inhibited, or leads to defeat, there is a depression of mood. Sometimes, however, the winning strategy is selected at the middle level, while the losing strategy is selected at the highest and lowest levels. This happened to a man who was falsely accused of sexually abusing his ten-year-old daughter. The accusation was made in public and permanently destroyed his reputation. At the cortical level he chose a losing strategy in that he refrained from taking legal action against the local authority on the grounds that further publicity would cause more harm to his daughter. At the lowest level the losing strategy was also selected with the result that he became severely depressed. However, at the limbic level, he continued to nurture a murderous rage against the social workers responsible for the initial grossly unjust accusation. His depression was consequently long-lasting and difficult to treat.

248

Intractable depressive disorders tend to occur when something appalling has been done to or by a patient and the normal processes of yielding, atonement, forgiveness and reconciliation have been unable to function. A man who, while drunk, caused a car crash in which his wife and children were killed developed a depression of this kind. Depression associated with post-traumatic stress disorder can follow a similar course.

ANXIETY AND PHOBIC DISORDERS

Research into the proximate causes of these disorders is already well advanced: their neurochemical and neuroanatomical bases are being investigated, and anxiolytic drugs as well as structured psychotherapies have been developed for their treatment. It is now clear that both serotonergic and noradrenergic systems (Soubrie, 1986; Robins and Everitt, 1995) play important roles in normal and exaggerated anxiety, and it seems that chronic anxiety states involve excessive activity in the hypothalamic–pituitary–adrenal axis (Stokes, 1985).

In Chapter 8 we argued that anxiety is probably a normally distributed trait throughout the whole population. Most of us experience enough anxiety to function efficiently. But some of us experience too little or too much. The homeostatic mechanism responsible for regulating anxiety has been compared to a 'smoke detection' system. In people who experience normal, appropriate anxiety, the system operates optimally. In anxiety disorders, the threshold for the system's activation is set too low, and the alarm is prone to go off capriciously ('false alarms') or may sound all the time. In antisocial personality disorder, on the other hand, the threshold is set too high and danger signals may go undetected. Such differences in threshold levels are set by a combination of proximal factors, including genetic predisposition (Fyer et al. 1995) and experiences of anxiety-evoking stimuli in the course of personal ontogeny.

The neuro-evolutionary perspective provides an indispensable framework for understanding these disorders. With regard to panic disorder, for example, each of MacLean's three processing assemblies is clearly involved:

1 brainstem nuclei, such as the locus coeruleus, mediate the symptoms of panic attack, especially the respiratory symptoms, which may be cardinal (Anderson et al. 1984);
2 limbic areas with high concentrations of GABA receptors are involved in anticipatory anxiety (the fear that a panic attack may occur);
3 frontal areas mediate the learned associations responsible for the release of panic as well as the avoidance behaviour (e.g., agoraphobia) typical of the disorder.

The practical usefulness of this triune concept of panic disorder is that it yields an integrated 'triune' approach to its treatment (Gorman et al. 1989), viz.

1 the prescription of serotonin re-uptake inhibitors and other antidepressants to inhibit the symptoms of panic disorder at the brainstem level;
2 the prescription of benzodiazepines to reduce anticipatory anxiety at the limbic level;
3 the use of psychotherapy or cognitive therapy to treat the conscious correlates of the disorder at the neocortical level.

Because of the advanced cerebral capacities of our species, the cognitive level of experience is central to both an understanding and the treatment of all anxiety and phobic disorders. The evolutionary approach to the psychotherapy of these disorders advocates the following principles:

1 The evolutionary origin of the anxiety should be explained clearly and evocatively in language that the patient can fully appreciate. This generally has the effect of demystifying the problem, even though it does not solve it. Terror of going out to do the shopping becomes more comprehensible and more acceptable if it is seen as an adaptive mechanism for keeping one's ancestors from straying off the home range, rather than as a personal weakness which is a cause for shame.
2 The agonistic and hedonic components of the anxiety should be differentiated. Social anxiety, for example, tends to occur, as we have seen, in situations where the sufferer anticipates failure in social competition with others. As most patients readily agree, there are essentially two kinds of situation which can induce this unpleasant anticipation – namely, fear that one will suffer defeat in an agonistic encounter, and fear that one will be found wanting or unacceptable by one's social group. The adaptive function of these anxieties should be explained to them as acting as inner sanctions against inappropriately assertive behaviour ('agonistic anxiety') and against making oneself unattractive ('hedonic anxiety').

   Since agonistic anxiety represents an anticipation of a personal attack from others, the history of agonistic encounters demands careful examination. Does the patient provoke such attacks by adopting an aggressive manner without the RHP to back it up? Or does he or she invite bullying by unconsciously adopting a victim role? When these basic issues have been determined, appropriate training can be devised – for example, training in social skills for the inappropriately aggressive patient, or training in assertiveness or the martial arts for the victim.

   Hedonic anxiety, on the other hand, is related to the patient's self-perception of not being liked or valued by the group. The grounds for this judgement need to be looked into, and treatment instituted to bring about its modification. Here the patient's attachment needs are often the crucial issue, the therapist becoming an attachment figure and the consulting room a secure base where the patient may be helped to form a more healthy 'internal working model' of the self as being worthy of love and affection (Bowlby, 1979).

250

3 Successful therapy has to take account of the fact that anxiety is almost invariably related to low RHP and low SAHP and, as a consequence, priority must be given to raising the patient's self-esteem. This will be discussed in the final section of this chapter.

4 Relaxation therapy is commonly prescribed for all forms of anxiety, but this can be ineffective because the adaptive function of the anxiety is overlooked. The anxiety sufferer is like a soldier on sentry-go, anticipating attack from the enemy. An ethological parallel is provided by the dwarf mongoose who adopts the role of lookout for predators (Alcock, 1989). Anxiety-prone people are anxious not only on their own account but for their nearest and dearest as well: their anxiety has an altruistic dimension (Akiskal, 1998). Akiskal makes the telling point that to ask anxious people to relax can be like asking a sentry to desert his post, and consequently can have the anti-therapeutic effect of making them more anxious still. Some anxious people are able to relax during a therapy session because they feel the therapist is performing the role of watch-keeper, but are unable to relax when on their own, even with the help of a comforting relaxation tape. Before advising relaxation, therefore, it is important to examine with the patient who precisely is going to take over the lookout function while he or she is relaxing. One successful line of approach to this problem has been developed by family therapists who endeavour to readjust family responsibilities when they have identified a patient as being overburdened with the task of fending off danger, such as debt, by obtaining a general agreement that another trustworthy member of the family should assume control of expenditure and use of the bank account. Another helpful technique is to prescribe communal 'worry sessions' at regular intervals, during which the day's worries are aired and shared so as to leave the rest of the day relatively free from anxiety.

ANOREXIA NERVOSA

In Chapter 9 we discussed one of the most mystifying features of anorexia nervosa – the inability of young women with this disorder to stop dieting when a reasonable degree of slimness has been achieved, so that the discipline of dieting persists to the point of emaciation and appears to assume the form of an addiction. We mentioned the explanation put forward by Ploog and Pirke (1987) that cerebral reward systems may have become linked to the hunger-regulating centres in these patients, increasing their satisfaction in being able to control their body weight and their social status, thus boosting their self-esteem.

An understanding of the evident association between excessive dietary control and raising self-esteem could well prove critical for successful outcome in treating the disorder. Clinically, the problem is that the achievement of a reasonably slim figure does not seem to produce a sufficient rise in self-esteem for the patient to be able to escape from her self-imposed dietary tyranny. If elevating self-respect is one of the anorexic's primary objectives, then it follows that treatment should be focused not on increasing the patient's weight but on providing the *anathetic* means necessary to boost her self-esteem. How can this be done? It is not an easy question to answer. On the whole, drug treatments and various forms of psychotherapy have proved ineffective, and the early successes claimed by family therapists have been hard to repeat. By the time she comes into treatment, the patient is usually too emaciated to be at all attractive to her peers, and too obsessed with the issues of food and thinness to be able to collaborate in any treatment programme which seeks to look beyond these preoccupations. However, one very promising approach to the problem has been advocated by De Giacomo, Professor of Psychiatry in Bari, Italy.

De Giacomo's method is quite unlike any other that has been tried. It consists of sending the anorexic patient away with her father for a month's holiday. Both father and daughter are instructed to devote their time during this period to finding out about each other, and to teaching each other about themselves. As may be imagined, this is not an easy arrangement to achieve and De Giacomo and his team have had to exert all their skills of diplomacy in persuading families to accept their prescription. Of the 22 families so treated, De Giacomo (1993) claimed success in 21.

In reviewing De Giacomo's work, it seems to us that he may have achieved what other therapeutic initiatives have failed to achieve – namely, the injection into the patient of a massive dose of high self-esteem. Probably for the first time in her life, the daughter is granted the undivided attention of her father, who, despite the cultural changes of recent decades, exerts the archetypal masculine qualities of power and authority, and exercises a profound influence over his daughter's sense of self-worth and mate value in relation to the world of men. If De Giacomo's success rate is confirmed, then it would seem likely that the long and intensive period of paternal attention has the effect of raising the patient's self-esteem to a level where it becomes possible for her to discontinue her dietary regime.

It might be argued that the positive therapeutic outcome achieved by De Giacomo could be attributed to the removal of the patient from the home situation in which the anorexia originated – in particular, enabling her to escape from the fraught emotions so characteristic of mealtimes in anorexic households. But this factor would seem to be of minor importance. Removal of the patient to a clinic, or to the home of a kindly aunt, does not achieve nearly the same degree of improvement as a month's exclusive holiday with her father.

It is to be hoped that this promising line of approach will be tried by treatment teams in other parts of the world, and that similar therapeutic strategies will be tried. It would be of great interest to know, for example, whether a month's holiday with the mother would achieve comparable benefits to those claimed by De Giacomo for a similar period spent alone with the father. This might go some way towards testing the psychoanalytic theory that anorexia is to do with rivalry between the daughter and her mother for her father's love. Following up changes in family dynamics subsequent to the holiday could also yield valuable material.

If our prediction is correct – that successful outcome in treating anorexia is critically dependent on greatly increasing the patient's self-esteem – then variations on De Giacomo's 'attention' method could prove to be the treatment of choice.

DREAMS

Dreams stir up powerful emotions which act as effective catalysts to change, and serious work on them can be crucial to success in psychotherapy. This is because it is extremely difficult to induce radical change in basic personality structures through rational discussion or deliberate exertion of the will, for the limbic structures involved are usually beyond the reach of consciousness. Cognitive behaviour therapy, though it can be helpful in many cases, suffers from the limitation that it proceeds almost exclusively at the conscious 'forebrain' level of functioning. In dreams, however, thinking is more flexible and emotions more dynamic than in wakefulness, and this increased fluidity makes it possible to try out more innovative possibilities than occur in waking life. To engage material arising from unconscious processes can become a matter of great therapeutic relevance, because dream symbols are energized thoughts: they provide the necessary drive to transform psychic structures from a dysfunctional to an adaptive mode of application. Without such engagement, emotions remain untouched, and little of lasting importance can be changed. For this reason, a more widespread understanding of the therapeutic implications of dreaming is to be encouraged.

THE LIMINAL STATE

One crucial area for research is the liminal state and its therapeutic implications. In non-psychotic patients, there may be much creative mileage to be obtained from enabling them to enter that borderline where dreams and psychosis meet, where limbic processes become dimly accessible to consciousness, and where, it appears, personal transformation can occur. Here again, Jung devised a therapeutic procedure for inducing this state of heightened awareness of unconscious processes: he called it **active imagination**. Jung experimented with this procedure while himself suffering a near-psychotic episode following his break with Freud, and out of this 'creative illness' came the basic principles and practices of analytical psychology (Ellenberger, 1970; Stevens, 1999). It is in the liminal state, as we have seen, that schizotypal personalities tend to live out much of their lives; and it is the very creativity of this state that, in appropriate circumstances, can make them powerfully charismatic. For a patient suffering from feelings of rejection and low self-esteem, it can be both healing and restorative to gain access to this state.

To attain it, one has to enter a kind of reverie, halfway between sleep and waking: for example, one may begin to fall asleep but stop short before consciousness is lost, remaining in that half-way condition to observe what occurs. As therapists familiar with the technique invariably stress, it is essential to record what has been experienced, so as to make it lastingly available to consciousness: it can be written down, painted or drawn, modelled in clay, or even danced or acted. Unfortunately, relatively few patients succeed in making use of this powerful therapeutic technique, either because they lack the time or patience to become proficient at it, or because they are, understandably, frightened of where it may lead. It is for this reason that careful research needs to be undertaken into the feasibility and effectiveness of its use.

THE THERAPEUTIC COMMUNITY

A further area for therapeutic development and research is suggested by evolutionary insights into the importance of group dynamics, particularly the powerful significance for human beings of co-operative ventures in small bands of the hunter-gatherer type. It may be that the use of outward-bound expeditions, treks, and vision quests under the guidance of skilled and (suitably restrained) charismatic leaders, well-versed in evolutionary theory, could achieve more in the development of self-value and the use of unlived archetypal potential than hours of individual or group therapy of the usual sedentary, verbal kind. In a world characterized by social fragmentation and 'anomie', one salient need which is frustrated for untold millions of our contemporaries is the need for **community** – a community functioning in the service of some guiding purpose or goal.

The 'therapeutic community movement' in vogue in the 1960s attempted to provide this, but, on the whole, failed, because it lacked all phylogenetic understanding of what it was attempting to achieve. Groups, usually established in mental hospital wards or 'villas', were generally too large and too open. Lacking a shared ethos and a sense of psychological direction, having few leaders with the necessary charismatic powers, and failing to develop any strong feelings of 'kinship' between group members, these 'therapeutic communities' were not real communities nor were they therapeutic; on the contrary, they often tended to degenerate into agonistic power struggles between politically motivated individuals.

To facilitate the health and well-being of its members, a community must provide social structures and group rituals which serve the archetypal needs of human beings. The only therapeutic community that attempted to do this, one of the first to be established, was the Withymead Centre, established by

Irene and Gilbert Champernowne at Exeter during the 1940s (Stevens, 1986). The Withymead experiment could be revised and extended in the light of evolutionary theory.

The mutuality of shared trust and dependence born of collaborative activity in adverse circumstances may well prove to be the best treatment for those believing themselves to be unloved, undervalued and under threat of imminent rejection, and it should be tried under controlled and verifiable conditions.

THE DOCTOR–PATIENT RELATIONSHIP

Research in recent decades has revealed some striking similarities between psychotherapy in Western society and healing in traditional societies. The numerous attempts to assess the effectiveness of different types of psychotherapy have met with varying degrees of success, but there seems to be fairly general agreement that, contrary to the assertions of neo-Freudian and Kleinian analysts, the application of psychoanalytic theories and the interpretation of the transference are not indispensable to favourable outcome. Certain basic characteristics appear to be conducive to positive results in all psychotherapies, and these include the prestige and genuineness of the therapist, the quality of the relationship established with the patient, and a belief on the part of the patient that the procedure will prove helpful. Parallel findings from the anthropological evidence suggests that people in traditional societies look to their healers for *authority*, or charisma, *attention* to their symptoms and personal history, *knowledge* of their condition, and the *power* to provide restoration to health (Leff, 1981).

These similarities would suggest that people look to their physicians for the same qualities and capacities that they have always sought in them, and that the doctor–patient relationship is an archetypal relationship (Rosen, 1992; Stevens, 1993). It has to be remembered that we evolved in circumstances of great vulnerability, threatened by the elements, by predators, by hostile neighbours, and by malevolent influences bringing disease and death. It is not surprising that in such conditions figures should emerge perceived as possessing great therapeutic power. The healer's ubiquitous activities reflect a demand for healing as old as our species, and the associated beliefs, rituals, and practices are among the most striking of all cultural universals. Seen in this light, healing is not just a matter of diagnosis and treatment; it is a question of channelling endogenous propensities that are as old as evolution itself. Evolution occurs, after all, when a dysfunctional gap existing between an organism and its environment is remedied by a genetic mutation that closes the gap and results in better adjustment or adaptation. If nature can be conceived as a great self-correcting process, then healing may be understood as the art of providing optimum circumstances in which these self-correcting powers can most efficiently achieve their purpose.

Unfortunately, Western physicians and psychiatrists tend to overlook these archetypal considerations and this could account for the remarkable renaissance of 'alternative' therapies in recent years. Conventional doctors are perceived as deficient in that they fail to meet the archetypal needs of their patients, leaving them to feel unconsidered, neglected, and misunderstood. Contemporary trends in psychiatry have tended to exacerbate this problem, for psychiatrists spend less time with individual patients than they did, devoting more of their energy to administration, teaching, and research. The same is true of psychiatric nurses. Even the traditional clinical interview has become more impersonal, the modern prejudice being in favour of the questionnaire, the personality inventory, and the test, rather than a personal consultation in depth. Reading the professional literature, one is left with the impression that patients are often regarded less as unhappy men and women in search of help and wise counsel than as assemblies of enzymes and neuronal circuits whose characteristics have to be corrected by the administration of appropriate drugs.

Psychotherapy is so ancient that it has a prior claim to be designated as 'the oldest profession'. It is a form of social grooming which probably arose out of the care-giving/care-receiving aspects of the parent–child bond. This might help to explain why therapists spend so much of their time trying to put right what went wrong in that bond. But the traditional Freudian view of the **transference** is unduly restrictive in its conception of the doctor–patient relationship as a mere recapitulation of the parent–child relationship. In the course of any treatment, especially if it is prolonged, archetypal images are stirred up and projected on to the person of the therapist, conferring great therapeutic (or destructive) power upon him or her – e.g., the witch-doctor, shaman, wise old man or woman. The therapist also receives the projection of previously unfulfilled archetypal needs – e.g., the wise, caring, understanding parent never experienced in childhood, the reassuring, appreciative peer who was never available at school, the mentor who never appeared when most needed, etc. Such patients, suffering as they are from the frustration of archetypal intent, need time to establish a working relationship with a therapist through which they can begin to conceive of themselves as capable of sustaining a lasting bond of intimacy with someone who grants them value as a human being. As most researchers agree, the primary factor in the therapeutic relationship is the attitude of the therapist – the provision of respect, attention, warmth, and acceptance capable of healing the patient's feelings of inadequacy, low self-esteem, and unworthiness.

Too often, psychiatrists neglect their patients' needs for status, fellow-feeling, and hedonic security. The patronizing attitudes so apparent among many health workers are essentially catathetic in effect – the condescending tone of voice, the use of Christian names from the very first encounter, irrespective of the age or status of the patient, etc. The interchangeability of staff in many clinics means that patients may see a different psychiatrist at each attendance, which effectively deprives them of the very kind of enduring intimacy that they most require. This tends to preclude the possibility that the healer archetype may be activated or that patients may be touched by its therapeutic power.

While there is little doubt that evolutionary theory can improve our understanding of the nature and function of the common psychiatric disorders, it is still too early to know how far it may help us to devise effective methods for the treatment of all of them. In the meantime, psychotherapies are mushrooming – new forms, new methods, new theories, new organizations, all offering new trainings, most of them under-researched and under-evaluated. It is likely, as we have seen, that all successful psychotherapies are based on a small number of principles which have been known to be effective in bringing psychological relief and personal transformation for many generations. What is needed now is a corpus of informed knowledge about the relationships between individual experience, social influences, and the phylogenetic propensities which guide and inform all human development. This is the programme which Freud and Jung embarked upon at the beginning of the twentieth century. We are now perhaps in a position to bring it to fruition.

21

RESEARCH

Research specifically designed to test evolutionary hypotheses concerning mental disorders and human behavioural traits is still a new and as yet undeveloped area of enquiry. There are considerable problems involved in reconstructing the evolutionary history of the human mind/brain, for this history is unrecorded. As a result, theories about it are essentially deductive, being derived from such sources as behavioural observations of different species and anthropological observations of different cultures. However, analysis of behaviour in terms of its adaptive function can not only yield valuable insights, as we have seen, but also give rise to testable statements – such as that care-giving will be more consistently and reliably provided to offspring by their biological parents than by step-parents.

From the research standpoint, it is probably most helpful to conceive evolutionary psychiatry as a branch of **behavioural ecology**, which uses evolutionary theory to interpret behavioural adaptations in relation to environmental characteristics, such as the availability of food, the presence of predators, and the particular habitat in which a species lives out its life cycle. In particular, behavioural ecology stresses that the adult phenotype is the result not of pure genetic determinism, but of complex interaction between genes and environmental factors prevailing during ontological development (Krebs and Davies, 1993).

Taking our cue from the behavioural ecologists, we would argue that psychiatric research programmes should in future be guided by Tinbergen's (1963) four ways of answering the question 'Why does this animal exhibit this particular form of behaviour?' The four ways of answering this question are in terms of (1) its adaptive function, (2) its proximate cause, (3) its developmental or ontogenetic history, and (4) its evolutionary or phylogenetic history. We shall adopt Tinbergen's perspective in discussing possible research programmes into obsessive-compulsive disorder, depression, schizophrenia, and the crucial importance for psychiatry of the concept of self-esteem.

OBSESSIVE-COMPULSIVE DISORDER (OCD)

In investigating this disorder we should ask:

1 What adaptive function does 'obsessional' behaviour perform in promoting individual survival and reproductive success?
2 What are the proximate factors that cause this kind of behaviour – i.e., what are the cerebral and biochemical mechanisms and environmental cues involved?
3 Why did the behaviour develop in the individual patient in the course of ontogeny (for example did the patient's father himself have an obsessional personality or was the mother unduly strict about potty training)?
4 At the phylogenetic level, when did such behaviour evolve, and is it shared with any other species?

Until recently, psychiatric research into all mental disorders has focused on the second and third of these questions while leaving the first and fourth of them out of account. Evolutionary psychiatry not only seeks to remedy this omission but to provide a global theoretical framework within which research designed to find answers to all four questions may be integrated.

While it is true that our efforts are hampered by the fact that there exists no video recording of human behavioural evolution that we can replay and study frame by frame, evolutionary psychiatrists nevertheless have at their disposal a wide range of scientific methods. Buss (1999) has contributed a summary of these. Potentially, the most productive of them makes use of the *comparative* approach which seeks analogies and homologues for a certain behavioural trait among members of different species so as to establish its phylogenetic continuity. Application of this approach has established, as we have already noted, that attachment behaviour between mothers and infants, between peers, and between mature males and females can be traced backwards from human beings through primates to their earliest mammalian origins.

Another productive comparison is that which can be made between male and female members of a species in order to explain their different behavioural strategies. One example is jealousy. Although both men and women display sexual jealousy, a man's jealousy, far more than a woman's, tends to be elicited by an admission of specifically *sexual* infidelity by his female partner. A woman's jealousy is more reliably elicited by evidence of her partner's *emotional* infidelity. The evolutionary explanation of this finding is that men, like male members of other species in which female fertilization occurs internally, face the adaptive problem of 'paternal uncertainty'. A man can never be certain beyond all shadow of doubt, that he is the genetic father of his mate's children. Women, however, do not have to confront this adaptive problem, for their children cannot be other than their own. This provides an important insight into the adaptive function of sexual jealousy.

A man's jealousy has the effect of repelling rivals and dissuading his mate from accepting other sexual partners. A female's jealousy, on the other hand, has the object of retaining her mate's emotional commitment to her and dissuading him from investing it in other female partners. Jealousy becomes an issue for psychiatrists when it is excessive, pathological, or 'morbid', causing great unhappiness, physical and emotional abuse, and sometimes murder.

Other useful comparisons can be made between different individuals within a certain species (e.g., comparing behaviours of people in different age groups, from different families, and from different cultural and social backgrounds, as in the study of schizophrenia) and between individuals functioning in different contexts (e.g., comparing the behaviours of depressed people in work and family situations in order to discover how they handle their aggression (see p. 263).

What light can comparisons such as these throw on obsessive-compulsive behaviour? In Chapter 7 we made certain suggestions concerning the function and evolution of obsessional behaviour, arguing that adequate checking is necessary for the defence of resources and for the preparation of weapons before embarking on hunting or warlike excursions, while washing and cleaning behaviour evolved as a defence against infection with microorganisms or infestation by parasites. We also proposed that, as a species, we possess a module to check, to verify, to ensure that things are in order.

How may these proposals be tested? What can use of the comparative method tell us? Do members of species other than humans exhibit checking and cleaning behaviour? Certainly, stereotyped and ritualized patterns of behaviour are apparent in a great number of animal species, as are grooming, cleaning, and bathing. Moreover, *excessive* or pathological grooming has been observed in animals of a type that bears a close phenomenological resemblance to compulsive handwashing in humans. Examples are hair-pulling in cats (what vets call 'psychogenic alopecia'), excessive preening in birds ('feather-pulling'), and compulsive paw-licking in dogs ('acral lick dermatitis'). What is even more interesting is that these conditions, like their compulsive human counterparts, usually respond therapeutically to serotonin re-uptake inhibitors. Research into the neuroanatomical basis of these disorders in animals should throw light on the neuroanatomy of human OCD.

Fascinating though these cross-species analogues are, the fact remains that the kind of careful checking and re-checking apparent in mathematicians, accountants, airline pilots, and obsessional personalities requires a degree of cognitive sophistication demanding the presence of a large and richly complex cerebral cortex. Anthropological data, derived from the study of hunter-gatherers, confirms that these people take enormous care in preparing themselves for rituals, whether these be religious or the preliminaries to embarking on the hunt or on warlike expeditions. Mutual grooming, washing and cleaning are also universally apparent. It seems reasonable to conclude, therefore, that the symptoms displayed by patients with obsessive-compulsive disorder have a long evolutionary history, and that their excessive checking and cleaning represents an exaggeration of ancient adaptations.

What evidence is there to support our suggestion that humans are equipped with a verification module which prompts us to check and sometimes double-check? This is an issue that research by cognitive scientists could settle. What role does verification play in all cognitive acts? Is cognitive efficiency possible without it? Or is verification necessary only in some cognitive procedures and not in others? Answers to questions such as these could throw light on the precise capacities which have become dysfunctional or exaggerated in patients with obsessive-compulsive disorder.

Productive research lies in asking the right questions. Important questions can arise haphazardly, but they are more likely to be guided by the theoretical paradigm within which the researcher operates. For example, research into the differences between male and female jealousy would lead us to predict that morbid or 'obsessive' jealousy would follow similar patterns – husbands would be obsessed with the possibility that their wives had been sexually unfaithful, while wives would be obsessed with the possibility of their husband's emotional infidelity. This research has yet to be done, and it provides an example of how evolutionary theory can yield testable predictions.

DEPRESSION

Research into depression, no less than into obsessive-compulsive disorder, can be profitably guided by Tinbergen's four levels of analysis:

1 What is the function of depression? We have argued that it promotes adaptation to loss of status or loss of an attachment figure.
2 What causes it? At what neurological or biochemical sites does the perception of loss operate to release the depressive reaction?
3 How does it develop in the individual patient? What are the relative roles of genetic predisposition, learning experiences in childhood and adolescence, and the effects of these experiences on self-esteem?
4 What is its evolutionary history?

We have proposed answers to questions 1, 3, and 4 in Chapter 5. Our hypothesis that depressed mood evolved as the ritualized yielding component of agonistic behaviour must draw attention to question 2, namely, what are the responsible neurological mechanisms in the corpus striatum of the reptilian forebrain? We would postulate that at this level two crucial decisions are made: (1) should the agonistic strategy be accessed? If so, (2) which form of the strategy should be activated – escalation or de-escalation?

Discovery of loci for these operations in the human brain would be of the greatest significance for the validity of the hypothesis.

A step in this direction has already been taken as the result of an adventitious observation made by Bejjani and colleagues (1999) while treating a woman with high-frequency deep-brain stimulation for the relief of intractable Parkinson's disease. Much to their surprise, she suffered brief but reproducible episodes of depression when a small area of tissue was stimulated by an electrode placed in the central region of the left substantia nigra in the reptilian brain. The patient wept and her verbal reports were compatible with a subjective reduction in RHP, SAHP, and Resource Value: 'I don't want to live anymore . . . Everything is useless, always feeling worthless, I'm scared of this world . . . I'm crying over myself . . . I'm hopeless, why am I bothering you . . . ?' Ninety seconds after stimulation was stopped, the depression disappeared, to be replaced by a rebound elevation of mood during which the patient laughed and joked with the examiner, playfully pulling his tie.

Commenting on this finding, Yudofsky (1999) declared: 'This effect is remarkable, not only because the patient had no previous known episodes of depression (thus diminishing the likelihood that the memory of a previously experienced mood state was evoked) but also because only a few cubic millimeters of neural tissue were being stimulated in a part of the brain not usually associated with mood regulation. This discovery will spark a plethora of new hypotheses related to the neuropathological features of both Parkinson's disease and depression . . . '.

Though not himself an evolutionary psychiatrist, Yudofsky, nevertheless, raises fundamental questions closely related to our own perspective: 'If the full constellation of depressive symptoms can be evoked by the electrical stimulation of a minute region of the brain in a person with no history of depression, does this indicate that depression may be "hard-wired" in the brain? Could there be an evolutionary advantage or purpose for depression . . . ?'.

Neurological and molecular biological investigations of relevant structures in the limbic system and the neocortex could also further our understanding of the emotional and cognitive correlates of depressive disorder. The possible significance of these three assemblies – the reptilian, the limbic, and the cortical – in contributing to the clinical manifestations of depression and their treatment have already been described on pages 243–48. Here again the findings of Bejjani et al. could be of significance, for during the episode of depression evoked by stimulation of the left substantia nigra, coincidental positron-emission tomography indicated an increase in blood flow in the left orbito-frontal cortex, the right parietal lobe, the left globus pallidus, and in the left amygdala and anterior thalamus. Clearly, Bejjani et al.'s observations need to be repeated, for they could represent a major breakthrough in our understanding of the evolved neurophysiological basis of depressive disorders.

As we observed, a depression may become resistant to treatment when the winning strategy is maintained at the limbic and cortical levels (causing the patient to remain angry, bitter, resentful, and aggressive), while the losing strategy has been selected at the reptilian level. This raises the whole issue of the relationship between hostility and depression which has been the subject of debate since Karl Abraham (1927) suggested that depression was the consequence of aggression turned against the self. Various studies of depressed patients have examined the relationship between 'inward hostility' and 'outward hostility' (Gottschalk *et al.*, 1963) or 'hostility-In' and 'hostility-Out' (Fernando, 1969; Millar, 1983), finding a low positive correlation with inward directed hostility and a low negative or negligible correlation with outward-directed hostility. Focusing on 'outward hostility' Weissman *et al.* (1971) found that depressed women showed more hostility to close relatives (particularly their children) than comparable women who were not depressed. However, none of these studies took into account the rank or status of these patients relative to the rank of the persons to whom they were hostile.

This is an unfortunate omission, for the rank theory of depression would predict that the expression of hostility will be directly affected by this vector: patients in whom the losing strategy has been selected at the reptilian level, while the winning strategy has been selected at the limbic and cortical levels, will be more likely to express hostility against persons perceived to be of lower rank and to inhibit its expression against persons perceived to be of higher rank. For example, we would anticipate that a depressed man would be seen by his boss at work as having become unduly 'quiet', while his wife and children would experience him as 'angry', 'touchy', and 'difficult' at home. Similarly, we would anticipate that in marriage, a depressed *dominant* spouse would tend to show increased hostility to his or her partner, while a depressed *sub*-dominant spouse would tend to show less hostility to his or hers. These predictions are readily testable and the results would enhance or diminish the value of the rank hypothesis of depression.

Another research project which could have interesting consequences for rank theory would be the effect of anathetic ('boosting') and catathetic ('down putting') signals on blood serotonin levels. If, for example, two comparable groups of subjects were given an identical task to perform, one group could be subjected to criticism every time they got something wrong, while the other group was given praise every time they got something right. Rank theory would predict that serotonin levels would fall in the first group and rise in the second, with a correlated fall or rise in subjective mood. Moreover, these effects might be expected to last longer (i.e., show greater refractoriness to recovery) in subjects with a history of bipolar disorder than in subjects with no such history.

SCHIZOPHRENIA

As the above examples may serve to demonstrate, research into the affective disorders will prove most productive, in our view, if they are considered primarily as disorders of *linkage* (rank and attachment), in that the capacity for mood change has evolved to maintain the cohesiveness of groups by facilitating an orderly distribution of the roles of leader and follower between group members. Most of the features of depression, which otherwise appear totally maladaptive, can be accounted for in this way. The schizophrenias and related spectrum disorders are, by contrast, 'spacing disorders', associated with the imperative to break the cohesiveness of early human groups so as to ensure group splitting and group dispersal. In view of these opposite biological functions, we should anticipate that different research initiatives and different therapeutic interventions would be necessary if promising results are to be achieved in those cases where 'spacing' as opposed to 'linking' processes have led to personal psychopathology.

The status of our group-splitting hypothesis of schizophrenia will be decided by advances in genetics linked to developments in the behavioural ecology of mental disorders. The crucial issues for research to decide are:

1 Is there a graded genetic predisposition to differing degrees of psychopathology in schizophrenia spectrum disorder?
2 What life events influence the extent to which the predisposition is expressed in the life of the carrier?
3 What evidence is there associating group splitting with the emergence of charismatic leaders possessing schizotypal traits?
4 Does a genetic loading of moderate degree predispose susceptible individuals to become charismatic prophets?
5 Is there a tendency for such prophets to become frankly schizophrenic if their message goes unheeded and followers fail to materialize?

It is not possible at this stage to predict how long will elapse before some or all of these questions may be answered. But there is one area in which our 'group-splitting' or 'dispersal phenotype' theory of schizophrenia could now be of practical significance and that is in guiding research into psychotherapy of the disorder. As Birchwood and Spencer (1999) have demonstrated, through well-controlled randomized trials, psychotherapeutic techniques are indeed able to modify the course of a schizophrenic illness, albeit to a moderate degree. We would suggest that greater success could be achieved if treatment programmes approached schizophrenia in the context of the biological function of the schizotypal propensity, so that instead of opposing this function by attacking it head on, therapists were to make use of the energy available for the function's realization. The essential point, from the perspective of the therapist, is that the schizophrenic is programmed to take direction from the delusional referents of his unconscious mind, and to socialize only with those who have been indoctrinated by his teaching. Having failed to recruit followers, the schizophrenic patient ends up not in the promised land but in a shop doorway or a psychiatric ward, his biological objective of leading an exodus from the natal group having conspicuously failed. However, from the purely psychological standpoint, the patient has, in a sense, already left his social milieu and created a new intrapsychic group, a *psychotic pseudocommunity*. It is this pseudocommunity that the therapist must enter, treating its members and its basic ideology with respect and, as far as is possible, with understanding. Therapy needs to take account of the major factor distinguishing a successful cult leader from a schizophrenic patient, namely, that the leader is surrounded by a group of devoted followers who hang on his words and adopt his beliefs (however crazy they might appear to outsiders). By granting the leader enthusiastic validation of his ideas, the followers boost his self-esteem and help to prevent him from lapsing into a psychosis. Accordingly, one might anticipate a powerful therapeutic effect were it possible to provide each schizophrenic patient with a cultic group of devoted members.

Unfortunately, this would hardly be possible, even in the most generously funded research project! But advances in computer technology provide an intriguing alternative. Might it not be possible for each patient to be provided with a computer system within which to create his own group of followers in 'virtual reality'? Could he not indoctrinate the robotic members of his cult with his own peculiar ideology and beliefs, sharing with them his visions, the hierophantic dictates of his voices, his neologisms, syntactical eccentricities, and his mission? Then he might succeed in forming a network of inspired communication with 'part personalities' projected from the recesses of his own psyche through the miracle of silicon into a virtually existent world of his own devising. The consequent sense of gratification, rather than frustration, of his politico-religious ambitions could well prove therapeutic, especially in relieving the negative symptoms of the disorder. Research along these lines could determine how the patient's general behaviour may be affected, together with his relation to society as a whole. It is possible that even the relative social withdrawal necessary for the computer work to be done might be balanced by a rise in sociability as a result of increased self-confidence.

Would such computerized cult following possess reality for the patient? There is reason to believe that it would. It is, after all, highly characteristic of the condition that patients have great difficulty in differentiating between outer and inner reality. Moreover, experiments have shown that it is relatively easy to persuade normal subjects, possessing no signs of psychiatric disorder, that they are communicating with real people, when in fact, they are interacting with a computer program. In one such study, a group of university students was told that they were communicating with others 'through a teletype', when the truth of the matter was that they were operating a simple computer program which was based on a mere hundred rules to generate replies. Afterwards, they were asked whether they had been communicating with a person or a computer. Ninety per cent of them answered that it was a person. Furthermore, 80 per cent stated categorically that it was *impossible* that they could have been communicating with a computer (McGuire and Troisi, 1998). This experiment was conducted in the 1960s when computer software was relatively primitive. At the present time, it seems not unreasonable to suppose that programs could be devised so that computer-generated followers would not only seem real and human but could elevate the schizophrenic patient into a leadership role.

Evidence that to be placed in a leadership role has beneficial effects in chronic schizophrenia comes from another study in which schizophrenic patients were allocated to work groups, initially facilitated by nurses. Later, the nurses withdrew, leaving the leadership position vacant. In five out of six groups, one patient gradually came to assume the leadership role. These showed clinical improvement, whereas the remaining patients showed no change (McGuire and Troisi, 1998). This promising study deserves to be repeated. It lends some weight to the supposition that to create a leadership role in relation to computer-generated followers may make it possible to benefit all patients, rather than confining the therapeutic effect to the emergent leader at the expense of the rest of the group.

Another experimental possibility would be to give each patient a website on which he could publicize his ideas on the internet and invite the participation of actual people in the fulfilment of his mission. It is not unlikely that a proportion of patients would recruit real followers: the ensuing communications could be monitored by researchers to assess the clinical response of the patient. For those patients whose messages and world views were too bizarre or incoherent to attract followers, members of the research team could themselves visit the website and provide appropriate validation. In some cases, a combination of real and research followers might result in a more marked therapeutic effect.

There are, of course, important ethical issues involved in carrying through such a research project, but a cursory search would indicate that a number of schizotypal or schizophrenic people are already recruiting followers on the web. In these circumstances, a randomized controlled trial of website exposure in schizophrenia may prove to be ethically and practically feasible.

Another potentially fruitful line of research would be to compare a group of schizophrenic patients whose delusional systems had received some form of validation with a group of comparable patients who received the more conventional form of treatment in which their belief systems were denied on rational grounds in the hope of granting 'insight' into their delusional nature. We would predict that a greater number in the first group would show improvement, whereas the latter would show a tendency to relapse into

266

chronicity. Such a project could provide critical evidence for the validation or refutation of our hypothesis.

We are sometimes asked to compare our theory of schizophrenia with those of other evolutionary theorists such as Crow (1995, 1997a, 1997b, 1998), Allen and Sarich (1988), and Horrobin (1998). Unfortunately, Crow's theory and ours belong to different logical categories, in that they are designed to provide different answers to the question 'Why?'. Whereas ours is an 'ultimate' theory which seeks to explain why schizotypal and schizophrenic behaviour evolved and why it has been maintained over generations, Crow's is a 'proximate' theory concerned with the neuroanatomical events which lead to psychosis.

Crow postulates that psychosis is a by-product of the evolution of language and of the hemispheric lateralization that the evolution of language seems to have required. He supports this contention with evidence that an association exists between early reading difficulties, incomplete development of handedness, and the later onset of schizophrenia. He does not, however, as do Allen and Sarich (1988), postulate 'phenotypic plasticity', by which the genotype conducive to schizophrenia may be expressed in a phenotype which can be either disadvantageous (e.g., result in schizophrenia) or advantageous (e.g., result in prophetic virtuosity). In other words, Crow does not offer an explanation of why the schizophrenogenic genotype evolved, but simply ascribes it to 'the price we pay for language'. This puts his theory in the same category as, for example, an explanation of lower back pain as a consequence of stresses imposed by bipedalism, or of visual hallucinations as the price we pay for evolution of the eye. By contrast, our theory, unlike Crow's, does not specify proximate mechanisms, and consequently it is not possible to make testable predictions on the basis of which one might choose between them. Nevertheless, we thoroughly endorse Crow's willingness to investigate schizophrenia from an evolutionary perspective and to draw attention to the anatomical structures responsible for language development in both schizophrenic and normal subjects.

While some theorists like Crow postulate proximate mechanisms, and some like us postulate ultimate mechanisms, to account for the existence of schizophrenia, others explicitly do both. For instance, Horrobin (1998) has suggested that schizotypy evolved because it 'increased the likelihood of high creativity, leadership qualities, achievements in many fields, high musical skills and an intense interest in religion ... ' We are human, Horrobin boldly asserts, 'because some members of the human race are schizophrenic.' In addition, Horrobin postulates the proximate theory that these schizotypic attributes evolved because of changes in lipid metabolism which had specific influences on development of the brain. The ultimate component of Horrobin's theory is wholly compatible with our own, for it emphasizes precisely those schizotypal traits which are characteristic of cult leaders. On the other hand, the theoretical component which postulates changes in lipid metabolism as a proximate cause of schizophrenia may indeed possess heuristic value but it carries him into areas we are not competent to enter.

In fact, our ultimate theory is compatible with *any* proximate theory (Price and Stevens, 1998). Even if it should be established beyond doubt, for example, that schizophrenia is due to a virus, this might well prove to be a form of symbiosis: it could be part of the 'extended phenotype' of the virus (Dawkins, 1982) to attack some specific part of the brain, thus converting a 'normal' genotype into a dispersal (schizotypal) phenotype. However well-advanced research into the proximate mechanisms of schizophrenia may become, there will remain an overriding concern to explain this bizarre condition's ultimate cause – to understand why it evolved in the first place.

It is of historical interest that our hypothesis that schizotypal personalities may possess the adaptive function of providing needy groups with charismatic prophets was first entertained by Erlenmeyer-Kimling and Paradowski (1969). They rejected the hypothesis, however, because they were under the impression that prophets have few children. Clearly, they were unaware at that time of the enormous reproductive advantage enjoyed by successful cult leaders (Stevens and Price, in press).

SELF-ESTEEM

Self-esteem is a pivotal subject for research, since people with low self-esteem appear susceptible to most psychiatric disorders, especially depression, anxiety states, personality disorders, and chronic schizophrenia. Ever since Abraham Maslow (1937) first revealed the enormous variation of individual self-ratings, investigators have confirmed again and again that people tend to give themselves a global rating on a self-concept scale and that this rating tends to remain fairly constant during adult life.

One of the first to study this concept was William James (1890), who suggested that the level of one's self-esteem is a function of the gap between one's level of aspiration and one's level of performance. He expressed this in the equation:

$$\text{self-esteem} = \text{successes} \div \text{pretensions}$$

We shall organize our approach to this subject using Tinbergen's four questions:

1 What adaptive function does a global self-concept rating perform in promoting survival and reproductive success?
2 What are the proximate factors that cause people to form such a self-concept: what intrapsychic mechanisms and environmental cues are involved?

3 How does an individual's level of global self-esteem develop in the course of ontogeny?

4 How did such a self-concept evolve? Is anything similar manifested in other animals?

The evolution and adaptive function of the self-concept

In Chapter 4 we have argued that self-esteem is the human equivalent of resource holding power or RHP, and that defeat in a dyadic contest can have similar effects on the behaviour and self-esteem of human beings as it does on the behaviour and RHP of reptiles, mammals, and non-human primates. We indicated that an essential aspect of high self-esteem is the subjective awareness of being able to control desired social outcomes, while low self-esteem is the awareness of not being able to control such desirable assets, and is associated with submissive or subordinate forms of behaviour, as well as with a liability to anxiety, depression, or social withdrawal. In order to answer the question how did such a self-concept come into existence, we have postulated that human self-esteem evolved out of a reptilian precursor, whose organization in the reptilian brain was laid down at a time when the only interaction between members of the same sex was agonistic behaviour.

As we have seen, behavioural ecologists introduced the term resource holding potential as a measure of an individual's fighting capacity which predicts the probable outcome of an agonistic encounter. RHP has the scientific status of an intervening variable, or hypothetical construct: that is to say, it is like a black box whose contents cannot be measured directly, but may be defined by its input and output. On the input side go all those influences which contribute to fighting capacity, such as previous successes or failures in combat, attributes of size, strength, weaponry, and skill, as well as the availability of allies. On the output side, there is the capacity to attack or withdraw when an agonistic encounter occurs, as well as the ability to make a 'display of RHP' through such behaviours as confident or diffident bearing, upright or slouched posture, and measured or furtive gait.

To summarize what has been established so far: the capacity for self-assessment arose out of the ability evolved by reptiles some 250 million years ago for comparing their own RHP with that of a rival. The adaptive function of this capacity is that it enables potential antagonists to make a rapid assessment of each other's RHP, so as to reduce time wasted in fighting and to minimize damage to the loser. Fighting capacity, or RHP, is a universal form of self-knowledge apparent in terrestrial vertebrates. Our own capacity to estimate our relative RHP in the form of a global rating of self-esteem has thus been with us for a very long time. There have, however, been changes with subsequent evolution, one of these being the shift from *agonistic* to *prestige* competition, which has had the effect of partly replacing a self-concept based on RHP with that based on social attention

269

holding potential or SAHP (Gilbert, 1997; Gilbert *et al.*, 1995). A further important evolutionary change has resulted in the development of social signals that have the effect of raising or lowering the RHP and SAHP of the recipient (Price, 1998), a capacity which has been enormously facilitated by the human development of language.

Thus, with the evolution of prestige competition, instead of intimidating their rivals, individuals began to compete for the approbation of significant others and even for the good opinion of the group as a whole. Age-old concerns about one's ability to fight gave place to worries about one's attractiveness.

Like RHP, SAHP resembles a black box and is defined by its input and output. Input to SAHP is determined by the perception of approbation or disapprobation by fellow group members, especially high-ranking and important members. Output, as with RHP, is partly manifested in a general bearing of confidence as opposed to diffidence and partly in the ability to make decisions whether to exhibit self-assertion or self-effacement on specific social occasions.

However, this new SAHP-linked self-concept has remained connected to the underlying reptilian complex, and although prestige competition has largely replaced agonistic competition in human affairs, there are still social situations in which agonistic competition prevails, particularly in all-male groups such as those found in prisons, in army units, on oil rigs, or in the Mafia and terrorist gangs. Agonistic competition is also evident in motorists, as in the phenomenon of 'road rage'.

In addition to SAHP, humans have evolved the concept of *mate value*, which is significant in determining both sexual and non-sexual behaviour. Thus, males relate their own perceived mate value to that of potential female partners. If they perceive their own mate value to be high, they will tend to court a female of high mate value, and vice versa. A female with high mate value is also more likely to reject male suitors whom she perceives as possessing low mate value. Both sexes go to great lengths to emphasize, and even falsify, their mate value. It has been suggested that the pursuit of high mate value underlies the behaviour of patients with such conditions as anorexia nervosa and antisocial and histrionic personality disorders. The same applies to extremes of body-building behaviour in men.

Another adaptive function of comparing oneself with others is noncompetitive, in the sense that it is concerned with 'belongingness' and with self-monitoring for signs of deviance which might expose one to criticism or social rejection. Such concerns become particularly salient in adolescence. In comparison with one's peer group, is one wearing the same uniform, speaking with the same accent, justifying the same opinions? Comparisons of this type, based on estimates of 'sameness' or conformity, are concerned with maintaining group membership rather than attaining and sustaining one's rank within the group, which is the objective of competitive comparison.

Having outlined the possible evolutionary history and adaptive function of self-assessment, we must proceed to the formulation of testable hypotheses as to the proximate and ontological factors involved.

The proximate and ontogenetic determinants of self-esteem

It must be acknowledged at once that we do not know how the variables of RHP, SAHP, and mate value combine in the brain to link up with other self-concepts and contribute to the formation of human self-esteem. This is a research area where contributions from neuroscience are eagerly awaited. However, we do know more about the psychology of how self-esteem is raised or lowered, both in the short term and in the long term. Research has established that we do indeed compare ourselves directly with others (Swallow and Kuiper, 1988), in the way that animals compare RHP. Thus we examine ourselves to determine whether we are bigger or shapelier, more handsome or beautiful, more eloquent or smartly dressed, better-connected, better-off, and so on. When this assessment is positive our esteem is boosted; when it is negative self-esteem is lowered. We bias this process to some extent by deciding with whom to compare ourselves, and much work has been done on the causes of 'upward comparison' and 'downward comparison' (Tennen and Affleck, 1993).

As such research is beginning to make clear, we classify social signals into those that raise self-esteem (*anathetic* or boosting signals), those that lower self-esteem (*catathetic* or putting-down signals), and those that have little or no effect on the self-esteem of the recipient (Price, 1992). We have suggested that the adaptive function of these signals is to maintain or increase the 'RHP gap' between higher-ranking and lower-ranking individuals so as to confirm the hierarchical asymmetry between them. McGuire and his colleagues have shown that the receipt of submissive signals by a dominant animal is associated with a rise in its blood serotonin (McGuire and Troisi, 1998) and it is possible that all boosting signals have a similar effect. An experiment designed to assess these effects in two groups of human subjects performing an identical task has already been proposed in the section on depression (p. 263). In real life, a particularly intense form of boosting occurs when an audience responds with great enthusiasm to a virtuoso performance by a concert pianist or an opera singer. One would anticipate a more marked rise in the performer's blood serotonin after a successful first night than after a dress rehearsal. Alternatively, one would anticipate a rise in catecholamines and/or corticosteroids in response to catathetic signals such as booing, hissing, and catcalls. Research designed to examine these different outcomes would not be easy to arrange, however, and a psychological experiment such as that suggested on page 263 might well prove more feasible.

Since an individual's level of self-esteem is largely conferred by others through signals of attention, respect, approval, praise, affection and love (or the reverse), each person sees his or her value mirrored in the eyes of society. This source of self-esteem was emphasized by Cooley (1902) and Mead (1934), and the process begins in early childhood. There would appear to be two critical periods for the development of self-esteem and this possibility needs to be carefully researched. The two periods are (1) early childhood (in relation to the parents), and (2) adolescence (in relation to the peer group).

Most parents appear highly motivated to make their children feel good about themselves. As Kohut put it, they mirror the child's 'grandiose self' (Seigel, 1996). Other children, however, are made by their parents to feel that they are worthless and bad, and even that their very existence has been a terrible mistake. Reports such as these are commonly received from patients attending psychiatric clinics. Parents, it seems, succeed in inculcating either a high self-esteem strategy or a low self-esteem strategy in their children, and it would appear that sometimes they hedge their bets by treating individual children differently (Price et al., 1994).

By the time adolescence is reached, mirroring is provided much less by the parents and more effectively by the peers. Clinically, many patients are seen who complain of low self-esteem, which they attribute to unfortunate experiences in adolescence. Some felt rejected because they were fat, ugly or clumsy, others because they had the bad luck to move into a strange peer group at a time when it was unready to welcome new members. The self-concept remains relatively plastic up to the end of adolescence but then seems to rigidify and become less open to influence, for good or ill. This squares with ethological findings which indicate that among social animals RHP is determined in adolescence. Adolescent baboons, for example, with few exceptions have settled disputes about relative RHP by the time their lethal canine teeth have erupted.

The majority of patients seen in psychiatric clinics suffer from low self-esteem and most answer 'No' to one or both of the following questions: (1) Did you feel loved and valued by your parents in early childhood? and (2) Did you feel accepted and valued by your adolescent peers? Many give negative answers to both questions, and, indeed, it seems likely – but this needs to be verified – that those who enter adolescence with low self-esteem induced by their parents are likely to find it more difficult to be accepted by their peers. Others, however, say that they were loved by their parents but rejected by their peers, while still others found peer group acceptance while they felt unloved and unvalued by their parents. The consequences for this differentiation in the later development of psychopathology have still to be worked out. It also gives rise to important issues concerning the provision of psychotherapy. One possibility that should be investigated is that individual psychodynamic therapy could, through the provision of a 'corrective emotional experience', compensate for the lack of positive mirroring from parents during the critical stage of early childhood; and that group therapy might be best designed to compensate for the lack of acceptance by the peer group during adolescence. This distinction is seldom, if ever, mentioned in accounts of patient assessment for psychotherapy and it could provide a most important avenue for research.

Research into the development and maintenance of high self-esteem, and into the treatment of those suffering from low self-esteem should, therefore, be given priority in view of the implications of this concept for the majority of psychiatric disorders. Moreover, it is possible that the human capacities for self-awareness, introspection, and consciousness itself, may prove to be evolutionary developments of those adaptations which have subserved agonistic competition between individuals for many millions of years.

FACTS, RESEARCH, AND PARADIGM SHIFTS

Thomas Kuhn (1962), the great authority on paradigm shifts in the history of science, was drawn to their study by his observation that such sciences as astronomy, physics, chemistry, and biology failed to evoke the intense controversies over fundamentals that seem endemic among psychologists and sociologists. He came to see that the source of this difference lay in the relative elegance, comprehensiveness, and precision of the paradigms which prevailed in these different sciences. A sequence of paradigm evolution occurs throughout the history of every science. Being the most recent, the behavioural sciences have much ground to make up before they attain the degree of paradigmatic sophistication achieved by the physical and biological sciences.

New paradigms gain their status because they are seen to be more successful than their predecessors and competitors in solving the central problems of the science concerned. Then the practitioners of that science undergo a process that can be likened to a political or religious 'conversion'. An earlier historian of science, Herbert Butterfield (1949), described a science's reorientation by paradigm change as a process that involves 'handling the same bundle of data as before, but placing them in a new system of relations with one another by giving them a different framework'.

For his part, Kuhn compared this aspect of scientific advance to the changes that can occur in a visual *Gestalt*, according to the mental orientation of the viewer – as, for example, when staring at an ambiguous figure like a cube, in which all sides are visible and not drawn in perspective. 'The decision to reject one paradigm', he wrote, 'is always simultaneously the decision to accept another, and the judgement leading to that decision involves the comparison of both paradigms with nature *and* with each other.'

Throughout the past century psychiatry has been juggling with two paradigms, the Standard Social Science Model and the Medical Model, and these have been of only limited success in explaining the nature of mental disorders. They have not, for example, been able to account for why it is that

273

when human beings become mentally and socially dysfunctional, they develop the kind of 'syndromes' that they do – the clusters of symptoms that are diagnosed as 'illnesses' such as 'depression', 'anxiety disorder', or 'schizophrenia'. What evolutionary psychiatry has set itself to explain is how our species developed the capacity to become dysfunctional in these ways. To achieve this it looks beyond the personal and social history of the individual to the natural history and evolutionary history of the human race. This perspective yields a more spacious explanatory framework within which 'the bundle of data' psychiatry has accumulated may be contained and understood. The search for ontogenetic and proximate causes will continue within this new paradigm, enabling us to frame new questions whose answers will refine our understanding. As Theodosius Dobzhansky said, 'Nothing in biology makes sense except in the light of evolution.'

One fascinating analogy drawn by Kuhn, particularly relevant to our project, was between the evolution of scientific ideas and the evolution of organisms. Resolution of the conflict between rival paradigms is a process, according to Kuhn, of

> selection by conflict within the scientific community of the fittest way to practice future science. The net result of a sequence of such revolutionary selections, separated by periods of normal research, is the wonderfully adapted set of instruments we call modern scientific knowledge. Successive stages in that developmental process are marked by an increase in articulation and specialization. And the entire process may have occurred, as we now suppose biological evolution did, without benefit of a set goal . . . .

The evolutionary revolution in psychiatry is still in its initial stages, and it will be a generation or more before it is complete. As yet it has only begun to tackle the problems confronting it, but that, Kuhn assures us, is in the nature of new paradigms, whose success is 'at the start largely a promise of success discoverable in selected and still incomplete examples. Normal science consists in the actualization of that promise . . . '. It is a promise that beckons us forward, with greater hope than ever possible before, of establishing a new and all-embracing science of humanity.

22

TOWARDS A SCIENCE OF HUMANITY

What brought the authors together to write this book was a shared ambition (though we were not aware of this until we met in the summer of 1992) to contribute to the development of a coherent theory of human nature. For many years we had independently held the view that no theory in psychology or psychiatry could hope to possess any lasting value unless it was securely founded on knowledge of the evolution of our species. This shared view had emerged over a professional lifetime which followed a different course in each case, Price in psychological medicine, Stevens in psychotherapy and analytical psychology. We did, however, have one formative experience in common (in addition to a training in medicine and psychiatry): we both read 'PPP' (Psychology, Philosophy, and Physiology) at Oxford, Price between 1953 and 1955, Stevens between 1958 and 1959. Oxford – largely, we suspect, because of Niko Tinbergen's presence in the Department of Zoology – was to the forefront in seeking to build a bridge between psychology and behavioural biology, and this gave us a theoretical orientation which has influenced our thinking ever since.

We were both attracted by ethological descriptions of animals living in the wild (rather than the performance of endless experiments on rats running in mazes, which provided the primary focus of study in psychology departments at that time) and by the brilliant demonstration by Konrad Lorenz that behaviour could be studied *comparatively* – in precisely the same way as anatomy.

This crucial insight – that all species have behavioural characteristics which are as distinctive and as classifiable as their physical attributes – created an extraordinary situation: it made it possible to trace the evolutionary history of basic patterns of behaviour from reptiles through mammals and primates to ourselves (who are, needless to say, also mammals and primates). This would have a profound impact on all branches and applications of the human sciences, not least psychiatry, where it might permit a definition of the basic psychosocial adaptations with which human beings are equipped and an understanding of how their malfunction could result in mental disorder. We believed that a new science was in the making – a science in the Platonic meaning of the word, namely, *the discovery of things as they really are*.

Though unusual, we were not alone in sharing this vision. Bowlby's work, as well as that of the human ethologist Irenäus Eibl-Eibesfeldt, the socio-biologist E.O. Wilson, and the anthropologists Robin Fox and Lionel Tiger, encouraged a handful of psychologists and psychiatrists on both sides of the Atlantic to advocate an evolutionary approach to the facts of human be-haviour, while the majority of behavioural scientists remained indifferent or hostile to these theoretical developments.

There are several reasons for the anti-biological prejudices which have, to a greater or lesser extent, persisted through most of this century. Most prevalent of these is the fear that acceptance of genetic influences on human psychology will be put to reprehensible political ends, as was the case with Social Darwinism, which deservedly earned itself a bad name during the early part of this century. By misapplying the concept of 'the survival of the fittest' to political phenomena, Social Darwinism did great harm: imperial-ists used it to justify the extermination of primitive populations, Marxists used it to incite massacre in the name of the class struggle, Hitler used it to launch his genocide of the Slavs and the Jews, criminologists used it to advo-cate castration and capital punishment, eugenicists used it to argue for select-ive euthanasia, and militarists used it to justify war. With such a catalogue of crimes to its discredit, it is not surprising that there should have been a revulsion against the application of evolutionary theory to human behaviour and that the pendulum should have swung away from the 'innate' towards behaviourism, culturalism, and the triumph of *tabula rasa* empiricism.

Although there has been a retreat from this extreme position in recent decades and the pendulum has begun to swing back towards acceptance of biological influences on human behaviour, there is still no shortage of critics who will find the approach to psychiatric disorders adopted throughout this book both dangerous and misguided. Some politically motivated writers, such as Lerner (1992), for example, still cling to a rigidly anti-biological position, maintaining that to acknowledge the existence of social hierarchies in human populations, and to trace their evolutionary origins, is to condone them at best and to promote fascism at worst. If we are unsympathetic to such arguments, it is because we feel that authors like Lerner would have us become scientific ostriches, burying our heads in the sand of political cor-rectness, in the pious hope that those powerful competitive propensities that behavioural biology has revealed, will, if we refuse to acknowledge them, quietly go away. This is as logical as arguing that AIDS would cease to exist if only scientists would stop studying the virus responsible for it. The current British enthusiasm for that carnival of inequity, the National Lottery, testi-fies to the strength of an imperative to achieve the power and social status that wealth can bring. To deny the evolutionary basis of such behaviour will not stop it from occurring, any more than the systematic imposition of

Marxism over a period of sixty years succeeded in eradicating the desire for personal property and social status among the peoples of the Soviet empire.

The often repeated criticism made of evolutionary psychologists by their opponents that they are ideologically motivated by a private 'right wing' political agenda is unjustified. Not only is it untrue of ourselves, but we believe it to be untrue of those evolutionary psychologists who are known to us personally. Those non-biological psychologists, behaviourists, and sociologists who, with a clear conscience and in defence of liberal democracy, accuse evolutionists of fascism too readily forget that the laws of learning and conditioning worked out during the heyday of behaviourism have been used by modern tyrants throughout the world to torture, intimidate, and brainwash their hapless subjects. That scientific discoveries can be put to evil uses is undeniable, but to hold scientists responsible for these crimes is to blame the Wright brothers for the destruction of Dresden and Hiroshima.

Instead of wishing to promote some political ideology, our more modest ambition is to work towards the provision for psychiatry, and for the social sciences generally, of a firm, neutral scientific foundation on which they may build. In fact, as Buss (1995) has pointed out, it is the *critics* of evolutionary psychology who are ideologically motivated: it is *their* strong political conviction that forms the basis of their approach to social and psychological issues rather than the scientific objectivity aspired to by the evolutionists. By denying their own political motives and projecting such motives on to others, these critics seem to be displaying that incipient paranoia which typically occurs when human communities divide.

But it is not profitable to debate this issue any further: we believe the argument has been won. The evidence for a biologically determined propensity for human and non-human primates to form hierarchically structured societies, in which individual rank has important social and psychological consequences, is so overwhelming that the onus is now on those who refuse to believe it to prove their case. We contend that evolutionary theories will prevail over non-evolutionary theories because they give a better explanation of the facts. Application of the usual procedures of empirical science will determine the matter over the next few years, and we are content to abide by the outcome.

Whatever the result, the primary duty of the psychiatrist will remain the same: to put skill, empathy, knowledge, and professional commitment at the service of the patient. To adopt an evolutionary approach is not to espouse a political cause, nor is it an invitation to submit to 'biological determinism' or an encouragement to abandon a proper concern with ethical or value-oriented premises. However sophisticated our understanding of neural mechanisms and brain chemistry may become in the years ahead, human beings will continue to live in their minds rather than their brains and the primacy of the psyche will remain paramount in all human endeavours – not least in the treatment of mental suffering.

Of the genetically based disciplines that have received most hostile attention from the non-biological psychologists, **sociobiology** has consistently come under attack for being both reductive and determinist in its analysis of human behaviour. While we share the same evolutionary principles as the sociobiologists, we do not however subscribe to their simplistic view of human beings as mere fitness-maximizing genetic vehicles, a view which Buss (1995) calls 'the sociobiological fallacy'. If men were blindly programmed to maximize their fitness, then why, asks Buss, are they not queuing up to donate their semen to sperm banks? Men do not look at erotic photographs in order to maximize their fitness, but because they are equipped with evolved psychological mechanisms which cause them to find images of nubile females sexually stimulating. They are manipulating components of the psychosexual system (which *can* result in reproduction) purely for their own enjoyment. As Buss observes, sociobiologists seem to have missed out the psychological level of analysis altogether. Our genes are powerful influences but they do not turn us into unconscious automata. The social matrix in which we grow up, its rules, values, language, customs, and ideals, are mediating factors between our basic human nature and the kind of individual human being we become.

Our evolved capacity for consciousness not only enables us to monitor what is going on about us in the interests of survival and reproductive success but makes us aware of the *meaning* and *quality* of events as they occur. In the words of Saint Augustine, we both exist and know that we exist, and rejoice in this existence and this knowledge. It is commonly observed that we are the only animal that knows that it must die. But we are also, as Robin Fox has said, the only animal that knows that it is alive. Evolutionary psychiatry can provide an insight into the natural history of this extraordinary achievement and, by granting a cosmic perspective, enable us to relate people's sufferings to the totality of human experience, as it is now and always has been.

The phenomena of mental life are infinitely varied and there is a great multiplicity of factors responsible for their functional development, but a growing understanding of the role of our archetypal dispositions, and the way in which they become integrated with features of the human *Umwelt*, is at last bringing a semblance of order and meaning into a field of daunting complexity. There is now hope that evolutionary psychology can begin to define what our basic needs are and what kinds of environmental characteristics can satisfy them. This, we believe, will have inestimable advantages not only for understanding the nature of mental disorders but in providing effective measures for their prevention, treatment, and cure.

GLOSSARY

Aetiology: that part of medical science which investigates the causes of disease.

Agonic competition: competition by intimidation.

Agonic mode: a mode of social interaction characteristic of hierarchically organized societies where individuals are concerned with warding off threats to their status and inhibiting overt expressions of aggressive conflict.

Agonistic mode: an episode in a relationship in which social asymmetry is being negotiated or renegotiated by **ritual agonistic behaviour**.

Algorithm: a genetically acquired learning mechanism which organizes experience into adaptive patterns specific to certain typical activities, such as mate selection, predator avoidance, site selection, and so on.

Anaclitic depression: depression due to the loss of a supportive attachment figure; first used by René Spitz to describe the physical, social, and intellectual impairment which may occur in an infant following separation from or loss of its mother or primary caretaker.

Analytical psychologist: an analyst who subscribes to the theories and who practices the therapeutic techniques devised by C.G. Jung. To be distinguished from **psychiatrist**, **psychoanalyst**, **psychologist**, and **psychotherapist**.

Anathetic behaviour: term derived from Greek *ana* = up, *thesis* = put or place, i.e., to put up; behaviour which has the effect of raising the **RHP** of the recipient. The opposite of **catathetic behaviour**.

Ancestral environment: the **environment of evolutionary adaptedness** or **EEA**; the environment in which our species evolved and in which it is adapted to live.

Ancestral society: the kind of intimate community characteristic of human beings living in the **ancestral environment**; the kind of society in which our species is probably best adapted to live.

Anhedonia: the inability to experience pleasure.

Anxious attachment: a term introduced by Bowlby to describe the state of those who suffer from the fear that their attachment figures may either be lost or prove inaccessible to them.

Archetypes: innate neuropsychic centres possessing the capacity to initiate, control, and mediate the common behavioural characteristics and typical experiences of all human beings irrespective of race, culture, creed, or historical epoch.

Arousal: neurophysiological state which accompanies intense emotions such as sex, anger and aggression or the perception of actual or potential threat; mobilized by hypothalamic structures in the **limbic system**, acting through the **sympathetic nervous system** and its connections with the endocrine glands.

Attachment: a tie of affection formed by one person or animal for another; in the sense used by Bowlby, the tie formed between an infant and its mother or mother-substitute.

Attachment behaviour: the characteristic forms of behaviour by which attachment bonds between individuals are expressed.

Basic trust: term introduced by Erik Erikson for the conviction that a good maternal figure can engender in a child, through the development of a strong attachment bond, that it can trust her, the world, and itself.

Behavioural ecology: a discipline concerned with the functional analysis of behaviour in relation to the environment; particularly concerned with the costs and benefits of alternative strategies employed in environmental exploitation.

Behavioural systems: term introduced by Bowlby for goal-directed mechanisms operating cybernetically (like electronic systems, through positive and negative feedback) in both mother and child which are responsible for **attachment behaviour** and for mediating the development and maintenance of attachment bonds.

Biosocial goals: the social goals for which we are biologically equipped to strive, such as care, protection, love, and status.

Borderline personality: concept applied to individuals whose abnormal personalities combine features of neurotic and psychotic symptomatology.

Catathetic behaviour: term derived from Greek *kata* = down, *thesis* = put or place, i.e., to put down; behaviour which has the effect of lowering the **RHP** of the recipient. The opposite of **anathetic behaviour**.

Charisma: term derived from New Testament Greek meaning the gift of grace; introduced into sociology by Max Weber to describe an 'extraordinary quality' possessed by persons or objects, which is thought to give them a unique, magical quality.

Chromosome: a complex, thread-like structure, numbers of which occur in every cell of animals and plants. Chromosomes carry the **genes**, which are the basic units of heredity.

Collective unconscious: term introduced by C.G. Jung to designate those aspects of the psyche which are common to all humanity; synonymous with **phylogenetic psyche**.

Complex: a group or cluster of interconnected ideas and feelings which exert a dynamic effect on conscious experience and on behaviour. Complexes are to the **ontogenetic psyche** (or personal unconscious) what **archetypes** are to the **phylogenetic psyche** (or collective unconscious), the one being dependent on the other in the sense that complexes are 'personations' of archetypes.

Conspecific: a member of the same species.

Cybernetics: term introduced by Norbert Wiener (1948) for the theoretical study of control and communication in machines and physiological systems.

Cyclothymia: a disposition to mood swings between episodes of depression and hypomania.

De-escalating strategy: a strategy of withdrawal, submission, and appeasement. A component of the **agonistic** strategy set, it may be deployed at any or all of the three levels of the **triune brain**: at the neocortical level it takes the form of a conscious decision to submit, at the **limbic** level it manifests as depressed emotion and at the **reptilian** level as depressed mood.

Delusions: false beliefs; a distinction is made between primary and secondary delusions. A **primary delusion** occurs suddenly and with complete conviction, and without any clearly identifiable preceding events. For example, a patient may be seized by the conviction that she is the reincarnation of Catherine the Great, without having thought of the idea before. A **secondary delusion** arises from a preceding experience, such as a hallucination or a powerful affect. Secondary delusions sometimes have an explanatory function, in that they make sense of the original experience. Thus a man who heard voices telling him to save the world may come to believe that he is the second incarnation of Christ.

Diathesis: a constitutional disposition that renders an individual liable to a certain disease.

DNA: deoxyribonucleic acid; the basic hereditary material of all living organisms, making up the **genes** and located within the **chromosomes.**

DSM-IV: *Diagnostic and Statistical Manual of Mental Disorders*, 4th edition (1994), American Psychiatric Association, Washington.

Dysphoria: a state of lowered mood.

ECT: electro-convulsive therapy.

Environment: everything external to an organism that affects its probability of survival and reproduction.

Environment of evolutionary adaptedness or **EEA:** see **Ancestral society**.

Epigenesis: term derived from Greek *epi* = upon, *genesis* = generation; a biological theory of development proposed by C.H. Waddington (1957). It holds that the development of all biological characteristics, whether they be relatively sensitive or insensitive to environmental variation, is governed by the **genome.**

Epistemology: study of the basis of knowledge.

Escalating strategy: a strategy of fighting on, raising the stakes, responding to aggression with retaliation. An alternative to the **de-escalating strategy**, it may be deployed at any or all of the three levels of the **triune** brain: at the **neocortical** level it takes the form of a conscious decision to fight; at the **limbic** level it manifests as an emotion of anger; and at the **reptilian** level as elevated mood (mania).

Ethogram: a schematic representation of the behavioural repertoire of an animal species.

Ethology: the study of the behaviour of organisms living in their natural habitats.

Free-rider: an individual who seeks to acquire an undue proportion of the group's resources without first satisfying the usual requirement of achieving high social rank.

Gene: the basic unit of heredity, made up of **DNA**.

Genome: the complete genetic constitution of an organism; the entire genetic programme characterizing the species.

Genotype: the genetic constitution of the individual.

Group selection: a sub-set of natural selection in which groups (rather than individuals) are the units of selection. If it occurs (which is a matter of controversy) it permits the evolution of a character that benefits the group at a cost to the individual.

Gynaephilic paedosexual behaviour: paedosexual behaviour directed towards females.

Hallucinations: false sensory perceptions in the absence of external stimuli; characteristic of **psychosis**; may be induced by emotional and other factors such as drugs, alcohol, and stress; they may occur in any sensory modality.

Hedonic competition: competition by attraction.

Hedonic mode: a mode of social interaction in which underlying dominance relations are not being challenged and agonic tensions are consequently absent, permitting individuals to be affiliative and to give their attention to recreational or task-oriented activities.

Homeorhesis: term used by C.H. Waddington (1957) to describe the tendency of growing organisms to persist in their course along specific pathways of development once they have started on them, despite environmental variations.

Homeostasis: maintenance of balance between opposing mechanisms or systems.

ICD 10: Classification of Mental and Behavioural Disorders: Clinical Descriptions and Guidelines (1992), World Health Organization, Geneva.

Inclusive fitness: refers to the number of copies of an individual's genetic material that survive him, not only in his direct descendants, but in other than direct descendants as well – nephews, nieces, cousins, brothers, and sisters, all of whom share a proportion of his genes.

Individuation: term used by C.G. Jung to designate the process of personality development which leads to the fullest possible actualization of the archetypal endowment of an individual: 'Individuation means becoming a single, homogeneous being, and, insofar as "individuality" embraces our innermost, last, and incomparable uniqueness, it also implies becoming one's own self. We could therefore translate individuation as "coming to selfhood" or "self-realization" ' (CW7, para. 266).

Innate releasing mechanism (IRM): postulated neuronal centre responsible for the release and co-ordination of instinctively determined patterns of behaviour when appropriate **sign stimuli** are encountered by an organism in the environment.

Internal working model: hypothetical construct introduced by John Bowlby; an inner, psychic representation of the self as capable (or incapable) of giving and receiving care and affection and of forming lasting bonds of **attachment**.

Intrasexual selection: the type of selection that promotes the evolution of characteristics which benefit an animal when it competes with others of the same sex for the favours of a sexual partner (e.g., in a male, size, strength, dominance, assertiveness).

Kin selection: refers to the selection of genes which cause individuals to favour close kin on account of the high probability that they will share those genes. Strictly speaking 'kin' should include direct offspring (sons and daughters), but many biologists have come to apply the term 'kin selection' solely to kin other than offspring (e.g., nephews and nieces). Kin selection is sometimes confused with group selection, from which it is logically distinct, although, where species happen to live in discrete kinship groups, the two may incidentally amount to the same process – what Dawkins (1982) has called 'kin group selection'.

Lamarckism: the discredited theory originally advanced by the French biologist, Jean-Baptiste Lamarck (1744–1829) which held that experiences acquired by one generation could be transmitted genetically to the next.

Limbic system: the cortex of the great limbic lobe described by the French surgeon Paul Broca (1824–1886) and the structures of the brainstem with which it is primarily connected; part of the paleomammalian brain.

Liminal: derived from the Latin *limen*, meaning threshold or doorway: used in psychology to refer to the threshold between conscious and unconscious levels of experience.

Mate selection: the kind of selection that promotes the evolution of characteristics which make an animal attractive to the opposite sex as a potential breeding partner (plumage, colouring, physique, etc.).

Mate value: an individual's reproductive value for a potential sexual partner.

Mirroring: psychoanalytic concept introduced by H. Kohut; the process whereby a parent feeds back pride and delight in a child's activities, thus allowing the child to internalize a concept of self as valued in the eyes of a significant other; important in the development of self-esteem and the formation of an **internal working model** of self as capable of giving and receiving care and affection and of forming lasting bonds of **attachment**.

Monogamy: in human beings, the custom of being married to only one person at a time; in non-human animals, the habit of living in pairs, or having only one mate.

Natural selection: the principle mechanism of evolutionary change, originally proposed by Darwin (1859). The theory holds that of the range of different individuals making up the population of a given species, those individuals possessing certain advantageous characteristics contribute more offspring to the succeeding generation (i.e., they have greater **reproductive success**) than those lacking these characteristics. Provided these advantageous attributes have an inherited basis, they will eventually become established as standard components of the genetic structure of the species (i.e., they will be **selected** by a natural process).

Neocortex: the neo-mammalian brain, responsible for cognition and sophisticated perceptual processes as opposed to instinctive and affective behaviour.

Neurosis: term dating from the second half of the eighteenth century which originally meant a disease of the nerves; since the work of Jean Martin Charcot (1825–1893) and Freud on hysteria towards the end of the nineteenth century, however, neurosis came to be applied precisely to mental disorders which were *not* diseases of the nervous system. Although used less frequently than hitherto, neurosis remains a convenient term for a group of psychiatric disorders which do not involve hallucinations, delusions, or loss of insight.

Nosology: the branch of medical science which deals with the systematic classification of diseases.

Ontogenetic psyche: those psychic attributes which are dependent for their functional development on the personal history of the individual.

Ontogeny: the development of an organism through the course of its life-cycle.

Open programme: term introduced by Ernst Mayr to designate those forms of instinctive behaviour which permit an organism to adapt appropriately to environmental variations.

Operant conditioning: learning to perform certain acts which initially occur as random or spontaneous movements through rewards (e.g., food) or punishments (e.g., electric shock).

Paedophilia: sexual attraction to prepubertal children; in common usage, the term has come to be applied to sexual attraction to all young people below the age of consent.

Paedosexual behaviour: actual sexual behaviour between an adult and a prepubertal child.

Paleolithic: pertaining to the earlier part of the prehistoric Stone Age (Greek *paleo* = old + *lithos* = stone).

Paradigm: term given a technical meaning within the philosophy of science by T.S. Kuhn in his *The Structure of Scientific Revolutions* (1962). Denying that scientific theories are mere products of induction from sensory experience, Kuhn argued that theories give *meaning* to facts rather than simply arising out of them. A paradigm is the theoretical framework within which all thinking in a given scientific discipline proceeds. A **paradigm shift** occurs when one theoretical framework is replaced by another.

Parental investment: term used to denote the time and energy a parent invests in an existing offspring: the greater the investment, the less the parent's chances of producing additional offspring in the future.

Participation mystique: term introduced into anthropology by Lévi-Brühl to describe the psychic state in which a subject experiences a sense of identification with an object.

Phenotype: the characteristics of an organism as a manifestation of the genes possessed by it. It is possible for organisms to possess the same genotype (e.g., identical twins) yet to have different phenotypes, owing to environmentally induced variations in their ontological development.

Phylogenetic psyche: those psychic structures and functions which are characteristic of all members of the human species; synonymous with Jung's term **collective unconscious**.

Phylogeny: the evolutionary origin and development of a species.

Pleistocene: term derived from Greek *pleistos* = most + *kainōs* = new, recent; the most recent division of the Pliocene; the geological formation that contains the greatest number of fossils of still existing species; the geological period which covers the last 2 million years.

Polyandry: that form of marriage in which one woman has two or more husbands at the same time.

Polygamy: among humans, the custom according to which one man has two or more wives; among animals, the habit of mating with more than one member of the opposite sex.

Polygyny: the practice by which one man has two or more female sexual partners, whether he is married to them or not.

Proximate cause: term used in evolutionary psychiatry to denote an aetiological factor which operates on and through the **phenotype** (i.e., on and through the constitution and the life experience of the individual).

Pseudospeciation: term used by Erik Erikson to describe the propensity of members of one human community to treat members of another as if they belonged to a nonhuman species.

Psychiatrist: a medically qualified practitioner who specializes in the diagnosis and treatment of mental disorder.

Psychoanalyst: an analyst who subscribes to the theories and who practises the therapeutic techniques devised by Sigmund Freud and developed by Freud's followers.

Psychologist: a pure scientist who studies all behaviour, normal and abnormal, human and animal.

Psychosis: a broad term used to cover those relatively severe psychiatric disorders in which hallucinations and delusions occur in people with relatively poor insight into their condition.

Psychotherapist: a generic term for therapists who use their own minds to treat the minds of others, with or without reference to unconscious processes or using the techniques of any particular school of analysis.

RAB: see **Ritual agonistic behaviour**.

REM sleep: rapid eye movement sleep, which is reliably associated with the experience of dreams and with characteristic physiological changes in the body of the dreamer.

Reproductive success: the number of surviving offspring produced by an individual.

Reptilian brain (syn. **reptilian complex, R-complex**): the most primitive component of the human brain which evolved in our reptilian ancestors about 300 million years ago; its main structural components are the basal ganglia, including the olfactostriatum and part of the corpus striatum.

Resource holding potential or **RHP:** an estimate of fighting capacity defined on the input side by size, strength, skill, weapons, allies, and other resources; and on the output side by the probability of escalating a **ritual agonistic encounter** (rather than withdrawing or submitting). Hence **relative RHP**, the estimate an individual makes of the difference between his own RHP and the RHP he ascribes to an adversary in a **ritual agonistic encounter**. In the simplest case, the estimate may be either favourable (i.e., his own RHP is estimated as equal to, or superior to, the adversary's) or unfavourable (i.e., his own RHP being estimated as inferior to the adversary's).

Reverted escape: the subsequent return after an initial withdrawal by a threatened subdominant animal to the proximity of the dominant animal that has threatened him or her.

RHP: see **Resource holding potential**.

Ritual agonistic behaviour or **RAB:** a process of signalling between two individuals that converts a symmetrical relationship into an asymmetrical complementary relationship.

Ritual agonistic encounter: an episode involving two (or more) individuals in which **ritual agonistic behaviour** takes place. A stage of mutual assessment may be followed by a stage of engagement.

SAHP: see **Social attention holding potential**.

Schizotypy: a genetic or developmental predisposition to withdrawal and alienation from members of the ingroup, who are perceived as members of an outgroup; in certain individuals and in certain social situations (i.e., those conducive to group schism) it can result in charismatic leadership, but the condition also carries an attendant risk of schizophrenia. As a genetically transmitted social strategy, we have suggested that schizotypy evolved in the context of a runaway process of group splitting, rapid group elimination, externally mediated **sexual selection**, and selection between groups.

Seasonal affective disorder (SAD): recurrent episodes of depression in late autumn, winter or early spring.

Separation anxiety: anxiety experienced at the prospect of becoming separated from a person to whom a bond of attachment has been formed.

Sexual selection theory: this holds that in every generation for the last 300 million years, the population has been stratified by social competition into those who are successful and those who are not.

Sign stimulus: a specific perceptual stimulus possessing the capacity to trigger a specific **innate releasing mechanism (IRM)**.

Social attention holding potential (SAHP): a self-construct which reflects an individual's confidence (or lack of it) that he or she can command the attention and investment of other group members.

Sociobiology: term introduced by E.O. Wilson for his approach to the study of behaviour; it is based on the assumption that the survival of the gene ultimately determines the form of the behaviour studied.

Superego: a term originally introduced by Freud which has come to designate that inner moral authority or ethical complex which monitors individual behaviour in such a way as to make it acceptable first to the parents and later to society.

Sympathetic nervous system: the part of the autonomic nervous system that enables an organism to act in an emergency, thus preparing it to respond to an imagined or actual threat with **arousal** and with appropriate physical activity – the so-called 'flight or fight' response.

Triune brain: conception introduced by Paul MacLean, who proposed that the human brain is not a unity but composed of three brains – the **reptilian brain**, the **paleo-mammalian brain**, and **neo-mammalian brain** – each with a different phylogenetic history, each with 'its own special intelligence, its own special memory, its own sense of time and space, and its own motor functions' (MacLean, 1976).

Ultimate cause: a factor contributing to the structure of the human genome over millions of years of selection pressure.

Umwelt: term introduced by von Uexküll to designate the perceptually selective and essentially subjective world in which each organism lives.

Westermarck effect: the tendency for young people to lack sexual interest in individuals with whom they have grown up (e.g., brothers, sisters, and fellow kibbutz members) and to seek sexual relationships with individuals previously unfamiliar to them.

Yielding subroutine: also called the 'involuntary subordinate strategy (ISS)'. A behavioural programme adopted by a contestant losing in a **ritual agonistic encounter**, which is contingent on a reduction in subjective RHP, SAHP, Resource Value, and Ownership. It terminates challenge by signalling submission and it facilitates voluntary yielding by inducing a mental and behavioural state of 'giving up', 'giving in', and 'giving way'. When prolonged it may manifest as a depressive state.

BIBLIOGRAPHY

Abraham, K. (1927) 'Notes on the psycho-analytical investigation and treatment of manic-depressive insanity and allied conditions', *Selected Papers of Karl Abraham*, pp. 137–156. Hogarth Press, London.

Ainsworth, M. D. (1964) 'Patterns of attachment behaviour shown by the infant in interaction with his mother', *Merrill-Palmer Quarterly*, 10, pp. 51–58.

Akiskal, H. S. (1985) 'Interaction of biologic and psychologic factors in the origin of depressive disorders', *Acta Psychiatrica Scandinavica*, 71, pp. 131–139.

—— (1988) 'Personality as a mediating variable in the pathogenesis of mood disorders: implications for theory, research, and prevention', in T. Helgason and D. J. Daly (eds) *Depressive Illness: Prediction of Course and Outcome*. Springer-Verlag, New York.

—— (1989) 'The classification of mental disorders', in H. I. Kaplan and B. J. Sadock (eds) *Comprehensive Textbook of Psychiatry* (5th edition), Volume 5, pp. 583–598. Williams & Wilkins, Baltimore, Md.

—— (1998) 'Toward a definition of generalized anxiety disorder as an anxious temperament type', *Acta Psychiatrica Scandinavica*, Supplement 393, pp. 66–73.

Alcock, J. (1989) *Animal Behavior: An Evolutionary Approach*, 4th edition. Sinauer Associates, Sunderland, Mass.

Allen, J. S., and Sarich, V. M. (1988) 'Schizophrenia in an evolutionary perspective', *Perspectives in Biology and Medicine*, 32, pp. 132–153.

Allen, N. (1995) 'Towards a computational theory of depression', *ASCAP, The Newsletter of the Society for Sociophysiological Integration*, vol. 8, no. 7, pp. 3–12.

Anderson, D. J., Noyes, R., and Crowe, R. R. (1984) 'A comparison of panic disorder and generalized anxiety disorder', *American Journal of Psychiatry*, 141, pp. 572–575.

Angyal, A. (1951) *Neurosis and Treatment: A Holistic Theory*. Wiley, New York.

Archer, J. (1992) *Ethology and Human Development*. Harvester/Wheatsheaf, New York.

Axelrod, R. (1984) *The Evolution of Co-operation*. Basic Books, New York.

Axelrod, R. and Hamilton, W. D. (1981) 'The evolution of co-operation', *Science*, 211, pp. 1390–1396.

Bailey, K. (1987) *Human Paleopsychology: Applications to Aggression and Pathological Processes*. Lawrence Erlbaum Associates, Hove and London; Hillsdale, NJ.

Bailey, P. (1982) *An English Madam: The Life and Work of Cynthia Payne*. Jonathan Cape, London.

Bakan, D. (1966) *The Duality of Human Existence*. Beacon Books, Boston.

Bancroft, J., Skrimshire, A., Casson, J., Harvard-Watts, O., and Reynolds, F. (1977)

'People who deliberately poison or injure themselves: their problems and their contacts with helping agencies', *Psychological Medicine*, 7, pp. 289–304.

Barkow, J. H. (1980) 'Prestige and self-esteem: a biosocial interpretation', in D. R. Omark, D. R. Strayer and J. Freedman (eds) *Dominance Relations: An Ethological View of Social Conflict and Social Interaction*. Garland STPM Press, New York.

Beck, A. T. (1967) *Depression: Clinical, Experimental and Theoretical Aspects*. Harper & Row, New York.

—— (1983) 'Cognitive therapy of depression: new perspectives', in P. J. Clayton and A. E. Barrett (eds) *Treatment of Depression: Old Controversies and New Approaches*. Raven Press, New York.

Bejjani, B.-P., Damier, P., Arnulf, I., *et al.* (1999) 'Transient acute depression induced by high-frequency deep-brain stimulation', *New England Journal of Medicine*, 340, pp. 1476–1480.

Bell, A. P., Weinberg M. S., and Hammersmith, S. K. (1981) *Sexual Preference: Its Development in Men and Women*. Indiana University Press, Bloomington.

Belsher, G., and Costello, C. G. (1988) 'Relapse after recovery from unipolar depression: a critical review', *Psychological Bulletin*, 104, pp. 84–86.

Belsky, J., Steinberg, J., and Draper, P. (1991) 'Childhood experience, interpersonal development and reproductive strategy: an evolutionary theory of socialization', *Child Development*, 62, pp. 647–670.

Biller, H. B. (1974) *Paternal Deprivation*. Lexington Books, Lexington, Mass.

Birchwood, M., and Spencer, E. (1999) 'Psychotherapies for schizophrenia: a review', in M. Maj and N. Sartorius (eds) *Schizophrenia*, pp. 147–214. Volume 2 of WPA series 'Evidence and Experience in Psychiatry'. John Wiley, Chichester.

Birtchnell, J. (1990) 'Interpersonal theory: criticism, modification and elaboration', *Human Relations,* 43, pp. 1183–1201.

—— (1993) *How Humans Relate: A New Interpersonal Theory*. Praeger, Westport, Conn.

—— (1994) 'On the cartoonization of Birtchnell', *ASCAP, The Newsletter of the Society for Sociophysiological Integration*, vol. 7, no. 8, pp. 6–10.

Blatt, S. J. (1974) 'Levels of object representation in anaclitic and introjective depression', *Psychoanalytic Study of the Child*, 29, pp. 107–157.

Bleuler, P. E. (1911) *Dementia Praecox, oder die Gruppe der Schizophrenien*. Translated by J. Zinkin (1950) as *Dementia Praecox, or the Group of Schizophrenias*. New York.

Boehm, C. (1993) 'Egalitarian behaviour and reverse dominance hierarchy', *Current Anthropology*, 34, pp. 227–254.

Bowen, M. (1966) 'The use of family theory in clinical practice', *Comprehensive Psychiatry*, 7, pp. 345–374.

Bowlby, J. (1941) *Maternal Care and Mental Health*. WHO, Geneva; HMSO, London; Columbia University Press, New York.

—— (1958) 'The nature of the child's tie to his mother', *International Journal of Psycho-Analysis*, 39, pp. 350–373.

—— (1969) *Attachment and Loss, vol. 1, Attachment*. Hogarth Press and the Institute of Psycho-Analysis, London.

—— (1973) *Attachment and Loss, vol. 2, Separation: Anxiety and Anger*. Hogarth Press and the Institute of Psycho-Analysis, London.

—— (1979) *The Making and Breaking of Affectional Bonds*. Tavistock Publications, London.

Brown, G. W. and Harris, T. (1978) *Social Origins of Depression*. Tavistock Publications, London.

Bruch, H. (1965) 'The psychiatric differential diagnosis of anorexia nervosa', in

J. E. Meyer and H. Feldmann (eds) *Symposium on Anorexia Nervosa*, Göttingen, Thieme Verlag, Stuttgart.

Bullough, V. L. (1990) 'History in adult human sexual behavior with children and adolescents in western societies', in J. R. Feierman (ed.) *Pedophilia: Biosocial Dimensions*. Springer-Verlag, New York.

Burton, R. V. (1972) 'Cross-sex identity in Barbados', *Developmental Psychology*, 6, pp. 365–374.

Buss, D. M. (1989) 'Sex differences in human mate preferences: evolutionary hypotheses tested in 37 cultures', *Behavioral and Brain Sciences*, 12, pp. 1–49.

—— (1991) 'Evolutionary personality psychology', *Annual Review of Psychology*, 45, pp. 459–491.

—— (1995) 'Evolutionary psychology: a new paradigm for psychological science', *Psychological Enquiry*, vol. 6, no. 1, pp. 1–30.

—— (1999) *Evolutionary Psychology: The New Science of the Mind*. Allyn & Bacon, Boston, Mass.

Butler, A. B., and Hodos, W. (1996) *Comparative Vertebrate Neuroanatomy*. Wiley-Liss, New York.

Butterfield, H. (1949) The Origins of Modern Science 1300–1800. London.

Cannon, W. B. (1929) *Bodily Changes in Pain, Hunger, Fear and Rage*. Appleton, New York.

Chadwick, P. K. (1997) *Schizophrenia: The Positive Perspective. In Search of Dignity for Schizophrenic People*. Routledge, London.

Champion, L. A. and Power, M. J. (1995) 'Social and cognitive approaches to depression', *British Journal of Clinical Psychology*, 34, pp. 485–503.

Chance, M. R. A. (1988) 'Introduction', in M. R. A. Chance (ed.) *Social Fabrics of the Mind*. Lawrence Erlbaum Associates, Hove and London; Hillsdale, NJ.

Chance, M. R. A. and Jolly, C. (1970) *Social Groups of Monkeys, Apes and Men*. Jonathan Cape/E. P. Dutton, New York and London.

Chomsky, N. (1965) *Aspects of the Theory of Syntax*. MIT Press, Cambridge, Mass.

Claridge, G. (1985) *Origins of Mental Illness*. Basil Blackwell, Oxford.

—— (1987) 'The schizophrenias as nervous types revisited', *British Journal of Psychiatry*, 151, pp. 735–743.

Cloninger, C. (1978) 'The antisocial personality', *Hospital Practice*, August, pp. 97–104.

Cohn, N. (1970) *The Pursuit of the Millennium: Revolutionary Millenarians and Mystical Anarchists of the Middle Ages* (revised edition). Oxford University Press, Oxford and New York.

Cooley, C. H. (1902) *Human Nature and the Social Order*. Scribner's, New York.

Cosmides, L., and Tooby, J. (1989) 'Evolutionary psychology and the generation of culture, part I: case study: a computational theory of social exchange', *Ethology and Sociobiology*, 10, pp. 51–97.

Crawford, C., and Krebs, D. L. (1998) *Handbook of Evolutionary Psychology: Ideas, Issues, and Applications*. Lawrence Erlbaum Associates, Hillsdale, NJ.

Crick, F. H. C., and Mitchison, G. (1983) 'The function of dream sleep', *Nature*, 304, pp. 111–114.

Crisp, A. H. (1967) 'Anorexia nervosa', *Hospital Medicine*, 1, p. 713.

Crook, J. H. (1980) *The Evolution of Human Consciousness*. Oxford University Press, Oxford.

Crow, T. J. (1995) 'A Darwinian approach to the origins of psychosis', *British Journal of Psychiatry*, 167, pp. 12–25.

—— (1997a) 'Is schizophrenia the price *Homo sapiens* pays for language?' *Schizophrenia Research*, 28, pp. 127–141.

—— (1997b) 'Schizophrenia as a failure of hemispheric dominance for language', *Trends in Neurosciences*, 20, pp. 339–343.

—— (1998) 'Precursors of psychosis as pointers to the *Homo sapiens*-specific mate recognition system of language', *British Journal of Psychiatry*, 172, pp. 289–290.

Daly, M., and Wilson, M. (1989) 'Evolutionary psychology and family violence', in C. Crawford, M. Smith and D. Krebs. (eds) *Sociobiology and Psychology*. Lawrence Erlbaum Associates, Hove and London; Hillsdale, NJ.

Darwin, C. (1859) *On the Origin of Species by Means of Natural Selection*. John Murray, London.

—— (1871) *The Descent of Man and Selection in Relation to Sex*. John Murray, London.

—— (1872) *The Expression of Emotion in Man and Animals*. John Murray, London.

Dawkins, R. (1982) *The Extended Phenotype*. Oxford University Press, Oxford.

De Giacomo, P. (1993) *Finite Systems and Infinite Interactions: The Logic of Human Interaction and its Application to Psychotherapy*. Bramble Books, Norfolk, Conn.

De Vore, I. (ed.) (1965) *Primate Behavior*. Holt, Rinehart & Winston, New York.

Diamond, M. (1990) 'Selected cross-generational sexual behavior in traditional Hawaii: a sexological ethnography', in J. R. Feierman (ed.) *Pedophilia: Biosocial Dimensions*. Springer-Verlag, New York.

Dominian, J. (1980) *Marital Pathology: An Introduction for Doctors, Counsellors and Clergy*. Darton, Longmann & Todd and The British Medical Association, London.

DSM-IV: *Diagnostic and Statistical Manual of Mental Disorders,* 4th edition (1994). American Psychiatric Association, Washington.

Eckman, P., and Davidson, R. J. (eds) (1994) *The Nature of Emotion: Fundamental Questions*. Oxford University Press, Oxford and New York.

Eibl-Eibesfeldt, I. (1971) *Love and Hate*. Methuen, London.

—— (1990) 'Dominance, submission, and love: sexual pathologies from the perspective of ethology', in J. R. Feierman (ed.) *Pedophilia: Biosocial Dimensions*. Springer-Verlag, New York.

—— (1995) 'The evolution of familiarity and its consequences', *Futura*, no. 4, 10 Jahrgang, pp. 253–264.

Eliade, M. (1958) Patterns in Comparative Religion, R. Sheed (trans.). Sheed & Ward, London and New York.

—— (1964) *Shamanism: Archaic Techniques in Ecstasy*. Routledge & Kegan Paul, London.

Ellenberger, H. (1970) *The Discovery of the Unconscious.* Basic Books, New York.

Ellis, H. Havelock (1899) 'The stuff that dreams are made of', *Popular Science Monthly*, 54, 721.

—— (1926) *Studies in the Psychology of Sex*, vol. III, *Analysis of the Sexual Impulse, Love and Pain, The Sexual Impulse in Women*. (2nd edition, revised and enlarged). F. A. Davis, Philadelphia.

Erikson, E. H. (1959) *Identity and the Life Cycle*. Psychological Issues, vol. I, no. 1, monograph 1, International Universities Press, New York.

Erikson, M. T. (1993) 'Rethinking Oedipus: an evolutionary perspective of incest avoidance', *American Journal of Psychiatry*, 150, pp. 411–416.

Erlenmeyer-Kimling, L., and Paradowski, W. (1969) 'Selection and schizophrenia', *American Naturalist*, 100, pp. 651–665.

Evans, C. (1983) *Landscapes of the Night: How and Why We Dream*, P. Evans (ed.). Viking, New York.

Eysenck, H. J. and Eysenck, S. B. G. (1976) *Psychoticism as a Dimension of Personality*. Hodder & Stoughton, London.

Fairbairn, W. R. D. (1956) 'A critical evaluation of certain basic psycho-analytical conceptions', *British Journal of Philosophy and Science*, 7, pp. 49–60.

Feierman, J. R. (1982) 'Nocturnalism: an ethological theory of schizophrenia', *Medical Hypotheses*, 9, pp. 455–479.

—— (1990) 'Human erotic age orientation: a conclusion', in J. R. Feierman (ed.) *Pedophilia: Biosocial Dimensions*. Springer-Verlag, New York and London.

—— (1994) 'A testable hypothesis about schizophrenia generated by evolutionary theory', *Ethology and Sociobiology*, 15, pp. 263–282.

Feldman, M. P. and MacCullough, M. J. (1971) *Homosexual Behaviour: Therapy and Assessment*. Pergamon, New York.

Fernando, S. J. M. (1969) 'Cultural differences in the hostility of depressed patients', *British Journal of Medical Psychology*, 42, pp. 67–74.

Festinger, L. (1957) *A Theory of Cognitive Dissonance*. Stanford University Press, Stanford, Calif.

Fisher, R. A. (1930) *The Genetical Theory of Natural Selection*. Clarendon Press, Oxford.

Flor-Henry, P. (1976) 'Lateralized temporal-limbic dysfunction and psycho-pathology', *Annals of the New York Academy of Sciences*, 380, pp. 777–797.

Fodor, J. A. (1985) 'Precis of the modularity of mind (plus peer commentary)', *Behavioral and Brain Sciences*, 8, pp. 1–42.

Fox, R. (1989) *The Search for Society: Quest for a Biosocial Science and Morality*. Rutgers University Press, New Brunswick and London.

Freedman, D. G. (1979) *Human Sociobiology: A Holistic Approach*. Free Press, New York.

Freud, S. (1900; 1976) *The Interpretation of Dreams*. Pelican Books, London.

—— (1905) *Three Essays on the Theory of Sexuality*, Standard Edition, vol. 7 (1962). The Hogarth Press and the Institute of Psycho-Analysis, London.

—— (1917) 'Mourning and melancholia', Standard Edition, vol. 14 (1957). The Hogarth Press and the Institute of Psycho-Analysis, London.

—— (1920) *Beyond the Pleasure Principle*, Standard Edition, vol. 18 (1961). The Hogarth Press and the Institute of Psycho-Analysis, London.

—— (1930) *Civilization and Its Discontents*, Standard Edition, vol. 21. The Hogarth Press and the Institute of Psycho-Analysis, London.

—— (1938) *The Basic Writings of Sigmund Freud*, A. A. Brill (trans. and ed.). Modern Library, New York.

Frith, C. D. (1994) 'Theory of mind in schizophrenia', in A. S. David and J. C. Cutting (eds) *The Neuropsychology of Schizophrenia*. Lawrence Erlbaum Associates, Hove.

Fyer, A. J., Mannuzza, S., Chapman, T. F., Martin, L. Y., and Klein, D. R. (1995) 'Specificity in familial aggregation of phobic disorders', *Archives of General Psychiatry*, 52, pp. 564–573.

Galanter, M. (1989) 'Cults and new religious movements', in M. Galanter (ed.) *Cults and New Religious Movements*, pp. 25–40. American Psychiatric Association, Washington, DC.

Gardner, H. (1985) *Frames of Mind*. Paladin, London.

Gardner, R. (1988) 'Psychiatric syndromes as infrastructure for intra-specific communication', in M. R. A. Chance (ed.) *Social Fabrics of the Mind*. Lawrence Erlbaum Associates, Hove and London; Hillsdale, NJ.

Garland, R. J., and Daugher, M. J. (1990) 'The abused/abuser hypothesis of child sexual abuse', in J. R. Feierman (ed.) *Pedophilia: Biosocial Dimensions*. Springer-Verlag, New York.

Gebhard, P. H. (1969) 'Fetishism and sadomasochism', in J. H. Masserman (ed.) *Dynamics of Deviant Sexuality*. Grune & Stratton, New York.

Geist, V. (1978) *Life Strategies, Human Evolution, Environmental Design: Toward a Biological Theory of Health*. Springer-Verlag, New York.

—— (1994) 'Culture and its biological origins: a view from ethology, epigenesis and design', in R. A. Gardner, B. T. Gardner, B. Chiarelli, and F. X. Plooij (eds) *The Ethological Roots of Culture*, pp. 441–459. Kluwer Academic, Dordrecht.

Gilbert, P. (1989) *Human Nature and Suffering*. Lawrence Erlbaum Associates, Hove and London; Hillsdale, NJ.

—— (1992) *Depression: The Evolution of Powerlessness*. Lawrence Erlbaum Associates, Hove and London; Hillsdale, NJ.

—— (1997) 'The evolution of social attractiveness and its role in shame, humiliation, guilt and therapy'. *British Journal of Medical Psychology*, 70, pp. 113–148.

Gilbert, P., and Bailey, K. (eds) (1999) *Genes on the Couch: Explorations in Evolutionary Psychotherapy*. Psychology Press, Hove.

Gilbert, P., Price, J., and Allan, S. (1995) 'Social comparison, social attractiveness and evolution: how might they be related?', *New Ideas in Psychology*, 13, pp. 149–165.

Glantz, K., and Pearce, J. (1989) *Exiles From Eden: Psychotherapy From An Evolutionary Perspective*. Norton, New York.

Gorman, J. M., Liebowitz, M. R., Fyer, A. J., and Stein, J. (1989) 'A neuroanatomical hypothesis for panic disorder', *American Journal of Psychiatry*, 146, pp. 148–161.

Gosselin, C., and Wilson, G. (1980) *Sexual Variations: Fetishism, Transvestism and Sado-Masochism*. Faber & Faber, London.

Gottesman, I. I., and Shields, J. (1982) *Schizophrenia: The Epigenetic Puzzle*. Cambridge University Press, Cambridge.

Gottschalk, L., Cleser, C., and Springer, K. (1963) 'Three hostility scales applicable to verbal samples', *Archives of General Psychiatry*, 9, pp. 254–279.

Gould, S. J. (1992) 'Ontogeny and phylogeny revisited and reunited', *Bioessays*, 14, pp. 275–279.

Green, R. (1987) *The 'Sissy Boy Syndrome' and the Development of Homosexuality*. Yale University Press, New Haven, Conn.

Guisinger, S., and Blatt, S. J. (1994) 'Individuality and relatedness: evolution of a fundamental dialectic', *American Psychologist*, 49, no. 2, pp. 104–111.

Haldane, J. B. S. (1955) 'Population genetics', *New Biology*, 18, pp. 34–51.

Hall, C. S., and Nordby, Vernon J. (1972) *The Individual and His Dreams*. New American Library, New York.

Hamilton, William D. (1963) 'The evolution of altruistic behaviour', *American Naturalist*, 97, pp. 354–356.

Harlow, H. F., and Harlow, M. K. (1965) 'The affectional systems', in A. M. Schrier, H. F. Harlow and F. Stollnitz (eds) *Behaviour of Nonhuman Primates*. Academic Press, London.

Harpending, H. C., and Sobus, J. (1987) 'Sociopathy as an adaptation', *Ethology and Sociobiology*, 8, no. 3S, pp. 63–72.

Hawkins, R. C., and Clement, P. F. (1980) 'Development and construct validation of a self-report measure of binge-eating tendencies', *Addictive Behavior*, 5, pp. 219–226.

Henry, J. P., and Stephens, P. M. (1977) *Stress, Health and the Social Environment: A Sociobiological Approach to Medicine*. Springer-Verlag, New York.

Heston, L. L. (1966) 'Psychiatric disorders in foster home reared children of schizophrenic mothers', *British Journal of Psychiatry*, 112, pp. 819–825.

Hobson, J. Allan (1988) *The Dreaming Brain*. Basic Books, New York.

Hobson, J. Allan, and McCarley, R. W. (1977) 'The brain as a dream-state generator: an activation-synthesis hypothesis of the dream process', *American Journal of Psychiatry*, 134, pp. 1335–1368.

Hoffman, L. (1981) *The Foundations of Family Therapy*. Basic Books, New York.

Horrobin, D. F. (1998) 'Schizophrenia: the illness that made us human', *Medical Hypotheses*, 50, pp. 269–288.

Hufford, D. J. (1992) 'Commentary: paranormal experiences in the general population', *The Journal of Nervous and Mental Disease*, 180, pp. 362–368.

ICD 10 Classification of Mental and Behavioural Disorders: Clinical Descriptions and Guidelines (1992). World Health Organization, Geneva.

Jackson, M. (1997) 'Benign schizotype? The case of spiritual experience', in G. Claridge (ed.) *Schizotypy: Relations to Illness and Health*, pp. 227–250. Oxford University Press, Oxford.

James, W. (1890) *Principles of Psychology*, vol. 1. Henry Holt, New York.

Jensen, P. S., Mrazek, D., Knapp, P., Steinberg, L., Pfeffer, C., Schowalter, J., and Shapiro, T. (1997) 'Evolution and revolution in child psychiatry: ADHD as a disorder of adaptation', *Journal of American Academy of Child and Adolescent Psychiatry*, 36, pp. 1672–1681.

Jones, D. C. (1985) 'Dominance and affiliation as factors in the social organization of same-sex groups of elementary schoolchildren', *Ethology and Sociobiology*, 5, pp. 193–202.

Jouvet, Michel (1967) 'The states of sleep', *Scientific American*, 216, pp. 62–72.

—— (1975) 'The function of dreaming: a neurophysiologist's point of view', in M. S. Gazzaniga and C. Blakemore (eds) *Handbook of Psychobiology*. Academic Press, New York.

Jung, C. G. Quotations in the text are taken from *The Collected Works of C. G. Jung* (1953–78), H. Read, M. Fordham and G. Adler (eds), published in London by Routledge and in New Jersey by Princeton University Press. Sources are indicated by the volume number followed by the number of the paragraph from which the quotation is taken, e.g., CW16, para. 351.

—— (1933) *Modern Man in Search of a Soul*. Kegan Paul, London.

Kamel, G. W. Levi (1983) 'Leathersex: meaningful aspects of gay sadomasochism', in T. Weinberg and G. W. Levi Kamel (eds) *S and M: Studies in Sadomasochism*. Prometheus Books; New York.

Kane, F. J., Lipton, M. A., and Ewing, J. A. (1969) 'Hormonal influences in female sexual response', *Archives of General Psychiatry*, 20, pp. 202–209.

Kaufman, I. C., and Rosenblum, L. A. (1967) 'Depression in infant monkeys separated from their mothers', *Science,* 155, pp. 1030–1031.

Kemper, T. D. (1984) 'Power, status and emotions: a sociobiological contribution to a psychological domain', in K. R. Scherer and P. Ekman (eds) *Approaches to Emotion*. Lawrence Erlbaum Associates, Hove and London; Hillsdale, NJ.

—— (1990) 'Social relations and emotions: a structural approach', in T. D. Kemper (ed.) *Research Agendas in the Sociology of Emotions*. State University of New York Press, Albany.

Kendler, K. S., Kessler, R. C., Heath, A. C., Neale, M. C., and Aevas, L. J. (1991) 'Coping: a genetic epidemiological investigation', *Psychological Medicine*, 21, pp. 337–346.

Kennedy, J. L., and McKenzie, K. R. (1986) 'Dominance hierarchies in psychotherapy groups', *British Journal of Psychiatry*, 148, pp. 625–631.

Kessel, W. I. N. (1965) 'Self poisoning', *British Medical Journal ii*, pp. 1265–1270, pp. 1336–40.

Kevles, B. (1986) *Females of the Species: Sex and Survival in the Animal Kingdom*. Harvard University Press, Cambridge, Mass.

Kinsey, A. C., Pomeroy, W. B., and Martin, C. E. (1948) *Sexual Behavior in the Human Male*. Saunders, Philadelphia.

Klein, D. F. (1993) 'False suffocation alarms, spontaneous panics, and related conditions: an integrative hypothesis', *Archives of General Psychiatry*, 50, pp. 306–317.

Klein, M. (1948) *Contributions to Psycho-Analysis 1921–1945*. Hogarth Press, London: Anglo Books (1952), New York.

Klein, M., Heimann, P., Isaacs, S., and Riviere, J. (1952) *Developments in Psycho-Analysis*. The Hogarth Press, London.

Klerman, G. L. (1988) 'The current age of youthful melancholia', *British Journal of Psychiatry*, 152, pp. 4–14.

Kohut, H. (1977) *The Restoration of the Self*. International Universities Press, New York.

Kraemer, G. W., and McKinney, W. T. (1979) 'Interactions of pharmacological agents which alter biogenic amine metabolism and depression', *Journal of Affective Disorders*, 1, pp. 33–54.

Krafft-Ebing, R. von, (1885/1965) *Psychopathia Sexualis*. Stein & Day, New York.

Krebs, J. R., and Davies, N. B. (1993) *An Introduction to Behavioural Ecology* (3rd edition). Blackwell Scientific Publications, Oxford.

Kuhn, T. S. (1962) *The Structure of Scientific Revolutions*. University of Chicago Press, Chicago.

Kummer, H. (1995) *In Quest of the Sacred Baboon*. Princeton University Press, Ewing, NJ.

LaBerge, S. (1985) *Lucid Dreaming*. Ballantine Books, New York.

Laing, R. D. (1960) *The Divided Self: A Study of Sanity and Madness*. Tavistock Publications, London.

Leary, M. R., and Downs, D. I. (1995) 'Interpersonal functions of the self-esteem motive: the self-esteem system as a sociometer', in M. H. Kernis (ed.) *Efficacy, Agency and Self-esteem*. Plenum, New York.

Leary, T. (1957) *Interpersonal Diagnosis of Personality*. Ronald Press, New York.

Le Bon, G. (1952) *The Crowd: A Study of the Popular Mind*. Ernest Benn, London.

Leff, J. (1981) *Psychiatry around the Globe: A Transcultural View*. Gaskell (The Royal College of Psychiatrists), London.

Leichty, M. M. (1960) 'The effect of father-absence during early childhood upon the oedipal situation as reflected in young adults', *Merrill-Palmer Quarterly*, 6, pp. 212–217.

Lemert, E. M. (1967) 'Paranoia and the dynamics of exclusion', in T. J. Scheff (ed.) *Mental Illness and Social Processes*, pp. 271–293. Harper & Row, New York.

Lerner, R. M. (1992) *Final Solutions: Biology, Prejudice and Genocide*. Pennsylvania State University Press, Penn.

Levitt, E. E. (1971) 'Sadomasochism', *Sexual Behaviour*, 1, no. 6, pp. 69–80.

Lindholm, C. (1990) *Charisma*. Basil Blackwell, Cambridge, Mass. and Oxford.

Lippitt, Ronald *et al.* (1958) 'The dynamics of power: a field study of social influence in groups of children', in Maccoby, E. E., Newcombe, T. M., and Hartley, E. L., *Readings in Social Psychology*. Holt, Rinehart & Winston, New York.

Loewenthal, K., Goldblatt, V., Gorton, T., Lubitsch, G., Bicknell, H., Fellowes, D., and Sowden, A. (1995) 'Gender and depression in Anglo-Jewry', *Psychological Medicine*, 25, pp. 1051–1063.

Loney, J. (1974) 'Background factors, sexual experiences and attitudes towards treatment in two 'normal' homosexual samples', *Journal of Consulting and Clinical Psychology*, 38, pp. 57–65.

Low, B. S. (1989) 'Cross-cultural patterns in the training of children: an evolutionary perspective', *Journal of Comparative Psychology*, 103, pp. 311–319.

Lumsdon, C. J., and Wilson, E. O. (1983) *Promethean Fire: Reflections on the Origin of Mind*. Harvard University Press, Cambridge, Mass. and London.

McAdams, D. P. (1980) 'A thematic coding system for the intimacy motive', *Journal of Research in Personality*, 14, pp. 413–432.

McClelland, D. C. (1980) 'Motive dispositions: the merits of operant and respondent measures', in L. Wheeler (ed.) *Review of Personality and Social Psychology*, vol. 1, pp. 10–41.

McClennon, J. (1997) 'Shamanic healing, human evolution, and the origin of religion', *Journal of the Scientific Study of Religion*, 36, pp. 345–354.

McGuire, M. T., and Troisi, A. (1998) *Darwinian Psychiatry*. Oxford University Press, New York.

MacLean, P. D. (1973) *A Triune Concept of the Brain and Behaviour*, University of Toronto Press, Toronto.

—— (1976) 'Sensory and perceptive factors in emotional function of the triune brain', in R. G. Grennell and S. Gabay (eds) *Biological Foundations of Psychiatry*, vol. 1, pp. 177–198.

—— (1985) 'Evolutionary psychiatry and the triune brain', *Psychological Medicine*, 15, pp. 219–221.

Malik, K. (1998) 'The Darwinian fallacy', *Prospect*, December, pp. 24–30.

Mapother, E., and Lewis, A. J. (1937) in *Price's Textbook of Medicine* (5th edition). Oxford University Press, London.

Marks, I. M. (1969) *Fears and Phobias*. Heinemann, London.

Maslow, A. H. (1937) 'Dominance-feeling, behavior, and status', *Psychological Review*, 44, pp. 404–429.

Matthiessen, P. (1962) *Under the Mountain Wall*. Viking, London.

Mayr, E. (1982) *The Growth of Biological Thought*. Harvard University Press, Cambridge, Mass.

Mead, G. H. (1934) *Mind, Self and Society*, pp. 253–257. University of Chicago Press. Reprinted as 'Taking the role of the other', in T. Parsons, E. Shild, K. D. Naegele, and J. R. Pitts (eds) *Theories of Society: Foundations of Modern Sociological Theory*, vol. 1, pp. 739–740. Free Press of Glencoe, New York, 1961.

Medicus, G., and Hopf, S. (1990) 'The phylogeny of male/female difference in sexual behavior', in J. R. Feierman (ed.) *Pedophilia: Biosocial Dimensions*. Springer-Verlag, New York.

Mednick, S., and Christiansen, K. (eds) (1977) *Biosocial Bases of Criminal Behavior*. Gardner, New York.

Meyersburg, H. A., and Post, R. M. (1979) 'A holistic developmental view of neural and psychobiological processes: a neurobiologic-psychoanalytic integration', *British Journal of Psychiatry*, 135, pp. 139–155.

Milgram, S. (1974) *Obedience to Authority*. Harper & Row, New York.

Millar, D. G. (1983) 'Hostile emotion and obsessional neurosis', *Psychological Medicine*, 13, pp. 813–819.

Money, J. (1990) 'Pedophilia, a specific instance of a new phylism theory as applied to paraphilic lovemaps', in J. R. Feierman (ed.) *Pedophilia: Biosocial Dimensions*. Springer-Verlag, New York.

Montagu, A. (1979) 'The skin, touch, and human development', in S. Weitz (ed.) *Nonverbal Communication* (2nd edition). Oxford University Press, Oxford and New York.

Morris, D. (1969) *The Human Zoo*. Jonathan Cape, London.

Moser, C., and Levitt, E. E. (1987) 'An exploratory-descriptive study of a sadomasochistically orientated sample', *Journal of Sex Research*, 23, no. 3, pp. 322–337.

Moyer, K. E. (1976) *The Psychology of Aggression*. Harper & Row, London.

Nesse, R. M. (1987) 'An evolutionary perspective on panic disorder and agoraphobia', *Ethology and Sociobiology*, 8, no. 3s, pp. 73–84.

Nesse, R. M., and Williams, G. C. (1995) *Evolution and Healing: The New Science of Darwinian Medicine*. Weidenfeld & Nicolson, London.

Okami, P. (1990) 'Sociopolitical biases in the contemporary scientific literature on adult human sexual behavior with children and adolescents', in J. R. Feierman (ed.) *Pedophilia: Biosocial Dimensions*. Springer-Verlag, New York.

Olds, J. (1956) 'Pleasure centres in the brain', *Scientific American*, 195, no. 4, p. 104.

Ornstein, R. (1986) *Multimind: A New Way of Looking at Human Behavior*. Macmillan, London.

Parker, G. (1984) 'The measurement of pathological parental style and its relevance to psychiatric disorder', *Social Psychiatry*, 19, pp. 75–81.

Parkes, C. M. (1973) 'Factors determining the persistence of phantom pain in the amputee', *Journal of Psychosomatic Research*, 17, pp. 97–108.

Patrias, D. (1978) 'The sociology of secret deviation', unpublished PhD thesis, New York University. Quoted in Thompson, B. (1994).

Pengelley, E. T. (1978) *Sex and Human Life* (2nd edition). Addison-Wesley, Menlo Park, Calif.

Pfohl, B., Stangl, D. D., and Tsuang, M. T. (1983) 'The association between early parental loss and diagnosis in the Iowa 500', *Archives of General Psychiatry*, 40, p. 965.

Pinker, S. (1994) *The Language Instinct*. Morrow, New York.

—— (1997) *How the Mind Works*. Allen Lane, London.

Ploog, D. W., and Pirke, K. M. (1987) 'Psychobiology of anorexia nervosa', *Psychological Medicine,* 17, pp. 843–859.

Pratto, F., Sidanius, J., Stallworth, L. M., and Malle, B. F. (1994) 'Social dominance orientation: a personality variable predicting social and political attitudes', *Journal of Personality and Social Psychology*, 67, pp. 741–763.

Price, J. S. (1967) 'Hypothesis: the dominance hierarchy and the evolution of mental illness', *Lancet*, 2, pp. 243–246.

—— (1969) 'Neurotic and endogenous depression: a phylogenetic view', *British Journal of Psychiatry*, 114, pp. 119–120.

—— (1988) 'Alternative channels for negotiating asymmetry in social relationships', in M. R. A. Chance (ed.) *Social Fabrics of the Mind*. Lawrence Erlbaum Associates, Hove and London; Hillsdale NJ.

—— (1991) 'Homeostasis or change? A systems theory approach to depression', *British Journal of Medical Psychology*, 62, pp. 331–334.

—— (1992) 'The agonic and hedonic modes: definition, usage, and the promotion of mental health', *World Futures*, 35, pp. 87–115.

—— (1998) 'The adaptive function of mood change', *British Journal of Medical Psychology*, 71, pp. 465–477.

Price, J. S., and Gardner, R. (1995) 'The paradoxical power of the depressed patient: a problem for the ranking theory of depression', *British Journal of Medical Psychology*, 68, pp. 193–206.

Price, J. S., and Sloman, L. (1987) 'Depression as yielding behaviour: an animal model based upon Schjelderup-Ebbe's pecking order', *Ethology and Sociobiology*, 8, pp. 85s–98s.

Price, J. S. and Stevens, A. (1998) 'The human male socialization strategy set: co-operation, defection, individualism and schizotypy', *Evolution and Human Behavior*, 19, pp. 57–70.

Price, J. S., Sloman, L., Gardner, R., Gilbert, P., and Rohde, P. (1994) 'The social competition hypothesis of depression', *British Journal of Psychiatry*, 164, pp. 309–335.

Price, V. A. (1982) *Type A Behaviour Pattern: A Model for Research and Practice*. Academic Press, New York.

Radcliffe-Brown, A. R. (1922) *The Andaman Islanders*. Cambridge University Press, Cambridge.

Raleigh, M., and McGuire, M. (1991) 'Serotonin in vervet monkeys', *Brain Research*, 559, pp. 181–190.

Reik, T. (1941) *Masochism in Modern Man*. Farrar, Straus & Co., New York.

Robins, T. W., and Everitt, B. J. (1995) 'Central norepinephrine neurons and behavior', in F. E. Bloom and D. J. Kupfer (eds) *Psychopharmacology: The Fourth Generation of Progress*, pp. 363–372. Raven Press, New York.

Rosen, D. H. (1992) 'Inborn basis for the healing doctor–patient relationship', *Pharos*, 55, pp. 17–21.

Rosen, D., and Luebbert, M. (eds) (1999) *Evolution of the Psyche*. Praeger, Westpoint, Conn.

Rossi, E. L. (1972) *Dreams and the Growth of Personality*. Pergamon, New York.

Russell, C., and Russell, W. M. S. (1998) 'Population crises and population cycles – 11. Some societies without recorded history', *ASCAP*, 11 (12), pp. 20–23.

Russell, G. F. M. (1970) 'Anorexia nervosa, its identity as an illness and its treatment', in J. H. Price (ed.) *Modern Trends in Psychological Medicine* (2nd edition). Butterworth, London.

Rutter, M. (1987) 'Temperament, personality and personality disorder', *British Journal of Psychiatry*, 150, pp. 443–458.

Rycroft, C. (1970) *Anxiety and Neurosis*. Penguin Books, Harmondsworth.

Sagan, C. (1977) *The Dragons of Eden*. Hodder & Stoughton, London.

Saghir, M. T., and Robins, E. (1973) *Male and Female Homosexuality: A Comprehensive Investigation*. Williams & Wilkins, Baltimore.

Sartorius, N., Davidian, H., and Ernberg, G. (1983) *Depressive Disorders in Different Cultures: Report on the WHO Collaborative Study on Standardized Assessment of Depressive Disorders*. World Health Organization, Geneva.

Savin-Williams, R. C. (1979) 'Dominance hierarchies in groups of early adolescents'. *Child Development*, 50, pp. 923–935.

Schad-Somers, S. P. (1982) *Sadomasochism*. Human Sciences Press, New York.

Schiefenhövel, W. (1990) 'Ritualized adult-male/adolescent-male sexual behaviour in Melanesia: an anthropological and ethological perspective', in J. R. Feierman (ed.) *Pedophilia: Biosocial Dimensions*. Springer-Verlag, New York.

Schopenhauer, A. (1862) 'Versuch über das Geisterschen und Was Damit Zusammenhängt', in *Parerga und Paralipomena* (Essay 5), vol. l, 313 (2nd edition), Berlin (1st edition, 1851, Leipzig).

Schumaker, J. F. (1995) *The Corruption of Reality: A Unified Theory of Religion, Hypnosis and Psychopathology*. Prometheus Books, Amherst, NY.

Schwab, J. J. (1989) 'The epidemiology of the affective disorders', in J. G. Howells (ed.) *Modern Perspectives in the Psychiatry of the Affective Disorders. Modern Perspectives in Psychiatry no. 13*. Brunner/Mazel, New York.

Schwartz, G. E., Davidson, R. J., and Maer, F. (1975) 'Right hemisphere lateralization for emotion in the human brain: interactions with cognition', *Science*, 190, pp. 286–288.

Seghorn *et al.* (1987) 'Childhood sexual abuse in the lives of sexually aggressive offenders', *Journal of the American Academy of Child and Adolescent Psychiatry*.

Seigel, A. M. (1996) *Heinz Kohut and the Psychology of the Self*. Routledge, London.

Seligman, M. E. P. (1975) *Helplessness: On Depression Development and Death*. W. H. Freeman, San Francisco.

Selye, H. (1974) *Stress Without Distress*. Hodder & Stoughton, London.

Sheehan, H. L., and Summers, V. K. (1949) *Quarterly Journal of Medicine*, 42, p. 319.

Shneidman, E. S. (1989) 'Overview: a multidimensional approach to suicide', in D. Jacobs and H. N. Brown (eds) *Suicide: Understanding and Responding*. Harvard Medical School Perspectives: International Universities Press, Conn.

Siever, L. J., and Gunderson, J. G. (1979) 'Genetic determinants of borderline conditions', *Schizophrenia Bulletin*, 5, pp. 59–86.

Silverman, I., and Eals, M. (1992) 'Sex differences in spatial abilities: evolutionary theory and data', in J. Barkow, L. Cosmides and J. Tooby (eds) *The Adapted Mind*. Oxford University Press, Oxford and New York.

Sims, A. (1995) *Symptoms in the Mind: An Introduction to Descriptive Psychopathology* (2nd edition). W. B. Saunders, London.

Slavin, M. O., and Kriegman, D. (1992) *The Adaptive Design of the Human Psyche: Psychoanalysis, Evolutionary Biology and the Therapeutic Process*. Guilford Press, New York.

Sloman, L., and Gilbert, P. (eds) (2000) *Subordination and Defeat: An Evolutionary Approach to Mood Disorders and Their Therapy*. Lawrence Erlbaum Associates, Hillsdale, NJ.

Sloman, L., Gardner, R., and Price, J. S. (1989) 'Biology of family systems and mood disorders', *Family Process*, 28, pp. 387–398.

Sober, E., and Wilson, D. S. (1998) *Unto Others: The Evolution and Psychology of Unselfish Behaviour*. Harvard University Press, Cambridge, Mass.

Sommer, V. (1990) *Wider die Natur? Homosexualität und Evolution*. C. H. Beck Verlag, Munich.

Soubrie, P. (1986) 'Reconciling the role of central serotonin neurones in human and animal behaviour', *Behavioural Brain Science*, 9, pp. 319–364.

Spengler, A. (1977) 'Manifest sadomasochism of males: results of an empirical study', *Archives of Sexual Behaviour*, 6, pp. 441–456.

Spitzer, R. L., Endicott, J., and Gibbon, M. (1979) 'Crossing the border into borderline personality and borderline schizophrenia: the development of criteria', *Archives of General Psychiatry*, 36, pp. 17–24.

Steele, C. M. (1986) 'What happens when you drink too much?' *Psychology Today*, 20, pp. 48–52.

Stein, D. J., and Bouwer, C. (1997) 'A neuro-evolutionary approach to the anxiety disorders', *Journal of Anxiety Disorders*, 11, no. 4, pp. 409–29.

Stein, D. J., and Bouwer, C. (1997) 'Blushing and social phobia: a neuroethological speculation', *Medical Hypotheses*.

Stevens, A. (1982) *Archetype: A Natural History of the Self*. Routledge & Kegan Paul, London; William Morrow & Co., New York.

—— (1986) *Withymead: A Jungian Community for the Healing Arts*. Element Books, Shaftesbury, Dorset.

—— (1989) *The Roots of War*. Paragon House, New York.

—— (1993) *The Two Million-Year-Old Self*. Texas A&M University Press, College Station, Texas.

—— (1994) *Jung*. Oxford University Press, Oxford and New York.

—— (1995; 1996) *Private Myths: Dreams and Dreaming*. Hamish Hamilton, London; Harvard University Press, Cambridge, Mass.

—— (1998) *An Intelligent Person's Guide to Psychotherapy*. Duckworth, London.

—— (1999) *On Jung* (2nd edition). Penguin, London.

Stevens, A., and Price, J. (in press) *The Voices of God: Charisma, Sex and Madness*. Duckworth, London.

Stoddard, D. M. (1990) *The Scented Ape: The Biology and Culture of Human Odour*. Cambridge University Press, Cambridge and New York.

Stokes, E. (1985) 'The neuroendocrinology of anxiety', in H. Tuma and J. Maser (eds) *Anxiety and Anxiety Disorders*. Lawrence Erlbaum Associates, Hillsdale, NJ.

Stone, M. H. (1980) *The Borderline Syndromes*. McGraw-Hill, New York.

Storr, A. (1964) *Sexual Deviations*. Penguin Books, Harmondsworth.

—— (1972) *The Dynamics of Creation*. Secker & Warburg, London.

Summit, R. C. (1983) 'The child sexual abuse accommodation syndrome', *Child Abuse and Neglect*.

Surbey, M. K. (1987) 'Anorexia nervosa, amenorrhea, and adaptation', *Ethology and Sociobiology*, 8, no. 3s, pp. 47–62.

Swallow, S. R., and Kuiper, N. A. (1988) 'Social comparison and negative evaluations: an application to depression', *Clinical Psychology Review*, 8, pp. 55–76.

Symons, D. (1979) *The Evolution of Human Sexuality*. Oxford University Press, Oxford and New York.

Szasz, T. S. (1974) *The Myth of Mental Illness*. Harper & Row, New York.

Teasdale, J. D. (1988) 'Cognitive vulnerability to persistent depression', *Cognition and Emotion*, 2, pp. 247–274.

Tennen, H., and Affleck, G. (1993) 'The puzzles of self-esteem: a clinical perspective, in R. F. Baumeister (ed.) *Self-Esteem: The Puzzle of Low Regard*, pp. 241–269. Plenum Press, New York.

Thompson, B. (1994) *Sadomasochism*. Cassell, London.

Tiger, L., and Fox, R. (1972) *The Imperial Animal*. Secker & Warburg, London.

Tinbergen, N. (1951) *The Study of Instinct*. Oxford University Press, London.

—— (1963) 'On aims and methods of ethology'. *Z. Tierpsychologie*, 20, pp. 410–433.

Tooby, J., and Cosmides, L. (1990a) 'On the universality of human nature and the uniqueness of the individual', *Journal of Personality*, 58, (l), pp. 17–67.

—— (1990b) 'The past explains the present: emotional adaptations and the structure of ancestral environments', *Ethology and Sociobiology*, 11, pp. 375–424.

Trivers, R. (1972) 'Parental investment and sexual selection', in B. Campbell (ed.) *Sexual Selection and the Descent of Man*. Aldine de Gruyter, Chicago.

de Waal, F. M. B. (1982) *Chimpanzee Politics*. Jonathan Cape, London.

—— (1988) 'The reconciled hierarchy', in M. R. A. Chance (ed.) *Social Fabrics of the Mind*. Lawrence Erlbaum Associates, Hove and London; Hillsdale, NJ.

Waddington, C. H. (1957) *The Strategies of the Genes: A Discussion of Some Aspects of Theoretical Biology*. George Allen & Unwin, London.

Wallace, A. F. C. (1956) 'Revitalization movements', *American Anthropologist*, 58, pp. 264–281.

—— (1966) *Religion: An Anthropological View*. Random House, New York.

Walters, S. (1994) 'Algorithms and archetypes: evolutionary psychology and Carl Jung's theory of the collective unconscious', *Journal of Social and Evolutionary Systems*, 17 (3), pp. 287–306.

Wasser, S. K., and Barash D. P. (1983) 'Reproductive suppression among female mammals: implications for biomedicine and sexual selection theory', *Quarterly Review of Biology*, 58, pp. 513–538.

Watson, D., and Clark, L. A. (1984) 'Negative affectivity: the disposition to experience aversive emotional states', *Psychological Bulletin*, 96, pp. 465–490.

—— (1994) 'Emotions, moods, traits and temperaments: conceptual distinctions and empirical findings', in P. Eckman, and R. J. Davidson (eds) *The Nature of Emotions: Fundamental Questions*. Oxford University Press, New York.

Webster, P. (1979) *Rua and the Maori Millennium*. Victoria University Press, Wellington.

Webster, R. (1998) *The Great Children's Home Panic*. The Orwell Press, Oxford.

Weinberg, T., and Kamel, G. W. L. (1983) *S and M: Studies in Sadomasochism.* Prometheus Books, New York.

Weissman, M. M., Klerman, G. L., and Paykel, E. S. (1971) 'Clinical evaluation of hostility in depression', *American Journal of Psychiatry,* 128, pp. 261–266.

Wender, P., Kety, H., Rosenthal, D., Schulsinger, F., Orthmann, J., and Lunde, I. (1986) 'Psychiatric disturbance in the biological and adoptive families of adopted individuals with affective disorder', *Archives of General Psychiatry,* 43, pp. 923–929.

Wenegrat, B. (1984) *Sociobiology and Mental Disorder.* Addison-Wesley, Menlo Park, Calif.

Werner, D. (1995) *On The Evolution and Cross-cultural Variation of Male Homosexuality.* Institute for Human Biology, University of Hamburg, Germany.

Whiting, B. (ed.) (1963) *Six Cultures: Studies of Child Rearing.* Wiley, New York.

Wilhelm, K., and Parker, G. (1989) 'Is sex necessarily a risk factor to depression?' *Psychological Medicine,* 19, pp. 401–413.

Williams, George G. (1966) *Adaptation and Natural Selection: A Critique of Some Current Evolutionary Thought.* Princeton University Press, Princeton, N. J.

Wilson, D. R. (1993) 'Evolutionary epidemiology: Darwinian theory in the service of medicine and psychiatry', *Acta Biotheoretica,* 41, pp. 205–218.

Wilson, D. S. (1997) 'Altruism and organism; disentangling the themes of multilevel selection theory.[2] *The American Naturalist,* July, 150, supplement, pp. 122–34.

Wilson, D. S., and Sober, E. (1994) 'Reintroducing group selection to the behavioral sciences', *Behavioral and Brain Sciences,* 17, pp. 585–608 (open peer commentary 608–654).

Wilson, E. O. (1975) *Sociobiology: The New Synthesis.* The Belknap Press of Harvard University Press, Cambridge, Mass., and London.

Wilson, G. (1989) *The Great Sex Divide: A Study of Male–Female Differences.* Peter Owen, London.

Wilson, M., and Daly, M. (1985) 'Competitiveness, risk-taking, and violence: the young male syndrome', *Ethology and Sociobiology,* 6, pp. 59–73.

Winson, J. (1990) 'The meaning of dreams', *Scientific American,* November, pp. 42–48.

Wright, R. (1994) *The Moral Animal: Why We Are The Way We Are.* Little, Brown & Co., London.

Wright, S. (1931) 'Evolution in Mendelian populations', *Genetics,* 16, pp. 97–159.

—— (1948) 'Genetics of populations', *Encyclopaedia Britannica* (14th edition) 10, pp. 110–115.

—— (1980) 'Genetic and organismic selection', *Evolution,* 35, pp. 825–843.

Wynne-Edwards, V. C. (1962) *Animal Dispersion in Relation to Social Behaviour.* Oliver & Boyd, Edinburgh.

—— (1965) 'Self-regulating systems in populations of animals', *Science,* 147, pp. 1043–1048.

Yerkes, R. M., and Dodson, J. D. (1908) 'The relation of strength of stimulus to rapidity of habit-formation', *Journal of Comparative and Neurological Psychology,* 18, 459–482.

Yudofsky, S. C. (1999) 'Parkinson's disease, depression, and electrical stimulation of the brain', *New England Journal of Medicine,* 340, pp. 1500–1501.

Zillman, D. (1984) *Connections between Sex and Aggression.* Lawrence Erlbaum Associates, London and Hove; Hillsdale NJ.

INDEX

301